DISTURBING TIMES

Before you start to read this book, take this moment to think about making a donation to punctum books, an independent non-profit press,

@ https://punctumbooks.com/support/

If you're reading the e-book, you can click on the image below to go directly to our donations site. Any amount, no matter the size, is appreciated and will help us to keep our ship of fools afloat. Contributions from dedicated readers will also help us to keep our commons open and to cultivate new work that can't find a welcoming port elsewhere. Our adventure is not possible without your support.

Vive la Open Access.

Fig. 1. Hieronymus Bosch, *Ship of Fools* (1490–1500)

DISTURBING TIMES: MEDIEVAL PASTS, REIMAGINED FUTURES. Copyright © 2020 by the editors and authors. This work carries a Creative Commons BY-NC-SA 4.0 International license, which means that you are free to copy and redistribute the material in any medium or format, and you may also remix, transform and build upon the material, as long as you clearly attribute the work to the authors (but not in a way that suggests the authors or punctum books endorses you and your work), you do not use this work for commercial gain in any form whatsoever, and that for any remixing and transformation, you distribute your rebuild under the same license. http://creativecommons.org/licenses/by-nc-sa/4.0/

First published in 2020 by punctum books, Earth, Milky Way.
https://punctumbooks.com

ISBN-13: 978-1-950192-75-5 (print)
ISBN-13: 978-1-950192-76-2 (ePDF)

DOI: 10.21983/P3.0313.1.00

LCCN: 2020934654
Library of Congress Cataloging Data is available from the Library of Congress

Book design: Vincent W.J. van Gerven Oei
Cover image: The ruins of Old Dongola, the capital of the Kingdom of Makuria, along the river Nile in present-day Sudan. Photo by Vincent W.J. van Gerven Oei, 2018.

HIC SVNT MONSTRA

Disturbing Times
Medieval Pasts,
Reimagined Futures

edited by
Catherine E. Karkov,
Anna Kłosowska,
and Vincent W.J. van Gerven Oei

Contents

Disturbance   13
Catherine E. Karkov, Anna Kłosowska, and Vincent W.J. van Gerven Oei,

Scholarship as Biography: An Allegorical Reading of the Philological Work of G.M. Browne   29
Vincent W.J. van Gerven Oei

"Semper Novi Quid ex Africa": Redrawing the Borders of Medieval African Art and Considering Its Implications for Medieval Studies   73
Andrea Myers Achi and Seeta Chaganti

Disorienting Hebrew Book Collecting   107
Eva Frojmovic

The Etymology of *Slave*   151
Anna Kłosowska

The Exiles of Byzantium: Form, Historiography, and Recuperation   215
Roland Betancourt

Confederate Gothic   247
Joshua Davies

"Die, defenceless, primitive natives!": Colonialism, Gender,
and Militarism in *The Legacy of Heorot*   285
Alison Elizabeth Killilea

Twenty-five Years of "Anglo-Saxon Studies": Looking Back,
Looking Forward   317
*Catherine A.M. Clarke with Adam Miyashiro, Megan Cavell,
Daniel Thomas, Stewart Brookes, Diane Watt, and Jennifer
Neville*

The Medieval Literature Survey Reimagined: Intersectional
and Inclusive Praxis in a US College Classroom   351
Carla María Thomas

Acknowledgments

Maxine Waters's "Reclaiming my time" is the anthem of 2016–20. And reclaiming history? — As survivors, or descendants of survivors, some of us consciously work on publishing the past, while others create beauty and ideas as a survival strategy, recover sedimented meanings and erased histories, preserve a heritage or a language for which there are not enough survivors. Building present collectives and communities is always also first on our minds.

The editors want to thank the Medievalists of Color for their work and discussion of the issues addressed in the volume. The organization's mission statement reads: "As people of color, we share a collective socio-political identity that draws its strength from the varied backgrounds and experiences of its members. We represent the power of difference," and the members' activism and publications are reshaping the field. We thank the contributors to this volume, Roland Betancourt, Stewart Brookes, Megan Cavell, Seeta Chaganti, Catherine A.M. Clarke, Joshua Davies, Eva Frojmovic, Alison Elizabeth Killilea, Adam Miyashiro, Andrea Myers Achi, Jennifer Neville, Carla María Thomas, Daniel Thomas, and Diane Watt, for their kindness and generosity, and for the discussions, support, and critical questioning that improved this volume. We are proud and grateful that they chose this book, which originated in a couple of conference panels and then grew to encompass and imagine some of the best parts of medieval studies to come. We thank Nadia

Altschul, who participated in the original IMC panel organized by Catherine Karkov and Eva Frojmovic, "Creating the Medieval Studies We Want to Remember," but was unable to contribute to the volume.

We must focus on eradicating racism from the field, especially because of a strong record of contributions to other areas of social justice, including role models who opened the doors to us intellectually and practically. Carolyn Dinshaw and others founded *Gay and Lesbian Quarterly* in 1991; Bonne Wheeler established women's careers through her work at Palgrave Macmillan; the art historian Michael Camille, decades after his death, is remembered in Yorkshire as a source of local pride: in the depressing class system, the person who gives hope; in the homophobic context, the brilliant, enviable genius. Medieval studies at the turn of the century included — as well as reactionaries — many powerful women, queers, first-generation descendants of working class and people of diasporas: economic, political, war-torn.

In the 2010s, enter the Babel Working Group, *postmedieval: a journal of medieval cultural studies,* and punctum books, with Eileen A. Joy's superpowers, envisioning the issues for which it will be important to fight in 5–15 years, such as funding for open access publishing. As Olga Tokarczuk says — like Joy, opening a path for others in a hopeless context — "when you imagine that things can get better, they already are better." Typically, Joy advertised her Harvard lecture by a still from Wes Anderson's *Royal Tenenbaums*: Gwyneth Paltrow with running kohl, cocooned in a *Grey-Gardens*-moth-eaten fur; Luke Wilson in a brown suit, holding a cigarette and a very alert falcon, Mordechai. Babel-the-collective grew, supported by the courage of graduate students and adjuncts, and the established scholars who used the resources of their powerful institutions to feed Babel: at the same time a real institution and a real departure that made medieval studies better and more utopian.

We want to thank Vincent W.J. van Gerven Oei, whose genius, indefatigable hard work, and serenity borne of having taken greater risks and having a bigger picture than anyone we know helped this collection all through; Anna for her eternal diplomacy and good cheer; and Catherine Karkov for the lion's share of the work, for her generous hospitality, for creating the panels, promoting early career scholars, and for her beautiful, important work on women, art, and time.

Anna also thanks Natasha the Princess Cat for sitting under the purple blooms that set off the green of her eyes the best. In a world where we solve real problems, it is often important to work on preserving the magic, as does Natasha. When they say you should dress for the job you want, they obviously mean tiaras. Boris's supporting role is crucial. Also, the unforgettable few days of brilliant, freshly-rained misty summer walks, with sustenance from Etna (for the wine) and Yorkshire (for the milk) is the closest I got to live in some impossible novel version of writer's retreat. I am so grateful for that well-remembered magic.

Introduction

Disturbance

*Catherine E. Karkov,
Anna Kłosowska,
and Vincent W.J. van Gerven Oei*

These are disturbing times. Scholars in medieval and premodern studies are tired of explaining why, yet this labor continues to be performed by those who often have the least personal and professional security.[1] A case in point here is Mary Rambaran-Olm, who consistently advocated, and with considerable risk for her own scholarly career and personal well-being, for the retirement of the racist term "Anglo-Saxon" in academic scholarly contexts.[2] One would think that medieval scholars would be lining up around the block to discontinue such a label, given that

---

1 See the excellent summaries of the problem by Matthew Gabriele and Mary Rambaran-Olm, "The Middle Ages Have Been Misused by the Far Right. Here's Why It's So Important to Get Medieval History Right," *Time*, November 21, 2019, https://time.com/5734697/middle-ages-mistakes/; Coleen Flaherty, "It's About More Than a Name," *The Chronicle of Higher Education*, September 20, 2019, https://www.insidehighered.com/news/2019/09/20/anglo-saxon-studies-group-says-it-will-change-its-name-amid-bigger-complaints-about.
2 Mary Rambaran-Olm, "Anglo-Saxon Studies [Early English Studies], Academia and White Supremacy," *Medium*, January 27, 2018, https://medium.com/@mrambaranolm/anglo-saxon-studies-academia-and-white-supremacy-17c87b360bf3

white supremacists engrave it on their weapons of choice.³ Yet the academics who protest the protest against "Anglo-Saxon" and other racist terms claim to be the ones oppressed! This is a classic situation that Sara Ahmed calls out so well: "When you expose a problem you pose a problem."⁴ And: "When people give accounts of sexist and racist harassment they are often dismissed as having a wrong or faulty perception, as not receiving the intentions or actions of others fairly or properly." Also, those who protest against the protest see "Anglo-Saxon" and racist uses of the medieval past as an image problem, a problem of perception or perspective — "a US problem" — and that, too, is classic: as Ahmed explains, for the prejudiced, the prejudice "is 'in the image' rather than 'in the organization' as an effect of what it does."⁵

The initial impetus of this collection of essays was a disturbance, when at the 2017 International Medieval Congress (IMC) in Leeds the opening plenary lecture was introduced with a racist joke, and the complaints of many medievalists about both the

---

3   See, for a recent overview of the ways in which "Anglo-Saxon" and white supremacy are intimately linked, Donna Beth Ellard, *Anglo-Saxon(ist) Pasts, postSaxon Futures* (Earth: punctum books, 2019).
4   We thank David Carillo-Rangel for the reference to Sara Ahmed's work in this context.
5   Ahmed concludes: "What we have here from my data are two contrasting accounts: in one, the perception is accepted as true and the demand is for self-modification; in the other, the perception is taken as false and the demand is for a new image. How can we account for this difference? We need to show how these perceptions have quite different social careers. That is a difference that matters. In both cases, whether or not it is the perception that becomes the problem is a way of distributing the problem. Whether or not a perception is of a problem, a perception is about making some and not others into the problem. I have learnt so much from how the language of inclusion and repair make those who are to be included into the problem. And once the 'to be included' or 'not yet included' are the problem, then those already given place by the institution, and even the institution itself, can maintain themselves not only as not the problem, but also as the solution to the problem" (Sara Ahmed, "The Problem of Perception," *Feministkilljoys*, February 17, 2014, https://feministkilljoys.com/2014/02/17/the-problem-of-perception/).

joke and the atmosphere of racism and exclusion that pervaded much of the conference went unheeded.[6] Of course, there were problems in and with Medieval Studies long before that. There was Mathew Parker in the sixteenth century, who used his collection and study of the medieval manuscripts dispersed at the dissolution of the monasteries to create an image of the primacy and exceptionalism of the English Church. There were medieval architectural styles used in the European claiming of imperial colonies from India to Mexico throughout the centuries. There was the nationalism of many of the nineteenth- and early twentieth-century figures who established the formal disciplines that comprise the field. At the same time, while medievalist expressions of misogyny and homophobia have emerged from various corners in the last several years, it is important to note that medievalists have consistently used these often oppressive and even violent moments as opportunities to advocate for change in the field, illustrated, for instance, through Jonathan Hsy's thoughtful and prescient response piece, "Femfog Medievalism: Lessons Learned."[7] Yet there is the continuing tolerance of senior academics such as Andy Orchard, who are known harassers of their students, and a continued harassment of those scholars — especially PhD students, early career researchers, and medievalists of color — who are working for a more just and inclusive Medieval Studies.

The problem of premodern and medieval scholars condoning or siding with contemporary forms of oppression is not a problem that only affects scholars dealing with the US or Western

---

6   J. Clara Chan, "Medievalists, Recoiling from White Supremacy, Try to Diversify the Field," *Chronicle of Higher Education,* July 16, 2017, https://www.chronicle.com/article/Medievalists-Recoiling-From/240666.

7   Jonathan Hsy, "#FemFog Medievalism: Lessons Learned," *In the Middle,* January 18, 2016, http://www.inthemedievalmiddle.com/2016/01/femfog-medievalism-lessons-learned.html. See also Eileen A. Joy, "CFP: Defenestrating Frantzen: A Fistschrift," *punctum books comms,* January 8, 2020, https://punctumbooks.pubpub.org/pub/cfp-defenestrating-frantzen-fistschrift.

Europe. In the same way that we need to question the ways in which the scholarly deployment of tropes such as "Anglo-Saxon" (not so) tacitly feed into white supremacist ideologies, archeological, anthropological, historical, and linguistic researchers of past and present cultures in countries such as Egypt, Sudan, India, and China, have to come terms with the way in which their work might enable nationalist tropes and symbolically prop up regimes that are not only oppressive or autocratic in nature, but moreover violate human rights on a large scale.

A concrete example was the response of the Nubiological community to the political developments in Sudan starting with the massive protests and strikes in December 2018. For decades, the Nubiological community has depended on the autocratic and genocidal[8] Omar Al Bashir government for its concessions and excavation, travel, and documentation permits. Under the Al Bashir government in Sudan (as well as under consecutive autocratic Egyptian governments) Nubian and other minority cultural identities were purposefully erased and subjected to a process of state-enforced "Arabization," or worse.[9] Furthermore,

---

8 Al Bashir was officially indicted by the International Criminal Court for crimes against humanity, including genocide. See "Al Bashir Case: The Prosecutor v. Omar Hassan Ahmad Al Bashir ICC-02/05-01/09," *International Criminal Court*, https://www.icc-cpi.int/darfur/albashir.

9 For example: "Consequently, the culture of the Arabized Northern Sudanese and the Islamization have been presented as the unifying genius of the Sudan bringing together diverse 'primitive' tribal groups within common identity through the mechanisms of Arabization and Islamization" (Amir Idris, *Conflict and Politics of Identity in Sudan* [New York: Palgrave Macmillan, 2005], 15–16), and: "Given the determined commitment of the government of Sudan to execute its ideology of homogenizing Sudan to become an Arab and Islamic country, the largest African state has been ravaged by war leading to the death of over two million Sudanese" (Jok Madut Jok, *War and Slavery in Sudan* [Philadelphia: University of Pennsylvania Press, 2001], 99). For an analysis of the Bashir regime's (ab)use of Islamism in relation to foreign policy, see Dimah Mahmoud, *Dynamics of Sudanese Foreign Policy (1998–2010): Attempts to Regain International Legitimacy*, PhD Thesis, University of Exeter.

the Sudanese government sponsored scholars to attend Nubiological conferences, where they often reinforced the nationalist narrative that "Nubia is Sudan."[10] All of this went unopposed and was therefore tacitly endorsed by the large majority of the Nubiological community, afraid to lose access to their research subject.[11] When the December 2018 protests and strikes continued into 2019 and were met by lethal violence, rape, and destruction of the Bashir regime, the Union for Nubian Studies widely circulated a petition among Nubiologists denouncing the violence of the regime.[12] The response was underwhelming, with only very few (senior) Nubian scholars willing to risk "disturbing" the regime. Meanwhile, Al Bashir's security forces raided and destroyed the University of Khartoum.[13]

Similarly in Sanskrit studies, humanists are battling the onslaught of state-endorsed Hindu nationalism, which projects a pure "Hindu period" into antiquity and the Middle Ages,[14] and is itself in part a reflex of Western colonialist and Orientalist ideas of Sanskrit speaking Aryans as "a lost wing of early European culture."[15] This Hindu nationalism comes with a virulent anti-

---

10 During one particular incident during the 14th International Conference for Nubian Studies at the Musée du Louvre and Sorbonne University, one of the editors, opposing unfounded demands that scholars ought to use "Sudan" instead of "Nubia," was threatened by one such scholar: "If you don't like this, you are no longer welcome in Sudan."
11 Those few that spoke out, such as Alexandros Tsakos, were banned from entering Sudan.
12 "UNS Declaration Regarding the Recent Human Rights Violations in Sudan," *Union for Nubian Studies,* February 22, 2019, http://unionfornubianstudies.org/2019/02/22/uns-declaration-regarding-the-recent-human-rights-violations-in-sudan/.
13 "Report: Large Parts of University of Khartoum Destroyed on June 3," *Dabanga,* August 7, 2019, https://www.dabangasudan.org/en/all-news/article/report-large-parts-of-university-of-khartoum-destroyed-on-june-3.
14 See Romila Thapar, "They Peddle Myths and Call It History," *New York Times,* May 17, 2019, https://www.nytimes.com/2019/05/17/opinion/india-elections-modi-history.html. We thank Dan Rudmann for pointing us to some of these sources, which, we realize, are in no way exhaustive.
15 Romila Thapar, "Interpretations of Ancient Indian History," *History and Theory* 7, no. 3 (1968): 318–35, at 319.

Islam politics, which has led to many deaths and the destruction of religious buildings. This has also affected scholars directly, in issues relating to the representation of Hinduism in textbooks,[16] the recall of a history textbook in India by Penguin after bowing to political pressure,[17] and petition to remove Sheldon Pollock as general editor of the Murty Classical Library of India at Harvard University Press because he would have "shown disrespect for the unity and integrity of India."[18] Scholars in India suffer even worse fates, being removed from their posts because of their purported "anti-Hindu" sentiments.[19]

Whether it is white, Arabist, or Hindu nationalist, all forms of fascism, the "mobilization of the identificatory emotions of the masses"[20] that turn a single ideological discourse into a hegemonic weapon of symbolic and physical oppression, need to be disturbed. It is our duty, as scholars and as human beings, to disturb them, to dissolve their hegemony.

This book is a disturbance. It participates in the current movement whose aim is to break up the tranquility, the settled condition that has been accepted as Medieval Studies for far too long — the settled condition that led to so many of our colleagues tolerating a racist joke or feeling that the appropriation

---

16 Teresa Watanabe, "A Textbook Debate over Hinduism," *Los Angeles Times*, February 27, 2006, https://www.latimes.com/archives/la-xpm-2006-feb-27-me-hindu27-story.html.

17 John Williams, "Author Resigned to Ill Fate of Book in India," *New York Times*, February 16, 2014, https://www.nytimes.com/2014/02/17/books/author-resigned-to-ill-fate-of-book.html.

18 Scott Jaschik, "Nonscholarly Litmus Tests for Key Scholarly Role," *Inside Higher Ed*, March 1, 2016, https://www.insidehighered.com/news/2016/03/01/scholars-india-demand-harvard-u-press-drop-its-well-respected-editor; Elizabeth Redden, "The Religious War against American Scholars of India," *Inside Higher Ed*, April 12, 2016, https://www.insidehighered.com/news/2016/04/12/scholars-who-study-hinduism-and-india-face-hostile-climate.

19 Aatish Taseer, "The Right-Wing Attack on India's Universities," *New York Times*, January 27, 2016.

20 Philippe Lacoue-Labarthe, *Heidegger, Art and Politics: The Fiction of the Political*, trans. Chris Turner (London: Basil Blackwell, 1990), 95.

of medieval symbols and the violence instigated by supremacists in Charlottesville or Ayodhya are not their concerns. It looks both backwards and forwards, working to decenter and recenter the medieval that we study, the disciplines that have constructed the medieval as a safe and distant place in the past far removed from the concerns of the contemporary world, and the medievalism that has used the medieval to construct and maintain racist, misogynistic, and oppressive agendas and power structures.

Disturbance is also the title of an exhibition by the photographer and video artist Willie Doherty, whose work explores the terror and violence that have left their traces in ancient landscapes, and the events that drop and ripple through history or that float like ghosts beneath its surfaces. The essays in this book explore the terror and violence that have left their traces in the historical record, especially in medieval history and culture, that continue to ripple through history in the form of medievalist texts or buildings, or in the way we think about and teach medieval texts and languages. They survey the events that left wounds that are impossible to heal: the erasure of peoples, cultures, or places, or the ghosts that float beneath the surface of history waiting to be revived in new periods or by new forms of oppression — the separation and imprisonment of families, for example,[21] an act associated with historical slavery but now so prominent a feature of the horrors wrought by the Trump administration.

Not everyone in the Middle Ages was a racist, just as not all medievalists actively engage in racist behavior, but Medieval Studies has a racist past, a past that nationalist and far-right politics (and some medievalists) continue to (mis)appropriate in their disturbing vision for the future. As Catherine Karkov says, "among other things, to value an outdated term — "Anglo-Saxon" — over the lives and careers of colleagues is both absurd

---

21 Discussed by both Anna Kłosowska and Joshua Davies in their chapters below.

and horrific. It is a clinging to the past that remains stubbornly blind to the racism of the past and its direct connections with the racism of the present."[22] The incredible resistance to change related to "Anglo-Saxon" is a symptom, and it's not a symptom of anything remotely pleasant. Consider that studies of slavery have been able to transition from "slave" to "enslaved person" in some five years ca. 2010 (there was discussion); French Literature of the 1970s became Francophone Studies of the 1980s; Women's Studies renamed themselves Gender Studies ca. 2005, so they would not sound Edwardian ca. 1905; "he/she" became "they" in a space of about 5 years. Change is difficult and involves fight and conflict, but the society does change for the better. We acknowledge the field's racist past, and we disturb it and the uses to which it has been put in order to help to create a radical and inclusive future.

The volume begins and ends with two very different experiences of working on the medieval in academia, and two very different experiences of research communities and teaching universities: the first a highly ranked research institution experienced as a tedious cultural wasteland, and the second a large urban public university enlivened by an intersectional approach to teaching designed to engage students from a variety of racial, ethnic, and cultural backgrounds. We open with a study that looks at the way a field struggles to connect the lives and deaths of past scholars to those who live and work in the field today. We end with a case study of the way in which caring about and incorporating the concerns and lived experiences of ourselves and our students can enrich teaching and research on the medieval past. And, following Vincent W.J. van Gerven Oei, we ask: "What is the purpose of the past if not to allow us to imagine a better future?"

---

22 Catherine E. Karkov, "Post 'Anglo-Saxon' Melancholia," *Medium*, December 10, 2019, https://medium.com/@catherinekarkov/post-anglo-saxon-melancholia-ca73955717d3.

The essays that follow weave a network of correspondences, and this section lays out some of these connections. The first is a focus on Northeast African history, cultures, and art. It is one of the areas in global medieval studies that has had the most impact recently. Two essays represent that area in the volume. The first is Vincent W.J. van Gerven Oei's "Scholarship as Biography." In the essay's conclusion, Van Gerven Oei focuses on political stakes and ethical imperatives and commitments in the archaeology and study of the area, a social context contrasted with the loneliness in the life and career of the eminent Old Nubian scholar Michael Browne that forms the core of the chapter. The second essay, by Andrea Myers Achi and Seeta Chaganti, "'Semper Novi Quid ex Africa," analyzes W.E.B. Du Bois's theories and metaphors of Africa as a map to radically rethink and open the perception and curation of medieval African art. The coauthored essay is also an important sequel to Achi's previous work on the history of epistemology of art-historical knowledge, and classification systems that affect our understanding and reception of African art.

The second cluster of texts deals with languages often thought to be "peripheral" to Medieval Europe, while in fact being integral to its cultural history. Eva Frojmovic's chapter, "Disorienting Hebrew Book Collecting" also discusses epistemology of knowledge. Frojmovic traces across centuries the circulation of a thirteenth century Hebrew manuscript to demonstrate how the condition of the volume's survival was that it was stripped of its original ritual and cultural function, its identity erased by Christian collectors. This powerful chapter demonstrates in succinct ways how Orientalist epistemology manipulates knowledge to obscure genocide and culturecide: as early as the sixteenth century, a European Jewish manuscript has become the subject of study for "Orientalism," and by corollary Jewish European culture is also "Oriental," that is, "other" than European. Similarly, Anna Kłosowska's chapter on the medieval history of the word slave reminds us that an estimated two million people were enslaved and deported from Ukraine and Crimea between the Middle Ages and the eighteenth century. That slave trade is the subject of important recent publications, and it is also connected to several epochal events in medieval history. Like Frojmovic, Betancourt's "The Exiles of Byzantium: Form, Historiography, and Recuperation" aims to disturb and subvert the paradigms that continue to define art-historical and manuscript studies and opens with a view of the global medieval world, people traversing space to create new collective communities, bringing with them diachronic traditions and emotions, recomposing them in the new, hybrid time and space. What are the ethics of such spatial and time travels? Colonialism shows the genocidal side of exile, while exile can also serve as the model for a radical opening up, decentering, resisting detrimental movements.

The third cluster of essays focuses on medievalisms, that is, the later uses of the medieval culture in Neo-Gothic architecture in the U.S. and in the 1980s macho Beowulf fan fiction. In "Confederate Gothic," Joshua Davies explains the role of Gothic architecture in creating a simulacrum of history that erased Native American history and the history of slavery. Built on the land stolen from Native Americans and often also built by enslaved people, nineteenth-century American Gothic buildings are a tragic legacy that Davis helps us understand as a legacy of colonialism and genocide, both in the North and South of the US. Focused on Beowulf fan fiction in the Reagan era, Alison Elizabeth Killilea's "*Die, defenseless, primitive natives!*" in turn explores the anti-women and anti-gay politics of the AIDS crisis period. Highlighting conservative and right-wing groups' misappropriation of medieval literature, Killilea reminds us of the enormous task that befalls all of us.

The final cluster includes the round table on "Twenty-five Years of 'Anglo-Saxon Studies'" by Catherine A.M. Clarke, Adam Miyashiro, Megan Cavell, Daniel Thomas, Stewart Brookes, Diane Watt and Jennifer Neville, and Carla María Thomas's "The Medieval Literature Survey Reimagined." The roundtable brings together important voices that have reshaped medieval studies, in particular as regards the discontinuation of the term "Anglo-Saxon." To mention only two of the participants, Watt's publications redefined both women's and queer studies, while Miyashiro's contributions shape the current fight to make medieval studies powerfully inclusive, not only nominally diverse. In the final chapter, Thomas stresses that in order to achieve an inclusive approach to the field we must engage with intersectionality in both theory and praxis, and she gives medievalists both theoretical and practical help, the latter in the form of a detailed syllabus including a statement of inclusivity, and an "ungrading policy." Thomas's description of her teaching practices will be inspirational in curriculum planning and class design, because, to once again quote Sara Ahmed: "no wonder diversity work is so trying: it takes a conscious willed effort not to reproduce how things tend to fall."[23]

---

23 Ahmed, "The Problem of Perception."

Bibliography

Ahmed, Sara. "The Problem of Perception." *Feministkilljoys*, February 17, 2014. https://feministkilljoys.com/2014/02/17/the-problem-of-perception/.

"Al Bashir Case: The Prosecutor v. Omar Hassan Ahmad Al Bashir ICC-02/05-01/09," *International Criminal Court*, https://www.icc-cpi.int/darfur/albashir.

Chan, J. Clara. "Medievalists, Recoiling from White Supremacy, Try to Diversify the Field." *Chronicle of Higher Education*, July 16, 2017. https://www.chronicle.com/article/Medievalists-Recoiling-From/240666.

Ellard, Donna Beth. *Anglo-Saxon(ist) Pasts, postSaxon Futures.* Earth: punctum books, 2019.

Flaherty, Coleen. "It's About More Than a Name." *The Chronicle of Higher Education*, September 20, 2019. https://www.insidehighered.com/news/2019/09/20/anglo-saxon-studies-group-says-it-will-change-its-name-amid-bigger-complaints-about.

Gabriele, Matthew, and Mary Rambaran-Olm. "The Middle Ages Have Been Misused by the Far Right. Here's Why It's So Important to Get Medieval History Right." *Time*, November 21, 2019. https://time.com/5734697/middle-ages-mistakes/.

Hsy, Jonathan. "#FemFog Medievalism: Lessons Learned." *In the Middle*, January 2016. http://www.inthemedievalmiddle.com/2016/01/femfog-medievalism-lessons-learned.html.

Idris, Amir. *Conflict and Politics of Identity in Sudan.* New York: Palgrave Macmillan, 2005.

Jaschik, Scott. "Nonscholarly Litmus Tests for Key Scholarly Role." *Inside Higher Ed*, March 1, 2016. https://www.insidehighered.com/news/2016/03/01/scholars-india-demand-harvard-u-press-drop-its-well-respected-editor.

Jok, Jok Madut. *War and Slavery in Sudan.* Philadelphia: University of Pennsylvania Press, 2001.

Eileen A. Joy, "CFP: Defenestrating Frantzen: A Fistschrift." *punctum books comms*, January 8. 2020. https://punctumbooks.pubpub.org/pub/cfp-defenestrating-frantzen-fist-schrift.

Karkov, Catherine. "Post 'Anglo-Saxon' Melancholia." *Medium*, December 10, 2019. https://medium.com/@catherinekarkov/post-anglo-saxon-melancholia-ca73955717d3.

Lacoue-Labarthe, Philippe. *Heidegger, Art and Politics: The Fiction of the Political*. Translated by Chris Turner. London: Basil Blackwell, 1990.

Mahmoud, Dimah. *Dynamics of Sudanese Foreign Policy (1998–2010): Attempts to Regain International Legitimacy*. PhD Thesis, University of Exeter.

Rambaran-Olm, Mary. "Anglo-Saxon Studies [Early English Studies], Academia and White Supremacy." *Medium*, January 27, 2018. https://medium.com/@mrambaranolm/anglo-saxon-studies-academia-and-white-supremacy-17c87b360bf3.

Redden, Elizabeth. "The Religious War against American Scholars of India." *Inside Higher Ed*, April 12, 2016. https://www.insidehighered.com/news/2016/04/12/scholars-who-study-hinduism-and-india-face-hostile-climate.

"Report: Large Parts of University of Khartoum Destroyed on June 3." *Dabanga*, August 7, 2019. https://www.dabangasudan.org/en/all-news/article/report-large-parts-of-university-of-khartoum-destroyed-on-june-3.

Taseer, Aatish. "The Right-Wing Attack on India's Universities." *New York Times*, January 27, 2016.

Thapar, Romila. "Interpretations of Ancient Indian History." *History and Theory* 7, no. 3 (1968): 318–35. DOI: 10.2307/2504471.

———. "They Peddle Myths and Call It History." *New York Times*, May 17, 2019. https://www.nytimes.com/2019/05/17/opinion/india-elections-modi-history.html.

"UNS Declaration Regarding the Recent Human Rights Violations in Sudan." *Union for Nubian Studies*, February 22, 2019. http://unionfornubianstudies.org/2019/02/22/uns-declaration-regarding-the-recent-human-rights-violations-in-sudan/.

Watanabe, Teresa. "A Textbook Debate over Hinduism." *Los Angeles Times,* February 27, 2006. https://www.latimes.com/archives/la-xpm-2006-feb-27-me-hindu27-story.html.

Williams, John. "Author Resigned to Ill Fate of Book in India." *New York Times,* February 16, 2014. https://www.nytimes.com/2014/02/17/books/author-resigned-to-ill-fate-of-book.html.

1

Scholarship as Biography: An Allegorical Reading of the Philological Work of G.M. Browne

Vincent W.J. van Gerven Oei[1]

A little over a year after his retirement, on August 30, 2004, Gerald M. Browne, known to his colleagues as Michael,[2] com-

---

1 My thanks go out to Alexandros Tsakos, a fellow lone Nubiologist. A passionate conversation on the plane from Rome to Amsterdam provided many of the sparks that lit this text. I am indebted to Stephen M. Bay, one of Gerald M. Browne's last PhD students, for generously sharing his stories and experiences concerning his *Doktorvater* with me. I want to thank Hans Henrich Hock and Dan Rudmann, who helped me with the Sanskrit, and Shayla Monroe and Claudia Näser for pointing me to valuable sources concerning Nubian archeology. Thanks also go out to Geoffrey Smith, who kindly shared photographs of the Old Nubian amulets with me. I also thank José Andrés Alonso de la Fuente for his critical remarks to improve this paper.

2 Even though his scholarly work is consistently signed "Gerald M. Browne," no one except his parents referred to him by his first name (Stephen M. Bay, p.c.). Even so, it appears that some colleagues also referred to him as "Gerald" rather than "Michael." See Gerald M. Browne, "Valedictory Address," in *Studia Palaeophilologica: Professoris G.M. Browne in honorem oblata*, ed. Stephen M. Bay (Champaign: Stipes Publishing, 2004), xv–xviii, at xv. However, note that Bay himself explicitly called him "G. Michael Browne" in Stephen M. Bay and Maryline G. Parca, "†G. Michael Browne

29

mitted suicide. This fact has been largely repressed within the scholarly community of Nubian Studies, as no one has yet tried to understand the context of his suicide and its relation to the way in which our field constitutes itself. This chapter offers a first attempt to do so, by reading Browne's scholarship not only as the virtuoso philological performance it represents, but also as an allegory of the way in which Nubian Studies continues to struggle to connect the lives and deaths of the people from the past it studies with those who live in the present.

Browne was a Professor of Classics at the University of Illinois at Urbana-Champaign and by far one of the most important and prolific scholars of Old Nubian, one of the literary languages of Makuria during what Artur Obłuski has termed the Two Kingdoms period.[3] As a scholar he was a true polymath, publishing editions in Arabic, Armenian, Blemmyan, Coptic, Geʿez, Georgian, Greek, Latin, Lydian, Old Nubian, Sanskrit, and Syriac.[4] For example, in 2003 he published a Latin edition of a piece of pottery inscribed with the Cushitic language Blemmyan written in Greek characters,[5] no doubt one of the very few scholarly publications published in Latin that year.[6] By choosing to express himself in this ancient language, he placed himself in a scholarly tradition stretching back centuries in time, as one of

---

(1943–2004)," *The Bullettin of the American Society of Papyrologists* 41, no. 1 (2004): 13–37.

3   Ca. 700–1450 CE. See Artur Obłuski, *The Rise of Nobadia: Social Changes in Northern Nubia in Late Antiquity,* trans. Iwona Zych (Warsaw: Raphael Taubenschlag Foundation, 2014), 9.

4   Stephen M. Bay, "Gerald Michael Browne," *Beiträge zur Sudanforschung* 9 (2006): 5–23, at 6.

5   Gerald M. Browne, *Textus Blemmyicus Aetatis Christianae* (Champaign: Stipes Publishing, 2003).

6   In fact, Browne published several articles in Latin in the last years of his life: Gerald M. Browne, "Ad Sphujidhvajae *Yavanajātakam*," *Illinois Classical Studies* 27–28 (2002–2003): 175–76; Gerald M. Browne, "Blemmyica," *Zeitschrift für Papyrologie und Epigraphik* 148 (2004): 245–46. An earlier Latin publication is his edition of the "Nubian Bible," *Bibliorum Sacrorum Versio Palaeonubiana* (Leuven: Peeters, 1994). Many of his other publications in English carry Latin titles.

the last authors proficient in the humanist language of scholarly inquiry, now all but abandoned and replaced by Browne's native tongue, English.

Browne started to publicly articulate his feeling of non-belonging midway through his scholarly career, only a few years after he first started to publish on Old Nubian.[7] In his article "Old Nubian Philology" from 1985, he draws a parallel between possible traces of a Makuritan philological tradition and his own scholarly practice. He ends the article by recalling an observation of his *Doktorvater*, the papyrologist Herbert C. Youtie,[8] about an Egyptian scribe, a "frustrated *érudit manqué*" from "an outpost of civilization on the verge of the Fayum's inhospitable desert," who "for no apparent reason other than playful desperation, translated Egyptian names into Greek."[9] Browne sees here an analogy not only with the Nubian scribes whose work he is studying, but also himself:

> But Egypt, at least in the areas responsible for the production and diffusion of texts, must have been more cosmopolitan and sophisticated than Nubia. For a more pertinent analogue I turn to the Egyptian village of Karanis, an outpost of civilization on the verge of the Fayum's inhospitable desert. There, in the last quarter of the second century of our era, scribes produced enormous tax rolls that have survived and provided papyrologists with many a problem of decipherment and interpretation. One of the scribes who drafted the rolls seems to have been a frustrated *érudit manqué*: such was Profes-

---

7   His first article on Old Nubian dates from 1979: Gerald M. Browne, "Notes on Old Nubian (I–III)," *Bulletin of the American Society of Papyrologists* 16, no. 4 (1979): 249–56. His first scholarly publication dates to 1967.
8   Herbert C. Youtie must have made a lasting impression on Browne, as he returns to him again, twenty years later, in his "Valedictory Address," xv.
9   Gerald M. Browne, "Old Nubian Philology," *Zeitschrift für Papyrologie und Epigraphik* 60 (1985): 291–96, at 296. See also Vincent W.J. van Gerven Oei, "The Disturbing Object of Philology," *postmedieval* 5, no. 4 (2014): 442–55, at 451.

sor H.C. Youtie's conclusion when he noted that this scribe at times, for no apparent reason other than playful desperation, translated Egyptian names into Greek; he reached the height of his powers when he rendered Πανπῖν "he of the mice" by ἀνδίκτης, a poetic word designating the tongue of a mousetrap and found elsewhere only in the erudite verses of Callimachus. "Not many Greeks or Graeco-Egyptians at Karanis were in the habit of entertaining themselves with Callimachus," writes Professor Youtie, in trying to understand the personality of a scribe who sought intellectual satisfaction by burying displays of linguistic virtuosity in gigantic money registers. I have a feeling that the men who translated Greek in Medieval Nubia would have been sympathetic with the Egyptian scribe's plight. Cultural wastelands can often be conductive to the refinement of intellectual pleasures: faced with a bleak and dismal landscape, the mind seeks solace within itself, and the gentle art of philology — as I have learned from practicing it in an area culturally not unlike Nubia — is a remarkably effective anodyne for boredom and despair.[10]

This quotation tells us much more about Browne's state of mind than about Nubia a thousand years ago. Because contrary to Browne's imagination, the Makuritan kingdom appears to have had a rich scribal culture and was anything but a "cultural wasteland." Rather than in a "bleak and dismal landscape," the Makuritans lived along the fertile grounds of the Nile river, on one of the main trade routes between sub-Saharan Africa and the Mediterranean, a society that "fused Greco-Roman legal forms and indigenous African social, cultural, and ceremonial practices."[11] In his description, Browne echoes the distinctively Egyptological view of Nubia, which, strongly influenced by

10 Ibid.
11 Giovanni R. Ruffini, *Medieval Nubia: A Social and Economic History* (Oxford: Oxford University Press, 2012), 21.

the way in which hieroglyphic texts portrayed Egypt's southern neighbors, viewed Nubia as a "poor and barbarous frontier province," to which they consistently applied the epithets "miserable" or "abominable."[12]

This uncritical application of Egyptological stereotypes serves not so much to depreciate his area of study, as to situate his own scholarly environment, the University of Illinois at Urbana-Champaign, as "an area culturally not unlike" a "cultural wasteland," where Browne himself practices philology as a "remarkably effective anodyne for boredom and despair." At the same time, casting Nubia as a region that is in need of development, scholarly or otherwise, allows Browne to claim that it "needed" him, as he states nearly twenty years later upon his retirement in his "Valedictory Address" from 2003, published in the *Festschrift, Studia Palaeophilologica*: "About Old Nubian I have only to say that I pursued it for the same reason that I bought a Yugo: I felt it needed me."[13] It appears, in another reversal, that Browne needed Old Nubian at least as much as it needed him:

> My 30 years in Urbana have been a wonderful time, filled with enough uninterrupted hours to pursue a philological career with some degree of success and with a great deal of personal satisfaction. Not having an orthodox belief system to support me, and refusing to succumb to the make-it-up-as-you-go-along spirituality of this our darkling and narcissistic age, I have ever sought solace in the secular salvation of textual criticism, remembering — with Erasmus — that

---

12 William Y. Adams, *Nubia: Corridor to Africa* (London: Allen Lane, 1977), 2, 17. See, for the Egyptian perceptions of Nubians, Stuart Tyson Smith, *Wretched Kush: Ethnic Identities and Boundaries in Egypt's Nubian Empire* (London: Routledge, 2003). See, for an overview of the racist tropes and colonialism in the history of Sudan archeology, Bruce G. Trigger, "Paradigms in Sudan Archaeology," *The International Journal of African Historical Studies* 27, no. 2 (1994): 323–45.

13 G.M. Browne, "Valedictory Address," xvii.

unless we purify our texts we can never hope to purify ourselves.[14]

Philology or textual criticism is here proposed as a secular belief system that offers "salvation" to its practitioners, a way to "purify" oneself. From these lines from both the 1985 article and his 2003 address, we gather an image of Browne clinging to his field of scholarship as a lifeline, as that which wards off a constant feeling of a deep despair and depression.

The lengths to which Browne went to "purify" the Old Nubian corpus are impressive. Not only did he publish new editions of nearly all previously edited material, but many of the texts went through series of revisions, leading to publications with baroque titles such as "Griffith's Old Nubian Lectionary: The Revision Revised."[15] Browne's tendency to constantly correct, refine, and expand his readings also seems not to have escaped his colleagues. In a transcription of a brief *encomium* at a dinner on the occasion of his retirement, his colleague Howard Jacobson said:

> To be sure, Michael is not always right. He too makes mistakes. One of the disadvantages — or perhaps advantages — of being the authority in the field is that no one out there recognizes that you've gone astray. Michael has even developed a technique to capitalize on this. Michael will publish a piece and then, down the road some, he will recognize that he was wrong. And so, he has published quite a number of deuterai phrontides, second-thoughts, self-corrections.[16]

---

14 Ibid., xvii–xviii.
15 Gerald M. Browne, "Griffith's Old Nubian Lectionary: The Revision Revised," *Bulletin of the American Society of Papyrologists* 24, nos. 1–2 (1987): 75–92.
16 Howard Jacobson, "Remarks upon G.M. Browne's Retirement," in *Studia Palaeophilologica: Proferessoris G.M. Browne in honorem oblata*, ed.

In fact, it seems Browne's career in Old Nubian set off with such a correction, albeit not of himself. Jacobson relates the story:

> An eminent scholar had published a papyrus which he identified (and translated) as a documentary text in Coptic about land. Michael then demonstrated, beyond any doubt, that it was in fact Old Nubian, not Coptic, and the text in question, far from being a document about land-possession, was a section from the gospel of Luke.[17]

Jacobson notes that Browne was particularly "proud" of this discovery, and indeed a reproduction of the fragment graces the cover of *Studia Palaeophilologica* as an emblem of his entire career.

The article in question, published in the *Zeitschrift für Papyrologie und Epigraphik* in 1980, is simply titled "A New Text in Old Nubian,"[18] and provides a completely revised reading of a manuscript fragment found in 1968 in the prothesis of the church in Sunnarti, first published by noted Coptologist C. Detlef G. Müller.[19] Browne rejects Müller's idea that the manuscript contains a Coptic documentary text, and identifies the text instead as an Old Nubian translation of Luke 1:27–29. This identification hinges on the suggestion of the insertion of an Old Nubian translation of the textual variant εὐηγγελίσατο αὐτὴν καὶ in verse 28 in order to make sure the word spacing works out correctly.

For seven years, Browne's new identification of the Sunnarti fragment stands uncontested. But in a chapter published in a

---

Stephen M. Bay (Champaign: Stipes Publishing, 2004): xi–xiii, at xii.

17 Ibid.
18 Gerald M. Browne, "A New Text in Old Nubian," *Zeitschrift für Papyrologie und Epigraphik* 37 (1980): 173–78. Jacobson erroneously dates this article to 1989 (Jacobson, "Remarks upon G.M. Browne's Retirement," xii).
19 C. Detlef G. Müller, "Ergänzende Bemerkungen zu den deutschen Texfunden in Nubien," *Oriens christianus* 62 (1978): 135–43, at 142–43.

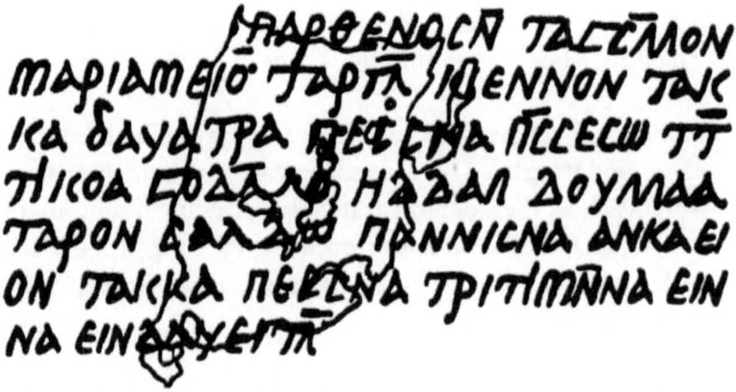

Fig. 1. Browne's reconstruction of the Sunnarti Luke. G.M. Browne, "The Sunnarti Luke," 293. The outline shows the actual fragment.

1987 *Festschrift* for Müller,[20] Rüdiger Unger severely criticizes the proposed variant reading. Although agreeing with the identification of the text as Old Nubian, Unger argues that Browne's variant reading is unverifiable as it mainly falls in a lost part of the fragment, while there is no evidence for the existence of this textual variant elsewhere in the Old Nubian corpus;[21] the Sunnarti fragment is the only part of the Gospel of Luke attested in Old Nubian.[22] Furthermore, Unger claims that this textual variant is very unlikely to have featured in the material that would have been available to Old Nubian scribes.[23] He thus proposes something of a compromise. The text is Old Nubian, but it cannot be securely identified as a fragment from Luke. It should be noted that Unger's article is the only published scholarly rebuttal

20 Rüdiger Unger, "Sunnarti — Fragment 203: Deutung und sprachliche Zuordnung," in *Nubia et Oriens Christianus: Festschrift für C. Detlef G. Müller zum 60. Geburtstag*, eds. Piotr O. Scholz and Reinhard Stempel (Cologne: Verlag Jürgen Dinter, 1987), 243–67.
21 Ibid., 259.
22 Ibid., 260. Cf. G.M. Browne, *Bibliorum Sacrorum Versio Palaeonubiana*, 10–11. Michael argues that there is also a short citation from Luke in St 35.5–9. See Gerald M. Browne, "The Sunnarti Luke," *Zeitschrift für Papyrologie und Epigraphik* 70 (1989): 292–96, at 296.
23 Unger, "Sunnarti," 263.

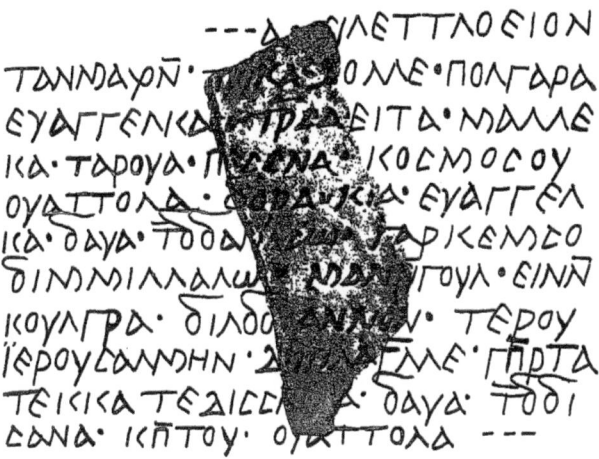

Fig. 2. Browne's reconstruction of the apocryphal text from Qasr Ibrim. G.M. Browne, "An Old Nubian Apocryphal Text from Qasr Ibrim," pl. 15.

Browne ever received regarding his Old Nubian work, a fact that will be relevant later on.

Browne doubles down two years later by providing a new edition of the fragment, which he now defiantly calls "The Sunnarti Luke," with a full reconstruction of the lost right and left margins of the text (fig. 1),[24] maintaining the translation of the textual variant εὐηγγελίσατο αὐτὴν καὶ in ll. 2–3 as [ⲧⲁⲕⲕⲁ ⲟ̄ⲁⲩ]ⲁ ⲧⲣⲁ [*takka jau*]*a tra*. He also dismisses Unger's criticism, claiming that it is "obvious" that "the Nubian translators of the New Testament followed a text that often deviated from [the standard edition] Nestle-Aland,"[25] adding in a footnote that biblical scholar and textual critic Bruce M. Metzger also has assured him

---

24 The same reconstruction is also shown on the cover of Browne's collection *Literary Texts in Old Nubian* (Vienna–Mödling: Verein der Förderer der Sudanforschung, 1989), published in the same year.
25 G.M. Browne, "The Sunnarti Luke," 294.

that his "methodology [was] 'entirely correct.'" Apart from this somewhat problematic appeal to authority, Browne's response to Unger is typical for his entire oeuvre: to overwhelm with the force of his own philological imagination.

The Sunnarti Luke is not the only fragment whose edition contains more reconstruction than actually attested text. An impressive example, allegedly an apocryphal text from Qasr Ibrim (fig. 2), again features a massive reconstruction based on a "scrap" on which only five words can be fully read.[26] The identification is even more shaky than in the case of the Sunnarti Luke, because there is no known Greek *Vorlage* and Browne reconstructs the Old Nubian "loosely" on the basis of several Biblical passages:

> Although only a small number of words survive undamaged, the general sense of the passage is clear enough: it is from an apocryphal text loosely based on Christ's instructions to his disciples as given at the end of the Gospels.[27]

Despite the great uncertainty of the actual wording of the original document, and in the absence of any true parallel text in Old Nubian, Greek, or any other scriptural language, Browne reconstructs several lines of text: "This reconstruction [...] is merely intended as an example of how the passage may have run. With so much lost, it would be reckless to claim any degree of certainty for restorations here offered."[28] Nevertheless, Browne's restoration "recklessly" provides the evidence for the

---

26 Alexandros Tsakos states that the edition is "characteristic of the extremes to which he was going with a language that back in his days he was the only one to claim an understanding of" ("In Search of Apocryphal Literature in Nubia," lecture at the 2019 Oslo Workshop on Apocrypha and Monastic Literary Culture, Faculty of Theology, University of Oslo, June 19, 2019).

27 Gerald M. Browne, "An Old Nubian Apocryphal Text from Qasr Ibrīm," *Journal of Coptic Studies* 3 (2001): 129–32, pls. 14–15, at 129.

28 G.M. Browne, "An Old Nubian Apocryphal Text from Qasr Ibrīm," 129.

apocryphal nature of the fragment which is then reinscribed onto it through the publication's title. As with the Sunnarti Luke, the title of the article suggests much more certainty than warranted by the textual evidence.

A final, similar example concerns the reconstruction of two passages from the *Liber Institutionis Michaelis Archangeli*,[29] based on Greek and Coptic versions of the same text. Even though this reconstruction is again "hypothetical,"[30] the differences between the original reconstruction and the new reconstruction proposed in this short article are considerable, and there is no way to objectively evaluate their quality except through our trust in Browne's philological prowess.

But Browne went even further than extensive reconstructions; he also *created* new Old Nubian texts. In the years after his death, University of Texas professor Geoffrey Smith acquired four framed "Old Nubian" documents on eBay, which he decided, after some research, had been forged, based on the fact that two of them contained nearly the same text (figs. 3, 4).[31]

One of the two papyri is identified as an "Old Nubian amulet" containing Luke 1:1, making it the second "identified" Old Nubian fragment containing the Gospel of Luke, besides the Sunnarti text. Browne's imagined fragment of Luke can be reconstructed on the basis of the two extant versions:

---

29 Gerald M. Browne, "Ad Librum Insitutionis Michaelis Archangeli," *Orientalia* 65 (1996): 131–35. See also Alexandros Tsakos, "The *Liber Institutionis Michaelis* in Medieval Nubia," *Dotawo: A Journal of Nubian Studies* 1 (2014): 51–62.

30 Ibid., 132.

31 I discovered the existence of these documents on Twitter, after Geoffrey Smith posted some photographs of them, stating: "Here's something fun: Old Nubian papyri of Luke 'forged' by Gerald M. Browne himself!" (@G_S_Smith, *Twitter*, November 18, 2019, 4:03PM, https://twitter.com/G_S_Smith/status/1196443754384764932). Professor Smith was kind enough to provide me with high-resolution images of the documents, as well as the information concerning their provenance.

Fig. 3. Old Nubian fragment of Luke 1:1 on papyrus, forged by Gerald M. Browne. Courtesy of Geoffrey Smith.

Fig. 4. "AMVLETVM PALAEONVBIANVM (Luc. 1,1 continens)." Old Nubian fragment of Luke 1:1 on papyrus, forged by Gerald M. Browne. Courtesy of Geoffrey Smith.

Fig. 5. Backside of "AMVLETVM PALAEONVBIANVM (Luc. 1,1 continens)" (fig. 4) with the dedication "For Charlotte — Love, Michael — Christmas 2000." Courtesy of Geoffrey Smith.

ⲅⲟⲩⲕⲁ ⲡⲁⲇ[- - -]
ⲛⲓⲁ̄ ⲁ̄ⲙⲁⲇⲟ̄[- - -]
ⲥⲁⲛⲛⲟⲇ̄ⲟⲩⲛ[- - -]

Browne has made sure only to include partial words, so as to minimize any room for errors on his side: -ⲅⲟⲩⲕⲁ -*gouka* is a plural accusative ending, perhaps forming the end of the object of the verb ⲡⲁⲇ *paj*, which means "to take away," and is difficult to place in Luke 1:1, perhaps rendering ἐπεχείρησαν "they have taken in hand." The sequence -ⲛⲓⲁ̄ ⲁ̄ⲙⲁⲇⲟ̄- *-nia amadj-* is no doubt inspired by SC 8.2 ⲕⲉⲛⲟⲩⲧⲟⲩⲣⲟ̄[ⲥⲉⲛ]ⲓⲁ ⲁⲙⲁⲇⲟ̄ⲕⲕⲁ *kenoutourosenia amadjokka* "that he has hastened to beach [his ship]"[32] but again difficult to reconcile with Luke 1:1. Perhaps the final ending -ⲛⲓⲁ̄ is supposed to render the infinitive ἀνατάξασθαι "to compose," but the possible role of the verb ⲁ̄ⲙⲁⲇⲟ̄ "to strive, hasten," remains obscure. -ⲥⲁⲛⲛⲟⲇ̄ⲟⲩⲛ *-sannojoun* is yet another bunch of verbal morphology without root, meaning "because they X-ed." Perhaps this is already supposed to be the beginning of Luke 1:2 καθὼς παρέδοσαν? In any case, even if these fragments were authentic, it would be impossible (for anyone not Browne), to assign them to the Gospel of Luke, or any other known text for that matter.

The backside of the "Old Nubian amulet" contains a dedication (fig. 5): "For Charlotte — Love, Michael — Christmas 2000."

---

32 Gerald M. Browne, *Chrysostomus Nubianus: An Old Nubian Version of Ps.-Chrysostom* In venerabile crucem sermo (Rome & Barcelona: Papyrologica Castroctaviana, 1984), 42–43.

Fig. 6. "Old Nubian Version of Apc 9,17.21; 10,1." Old Nubian fragment of Revelation 9:17 on paper, forged by Gerald M. Browne. Courtesy of Geoffrey Smith.

Fig. 7. Backside of "Old Nubian Version of Apc 9,17.21; 10,1" (fig. 6). Old Nubian fragment of Revelation 10:1 on paper, forged by Gerald M. Browne with the dedication "For Charlotte with love from Michael: Christmas 1994." Courtesy of Geoffrey Smith.

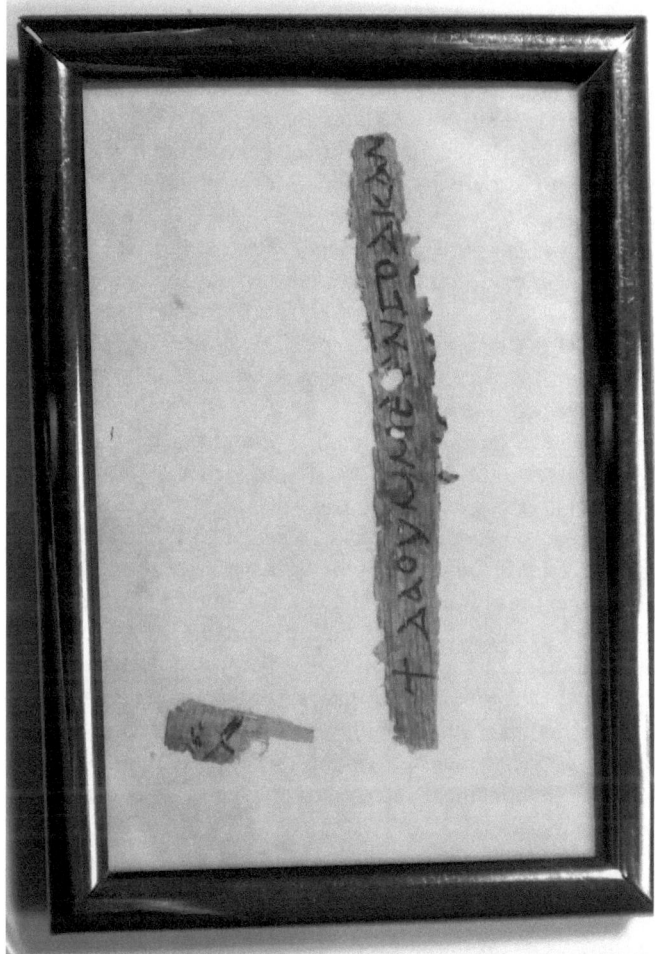

Fig. 8. Old Nubian fragment of a letter on papyrus, forged by Gerald M. Browne. Courtesy of Geoffrey Smith.

We find a similar dedication on another framed Old Nubian text, this time written on paper and dated 1994 (figs. 6, 7): "For Charlotte with love from Michael: Christmas 1994." We will return to the identity of "Charlotte" below.

As with the forged fragments of Luke, these fragments of Revelation clearly express Browne's own philological desires. Recto l. 2 (fig. 6) happens to show ογⲁ̄- *hua-*, no doubt meant to render (as a loan word) Revelation 9:17 ὑακίνθινος, which would provide a welcome "parallel" to his very shaky reconstruction of the hapax P.QI 1 10.C.i.10 <ογⲁ̄>ⲕⲛ̄ⲧ{ⲓⲣ}ⲟⲥⲕⲁ.[33] Verso l. 3 (fig. 7) [ⲉⲓ]ⲥ ⲁⲅⲅⲉⲗⲟⲥ[- - -] *eis aggelos-* is no doubt meant to render Revelation 10:1 ἄλλον ἄγγελον, again with nominal morphology conveniently omitted.

The fourth framed text (fig. 8), without title or dedication, neatly contains the opening greeting of a letter, ⲇⲁⲟⲩⲙⲙⲉⲗⲟ ⲉⲛ̄ ⲅⲟⲇⲕⲁⲛ[ⲉⲕⲁ] *daoummelo ein ŋodkaneka* "I greet Your Lordship." As the language of letters written in Old Nubian is significantly more difficult to comprehend, it makes sense that Browne here forges the only aspect of letter that is known relatively well: the greeting formula. Rather than showing us novel aspects of Old Nubian, which nearly all newly discovered documents do, no matter their size or provenance, the framed fragments that Geoffrey Smith acquired online show us a precise cross-section of Old Nubian knowledge while Browne was alive: the lacunas in his forgeries coincide precisely with Nubiology's philological blind spots.

The Sunnarti Luke, the Qasr Ibrim Apocryphon, the *Liber Institutionis Michaelis Archangeli,* and the forged papyri are all exam-

---

33 J. Martin Plumley and Gerald M. Browne, *Old Nubian Texts from Qasr Ibrīm I* (London: Egypt Exploration Society, 1988), 47. Cf. Gerald M. Browne, *Old Nubian Dictionary* (Peeters: Leuven, 1996), 187, s.v. *ογⲁ̄ⲕⲛ̄ⲧⲟⲥ-.

ples of Browne's philological skill, showing a masterful competence of a language not written for nearly a thousand years. The suspension of the philologist and their text between reality and imagination is, in fact, a prominent feature of Browne's practice. Its most pervasive feature is the reconstructed *Vorlage,* usually in Greek. Such *Vorlages* are retrotranslations from Old Nubian to Greek and are always "attempted"[34] or "hypothetical."[35] Nevertheless, their mere presence as typeset and published text inevitably lends them a sense of scholarly authority. What speaks from all of them is the "refinement of intellectual pleasures,"[36] the intense pleasure of creating, or even *inventing* language.[37] Again, Jacobson affirms so much in his *encomium*:

> Michael will even go to the extreme of *inventing* languages, more or less. There is a modern language, Beja, spoken in Sudan and Ethiopia, but we have no traces of an early version or forerunner of this language. I recently finished reading his latest monograph [...], *Textus Blemmyicus Aetatis Christianae,* in which he claims to have identified and deciphered fragments of this unknown language, Blemmyian.[38]

This is, one hopes, partially spoken in jest, but it contains a core of truth. Because Browne's philological imagination extended beyond the realm of reconstructions and *Vorlages,* into the invention of actual philological objects and even personae. In the same way that Browne imagined a Nubian scribe stuck in a "cultural wasteland" and imbued with his own feelings of "boredom

---

34 G.M. Browne, *Chrysostomus Nubianus,* 23.
35 Gerald M. Browne, *The Miracle of Saint Menas,* Beiträge zur Sudanforschung Beiheft 7 (Vienna-Mödling: Verein der Förderer der Sudanforschung, 1994), 3, 84.
36 G.M. Browne, "Old Nubian Philology," 296.
37 A parallel may perhaps be drawn here with the way in which Friedrich Nietzsche used his philological prowess to "reinvent" the Presocratics. See James I. Porter, *Nietzsche and the Philology of the Future* (Stanford: Stanford University Press, 2000), 228.
38 Jacobson, "Remarks upon G.M. Browne's Retirement," xiii. My emphasis.

and despair," he created scholarly alter-egos, called "stufflings." These were not a mere caprice of the imagination but can be analyzed as a projection of Browne's personal thoughts and emotions into the scholarly realm. Through the stufflings, philology becomes biography.

The first open acknowledgment of the stufflings' existence as Browne's scholarly companions appears in the footnote apparatus — yet another treasured tool of the philologist — of his "Valedictory Address," roughly a year before his suicide. The first footnote corrects Jacobson's claim that Browne no longer uses the pen as his main writing implement,[39] which would imply that he no longer operates in the philological tradition he imagined for himself:

> I still use the pen for composition, and only after I have finished the work in all its details do I entrust it — but only if the publisher insists — to the infernal word-processor (which, incidentally, the stufflings [see n. 2] and I will not keep in the sanctity of our home).[40]

Note here the use of "our home," in which the possessive pronoun refers to both Browne and the stufflings. This suggests a certain intimacy between Browne and his philological alter-egos, which is confirmed by what follows. The second footnote, to which this first one refers, is written entirely in Latin, in the time-honored manner of disguising potentially subversive material from the lay reader.[41] The footnote deals directly with

---

39 Ibid.
40 G.M. Browne, "Valedictory Address," xv, n. 1.
41 A notorious example is Richard von Krafft-Ebing's *Psychopathia Sexualis*, where he writes in the introduction: "In order that unqualified persons should not become readers, the author saw himself compelled to choose a title understood only by the learned, and also, where possible, to express himself in terminis technicis. It seemed necessary also to give certain particularly revolting portions in Latin rather than in German." In a footnote, he even adds, for good measure, that "the Latin is left untranslated" (*Psychopathia Sexualis, with Especial Reference to Contrary*

Browne's death, as it contains the inscription for his gravestone. This strongly suggests that his suicide was premeditated:[42]

> Cum non credam umquam fore librum memoriae meae dedicatum (qui germanice Gedenkschrift vocatur), hoc loco titulum sepulcri mei refero. quid significet intellegent qui me noverunt; confundantur reliqui. N.B. quod ad versiones quae sequuntur pertinet, si latina et graeca paulo magis priscae sunt quam ut fautoribus Ovidii et Callimachi placeant, ipsi suos versus componant!

> [As I do not believe there will ever be a book dedicated to my memory (usually called *Gedenkschrift*), I here convey my epitaph. Those who know me will understand what it means. Let others be confused. N.B. with respect to the versions that follow, if the Latin and Greek are a bit more old-fashioned than would please the supporters of Ovid and Callimachus,[43] let them write their own verses!][44]

What follows is an epitaph in English, followed by translations in Latin, Greek, Sanskrit, Old Nubian, and Sahidic Coptic. I give here only the English:

> Every bond is a bond to sorrow,
>   To sorrow and despair,
> Except the bond to stufflings,
>   Which removeth every care.[45]

   Sexual Instinct: A Medico-Legal Study, trans. Charles Gilbert Chaddock [Philadelphia: F.A. Davis; London: F.J. Rebman, 1894], v).
42 *Studia Palaeophilologica* was published before Browne's death (Stephen Bay. p.c., May 16, 2019).
43 Note that Callimachus also appears in the final paragraphs of "Old Nubian Philology," 296.
44 G.M. Browne, "Valedictory Address," xv, n. 2. My translation.
45 Ibid.

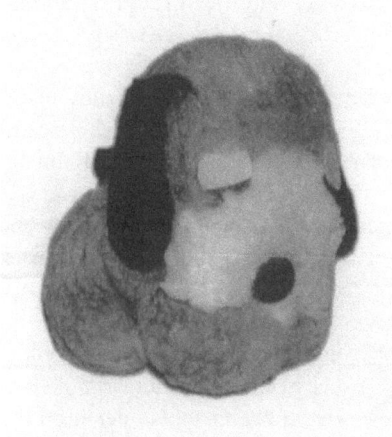

Fig. 9. Charlotte Stuffling. Courtesy of Stephen M. Bay.

In the Old Nubian translation of the inscription, the stufflings are poetically called ϩⲁⲣⲙⲓⲧⲟⲩ ⲅⲟⲫⲓⲧⲁⲕⲟⲗⲅⲟⲩⲗ *harmitou goñitakolgoul,* "constructed heavenly creatures."[46] *harmit-* is here an Old Nubian neologism, based on the noun ϩⲁⲣⲙ *harm* "heaven," and moreover forms a slightly macabre rhyme with ⲅⲁⲣⲙⲓⲧ *ngarmit,* the Old Nubian word for the Beast. The inscription thus testifies to the attachment Browne had to these stufflings, perhaps stronger than most human bonds he forged in his life — if we may believe the symbolic importance of an epitaph.

These stufflings were a group of stuffed animals, each with a different scholarly specialization, which Browne kept throughout his career. Charlotte the dog studied Old Nubian (fig. 9), Willie the racoon Sanskrit, Arthur the raven specialized in Coptic, and Freddy the floppy-eared dog was a numismatist.[47] In fact, Charlotte Stuffling made her first public appearance in

---

46 Ibid., xvi, n. 2.
47 Stephen M. Bay, p.c., June 13, 2018.

Browne's *Old Nubian Dictionary* from 1996, which is dedicated to "Charlotte. Thou from the first wast present."[48] This phrase derives from Milton's *Paradise Lost* and refers to the "Heav'nly Muse" inspiring the poet.[49] Charlotte, the same Charlotte who received the forged Old Nubian papyri for Christmas 1994 and 2000, was Browne's plush muse. The stufflings were thus essential to Browne's scholarly practice, his sole interlocutors in the "cultural wasteland" of Urbana-Champaign.

But the stufflings do not only appear as Browne's scholarly companions. In *Studia Palaeophilologica* they also appear as scholars in their own right. The volume contains two contributions by a Browne that is not Michael: W.S. Browne's "A Sanskrit Hymn to Durgā" (fig. 10) and C.S. Browne's "Tatianus Nubianus" (fig. 11).[50] W.S. stands for Willie Stuffling, the Sanskritist, while C.S. stands for Old Nubian specialist Charlotte Stuffling. As Stephen Bay, who published their contributions in the *Festschrift* narrated to me in an email:

> Anyway, the Festschrift project was not a secret. Michael sent me suggestions for colleagues around the world that might want to contribute to the volume. One morning I found that two manuscripts for inclusion in the Festschrift had been slipped under my door. One was by C.S. Browne (Charlotte Stuffling Browne), the other by W.S. Browne (Willie Stuffling Browne). Michael always claimed that his stuffed animals had dictated the articles to him and that I should include

---

48 Browne, *Old Nubian Dictionary*, v.
49 John Milton, *Paradise Lost: Books I. and II.*, ed. A.W. Verity (Cambridge: Cambridge University Press, 1934), Book I, ll. 19–20.
50 W.S. Browne, "A Sanskrit Hymn to Durgā," in *Studia Palaeophilologica: Proferessoris G.M. Browne in honorem oblata*, ed. Stephen M. Bay (Champaign: Stipes Publishing, 2004), 47–51; C.S. Browne, "Tatianus Nubianus," in *Studia Palaeophilologica: Proferessoris G.M. Browne in honorem oblata*, ed. Stephen M. Bay (Champaign: Stipes Publishing, 2004), 91–98.

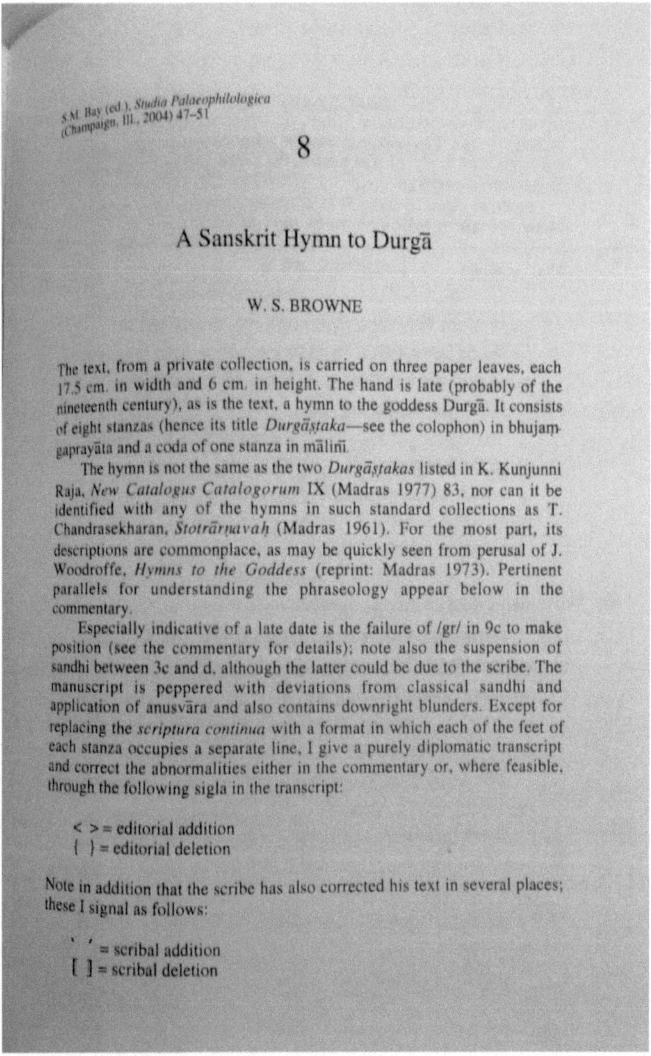

> S.M. Bay (ed.), *Studia Palaeophilologica*
> (Champaign, Ill., 2004) 47-51

8

A Sanskrit Hymn to Durgā

W. S. BROWNE

The text, from a private collection, is carried on three paper leaves, each 17.5 cm. in width and 6 cm. in height. The hand is late (probably of the nineteenth century), as is the text, a hymn to the goddess Durgā. It consists of eight stanzas (hence its title *Durgāṣṭaka*—see the colophon) in bhujaṃgaprayāta and a coda of one stanza in mālinī.

The hymn is not the same as the two *Durgāṣṭakas* listed in K. Kunjunni Raja, *New Catalogus Catalogorum* IX (Madras 1977) 83, nor can it be identified with any of the hymns in such standard collections as T. Chandrasekharan, *Stotrārṇavaḥ* (Madras 1961). For the most part, its descriptions are commonplace, as may be quickly seen from perusal of J. Woodroffe, *Hymns to the Goddess* (reprint: Madras 1973). Pertinent parallels for understanding the phraseology appear below in the commentary.

Especially indicative of a late date is the failure of /gr/ in 9c to make position (see the commentary for details); note also the suspension of sandhi between 3c and d, although the latter could be due to the scribe. The manuscript is peppered with deviations from classical sandhi and application of anusvāra and also contains downright blunders. Except for replacing the *scriptura continua* with a format in which each of the feet of each stanza occupies a separate line, I give a purely diplomatic transcript and correct the abnormalities either in the commentary or, where feasible, through the following sigla in the transcript:

< > = editorial addition
{ } = editorial deletion

Note in addition that the scribe has also corrected his text in several places; these I signal as follows:

ˋ ˊ = scribal addition
[ ] = scribal deletion

Fig. 10. Opening page of Willie Stuffling Browne's "A Sanskrit Hymn to Durgā." Photo by the author.

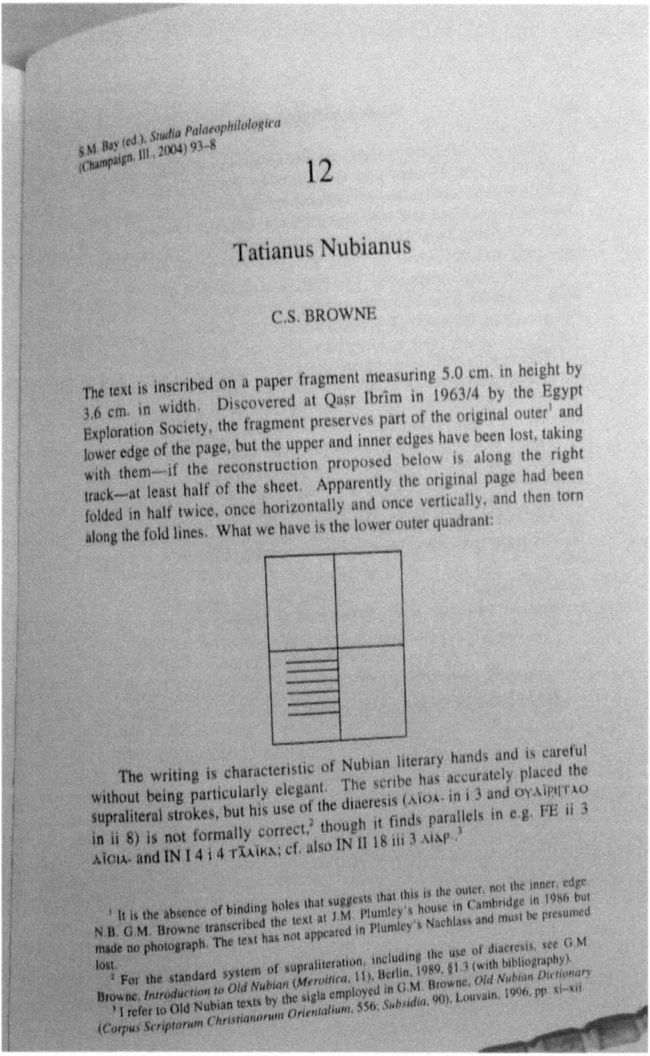

S.M. Bay (ed.), *Studia Palaeophilologica*
(Champaign, Ill., 2004) 93–8

12

Tatianus Nubianus

C.S. BROWNE

The text is inscribed on a paper fragment measuring 5.0 cm. in height by 3.6 cm. in width. Discovered at Qasr Ibrîm in 1963/4 by the Egypt Exploration Society,[1] the fragment preserves part of the original outer and lower edge of the page, but the upper and inner edges have been lost, taking with them—if the reconstruction proposed below is along the right track—at least half of the sheet. Apparently the original page had been folded in half twice, once horizontally and once vertically, and then torn along the fold lines. What we have is the lower outer quadrant:

The writing is characteristic of Nubian literary hands and is careful without being particularly elegant. The scribe has accurately placed the supraliteral strokes, but his use of the diaeresis (ΑΪΟΛ- in i 3 and ΟΥΛΙΡΗΤΛΟ in ii 8) is not formally correct,[2] though it finds parallels in e.g. FE ii 3 ΑΪΟΙΑ- and IN I 4 i 4 ΤΪΛΑΪΚΑ; cf. also IN II 18 iii 3 ΑΪΑΡ-.[3]

---

[1] It is the absence of binding holes that suggests that this is the outer, not the inner, edge. N.B. G.M. Browne transcribed the text at J.M. Plumley's house in Cambridge in 1986 but made no photograph. The text has not appeared in Plumley's Nachlass and must be presumed lost.

[2] For the standard system of supraliteration, including the use of diaeresis, see G.M. Browne, *Introduction to Old Nubian* (Meroitica, 11), Berlin, 1989, §1.3 (with bibliography).

[3] I refer to Old Nubian texts by the sigla employed in G.M. Browne, *Old Nubian Dictionary* (*Corpus Scriptorum Christianorum Orientalium*, 556; *Subsidia*, 90), Louvain, 1996, pp. xi–xii.

Fig. 11. Opening page of Charlotte Stuffling Browne's "Tatianus Nubianus." Photo by the author.

them in the volume as their work. It was a Festschrift for him, so what could I do?

So, unbeknownst to the rest of the world, I have introduced two stuffed animal scholars into the standard academic bibliographies and, consequently, into academia.[51]

Indeed, the textual evidence strongly suggests that Browne himself wrote both contributions. "Tatianus Nubianus" discusses a fragment deriving from Martin Plumley's 1963–64 Qasr Ibrim excavations, from which Browne published most of the Old Nubian material.[52] As in the other examples discussed above, Charlotte's reading and identification depend on a minimum of material, as only six words in the Old Nubian fragment appear to have survived completely. Furthermore, the breadth of sources cited from Arabic, Middle Dutch, and Middle Italian, the translation made from the Manichean Middle Persian made by the author herself, footnoted with a snarky comment about a prior, erroneous translation,[53] as well as the typical reconstructed Greek *Vorlage* and extensive reconstructions of the Old Nubian,[54] combined with a commentary that relies twice on Syriac,[55] all point to skillset and editorial style of a single scholar: Gerald Michael Browne.

---

51 Stephen M. Bay, p.c., June 13, 2018.
52 Plumley and G.M. Browne, *Old Nubian Texts from Qasr Ibrīm I*; Gerald M. Browne, *Old Nubian Texts from Qasr Ibrīm II* (London: Egypt Exploration Society, 1989); Gerald M. Browne, *Old Nubian Texts from Qasr Ibrīm III* (London: Egypt Exploration Society, 1991); Gerald M. Browne, "Old Nubian Studies: Past, Present, and Future," in *Egypt and Africa: Nubia from Prehistory to Islam*, ed. W.V. Davies (London: British Museum Press, 1991), 286–93; Gerald M. Browne, "A Survey of Old Nubian Texs from Qasr Ibrim," *Nubian Letters* 21 (1994): 7–10; Gerald M. Browne, "An Old Nubian Lectionary Fragment," *Orientalia* 70 (2001): 113–16; Browne, "An Old Nubian Apocryphal Text from Qasr Ibrīm."
53 C.S. Browne, "Tatianus Nubianus," 95, n. 7.
54 Ibid., 97.
55 Ibid., 98.

Whereas his article "Old Nubian Philology" from 1985 argues for the availability of the *Hexapla* in Makuria, "Tatianus Nubianus" uses the Qasr Ibrim fragment to argue for the availability in Nubia of another philological treasure, Tatian's *Diatessaron,* originally composed in Syriac. With this article, Browne thus recaptures — through Charlotte — the parallel between the deserts of Nubia and Urbana-Champaign, and the figure of the scribe purging his despair by leafing through rare philological tomes.

It is even questionable whether the Old Nubian fragment discussed by Charlotte actually exists, considering the fact that Browne actually did forge Old Nubian documents. The first footnote states: "G.M. Browne transcribed the text at J.M. Plumley's house in Cambridge in 1986 but made no photograph. The text has not appeared in Plumley's Nachlass and must be presumed lost."[56] The typewritten excavation registry lists under register number 64/24 "Old Nubian letters on paper, now with J.M.P. — church 1, south crypt," but no photographs were taken in situ or afterward.[57] Plumley's published excavation notes from the 1963–64 season mention them too: "manuscript fragments in Greek and Old Nubian, which had certainly originated from the Library of the Church,"[58] but no further specifics are mentioned in Plumley's article or Plumley and Browne's later publication of part of the Old Nubian material in 1988.[59] The state of the Old Nubian fragment, suspended between reality and imagination, therefore uncannily resembles the status of its edition's author.

The same uncertainty plagues us in the case of Willie Stuffling's "A Sanskrit Hymn to Durgā." Like Charlotte Stuffling's edition of the Old Nubian fragment from Qasr Ibrim, the existence of the original manuscript of this text cannot be veri-

---

56 Ibid., 93, n. 1.
57 I thank Giovanni Ruffini for providing me with photographs of the Qasr Ibrim excavation registries and the Egypt Exploration Society for allowing me to study them.
58 J. Martin Plumley, "Qasr Ibrim 1963–1964," *The Journal of Egyptian Archaeology* 50 (1964): 3–5, at 3.
59 G.M. Browne and Plumley, *The Old Nubian Texts from Qasr Ibrim I*, 1–2.

fied, as it resides in an unspecified "private collection."[60] Like the Old Nubian text, the hymn is a philological oddity. It is "not the same" as other published hymns to Durgā, "nor can it be identified with any of the hymns" recorded in standard collections. Moreover, "[t]he manuscript is peppered with deviations from classical sandhi and application of anusvāra and also contains downright blunders."[61] If we look at the structure of the verse, it is remarkably similar to the Sanskrit translation Browne produced of his epitaph in footnote 2 of the "Valedictory Address." And as in the case of "Tatianus Nubianus," it is impossible to verify whether this hymn actually exists or is a brilliant philological invention, as imaginary as the author who wrote it. But the "refined pleasure" that speaks from composing Sanskrit verse including "downright blunders" suggests, just like with Charlotte's article, that also this text may hover on the edge of existence.[62]

---

60 W.S. Browne, "A Sanskrit Hymn to Durgā," 47. Michael published relatively few texts from private collections, and most of his critical editions can be checked against publicly held manuscripts. There is, however, the publication of a bilingual Fayumic Coptic–Old Nubian papyrus fragment from a "private collection" that is equally suspect. The text was published in a Gedenkschrift for Coptologist Zbigniew Borkowski (G.M. Browne, "A Papyrus Document in Coptic and Old Nubian," *Journal for Juristic Papyrology* 23 (1993): 29–32). Not only would this be the only extant bilingual Coptic–Old Nubian letter, Browne also claims a very early 7th c. CE date, making it the earliest attestation of Old Nubian. Furthermore, it would be the only Old Nubian text on papyrus, and the text would contain — remarkably — the unattested and partially reconstructed Latin loanword ⲗⲓⲡⲉ[ⲣⲁⲗⲓⲥ(?) < *liberalis*. A remarkable coincidence of unique features, to say the least.
61 W.S. Browne, "A Sanskrit Hymn to Durgā," 47.
62 Hans Henrich Hock (p.c., May 23, 2019) vaguely recalls discussing Willie Stuffling's edition with Browne (cf. W.S. Browne, "A Sanskrit Hymn to Durgā," 48), but admits that "[he doesn't] think [they] talked about the text, or its provenance, in any detail." I also showed the edition to Dan Rudmann, a Sanskritist colleague, asking him for his opinion about the text without revealing my own suspicions. This is what he wrote: "I will say that the sandhi is off, as the intro points out, which by extension messes up the meter. I don't usually come across texts with dissonance

Neither article shows up in Browne's official bibliography,[63] and the original manuscripts have been respectively "lost" or are located in an inaccessible "private collection." They were published in a non-peer-reviewed, celebratory *Festschrift* printed in a small edition, and written semi-pseudonymically. If anything, the articles of Charlotte and Willie appear to be "displays of linguistic virtuosity" buried in the "vast registers" of philological scholarship.[64]

How then to read these two articles, written by imaginary scholars discussing probably invented texts? Why did Browne write them and what can they tell us? Perhaps the footnotes he attached to the "Valedictory Address" can give us a clue here: Browne's contributions to the *Festschrift* deal with his own impending death.[65] They are, following footnote 1 the *Gedenkschrift*, the *in memoriam* that was never written. In this reading, which brings us straight into the literary territory surveyed by Vladimir Nabokov's famous novel *Pale Fire,* in which a murder mystery unfolds itself in the scholarly apparatus to a poem,[66] the articles by Charlotte and Willie Stuffling should be read not only as works of (imaginary) scholarship, but as biography.

Read through such a biographical lens, the "Sanskrit Hymn to Durgā" suddenly becomes understandable. Durgā is a Hindu

---

like this — perhaps it's because what I read is much older and presumably more combed over. But sandhi strikes me as a strange thing to mess up if the writer has much experience in Sanskrit because it is so foundational. It could suggest that the work was translated into Sanskrit" (p.c., May 11, 2019. My emphasis).

63 Cf. Bay, "Gerald Michael Browne."
64 G.M. Browne, "Old Nubian Philology," 296.
65 This already seems to be intimated by Stephen Bay, when he suggests that Browne's "Valedictory Address does indeed read as if he meant it for such occasion [sc. as tribute to a departed colleague]" (Bay and Parca, "†G. Michael Browne (1943–2004)," 14).
66 Vladimir Nabokov, *Pale Fire* (London: Penguin, 2011).

goddess, a "defender of the dharmic order, an all-powerful warrior goddess who manifests unsurpassed martial skills to confront various demonic threats to world."[67] And reading the actual text of the hymn, one gets the strong impression that Browne, who professed to have "no orthodox belief system" to support him, found "secular salvation"[68] in composing and editing this hymn:

> 3. For a man hopeless, afflicted, violently suffering, sick of existence, terrified of (worldly) bondage, you, Goddess, are the cause of deliverance, the only refuge. [...] 4. In foreign land, in dreadful battle, in the midst of the enemy, or in water, in fire, in the palace, in the cemetery, you, Goddess, are the maker of deliverance, the only refuge. [...] 5. For the embodied ones who sink in the boundless, very hard-to-cross, extremely terrible ocean of misfortune, you, Goddess, are the raft of deliverance, the only refuge.[69]

The adjectives used in this passage are eerily reminiscent of Browne's own "plight," which he compared to a "frustrated *erudit manqué*" who, stuck in a "cultural wasteland," out of "playful desperation" sought "solace within [...] the gentle art of philology" as "anodyne for boredom and despair."[70] Durgā, in other words, figures here as goddess of philology, delivering those who are "hopeless, afflicted, violently suffering, sick of existence, [...] in foreign land, [... and] in the boundless very hard-to-cross, extremely terrible ocean of misfortune."[71]

---

67 Denise Cush, Catherine Robinson, and Michael York, eds., *Encyclopedia of Hinduism* (London: Routledge, 2008), s.v. "Durgā."
68 G.M. Browne, "Valedictory Address," xvii–xviii.
69 W.S. Browne, "A Sanskrit Hymn to Durgā," 51.
70 G.M. Browne, "Old Nubian Philology," 296.
71 W.S. Browne suggests that such descriptions are "commonplace," but I have only been able to find a few lines in a much longer hymn that could correspond to some of the imagery (but certainly not verse form) in W.S. Browne's hymn. See Arthur and Ellen Avalon, eds., *Hymns to the Goddess*, trans. John Woodroffe, 3rd edn. (Madras: Ganesh & Co., 1964), 144: "Thou

Whereas Willie's article can be straightforwardly read as a dirge, if not a cry for help, Charlotte's "Nubianus Tatianus," an Old Nubian version of Tatian's *Diatessaron,* is more subtle in the way in which it settles scores and plays with figures of absence and presence. I here reproduce the edition of the "lost" Qasr Ibrim fragment:

i

ⲡⲉⲥⲥⲁⲛⲁ ⲧ[ⲉⲇⲅ̄ⲗⲗⲉ·] (Lk 24:5)
ⲙⲛ̄ⲛⲉⲇⲟⲩⲛ [ⲁ̄ⲫⲗ̄ⲕⲁⲗⲟ]
ⲇⲓ̈ⲟⲗⲅⲟⲩⲇ[ⲇⲁⲗ ⲇⲟⲛⲛⲟ·]
ⲉⲛ̄ⲛⲟ ⲇⲟⲩⲙ[ⲙⲉⲛⲛⲁⲗⲟ·]
5 ⲥⲓⲥⲛⲁ̄ⲉⲛⲕ[ⲱ· ⲁⲛⲕⲁ]
ⲛⲁⲥⲟ· ⲉ̂ⲅⲉⲗ [ⲅⲁⲗⲓⲗⲁⲓ̈ⲁ̄]

ii

[ⲉⲓⲟ̄ ⲇⲟⲩⲛ ⲟⲩⲕⲕⲁ ⲉⲓⲁ̄]
[ⲧ̄ⲟ̄ⲇⲓ̈ⲥⲛⲁ̄ⲗⲟⲁ̄· ⲡⲉⲥⲗ̄· ⲉⲓ]
[ⲧⲛ̄ ⲧⲟⲧⲛⲁ̄ ⲥⲁⲡⲉⲕⲁⲉⲓ]
[ⲅⲟⲩⲛ ⲉⲓⲗⲱ ⲇⲟⲩⲙⲙⲓ]
5 [ⲧⲁⲕⲁ ⲧ̄ⲟ̄ⲇⲓ̈ⲇⲉⲛⲟⲩ ĉ]
[ⲧⲁⲩⲣⲟⲥⲗ̄]ⲇⲱ ⲟⲗⲗⲓⲇⲉ
[ⲛⲟⲩ ⲟⲩⲕⲟ]ⲩⲛ ⲧⲟⲩⲥⲕ̄ⲧⲓ
[ⲗⲟ ⲥⲓⲇⲉ]ⲛⲉⲛ· ⲟⲩⲇⲓⲣⲓ (Mt 28:7)
[ⲧⲗⲟ̄ ⲇ̂ⲟⲣ]ⲁⲉⲓⲟⲛ ⲧⲁⲛ ⲙⲁ
10 [ⲉⲏⲧⲓⲥⲟⲩ]ⲅⲟⲩⲇⲇⲉ ⲡⲉ (Mk 16:7)
[ⲧⲣⲟⲥⲓⲇⲉ]ⲕⲉⲗⲅⲗ̄ⲗⲉ/ [ⲡⲉⲥⲁⲛⲁⲥⲱ

(Lk 24:5) ... they said to them: "Why [do you seek the living with] the dead? (6) He is [not] here but he arose. [Remember

art called Durgā by all because Thou savest men from difficulty. / Whether in dangerous lands or sinking in the great ocean, / Thou art the sole refuge of men. / When assailed by robbers, when crossing streams and seas, / As also in wilderness and great forests, / Those who remember Thee, O Māhadevī! are never lost."

that, when he was] still [in Galilee, he spoke to you, (7) saying that the son of man will be delivered to the hands of sinner and will be crucified and] will [arise on] the third day. (Mt 28:7) And going quickly, [say] to his disciples (Mk 16:7) and to Peter…"⁷²

The first thing that should be noted is that, through a remarkable coincidence, the majority of the surviving — and extensively reconstructed — Old Nubian text contains a long fragment from the Gospel of Luke, the very same Gospel whose existence in Old Nubian Unger questioned in his critique of Browne's Sunnarti Luke. As Unger was the only scholar ever to publicly dispute one of Browne's Old Nubian identifications — an identification which initiated his Old Nubian career and an accomplishment he was proud of — the edition of this fragment reads like a firm rebuttal.

Furthermore, as may be clear from the translation, much of the material that is "actually" in the Old Nubian is highly suggestive. Only i.3 ⲇⲓⲟⲗⲅⲟⲩⲇ- *diolgoud-* "the dead" are found in the manuscript, while ⲁ̄ⲫⲗ̄- *añil-* "the living" are under erasure, reconstructed. Equally mesmerizing is the reconstructed negation in i.4 ⲇⲟⲩⲙ[ⲙⲉⲛⲛⲁⲗⲟ·] *doum[mennalo]* "He is [not] here." Both reconstructions thematize the suspension of the dichotomy of absence and presence, life and death.⁷³

A similar game with a reconstructed negation can be found in another article from 2003. The article, entitled "Ad Sphujidhvajae *Yavanajātakam*," and, like footnote 2 of the "Valedictory Address," composed in Latin, comprises a single comment on a verse from the Sanskrit horoscope *Yavanajātakae* by Sphujidhvajae. According to the opening paragraph, its publication was occasioned by the death of Miroslav Marcovich, who was

---

72 C.S. Browne, "Tatianus Nubianus," 97.
73 We may perhaps also note that there are two parallel texts adduced by Charlotte that don't have "Peter" in the last phrase. The Arabic Harmony has instead "Céphas," whereas the Turfan (Manichean) Fragment has "Simon": C.S.

head of the Classics Department at the University of Illinois at the time Browne was first hired as Assistant Professor in 1974.[74] Both the use of Latin and the personal dedication "ad memoriam collegae mei" should alert us to the biographical relevance of this text.

The verse reads as follows in English translation:

> One should say that a man born under sunaphā of Saturn is a clever and prosperous person who is secretive in his actions [*kriyāsu guptaṃ*], a man who is honored or is the mahattara of a city or town, a greedy fellow of impure character but healthy body.

Browne emends, based on a Greek parallel from Manetho's *Apothelesmatica*, the reading *kriyāsu guptaṃ* to *kriyāsv <a>guptaṃ*, rendering "secretive in his actions" into "non-secretive in his actions."[75] Taken within the context of Browne's other philological interventions from the same period, this emendation is highly suggestive. It appears that Browne, yet again, buried here a "display of linguistic virtuosity" doubling as biographical note.

There is increasing evidence for a mental health crisis in academia,[76] which may not be entirely unrelated to the pressures and inhospitality created by the continuous submission of the university to the logic and forces of the neoliberal market at the hands of a well-remunerated cadre of managers and bureaucrats without any personal stake in scholarship or education.[77]

---

74   Again, explicitly acknowledged in Browne's "Valedictory Address," xvi.
75   G.M. Browne, "Ad Sphujidhvajae *Yavanajātakam*," 175.
76   See, e.g., Teresa M. Evans et al., "Evidence for a Mental Health Crisis in Graduate Education," *Nature Biotechnology* 36, no. 3 (2018): 282–84.
77   In his "Valedictory Address," Browne touches upon this subject and finds also himself to blame: "For years the U[niversity] of I[llinois] maintained its position as a research institution, but recently — within the time of my

However, I would like to think through Browne's death precisely in relation to his scholarship and its broader academic context. Much of Nubian Studies is built upon death and erasure. Not only is the archeological enterprise continuously engaged with recovering the remainders of past lives, the blossoming of the scholarly field of Nubian Studies itself is predicated on a massive erasure of living culture and human displacement caused initially by the construction of the Aswan Dam, which destroyed many lives and even more livelihoods. In Egypt, the Nubians fruitlessly wait for their constitutional right to return to their ancestral lands to be enacted,[78] while in Sudan the ancient Meroitic word *kandaka* continues to resonate as Sudanese from all backgrounds wage a struggle to oust a military dictatorship and combat its deeply rooted legacy.[79] Yet, much of Nubian Studies' progress remains predicated on dam construction.

Even though Browne's oeuvre is to a certain extent unique in the way it allegorizes his depression and suicide, we should take seriously his deeply felt, if amorphous, sentiment that Old Nubian "needed" him. What is this feeling of need? A need for rec-

---

tenure — an administration filled with failed academics actually began to believe that the purpose of a university is to educate the young. If our administrators were scholars, they never would have entertained such a preposterous notion. The university exists primarily to expand the limits of human thought; [...] The fault for the mess in which our university now finds itself lies at least in part with me and with those other scholars who have steadfastly refused to dirty their hands with administration" (G.M. Browne, "Valedictory Address," xvii).

78 See, e.g., Amy Austin Holmes, "What Egypt's Racist Campaign against Nubians Reveals about Sissi's Regime," *Washtington Post*, April 19, 2018, https://www.washingtonpost.com/news/global-opinions/wp/2018/04/19/what-egypts-racist-campaign-against-nubians-reveals-about-sissis-regime/.

79 See, e.g., Nisrin Elamin and Tahani Ismail, "The Many Mothers of Sudan's Revolution," *Aljazeera*, May 4, 2019, https://www.aljazeera.com/indepth/opinion/alaa-salah-sudanese-mothers-190501175500137.html. By the time this chapter was published, the military dictatorship had been replaced by a transitory government in a power-sharing arrangement between civilians and the military.

ognition of a language and culture which continues to remain erased from so many maps — including the "medieval" one; a need to recognize that our field of Nubian Studies, by largely continuing to ignore the very real struggle of the currently living inheritors of Nubian culture, out of a fear this may "politicize" the field, or, even worse, threaten our state-sanctioned access to the archeological sites, we ignore the very reason that makes being engaged in our field worthwhile: that it relinks the dead with the living, that it scrutinizes the past so that we may imagine a future. And this activity — and here I disagree with Browne — is not merely to "expand the limits of human thought,"[80] but also to expand the possibilities of human *life*.

This is not to say that no reflection on the ethical and political implications of our research has taken place at all. A recent turning point was the construction of the Merowe Dam on the Fourth Cataract of the Nile in Sudan, which was inaugurated by ousted Sudanese president Omar al-Bashir in 2009. The construction was accompanied by several salvage-archeological missions, which encountered resistance from the local Manasir population, who argued that the archeological work legitimized the government's project of forced and violent expropriation and displacement.

Claudia Näser and Cornelia Kleinitz, who were involved in salvage archaeology at the Fourth Cataract through the mission of the Humboldt University, provide great detail on the interactions and tensions between archaeologists and the local community, and critically analyze the "idealised self-understanding"[81] with which many of the archaeologists involved framed their own commitment to the project:

80 G.M. Browne, "Valedictory Address," xvii.
81 Claudia Näser and Cornelia Kleinitz, "The Good, the Bad and the Ugly: A Case Study on the Politicisation of Archaeology and its Consequences from Northern Sudan," in *"Nihna nâs al-bahar — We Are the People of the River": Ethnographic Research in the Fourth Nile Cataract Region, Sudan,* eds. Cornelia Kleinitz and Claudia Näser (Wiesbaden: Harrassowitz, 2012), 269–304, at 287.

> The archaeologists working in the Fourth Cataract acted upon the deep conviction that salvage i.e., the documentation of archaeological heritage along the western notion of its innate value, is a universal goal of first priority and that the value system along which western archaeologists act is objective and universally valid. Moreover, they often had a "romantisised" [sic] involvement with the research area and its inhabitants.[82]

They also offer a withering critique of the response of Derek Welsby, former president of the International Society for Nubian Studies (ISNS), who stated that "by banning archaeologists from the region the Manasir Higher Committee is wantonly destroying the heritage of the people it is there to represent."[83] Näser and Kleinitz conclude: "These are strong words against people who faced the irretrievable loss of their ancestral land and their previous way of life as riverine farmers, in exchange for an uncertain future due to the development project that also brought in the archaeologists."[84]

Henriette Hafsaas offers an extensive review and analysis of the responses from the Nubiological community and their interactions with the Manasir and Sudanese government, remarking that "we still lack a self-reflexive critique that would involve a deconstruction of the Merowe Dam Archaeological Salvage Project — its truths, motives, knowledge, and power relationships,"[85] while pointing out that ISNS members continue

---

82 Ibid.
83 Derek Welsby, "Dams on the Nile: From Aswan to the Fourth Cataract," *Sudan Studies* 37 (2008): 5–18, at 14.
84 Näser and Kleinitz, "The Good, the Bad and the Ugly," 288.
85 Henriette Hafsaas-Tsakos, "Ethical Implications of Salvage Archaeology and Dam Building: The Clash between Archaeologists and Local People in Dar al-Manasir, Sudan," *Journal of Social Archaeology* 11, no. 1 (2011): 49–76, at 67.

to operate without a "code of ethics regulating their professional conduct."[86] She urges us that:

> By uncritically participating in archaeological salvage projects, archaeologists run the risk of being accused of complicity in human rights abuses, forced resettlement, and violations of international environmental standards. [...] It is a global problem that archaeologists conduct their business as if they are not implicated in the representations and struggles of living people. In this way, we ignore the ethical dimensions of our work and hide behind research agendas and scientific objectivity. [...] The idea that our work is retrospective rather than prospective and passive rather than active needs to change.[87]

In another article dealing with the same project, Kleinitz and Näser conclude:

> Taking a "neutral stance" within this web of interests while at the same time failing to consult with local communities about their heritage values and views of the past proved extremely counter-productive for the archaeological missions. [...] The case of the MDSAP underlines the fundamental point that securing adequate conditions for human life and human rights cannot be considered separately from, or irrelevant to, the study and preservation of archaeological heritage.[88]

---

86 Ibid., 68.
87 Ibid.
88 Cornelia Kleinitz and Claudia Näser, "The Loss of Innocence: Political and Ethical Dimensions of the Meroe Dam Archaeological Salvage Project at the Fourth Nile Cataract (Sudan)," *Conservation and Management of Archaeological Sites* 13, nos. 2–3 (2011): 253–80, at 273. See also Cornelia Kleinitz and Claudia Näser, "Archaeology, Development and Conflict: A Case Study from the African Continent," *Archaeologies: Journal of the World Archaeological Congress* 9, no. 1 (2013): 162–91.

But it is not only archeology that needs this reflection: the entirety of Nubian Studies, including philology, needs to become aware of how its constant preoccupation with the past is firmly rooted in the present, and how the way we deal with our dead reveals much about how we treat those who are alive. Browne's oeuvre shows us, in its breathtaking scope, how the personal and biographical are deeply enmeshed with the scholarly. His case is perhaps extraordinary, but it therefore has the virtue of clarity. What Browne's philological oeuvre teaches us is that all research is inevitably biographical, and because it is biographical, it carries the imprint of our own ethics and politics. It is, because of its very existence as text in a community of scholars and a much broader community of readers present and future, a reflection of how we are with other people, whether real or imaginary.

Browne liked to quote Erasmus: "unless we purify our texts we can never hope to purify ourselves." I would like to turn that around and say, "unless we get our hands dirty, our texts will remain sterile."

Bibliography

Adams, William Y. Nubia: *Corridor to Africa.* London: Allen Lane, 1977.

Austin Holmes, Amy. "What Egypt's Racist Campaign against Nubians Reveals about Sissi's Regime." *Washington Post,* April 19, 2018. https://www.washingtonpost.com/news/global-opinions/wp/2018/04/19/what-egypts-racist-campaign-against-nubians-reveals-about-sissis-regime/.

Avalon, Arthur and Ellen, eds. *Hymns to the Goddess.* Translated by John Woodroffe with Lady Woodroffe. 3rd Edition. Madras: Ganesh & Co., 1964.

Bay, Stephen M. "Gerald Michael Browne." *Beiträge zur Sudanforschung* 9 (2006): 5–23.

——— and Maryline G. Parca. "†G. Michael Browne (1943–2004)." *The Bulletin of the American Society of Papyrologists* 41, no. 1 (2004): 13–37. https://www.jstor.org/stable/24519832.

Browne, C.S. "Tatianus Nubianus." In *Studia Palaeophilologica: Proferessoris G.M. Browne in honorem oblata,* edited by Stephen M. Bay, 91–98. Champaign: Stipes Publishing, 2004.

Browne, Gerald M. "Ad Librum Insitutionis Michaelis Archangeli." *Orientalia* 65 (1996): 131–35.

———. "Ad Sphujidhvajae *Yavanajātakam*." *Illinois Classical Studies* 27–28 (2002–2003): 175–76. https://www.jstor.org/stable/23065459.

———. "A New Text in Old Nubian." *Zeitschrift für Papyrologie und Epigraphik* 37 (1980): 173–78. https://www.jstor.org/stable/20185841.

———. "An Old Nubian Apocryphal Text from Qasr Ibrīm." *Journal of Coptic Studies* 3 (2001): 129–32, pls. 14–15.

———. "An Old Nubian Lectionary Fragment." *Orientalia* 70 (2001): 113–16. https://www.jstor.org/stable/43076738.

———. "A Papyrus Document in Coptic and Old Nubian." *Journal for Juristic Papyrology* 23 (1993): 29–32.

———. "A Survey of Old Nubian Texs from Qasr Ibrim." *Nubian Letters* 21 (1994): 7–10.

———. *Bibliorum Sacrorum Versio Palaeonubiana*. Leuven: Peeters, 1994.

———. "Blemmyica." *Zeitschrift für Papyrologie und Epigraphik* 148 (2004): 245–46. https://www.jstor.org/stable/20191864.

———. *Chrysostomus Nubianus: An Old Nubian Version of Ps.-Chrysostom* In venerabile crucem sermo. Rome & Barcelona: Papyrologica Castroctaviana, 1984.

———. "Griffith's Old Nubian Lectionary: The Revision Revised." *Bulletin of the American Society of Papyrologists* 24, nos. 1–2 (1987): 75–92. https://www.jstor.org/stable/24518950.

———. *Literary Texts in Old Nubian*. Beiträge zur Sudanforschung Beiheft 5. Vienna–Mödling: Verein der Förderer der Sudanforschung, 1989.

———. "Notes on Old Nubian (I–III)." *Bulletin of the American Society of Papyrologists* 16, no. 4 (1979): 249–56. https://www.jstor.org/stable/24518811.

———. *Old Nubian Dictionary*. Peeters: Leuven, 1996.

———. "Old Nubian Philology." *Zeitschrift für Papyrologie und Epigraphik* 60 (1985): 291–96. https://www.jstor.org/stable/20184318.

———. "Old Nubian Studies: Past, Present, and Future." In *Egypt and Africa: Nubia from Prehistory to Islam*, edited by W.V. Davies, 286–93. London: British Museum Press, 1991.

———. *Old Nubian Texts from Qasr Ibrīm II*. London: Egypt Exploration Society, 1989.

———. *Old Nubian Texts from Qasr Ibrīm III*. London: Egypt Exploration Society, 1991.

———. *Textus Blemmyicus Aetatis Christianae*. Champaign: Stipes Publishing, 2003.

———. *The Miracle of Saint Menas*. Beiträge zur Sudanforschung Beiheft 7. Vienna-Mödling: Verein der Förderer der Sudanforschung, 1994.

———. "The Sunnarti Luke." *Zeitschrift für Papyrologie und Epigraphik* 70 (1989): 292–96. https://www.jstor.org/stable/20187101.

———. "Valedictory Address." In *Studia Palaeophilologica: Proferessoris G.M. Browne in honorem oblata,* edited by Stephen M. Bay, xv–xviii. Champaign: Stipes Publishing, 2004.

Browne, W.S. "A Sanskrit Hymn to Durgā." In *Studia Palaeophilologica: Proferessoris G.M. Browne in honorem oblata,* edited by Stephen M. Bay, 47–51. Champaign: Stipes Publishing, 2004.

Cush, Denise, Catherine Robinson, and Michael York, eds. *Encyclopedia of Hinduism.* London: Routledge, 2008.

Elamin, Nisrin, and Tahani Ismail. "The Many Mothers of Sudan's Revolution." *Aljazeera,* May 4, 2019. https://www.aljazeera.com/indepth/opinion/alaa-salah-sudanese-mothers-190501175500137.html.

Evans, Teresa M., et al. "Evidence for a Mental Health Crisis in Graduate Education." *Nature Biotechnology* 36, no. 3 (2018): 282–84. DOI: 10.1038/nbt.4089.

Gerven Oei, Vincent W.J. van. "The Disturbing Object of Philology." *postmedieval* 5, no. 4 (2014): 442–55. DOI: 10.1057/pmed.2014.32.

@G_S_Smith. *Twitter.* November 18, 2019, 4:03PM. https://twitter.com/G_S_Smith/status/1196443754384764932.

Hafsaas-Tsakos, Henriette. "Ethical Implications of Salvage Archaeology and Dam Building: The Clash between Archaeologists and Local People in Dar al-Manasir, Sudan." *Journal of Social Archaeology* 11, no. 1 (2011): 49–76. DOI: 10.1177/1469605310388372.

Jacobson, Howard. "Remarks upon G.M. Browne's Retirement." In *Studia Palaeophilologica: Proferessoris G.M. Browne in honorem oblata,* edited by Stephen M. Bay, xi–xiii. Champaign: Stipes Publishing, 2004.

Kleinitz, Cornelia, and Claudia Näser. "Archaeology, Development and Conflict: A Case Study from the African Continent." *Archaeologies: Journal of the World Archaeological Congress* 9, no. 1 (2013): 162–91. DOI: 10.1007/s11759-013-9227-2.

———. "The Loss of Innocence: Political and Ethical Dimensions of the Meroe Dam Archaeological Salvage Project at the Fourth Nile Cataract (Sudan)." *Conservation and Management of Archaeological Sites* 13, nos. 2–3 (2011): 253–80. DOI: 10.1179/175355211X13179154166231.

Krafft-Ebing, Richard von. *Psychopathia Sexualis, with Especial Reference to Contrary Sexual Instinct: A Medico-Legal Study.* Translated by Charles Gilbert Chaddock. Philadelphia: F.A. Davis; London: F.J. Rebman, 1894.

Milton, John. *Paradise Lost: Books I. and II.* Edited by A.W. Verity. Cambridge: Cambridge University Press, 1934.

Müller, C. Detlef G. "Ergänzende Bemerkungen zu den deutschen Texfunden in Nubien." *Oriens christianus* 62 (1978): 135–43.

Nabokov, Vladimir. *Pale Fire.* London: Penguin, 2011.

Näser, Claudia, and Cornelia Kleinitz. "The Good, the Bad and the Ugly: A Case Study on the Politicisation of Archaeology and its Consequences from Northern Sudan." In *"Nihna nâs al-bahar — We Are the People of the River": Ethnographic Research in the Fourth Nile Cataract Region, Sudan,* edited by Cornelia Kleinitz and Claudia Näser, 269–304. Wiesbaden: Harrassowitz, 2012.

Obłuski, Artur. *The Rise of Nobadia: Social Changes in Northern Nubia in Late Antiquity.* Translated by Iwona Zych. Warsaw: Raphael Taubenschlag Foundation, 2014.

Plumley, J. Martin. "Qasr Ibrim 1963–1964." *The Journal of Egyptian Archaeology* 50 (1964): 3–5. DOI: 10.2307/3855736.

——— and Gerald M. Browne. *Old Nubian Texts from Qasr Ibrīm I.* London: Egypt Exploration Society, 1988.

Porter, James I. *Nietzsche and the Philology of the Future.* Stanford: Stanford University Press, 2000.

Ruffini, Giovanni R. *Medieval Nubia: A Social and Economic History.* Oxford: Oxford University Press, 2012.

Trigger, Bruce G. "Paradigms in Sudan Archaeology." *The International Journal of African Historical Studies* 27, no. 2 (1994): 323–45. https://www.jstor.org/stable/221028.

Tsakos, Alexandros. "In Search of Apocryphal Literature in Nubia." Lecture at the 2019 Oslo Workshop on Apocrypha and Monastic Literary Culture, Faculty of Theology, University of Oslo, June 19, 2019.

———. "The *Liber Institutionis Michaelis* in Medieval Nubia." *Dotawo: A Journal of Nubian Studies* 1 (2014): 51–62. DOI: 10.5070/D61110036.

Tyson Smith, Stuart. *Wretched Kush: Ethnic Identities and Boundaries in Egypt's Nubian Empire.* London: Routledge, 2003.

Unger, Rüdiger. "Sunnarti — Fragment 203: Deutung und sprachliche Zuordnung." In *Nubia et Oriens Christianus: Festschrift für C. Detlef G. Müller zum 60. Geburtstag,* edited by Piotr O. Scholz and Reinhard Stempel, 243–67. Cologne: Verlag Jürgen Dinter, 1987.

Welsby, Derek. "Dams on the Nile: From Aswan to the Fourth Cataract." *Sudan Studies* 37 (2008): 5–18.

2

"Semper Novi Quid ex Africa": Redrawing the Borders of Medieval African Art and Considering Its Implications for Medieval Studies

Andrea Myers Achi and
Seeta Chaganti

Clues exist that the relationship between African American and African studies might be fruitfully negotiated through the medieval. Consider, for example, that Asa J. Davis, the founder of the historically significant Black Studies department at Amherst College, wrote a dissertation on a thirteenth-century Ethiopian manuscript.[1] We take that intersection as an invitation to consider the possibility of a collaboration between African American and medieval African art historical studies in the name of racial justice.

This essay stages such a collaboration: between a scholar of late antique art and archaeology (Andrea Myers Achi reading African art) and a literature scholar (Seeta Chaganti reading the

---

1 Fikru Negash Gebrekidan, "Ethiopia in Black Studies from W.E.B. Du Bois to Henry Louis Gates, Jr.," *Northeast African Studies* 15, no. 1 (2015): 1–34, at 17.

work of W.E.B. Du Bois). Together, we explore how emerging practices of curating art made in Africa from premodern historical periods might illuminate a specifically medievalist intervention into US-based discourses of race and racial justice. We contend, first, that curation offers important and necessary opportunities to broaden the meanings and definitions underlying African art. We ask: what specific national cultures on the African continent have and have not been considered African in scholarly perspectives? Our project, in other words, redefines what is considered African or medieval in predominantly US museum contexts. And second, we suggest that such broadening of definition can lead us toward curatorial practices, as well as responses to exhibitions, that further the critical examination of the very institutions that produce exhibitions. This means more than just introducing African objects into settings that visitors might expect to be Eurocentric. It means, as we shall ultimately argue, curating objects in such a way as to introduce a spectatorial practice of radical hesitation that intervenes into racialized epistemologies.

Our intervention requires a methodological and conceptual framework that acknowledges both the epistemology of hesitation and the facets of relation between the US-based racial politics, and the study of Africa. We find this critical framework in the work of W.E.B. Du Bois, whose conception of "Sociology Hesitant" has provided a springboard for other work that links readings of culture with social justice.[2] Furthermore, Du Bois's interest in African countries and pan-Africanism also informed, throughout his writing and activist life, his thoughts about race in the US. In addition, Du Bois incorporated into his perspective on Africa a consciousness not only of its particular history — one preceding the Atlantic slave trade — but also of

---

2 W.E.B. Du Bois, "Sociology Hesitant," *boundary 2* 27, no. 3 (2000): 37–44. See the important revisitings of this piece in Mark C. Jerng, "Race in the Crucible of Literary Debate," *American Literary History* 31, no. 2 (2019): 260–71 and Lisa Lowe, "History Hesitant," *Social Text* 33, no. 4 (2015): 85–107.

historical time more broadly, all crucial themes in the discussion of premodernity. Indeed, as Matthew X. Vernon has shown, Du Bois's writing frequently gestures toward the medieval. Like Vernon, we are interested in how Du Bois construed the "sphere of cultural production" as an important site in which to examine race and foster racial justice.[3] But while Vernon invokes Du Bois through the latter's explicit engagements with medieval European literature and history, we look to other aspects of Du Bois's work and other reasons to invoke him. Perhaps most significantly, Du Bois's writings explore how to shift in conceptual focus between the US and African countries, a mode of shifting that we bring to the US-sited exhibition of African art. Du Bois begins and ends his "Hands of Ethiopia" with the phrase "Semper novi quid ex Africa!" to designate the possibility of a meaningfully new, racially just, and anticolonial world.[4] He compels us to ask how focusing on the cultures of African countries might contribute to the creation of this world. As a medievalist using American critical race theory as a lens to read early Western literature and a medievalist who is an expert in Christian art of northeast Africa, we aim to triangulate the stakes of African art curation, its inflection in the realm of premodernity, and, finally, racial justice in the American settings that often provide the first public audiences for shows focusing on medieval Africa.

Ex Africa

The global turn in medieval studies coincides with a turn in the curation of American museum exhibitions of medieval art; in

3   Matthew X. Vernon, *The Black Middle Ages* (New York: Palgrave, 2018), 19–20, 48–49.
4   Ryan Schneider calls "The Hands of Ethiopia" a "call for de-colonization." "Sex and the Race Man: Imagining Interracial Relationships in W.E.B. Du Bois's Darkwater," *Arizona Quarterly* 59, no. 2 (2003): 59–80, at 60. On Du Bois's "anti-colonial" position, see also James Quirin, "W.E.B. Du Bois, Ethiopianism and Ethiopia 1890–1955," *International Journal of Ethiopian Studies* 5, no. 2 (2010–11): 1–26, at 18.

this sense, we might say that many medievalists interested in the global Middle Ages find themselves confronted with a stereoscopic view: one pairing US race and African art. The turn in museum curation — initiated several years ago in the long process of exhibition planning — manifests itself in the present to foreground the contributions of the African continent to the worldwide development of art and artifacts across the Middle Ages. Two shows exemplifying this commitment are *Caravans of Gold, Fragments in Time*, which premiered at Northwestern University's Block Museum (2019); and the Metropolitan Museum of Art's *Art and Peoples of the Kharga Oasis* (2017). In changing received narratives about medieval artistic traditions across Africa and Europe, such exhibitions raise, for us, a question about the extent to which a US-sited exhibition about medieval Africa is implicitly also an exhibition about race. For even though such shows often result from substantive collaboration with arts ministries and other representatives of African countries, we would suggest that their premiering, publicity, and viewing in the US necessitates understanding them through a filter of American racial politics.[5] Indeed, the Getty Museum's *Outcasts: Prejudice and Persecution in the Medieval World* (2018) at once brought up the topic of race as inflected by contemporary American political discourse and "inspired," through responses to it, a subsequent Getty exhibition focused on Africa, entitled *Balthazar: A Black African King in Medieval and Renaissance Art* (2019).[6]

---

5 *Caravans of Gold* has been produced in partnerships with museum officials in Nigeria, Mali, and Morocco.

6 Kristen Collins and Bryan C. Keene, "Scholars Respond to an Exhibition about Medieval Prejudice," *The Iris*, March 6, 2019, https://blogs.getty.edu/iris/scholars-respond-to-an-exhibition-about-medieval-prejudice/. In the development of *Outcasts*, the terms "diversity," "inclusivity," "tolerance," and "out groups," as well as the aim "to make connections between the Middle Ages and the contemporary world," appeared. While this terminology itself is not limited to a US context, the curators also cite as foundational to their aims Holland Cotter's *New York Times* manifesto, which refers to the urgency of connecting specifically American politics

In tandem with medievalists' push to use anti-racist approaches in their work, an adjacent discipline of Medieval African Studies and Art History seems to be emerging; these newer approaches in combination with a longer history of display and taxonomic practice foreground the need to re-examine what we mean by "medieval African art."[7] Books such as François-Xavier Fauvelle's *The Goldern Rhinoceros: Histories of the African Middle Ages* and Michael Gomez's *African Dominion: A New History of Empire in Early and Medieval West Africa* carefully examine primary sources from historical Africa and situate Africa within the global Middle Ages.[8] These publications broaden public understanding of the interconnectedness of medieval worlds. Work on "medieval" Africa, for the most part, applies to traditional African studies and a chronological period that approximates late antiquity and the European Middle

    to the artifacts of the past: "Right now America is in an emotionally and morally raw moment" (Holland Carter, "How to Fix the Met," *New York Times,* March 1, 2017, https://www.nytimes.com/2017/03/01/arts/design/how-to-fix-the-met-connect-art-to-life.html). See also Kristen Collins and Bryan C. Keene, "Dialogue: Exposing the Rhetoric of Exclusion through Medieval Manuscripts," *The Iris,* August 3, 2017, http://blogs.getty.edu/iris/dialogue-exposing-the-rhetoric-of-exclusion-through-medieval-manuscripts/ and, most recently, on the connection between the *Outcasts* and *Balthazar* shows, see Kristen Collins and Bryan C. Keene, "A New Exhibition Explores Balthazar, a Black African King in Medieval and Renaissance European Art," *The Iris,* November 19, 2019, http://blogs.getty.edu/iris/exhibition-to-examine-balthazar-a-black-african-king-in-medieval-and-renaissance-european-art/.

7 Kathleen Bickford Berzock, "Caravans of Gold, Fragments in Time: An Introduction," in *Caravans of Gold, Fragments in Time: Art, Culture, and Exchange across Medieval Saharan Africa,* edited by Kathleen Bickford Berzock (Princeton: Princeton University Press, 2019), 23–37. Also, at the recent International Congress of Medieval Studies and Medieval Academy of America conferences multiple sessions have addressed topics concerning medieval Africa.

8 François-Xavier Fauvelle, *The Golden Rhinoceros: Histories of the African Middle Ages* (Princeton: Princeton University Press, 2018); Michael A. Gomez, *African Dominion: A New History of Empire in Early and Medieval West Africa* (Princeton: Princeton University Press, 2018).

Ages (300–1500). To complicate matters further, the borders of Northeast Africa have expanded and waned not only geographically, but also, more importantly, within the mental landscape of both medieval and modern writers. As the term "Medieval African Art" begins to appear in museums, it creates an urgent need for reflective discussion. This conversation requires careful approaches to undoing the implicitly colonial elements of museum spaces, highlighting original contexts, and sharing understudied narratives.

Critiques aiming to "decolonize" museums often focus on West African art, but where does Christian art from Northeast Africa fit within these conversations? The artist Kader Attia opened an exhibition directly confronting the display of African art in his "Museum of Emotion" at the Hayward Gallery in London. In describing the exhibition, Farah Nayeri remarks:

> Through his installations, Mr. Attia (who won the Prix Marcel Duchamp, France's most prestigious art award, in 2016) critiques Western museums' approach to African heritage — their tendency to undervalue, misread and misrepresent its treasures, and to view it, still, through colonial eyes.[9]

Discussions of West African art exhibitions often entail such critiques. In considering the problems of African art displayed in museums, Suzzane Blier notes: "'Traditional' African arts are alternatively: a) too African (i.e., 'Exotic'); b) not where they should be displayed (in Western museums rather than in 'traditional' African shrines)."[10] Rarely, however, do these issues spill into a discourse concerning Northeast African art, particularly

---

9 Farah Nayeri, "We Need to Talk About Colonialism, This Artist Says," *New York Times*, March 5, 2019, https://www.nytimes.com/2019/02/25/arts/design/kader-attia-hayward-gallery.html.

10 Suzanne Preston Blier, "Nine Contradictions in the New Golden Age of African Art," *African Arts* 35, no. 3 (2002): 1–6.

Christian art from those regions.[11] In *Art History in Africa,* Jan Vansina addresses this issue:

> "African art" is the label usually given to the visual and plastic arts of the peoples south of the Sahara, especially those of western and central Africa. […] Thus defined "African art" is not the Art of Africa. […] We cannot amputate half of Africa then call a portion of what remains "African art."[12]

As a solution, Vansina labels North and Northeast African art as *Oikoumenical,* reflecting traditions centered on the Mediterranean. Already, many art historians and historians in late-antique, Byzantine and Medieval Studies accept the material culture of Christian Northeast Africa as integral to their fields. Consequently, Christian artworks from these regions are usually in museums' medieval galleries, not African galleries. Christian Northeast African art is seen as created "in" Africa, but not "of" the continent. The colonial division of Africa is apparent in the separateness of Egypt, Sudan, and Ethiopia in museums. Ethiopia, for example, an ancient Christian society, never colonized, is absorbed often into European galleries. While the presence of Ethiopian art in European galleries highlights the diversity of the medieval world, it also suggests a non-African character of Ethiopian art. When Ethiopian art is displayed in African sections in museums, it can seem equally out of place due to the art's Christian themes.

The Medieval *Oikoumenē* in Africa

Recently, significant exhibitions of Byzantine art have incorporated arts of Christian communities from Africa in an attempt

---

11 Earnestine Jenkins, "Egypt in Africa," ed. Theodore Celenko, *African Arts* 31, no. 2 (1998): 16–88.

12 J. Vansina, *Art History in Africa: An Introduction to Method* (London: Routledge, 1984), 1.

to counteract a longstanding misperception and separation of these particular African arts within a broader context.[13] The exhibitions allowed visitors to situate Christian artworks made in Africa within their real time and space. Still, the arts from Christian Egypt (Coptic), Nubia, and Ethiopia are perpetually understudied and misunderstood: understudied because they are not part of western art historical canons; misunderstood because they are often seen as low-quality iterations of Byzantine art and never as African art. While it is true that the medieval material cultures of Egypt, Nubia, and Ethiopia have meaningful links to the Mediterranean basin, the art cannot be claimed to be "non-African."[14] We can place the objects within "a broader African context without adhering to the concept of a unified African culture" and, by doing so, expand the collective mental geography of Africa.[15]

Stemming from the Arabic word *Qibt* and the Greek *Aiguptios*, the word *Coptic* has a provincial connotation in art historical discourse and has allowed room for racist perspectives in these discourses. The umbrella term "Coptic Art" designates an amalgamation of visual culture made by predominantly Christian communities in Egypt. To reflect the diversity of the art, specialists prefer inclusive phrasings such as Christian Egyptian, late antique Egyptian, Byzantine Egyptian, and medieval Egyptian.[16] The art from these periods encompasses a plurality

---

13 Among many examples, see Helen Evans, ed., *Byzantium and Islam: Age of Transition, 7th–9th Century* (New York: Metropolitan Museum of Art, 2012); Helen Evans, ed., *The Glory of Byzantium: Art and Culture of the Middle Byzantine Era, A.D. 843–1261* (New York: The Metropolitan Museum of Art, 1997); Barbara Drake Boehm and Melanie Holcomb, *Jerusalem, 1000–1400: Every People under Heaven* (New York: Metropolitan Museum of Art, 2016).
14 Peri M. Klemm and Leah Niederstadt, "Beyond Wide-Eyed Angels: Contemporary Expressive Culture in Ethiopia," *African Arts* 42, no. 1 (2009): 6–13.
15 Jenkins, "Egypt in Africa."
16 Scholarship over the past twenty-five years has firmly placed Egypt as an important region for the Roman and Byzantine empires. See Roger S.

of cultural influences, which merged Egyptian, Greek, Roman, Persian, and later Arab visual strains. Despite the richness of Egyptian Christian art, early scholarship on the material was often racist and derogatory. For example, Charles Rufus Morey's article "The Painted Covers of the Washington Manuscript of the Gospels" addressed the important book covers within the framework of early Christian art from Egypt that was either derivative of high-quality Greek art from cosmopolitan Alexandria or primitive, native Egyptian (i.e., Coptic) art from the rural regions along the Nile.[17] Likewise, Klaus Wessel's *Coptic Art* perpetuated the idea of an Alexandrian "sophisticated style" in contrast to a "crude style" created by ethnic Egyptians.[18]

One cannot help but wonder if recent efforts to incorporate Christian Egyptian art into the canon of Byzantine Art have overshadowed other narratives of interaction between the arts of Egypt and the art of its southern and western African neighbors. While the boundaries and material culture of Christian Egypt are well defined, the regions and peoples south of Egypt sway from tangible to fantastical. Greeks, Romans, and early Christians called these people *Aethiopians,* a descriptive term referring to their dark skin color.[19] As a geographic region, historic Nubia extended from the Nile's First Cataract (in modern Egypt) to sites between the Fifth Cataract and the Sixth Cataract (in modern Sudan). Medieval Nubia was not monolithic; it incorporated the Kingdoms of Nobadia, Makuria, and Alwa. The region converted to Christianity in 541 CE after the Byzantine

---

Bagnall, *Egypt in Late Antiquity* (Princeton: Princeton University Press, 1996); Thelma K. Thomas, *Late Antique Egyptian Funerary Sculpture: Images for This World and for the Next* (Princeton: Princeton University Press, 2000).

17 Charles R. Morey, "The Painted Covers of Washington Manuscript of the Gospels," in *Eastern Christian Paintings in the Freer Collection* (New York: Macmillian Company, 1914), 63–81, at 76.
18 Klaus Wessel, *Coptic Art* (New York: McGraw-Hill Book Company, 1965).
19 Frank Snowden lists the references to the primary sources on this topic. Frank M. Snowden, *Before Color Prejudice: The Ancient View of Blacks* (Cambridge: Harvard University Press, 1983), 5.

Figure 1. Bishop Marianos under the Protection of the Virgin and Child. Fresco, 1003-36, Great Cathedral, Faras Nubia. Muzeum Narodowe, Warsaw.

emperor Justinian and his wife Theodora sent separate groups of missionaries to the area. In 652 CE, the Nubian kingdoms held off Arab invasions, and Christianity remained a defining feature of Nubian society until the 15th century. During this period, hundreds of churches and monasteries were built throughout the region. With its clear links to Byzantine visual culture, medieval Nubian art is challenging to define.[20] It is of neither Byzantium nor Africa. The Nubians were of both worlds. Medieval Nubians spoke their indigenous language, but many were also fluent in Greek and Coptic, and later could correspond in Arabic.[21] The "complexity" and "richness" of Nubian material culture has only recently been acknowledged in medieval studies.[22] From large wall paintings in churches to the abundance of liturgical parchment manuscripts, Medieval Nubian art reflects direct contact with eastern Christian communities (fig. 1).[23] In

20 Kurt W. Weitzmann was one of the earliest and most prominent Byzantine art historians to publish on the connections between Byzantine and Nubian art. See Kurt W. Weitzmann, "Some Remarks on the Sources of the Fresco Paintings of the Cathedral of Faras," in *Studies in the Arts at Sinai* (Princeton: Princeton University Press, 1982), 187–211.
21 Grzegorz Ochała, "Multilingualism in Christian Nubia: Qualitative and Quantitative Approaches," *Dotawo: A Journal of Nubian Studies* 1, no. 1 (2014), 1–50.
22 Ibid., 3. Stanley M. Burstein, "When Greek Was an African Language: The Role of Greek Culture in Ancient and Medieval Nubia," *Journal of World History* 19, no. 1 (2008): 41–61.
23 For a brief summary of the links between medieval Nubian art and adjacent Christian communities, see Thelma K. Thomas, "Christians in the Islamic East," in *The Glory of Byzantium,* ed. Helen Evans (New York: The Metropolitan Museum of Art, 1997), 365–87. Nubiologists have long considered the links between Africa and eastern Christian communities. For recent discussions on the topic, see Vincent W.J. van Gerven Oei, "A Dance for a Princess: The Legends on a Painting in Room 5 of the Southwest Annex of the Monastery on Kom H in Dongola," *The Journal of Juristic Papyrology* 47 (2017): 117–36; Stefan Jakobielski, *Pachoras Faras: The Wall Paintings from the Cathedrals of Aetios, Paulos and Petros,* (Warsaw: Polish Centre of Mediterranean Archaeology, 2017); Dobrochna Zielińska, "The Iconography of Power — The Power of Iconography: The Nubian Royal Ideology and Its Expression in Wall Painting," in *The Fourth Cataract and Beyond: Proceedings of the 12th International Conference*

museum contexts, to separate this art from the corpus of African art negates the diversity of the art made on the continent.

In many ways, Christianity defined the art and material culture of Ethiopian society, which maintained significant contacts with Western Europe, Byzantium, and then the Church of the East, and other African kingdoms through both trade and diplomacy. One of the first Christian nations, the Kingdom of Aksum (ancient Ethiopia), converted to Christianity early in the fourth century before Rome became a Christian state. As Getachew Haille notes, the influences of Christianity were "layered atop a stratum of traditional African life, particularly in the areas of social organization, family life, art, and architecture."[24] Like the art of medieval Nubia, medieval Ethiopian art reflects close visual connections with orthodox Christian communities throughout the medieval world. Because of these links, the arts of Ethiopia, often seen as too different from sub-Saharan African art, have been explained within the context of "medieval European traditions."[25]

How can we reconcile past efforts to place northeast African arts within the framework of the Mediterranean world with the efforts we envision to undo museums' replications of colonialist perspectives in their own configurations? How can the setting of the museum reflect, for example, Suzanne Conklin Akbari's conception of medieval Ethiopia as "variable and multiple" in time and space?[26] The answer, we propose, is that museums can display northeastern African arts near related objects from European and Byzantine traditions, but signpost the art as being

---

for Nubian Studies, eds. Julie R. Anderson and Derek A. Welsby (Leuven: Peeters, 2014), 943–49.

24 Deborah Ellen Horowitz et al., eds., *Ethiopian Art: The Walters Art Museum* (Lingfield: Third Millennium, 2001), 27.

25 Klemm and Niederstadt, "Beyond Wide-Eyed Angels," 3.

26 Suzanne Conklin Akbari, "Where Is Medieval Ethiopia? Mapping Ethiopic Studies within Medieval Studies," in *Toward a Global Middle Ages: Encountering the World through Illuminated Manuscripts,* ed. Bryan Keene (Los Angeles: Getty Publications, 2019), 80–91, at 83.

made in Africa. This solution would address a persistent bind. On the one hand, one could argue that Egyptian, Nubian, and Ethiopian art in medieval galleries represents African heritage viewed through colonial eyes; those eyes render the objects exceptional due to their proximity to arts of Europe. On the other hand, it would misrepresent these objects to orphan them entirely from their original contexts within the Christian world of the Roman and Byzantine Empires. We should take care not to undervalue, misread, and oversimplify the art from these countries and its associations. We can speak about the art of the African continent in a way that discusses similarities between the Mediterranean basin cultures but also stresses differences. By doing this, we will shift the conceptual focus on northeast African art and incorporate it into the canons of both medieval and African art. We offer another approach to incorporating these artworks in medieval galleries: redrawing the boundaries of medieval African art. And what would it then mean for the fields of medieval art and African art if curators, collectively, put the word "Africa" on labels of objects that are made in Africa? In the next two sections, we will address this question first by outlining, through the work of W.E.B. Du Bois, a theoretical paradigm for such an experiment; and second, by offering an example of museum curation that engages in this experimental labeling in order to produce an experience of generative hesitation, both temporally and spatially.

Always Old, Always New

The previous section suggested changes to museum practices, which respond to the implicitly colonial impulses of the modern museum and in particular its treatment of African art. It is therefore worth briefly dwelling on the distinction between our goals in this essay and what is conventionally thought of as "decolonial" discourse, particularly because the latter has been subject to important critique specifically within medieval studies. Adam Miyashiro notes that "Until medievalists, and the wider academic world, can decolonize their fields, they will be (unwittingly or not) part of the problem of white supremacy and settler colonialism."[27] His comment encapsulates a shift crucial for medieval studies to make, but his exhortation specifies settler colonialism as the structure to which decoloniality responds. That specificity acknowledges Eve Tuck and K. Wayne Yang's critique of decolonization discourse as too easily absorbed into the field of metaphor and too easily conflated with other social justice initiatives. Because of its complexity in settler colonial contexts (which involve layers of different colonialist operations), decolonization is, according to them, readily transformed into a camouflage of figuration and analogy that conceals the real and material harms particular to the settler colonial structure.[28] The relationship between, on the one hand, US museum history's uses of medieval African objects; and, on the other hand, the settler colonial structure that decolonization should properly "unsettle," per Tuck and Yang, is complicated. The differences between those two poles should not be elided. Decolonization as they understand it counteracts settler appropriation of indigenous identity as heritage, and the attendant convenient "desire to *become without becoming*," by asserting an indigenous future that necessarily involves repatriation.[29] It becomes important for us, correspondingly, not to employ the language of decolonization to metaphorize the changing function of the museum space but rather to formulate other ways to describe how our model's counteraction of a colonial structure might interact with liberatory thought and action.

---

27 Adam Miyashiro, "Decolonizing Medieval Studies: A Response to ISAS in Honolulu," *In the Middle*, July 29, 2017, http://www.inthemedievalmiddle.com/2017/07/decolonizing-anglo-saxon-studies.html.
28 Eve Tuck and K. Wayne Yang, "Decolonization Is Not a Metaphor," *Decolonization: Indigeneity, Education & Society* 1, no. 1 (2012): 1–40, at 2–3, 7. Their explanation that the US's paradigm involves the simultaneity of internal and external colonialism, whereas we might think of North American museums' uses of African objects mostly as external colonialism (4–5).
29 Ibid., 13–14, 21.

We shall therefore argue that the medieval focus of the African museum exhibition can give us some tools for sharpening our own impulses to detect, question, and attempt to dismantle the structures of dispossession around us. This dynamic exists not because of a nostalgic or romanticized vision of a recaptured precolonial time but rather because, as Du Bois's model will suggest, self-determination depends upon inhabiting several different temporal and spatial strata at once, and antiracist thought and action can emerge in the experiences of hesitation existing between those strata.

Scholars of Du Bois have traced the relationship that he builds between his interest in Africa (and pan-Africanism), on the one hand, and his examination of race in the US, on the other. His writings on Africa cover a broad spectrum of genres, including, for example, *The Negro,* a 1915 history of Africa that Du Bois necessarily characterizes as incomplete because of the racism that has delayed and stymied the development of scholarly interest in this field (later updated as *Black Folk Then and Now* [1939]); to the short piece that seems both meditation and manifesto "The Hands of Ethiopia" in the 1920 *Darkwater* (discussed below); to *The World and Africa* (1947), which further develops his historical and cultural project.[30] James Quirin argues that over time Du Bois became "convinced that progress in African America would not be possible without progress in Africa and the African diaspora as a whole."[31] Du Bois's sense of what the US had to teach Africa, and vice versa, shifted over time, but Daniel Walden suggests that throughout, Du Bois saw the "colonial system" as extending to the US and as something that needed to be dismantled in order to activate "racial progress in general."[32] Fikru Negash Gebrekidan elaborates on Du

---

30 Sections of "The Hands of Ethiopia" appeared earlier in the *Atlantic* (May 1915) in the essay "The African Roots of War," a draft document published in *The Atlantic* World War I special issue (August 2014).

31 Quirin, "W.E.B. Du Bois, Ethiopianism and Ethiopia 1890–1955," 1.

32 Daniel Walden, "Du Bois' Pan-Africanism, a Reconsideration," *Negro American Literature Forum* 8, no. 4 (1974): 260–62, at 260–61.

Boisian thought about Ethiopia and Africa to argue that despite a history of controversy among Ethiopianists regarding Du Bois's depictions of Ethiopia and Africa, Du Bois has ultimately played a shaping role in negotiating the relationship between US-based Black studies and Ethiopian studies though his "counter-hegemonic" thesis concerning Africa and its history.[33] For these different reasons, the framework Du Bois provides — one that links African and African American studies — can further inform our response to museum curation as it re-examines art from Africa within a US setting.

We begin this juxtaposition of Du Bois's work with our art historical archive by noting that medieval art from Africa can help elucidate in new ways certain aspects of Du Bois's perspective. Du Bois sometimes seems to espouse distinctions and exceptions among certain African countries, but these are not always consistently characterized. For example, at the end of "The Hands of Ethiopia," Du Bois notes that "it is clear that for the development of Central Africa, Egypt should be free and independent, there along the highway to a free and independent India; while Morocco, Algeria, Tunis, and Tripoli must become a part of Europe, with modern development and home rule."[34] Ethiopia itself, the subject of this section, also potentially offers itself as a site of exceptionalism owing to the tradition of its "special meaning," encoded in Psalm 68:31, to African Americans.[35] At

---

33 See also Amy Kaplan, *The Anarchy of Empire in the Making of U.S. Culture* (Cambridge: Harvard University Press, 2005), on critiques of Du Bois as romanticizing and exoticizing African countries (197). To some degree Quirin demonstrates this critique of Du Bois. However, he also shows how Du Bois's knowledge of Ethiopia in particular deepened over time.

34 W.E.B. Du Bois, "The Hand of Ethiopia," in *Darkwater* [1920] (Clifton: African Tree Press, 2014), 79.

35 Quirin, "W.E.B. Du Bois, Ethiopianism and Ethiopia 1890–9155," 2. See also Gebrekidan, "Ethiopia in Black Studies from W.E.B. Du Bois to Henry Louis Gates, Jr.," 12–14, on discussions among American scholars and activists of the rumors and perceptions of anti-black racism in Ethiopia. On the one hand, according to Gebrekidan, "From the 1960s onward […] country specialization replaced the pan-African tradition on which earlier

the same time, however, in *The World and Africa,* Du Bois offers a different perspective on Egypt, critiquing the separation of not only Egypt but also Ethiopia from the rest of Africa, referring to those efforts as "contradictory" because of the illogic of the race science on which they might depend. He elaborates that the apparent exceptionality of both countries, as well as the appearance of fundamental dissociation between them, stems from the needs of modern slavery to perpetuate those narratives as self-rationalization.[36] We are struck by the ways that the fluctuation around this exceptionalism maps onto what we observed earlier regarding the curation of African art. In other words, we wonder about the extent to which the complex structures Du Bois creates to accommodate relations among African nations might subtly reflect complexities inherent to their older histories, and particularly the relationships to Christian arts that make these ambiguities especially visible. Furthermore, the dynamic relation of Ethiopia and Egypt speaks to the ways Du Bois deploys ideas about Blackness and specifically American Blackness. As Keisha A. Brown argues, Du Bois's representation of American Blackness shifted during his process of bringing his political ideas to an international arena, with Blackness becoming a "metonymic part of a huge…web of global struggles."[37] Questions about how Blackness might intersect with specific African countries — e.g., Egypt vs. Ethiopia — inevitably have multifarious answers in such a trajectory. Furthermore, the particular triangulation our study brings forth of American Blackness, African history, and Christian faith — along with the complexities this triangulation involves — also resonate with Du Bois's work.

---

writings about Africa were founded," but on the other hand African and African American scholars of Ethiopia continued to consider a "broader pan-African worldview" (16–17).

36 W.E.B. Du Bois, *The World and Africa* (New York: Cambridge University Press, 2007), 74–75.

37 Keisha A. Brown, "Blackness in Exile: W.E.B. Du Bois' Role in the Formation of Representations of Blackness as Conceptualized by the Chinese Communist Party," *Phylon* 53, no. 2 (2016): 20–33, at 21.

As Yolanda Pierce argues, the "souls" of *The Souls of Black Folk* (1903) refer not only to religious life but also, and more specifically, to the sorrow songs and other faith-based practices that, again, negotiate for Du Bois between a Black American present and an African past.[38]

In these ways we might consider Du Bois's political writings to run parallel to the complexities of the art historical dynamic as we have explored them. On the one hand, he reveals moments when the Christian European categorization of certain African cultures—particularly, but not exclusively, those with a geographically Mediterranean orientation—have subtended his political thought about African identity more broadly. On the other hand, while discussing aspects of culture distinct from the art historical, he recognizes the constructed nature of this narrative (a construction often by racist principles and serving colonialist ends) and perceives a more multifarious set of interrelations among African countries and their intersections in shaping this continent's historical past and consequently its cultural legacies.[39]

Indeed, looking at Du Bois's work from a medievalist perspective, we notice that he suggests not only the possibility of a new vision of the world emerging from Africa but also the dependence of that new vision on what is old, an attunement to a deep historical consciousness of Africa. This attunement manifests itself in Du Bois's impulses to write histories of the continent and to use those histories to trace a long narrative—one that extends beyond the Atlantic slave trade—of perceptions of Blackness. In *The Negro*, for instance, Du Bois notes: "The medieval European world, developing under the favorable physical

---

38 Yolanda Pierce, "The Soul of Du Bois' Black Folk," *The North Star: A Journal of African American Religious History* 7, no. 1 (2003): 1–4.

39 While Du Bois does not specifically discuss African art history here, this is not to suggest his lack of engagement with visual media more broadly; see, for instance, Whitney Battle-Baptiste and Britt Russert, eds., *W.E.B. Du Bois's Data Portraits: Visualizing Black America: The Color Line at the Turn of the Twentieth Century* (New York: Princeton Architectural Press, 2018).

conditions of the north temperate zone, knew the Black man chiefly as a legend or occasional curiosity, but still as a fellow man."[40] An extended history of African nations — sometimes even marked by Du Bois as the time of the European Middle Ages — forms an important part of an origin story about African culture intended to push against the modern conceptions of Africa and Africans that the Atlantic slave trade reified.

At the same time, "The Hands of Ethiopia" accomplishes something more complex than an origin story in deploying Africa's cultural past to counteract the harms of the present. The form of this text suggests a circuit between past and present as the crucial mechanism for generating African-centered concepts of the continent and rejecting Eurocentric ones.[41] We have noted this piece's refrain throughout, making it a refrain of our own as well: "Semper novi quid ex Africa."[42] By beginning and ending "The Hands of Ethiopia" with this phrase, Du Bois emphasizes the potential newness of oldness. When the second iteration echoes the first, that something new becomes an echo of the previous invocation; it is already deep in time, and its newness is not so much the unprecedented but rather what a now-old thing might reveal that is new. The form of this piece at once calls to mind a framing structure and at the same time challenges it. In this sense the piece illuminates what we want to see as the work of the American museum: at once signaling its awareness

---

40 W.E.B. Du Bois, *The Negro* [1915] (New York: Cosimo, 2007), 6.
41 On Du Bois's use of Afrocentricity, see Abdul Karim Bangura, "African-Centered Conceptualizations of Africa in W.E.B. Du Bois's Work: An Analysis of their Essentiality," in *W.E.B. Du Bois and the Africana Rhetoric of Dealienation*, ed. Monique Leslie Akassi (Newcastle upon Tyne: Cambridge Scholars Publishing, 2018), 19–44, at 19.
42 *Ex Africa semper aliquid novi* and other versions of this expression have been attributed to several authors from the classical period to the Renaissance. See Harvey M. Feinberg and Jospeh B. Solodow, "Out of Africa," *The Journal of African History* 43, no. 2 (2002): 255–61. While these authors mention Karen Blixen (Isak Dinesen)'s use of the phrase in the 1930s, along with other modern instances, Du Bois appears nowhere in their analysis.

of the frames and labels within which it necessarily works and at the same time challenging itself and viewers to unsettle them. Other aspects of Du Bois's text elaborate more specifically on the temporal dynamics of African history and American contemporaneity. Let's look, for instance, at the sentence "Always Africa is giving us something new or some metempsychosis of a world-old thing." The assertive shadow of America lies behind the similarly assertive assonance of "Always Africa"; the US is to some extent the "us" to which Du Bois refers. In addition, the final phrase "metempsychosis of a world-old thing" linguistically balances a classical Greek past with ancient Germanic monosyllables, and places both on a pivot across from "something new," repeated from the Latin. These elements of the sentence suggest a view of time that is not simply a historical sweep from past to present but rather a more obsessively wrought and even disorienting doubling back and turning. The structure seems to imply that for us to understand what Africa is saying to us on its own terms, to allow that "new thing" to be "a great humanity of equal men," will require that we dislocate and destabilize ourselves within, and challenge the boundaries of, temporal and historical structures.[43]

Du Bois's use of parallel construction emphasizes this point. He composes his coda to shift between scenes "twenty centuries before Christ" and "twenty centuries after Christ":

> Twenty centuries before Christ a great cloud swept over seas and settled on Africa, darkening and well-nigh blotting out the culture of the land of Egypt. For half a thousand years it rested there, until a black woman, Queen Nefertari, "the most venerated figure in Egyptian history," rose to the throne of the Pharaohs and redeemed the world and her people. Twenty centuries after Christ, Black Africa,—prostrated, raped, and shamed, lies at the feet of the conquering Philistines of Europe. Beyond the awful sea a black woman is weeping and

43 Du Bois, "Hands of Ethiopia," 80.

waiting, with her sons on her breast. What shall the end be? The world-old and fearful things,—war and wealth, murder and luxury? Or shall it be a new thing,—a new peace and a new democracy of all races,—a great humanity of equal men? "*Semper novi quid ex Africa!*"[44]

We teeter between one possibility and the other while the present of Africa continues to exist palimpestically with the past. Again, to see the possibility of worldwide emancipation emerging from Africa requires acknowledging this state of temporal and spatial disorientation. It is important to specify here that this temporalized proposal does not consider Africa the "Unhistorical […] Spirit" of Hegel's terms.[45] To the contrary, we propose a deepened precision of historical complexity rendered through the intersection of Du Bois's words with a material archive of objects.

In this way our point about the space of African countries above collaborates with Du Bois's point about the time of Africa here. More specifically, these perspectives on space and time reinforce each other in the service of racial justice in our own time and the space of the US museum exhibition of medieval African art. We might, for instance, ask how to respond to these shows in ways that acknowledge and challenge the limits of institutional spaces and the category boundaries they impose. In saying this, we don't simply mean considering museum spaces to be coded or configured as Western or non-Western in some general or visible sense; we refer to what strictures underlie the structures of cultural and intellectual institutions. In describing the possibilities and limits of working from within academic and other institutions, Jenn M. Jackson points out that systems such as university policing have ways of "expand[ing] them-

---

44 Ibid.
45 Cited in Howard W. French, "Africa's Lost Kingdoms," *The New York Review of Books,* June 29, 2019, https://www.nybooks.com/articles/2019/06/27/medieval-africa-lost-kingdoms/.

selves into other community spaces," with predictably harmful effects on those already marginalized.[46] Thinking about "The Hands of Ethiopia" as overlaying and complicating the categories of different spaces over time, we might ask: how can viewers respond to these exhibitions of medieval Africa in ways that similarly resist the impacts of the very institutional spaces that have produced them? To answer this question is to move toward an exhibition space that sharpens viewers' awareness of not only contemporary dispossession but also what is lashed to it across time. In other words, the aim might be to present objects in ways that allow viewers to engage them as what Jodi Melamed calls "race-radical" cultural artifacts. Such artifacts repudiate "liberal-multicultural affirmations" of capitalist policy, and state-sanctioned "liberal antiracism," in favor of a truly emancipatory and communal agenda.[47] We wonder if a "race-radical" potential in these newly-presented medieval objects, the *aliquid novi* that is also old, might assert itself through a different conception of the exhibition, one we posited in a general and theoretical way above but will specify further below. We envision museum presentation that dismantles precisely the oppressive epistemological structures that have hitherto dictated which objects occupy which spaces in the museum. We propose replacing the racist epistemologies that we discussed above in the reception of African cultural objects specifically with Du Bois's way of seeing, one that integrates past and present in order to illuminate a more just political future. Museum curation, we suggest, could go out of its way to trouble, perhaps uncomfortably for many, the institutionally constructed borders of premodern African space precisely to engage in temporally productive work that brings past and present into a radical dialogue. Rather than

---

46 Jenn M. Jackson, "Breaking Out of the Ivory Tower: (Re)Thinking the Inclusion of Women and Scholars of Color in the Academy," *Journal of Women, Politics & Policy* 40 (2019): 195–203, at 196–97.

47 Jodi Melamed, *Represent and Destroy: Rationalizing Violence in the New Racial Capitalism* (Minneapolis: University of Minnesota Press, 2011), xv–xviii.

treating the museum space as one that articulates colonization and decolonization metaphorically, we suggest drawing upon its concrete potential to create palimpsests, to use the centering of medieval Africa in particular as a way to complicate the viewer's experience of time as well as space and ultimately to create an immediate environment for thought and change.

We might elaborate on this possibility by extending the methodology that one exhibition, *Caravans of Gold,* articulates for itself. In the introduction to the exhibition's accompanying volume, Kathleen Bickford Berzock explains how the fragmentary nature of the archives with which they worked moved the curators "from the concrete to the imaginable." The archive engenders a methodology of "archaeological imagination" that affirms the validity of "informed supposition" in the absence of definitive evidence — an absence that characterizes so many premodern archives.[48] This willingness to acknowledge the impossibility of total recovery, and to find productive alternatives, is thought-provoking and useful. But can it go even further? In his essay "Sociology Hesitant," Du Bois points out a critical tendency to favor abstract structural arguments about social phenomena over reading the contingencies and complexities of more particular interactions.[49] Mark C. Jerng argues that a method of hesitation — in which "being made not to act can be understood as richly as being made to act" — plays a crucial role in how Black studies and other ethnic and area studies analyze race and in particular the relationship of the narrative to the social.[50] Thus, rather than following our impulses to fill in the gaps that fragments leave, what if we were instead more deliberately hesitant about what lies in those gaps? How would sitting with that particular confounding temporal and spatial inaccessibility further the connections we make between museum

---

48 Berzock, "Caravans of Gold, Fragments in Time," 29, 37, and passim.
49 Du Bois, "Sociology Hesitant," 37–40 and passim.
50 Jerng, "Race in the Crucible of Literary Debate," 7, 9. See also Lowe, "History Hesitant," 98, on the use of hesitation in the approach to archive.

objects — and their means of presentation — and the present realities surrounding the museum and us? We offer these questions to reconstitute the formal aspects of Du Bois's discussion of Africa as a method of response and interpretation when faced with the objects of premodern African countries.

A Solution: Exhibiting Art Made "in Africa," Not "of Africa"

In the following section, we propose a model for the placement of medieval objects within their broader African context, one that responds to the dynamics of hesitation outlined above by focusing on the complexities of interactions in Africa during the medieval period. In "Sociology Hesitant", Du Bois remarks upon the significant lacunae in Comte's study of "Society":

> So Comte and his followers noted the grouping of men, the changing of government, the agreement in thought, and then, instead of a minute study of men grouping, changing, and thinking, proposed to study the Group, the Change, and the Thought, and call this new created Thing Society.[51]

Following Du Bois's charge, exhibitions on medieval Africa should engage with the studies of the critical details of "men grouping, changing, and thinking." Medieval Africa should not be an abstract idea, relevant to medieval studies based only on chronological similarities, but it should represent real connections across the space of the museum and across time both within and beyond what we consider the Middle Ages.

The exhibition *Arts and Peoples of Kharga Oasis* (2017–2020) was able to convey real links among societies in Africa, Byzantium, and Western Europe by foregrounding narratives about object uses, movements, origins, and temporal placements not ordinarily communicated to the general public. In this way, the exhibition encouraged viewers to hesitate over the assumptions

---

51 Du Bois, "Sociology Hesitant," 39.

they might bring to the time and space of these objects, in Africa and in the museum, and thus in their own ways challenge the hegemonic paradigms that traditional museum culture might impose upon them. The exhibition presented a nuanced perspective on late antique Egyptian objects and worked against the tendency to see these objects as simply the "Thing."

Both the introductory panel of *Arts and Peoples* and the individual labels offered different opportunities to present the art in the exhibition as being made "in Africa" and of the Mediterranean world. Providing an overview of the material was not difficult, nor controversial; the archaeological data is not disputed.

The Kharga Oasis, located in the Western Desert of Egypt, was an important intersection connecting caravan roads from the Darfur province of Sudan (ancient Nubia) to the Nile Valley, a journey of 1,082 miles. As a result, objects and ideas from across Egypt, Nubia, and the eastern Mediterranean from the Pharaonic to early Byzantine periods made their way to Kharga. In late antiquity (fourth to seventh century), the region also bore witness to an expansive and vibrant Christian community, evidenced by new sacred spaces and the reuse of forts and temples as churches and monasteries. In 1908, The Metropolitan Museum of Art began excavations of late antique sites in Kharga. The Met's archaeologists uncovered two-story houses, painted tombs, and a church. A selection of objects from these sites is on view in this gallery, revealing the multiple cultural and religious identities of people who lived in the region between the third and seventh centuries, a time of transition between the Roman and Byzantine periods. The finds represent a society that integrated Egyptian, Greek, and Roman culture and art. Presenting objects according to the archaeological context in which they were discovered, this exhibition explores these ancient identities and artifacts and demonstrates how archaeological documentation can aid in understanding an object's original function.

Figure 2. Bowl with Interior Geometric Decoration, 4th–7th Century, Earthernware, slip decoration, from Kharga Oasis in Egypt, Africa. 5 3/16 × 11 ¼ in. The Metropolitan Museum of Art, New York, Rogers Fund, 1925, MMA 25.10.20.177.

The exhibition's daily life objects — pottery, writing materials, and textiles — represented unique narratives curators do not often tell the general public. For example, the labels in the exhibition noted original archaeological contexts, which allowed the viewer to understand how, why, and when the original owners used the art.

Describing broader contexts for some individual artworks, however, did prove complicated. Some of the pottery found near a late antique church in Kharga have motifs known from Nubian pottery of the same period (fig. 2). Nubians either made the pots and exported them, or Egyptian potters produced them locally and emulated the Nubian ornament, or Nubian potters made them in Egypt. Are these pots late-antique, Christian, or Byzantine? Are they Egyptian or Nubian? Are they African? How would the Homeric inscriptions on some of them affect viewers' perspectives on the time of literary genealogy (a timeline also of interest to Du Bois)? For the exhibition, in addition to the pots' date and general description, their labels included their exact find-spots (in Egypt) and descriptions of the pots' connection to Nubia. Labels like these can dismantle assumptions about authority, categorization, generalization, and subjectivity in ways that further the conceptual and activist projects that Du Bois advocated, and the instrument of the label itself can crucially inform the spectator's process in the real time and space of the museum experience. For while it is true that a visitor will look at an object before reading a label, visitor studies literature has shown that people do read and appreciate interpretative labels.[52] Effective labels "create a symbolic dialogue between the label and the object" and "answer the visitor's questions first, then try to tell them what you [the curator] think they should know."[53] The labels for the Nubian pots, displayed in the medieval galleries, enter both the museumgoer and the curation project itself into a dynamic of hesitation rather than authority. Even when archaeological data temporally fix us in one sense, we might in another sense experience hesitation over perceived boundaries of civilizational period, opening still larger questions about periodization and these objects' pasts in relation to our present. We might experience the spatial hesitation born from the complexities of attempting to categorize by nation.

Despite their importance, labels are not the only method that create spatial hesitation in galleries. An excellent example of innovative display strategies that push the limits of experimentation in museums is the Bode Museum's *Beyond Compare* exhibition, which juxtaposed medieval European sculpture with traditional African Art. In this exhibition, viewers were forced to confront their own biases of beauty and art historical canons through formal pairings of sculptures, which differed in both time and space. Likewise, the Metropolitan Museum of Art's *Crossroads: Power and Piety* exhibition in the Medieval Sculpture Hall (2020–2021) will experiment with groupings that

---

52   Chandler G. Screven, "Motivating Visitors to Read Labels," *ILVS Review: A Journal of Visitor Behavior* 2, no. 2 (1992): 183–211.

53   Stephen Bitgood, "The Role of Attention in Designing Effective Interpretive Labels," *Journal of Interpretation Research* 5, no. 2 (2000): 31–45, at 32.

highlight overarching concepts core to understanding medieval works of art, and that also resonate for works of art from other regions and time-periods. We hope that museums will extend these experiments even further, using curation not only to unsettle audiences but also to move toward dismantling their own reified claims to knowledge and ownership.

We are aware that we write from within powerful and dispossessing institutions ourselves: the predominantly white research university and museum. But we offer these thoughts with the hope that within such institutional spaces might exist ways for premodern artifacts to re-shape or even explode the spaces they occupy, generating new thought about race and racial justice by bringing needed change to our understanding of their histories. We hope museums will consider the idea that to create alternatives to Westernized perspectives on Africa requires an abyss of premodern time from which emerges not an inchoate, unexamined nostalgia but rather a time and space of strategic hesitation, an environment of perpetual interrogation and even disorientation. Perhaps this approach will encourage us to intervene more actively as medievalists into American political contexts when we occupy US sites — sites that themselves can intensify inequity — to re-examine art from Africa.

Bibliography

Akbari, Suzanne Conklin. "Where Is Medieval Ethiopia? Mapping Ethiopic Studies within Medieval Studies." In *Toward a Global Middle Ages: Encountering the World through Illuminated Manuscripts,* edited by Bryan Keene, 80–91. Los Angeles: Getty Publications, 2019.

Bagnall, Roger S. *Egypt in Late Antiquity.* Princeton: Princeton University Press, 1996.

Bailey, Martin. "V&A Opens Dialogue on Looted Ethiopian Treasures." *The Art Newspaper,* April 3, 2018. http://theartnewspaper.com/news/v-and-a-opens-dialogue-on-looted-ethiopian-treasures.

Bangura, Abdul Karim. "African-Centered Conceptualizations of Africa in W.E.B. Du Bois's Work: An Analysis of their Essentiality." In *W.E.B. Du Bois and the Africana Rhetoric of Dealienation,* edited by Monique Leslie Akassi, 19–44. Newcastle upon Tyne: Cambridge Scholars Publishing, 2018.

Battle-Baptiste, Whitney, and Britt Russert, eds. *W.E.B. Du Bois's Data Portraits: Visualizing Black America: The Color Line at the Turn of the Twentieth Century.* New York: Princeton Architectural Press, 2018.

Berzock, Kathleen Bickford. "Caravans of Gold, Fragments in Time." In *Caravans of Gold, Fragments in Time: Art, Culture, and Exchange across Medieval Saharan Africa,* edited by Kathleen Bickford Berzock, 23–37. Princeton: Princeton University Press, 2019.

Bitgood, Stephen. "The Role of Attention in Designing Effective Interpretive Labels." *Journal of Interpretation Research* 5, no. 2 (2000): 31–45. https://www.interpnet.com/nai/docs/JIR-v5n2.pdf.

Blier, Suzanne Preston. "Nine Contradictions in the New Golden Age of African Art." *African Arts* 35, no. 3 (2002): 1–6. DOI: 10.1162/afar.2002.35.3.1.

Boehm, Barbara Drake, and Melanie Holcomb. *Jerusalem, 1000–1400: Every People under Heaven.* New York: Metropolitan Museum of Art, 2016.

Brown, Keisha A. "Blackness in Exile: W.E.B. Du Bois' Role in the Formation of Representations of Blackness as Conceptualized by the Chinese Communist Party." *Phylon* 53, no. 2 (2016): 20–33. https://www.jstor.org/stable/phylon1960.53.2.20.

Burstein, Stanley M. "When Greek Was an African Language: The Role of Greek Culture in Ancient and Medieval Nubia." *Journal of World History* 19, no. 1 (2008): 41–61. DOI: 10.1353/jwh.0.0006.

Carter, Holland. "How to Fix the Met." *New York Times,* March 1, 2017. https://www.nytimes.com/2017/03/01/arts/design/how-to-fix-the-met-connect-art-to-life.html.

Collins, Kristen, and Bryan C. Keene. "A New Exhibition Explores Balthazar, a Black African King in Medieval and Renaissance European Art." *The Iris,* November 19, 2019. http://blogs.getty.edu/iris/exhibition-to-examine-balthazar-a-black-african-king-in-medieval-and-renaissance-european-art/.

———. "Dialogue: Exposing the Rhetoric of Exclusion through Medieval Manuscripts." *The Iris,* August 3, 2017. http://blogs.getty.edu/iris/dialogue-exposing-the-rhetoric-of-exclusion-through-medieval-manuscripts/.

———. "Scholars Respond to an Exhibition about Medieval Prejudice." *The Iris,* March 6, 2019. https://blogs.getty.edu/iris/scholars-respond-to-an-exhibition-about-medieval-prejudice/.

Du Bois, W.E.B. "Sociology Hesitant." *boundary 2* 27, no. 3 (2000): 37–44. DOI: 10.1215/01903659-27-3-37.

———. "The Hand of Ethiopia." In *Darkwater* [1920], 61–80. Clifton: African Tree Press, 2014.

———. *The Negro* [1915]. New York: Cosimo, 2007.

———. *The World and Africa.* New York: Oxford University Press, 2007.

Evans, Helen, ed. *Byzantium and Islam: Age of Transition, 7th–9th Century.* New York: Metropolitan Museum of Art, 2012.

———. "Recent Acquisitions, A Selection: 2005–2006." *The Metropolitan Museum of Art Bulletin* 64, no. 2 (Fall 2006): 19. http://resources.metmuseum.org/resources/metpublications/pdf/Recent_Acquisitions_A_Selection_2005_2006_The_Metropolitan_Museum_of_Art_Bulletin_v_64_no_2_Fall_2006.pdf.

———, ed. *The Glory of Byzantium: Art and Culture of the Middle Byzantine Era, A.D. 843–1261.* New York: Metropolitan Museum of Art, 1997.

Fauvelle, François-Xavier. *The Golden Rhinoceros: Histories of the African Middle Ages.* Princeton: Princeton University Press, 2018.

Feinberg, Harvey M., and Jospeh B. Solodow, "Out of Africa." *The Journal of African History* 43, no. 2 (2002): 255–61. DOI: 10.1017/S0021853701008118.

French, Howard W. "Africa's Lost Kingdoms." *The New York Review of Books,* June 27, 2019. https://www.nybooks.com/articles/2019/06/27/medieval-africa-lost-kingdoms/.

Gebrekidan, Fikru Negash. "Ethiopia in Black Studies from W.E.B. Du Bois to Henry Louis Gates, Jr." *Northeast African Studies* 15, no. 1 (2015): 1–34. DOI: 10.14321/nortafristud.15.1.0001.

Gerven Oei, Vincent W.J. van. "A Dance for a Princess: The Legends on a Painting in Room 5 of the Southwest Annex of the Monastery on Kom H in Dongola." *The Journal of Juristic Papyrology* 47 (2017): 117–36.

Gomez, Michael A. *African Dominion: A New History of Empire in Early and Medieval West Africa.* Princeton: Princeton University Press, 2018.

Horowitz, Deborah Ellen et al., eds. *Ethiopian Art: The Walters Art Museum.* Lingfield: Third Millennium, 2001.

Humphrey, Lyle. "Collecting Christianity on the Nile: J. Pierpont Morgan and The Metropolitan Museum of Art." In *Age of Transition: Byzantine Culture in the Islamic World,* edited by Helen Evans, 2–20. New York: Yale University Press, 2015.

Jackson, Jenn M. "Breaking Out of the Ivory Tower: (Re)Thinking the Inclusion of Women and Scholars of Color in the Academy." *Journal of Women, Politics & Policy* 40 (2019): 195–203.

Jakobielski, Stefan. *Pachoras Faras: The Wall Paintings from the Cathedrals of Aetios, Paulos and Petros.* Warsaw: Polish Centre of Mediterranean Archaeology, 2017.

Jenkins, Earnestine. "Egypt in Africa." Edited by Theodore Celenko. *African Arts* 31, no. 2 (1998): 16–88. DOI: 10.2307/3337514.

Jerng, Mark C. "Race in the Crucible of Literary Debate." *American Literary History* 31, no. 2 (2019): 260–71. DOI: 10.1093/alh/ajz007.

Kaplan, Amy. *The Anarchy of Empire in the Making of U.S. Culture.* Cambridge: Harvard University Press, 2005.

Klemm, Peri M., and Leah Niederstadt. "Beyond Wide-Eyed Angels: Contemporary Expressive Culture in Ethiopia." *African Arts* 42, no. 1 (2009): 6–13. DOI: 10.1162/afar.2009.42.1.6.

Lowe, Lisa. "History Hesitant." *Social Text* 33, no. 4 (2015): 85–107. DOI: 10.1215/01642472-3315790.

Melamed, Jodi. *Represent and Destroy: Rationalizing Violence in the New Racial Capitalism.* Minneapolis: University of Minnesota Press, 2011.

Miyashiro, Adam. "Decolonizing Medieval Studies: A Response to ISAS in Honolulu." *In the Middle,* July 29, 2017. http://www.inthemedievalmiddle.com/2017/07/decolonizing-anglo-saxon-studies.html.

Morey, Charles R. "The Painted Covers of Washington Manuscript of the Gospels." In *Eastern Christian Paintings in the Freer Collection*, 63–81. New York: Macmillian Company, 1914.

Nayeri, Farah. "We Need to Talk About Colonialism, This Artist Says." *New York Times,* March 5, 2019. https://www.nytimes.com/2019/02/25/arts/design/kader-attia-hayward-gallery.html.

Ochała, Grzegorz. "Multilingualism in Christian Nubia: Qualitative and Quantitative Approaches." *Dotawo: A Journal of Nubian Studies* 1, no. 1 (2014): 1–50. DOI: 10.5070/D61110007.

O'Connor, David B. *Ancient Nubia: Egypt's Rival in Africa.* Philadelphia: University Museum of Archaeology and Anthropology, University of Pennsylvania, 1993.

Pierce, Yolanda. "The Soul of Du Bois' Black Folk." *The North Star: A Journal of African American Religious History* 7, no. 1 (2003): 1–4. https://www.princeton.edu/~jweisenf/northstar/volume6/pierce.html.

Quirin, James. "W.E.B. Du Bois, Ethiopianism and Ethiopia 1890–1955." *International Journal of Ethiopian Studies* 5, no. 2 (2010–11): 1–26. https://www.jstor.org/stable/41757589.

Salam, Maya. "Brooklyn Museum Defends Its Hiring of a White Curator of African Art." *New York Times,* April 6, 2018. https://www.nytimes.com/2018/04/06/arts/brooklyn-museum-african-arts.html.

Schneider, Ryan. "Sex and the Race Man: Imagining Interracial Relationships in W.E.B. Du Bois's Darkwater." *Arizona Quarterly* 59, no. 2 (2003): 59–80. DOI: 10.1353/arq.2003.0024.

Screven, Chandler G. "Motivating Visitors to Read Labels." *ILVS Review: A Journal of Visitor Behavior* 2, no. 2 (1992): 183–211.

Snowden, Frank M. *Before Color Prejudice: The Ancient View of Blacks.* Cambridge: Harvard University Press, 1983.

Thomas, Thelma K. "Christians in the Islamic East." In *The Glory of Byzantium,* 365–87. New York: The Metropolitan Museum of Art, 1997.

———. *Late Antique Egyptian Funerary Sculpture: Images for This World and for the Next.* Princeton: Princeton University Press, 2000.

Tuck, Eve, and K. Wayne Yang. "Decolonization Is Not a Metaphor." *Decolonization: Indigeneity, Education & Society* 1, no. 1 (2012): 1–40. https://jps.library.utoronto.ca/index.php/des/article/view/18630.

Vansina, J. *Art History in Africa: An Introduction to Method.* London: Routledge, 1984.

Vernon, Matthew X. *The Black Middle Ages.* New York: Palgrave, 2018.

Weitzmann, Kurt W. "Some Remarks on the Sources of the Fresco Paintings of the Cathedral of Faras." In Kurt W. Weitzmann, *Studies in the Arts at Sinai*, 187–211. Princeton: Princeton University Press, 1982.

Wessel, Klaus. *Coptic Art.* New York: McGraw-Hill Book Company, 1965.

Zielińska, Dobrochna. "The Iconography of Power — The Power of Iconography: The Nubian Royal Ideology and Its Expression in Wall Painting." In *The Fourth Cataract and Beyond: Proceedings of the 12th International Conference for Nubian Studies*, edited by Julie R. Anderson and Derek A. Welsby, 943–49. Leuven: Peeters, 2014.

3

Disorienting Hebrew Book Collecting

Eva Frojmovic

The provenance of a book, that is, the history of a manuscript after its writing or a book after its printing, is in the case of Hebraica almost always bound up with the history of the Jews [...]. the movement of Hebrew books reflects the wandering of the Jews.[1]

My purpose in this essay is to re-think the biography of a seemingly neutral Hebrew codex of biblical commentary (Bayerische Staatsbibliothek, henceforth BSB, Cod. Hebr. 5) as the fortuitous survivor of traumatic events, whose scars are barely visible on its parchment skin. After escaping late medieval persecutions and expulsions of Jews from imperial cities north of the Alps, and censorship against Hebrew books, the acquisition for the Catholic Augsburg merchant-collector Johann Jakob Fugger in Venice ca. 1549 saved it from subsequent Counter-Reformation confiscation or destruction in Italy. Yet, this entry into a Catholic collection irrevocably removed it from the environment of a Jewish community and transferred it into a Christian Hebraist

1   Brad S. Hill, *Hebraica from the Valmadonna Trust / Hebraica (saec. X ad saec. XVI): Manuscripts and Early Printed Books from the Library of the Valmadonna Trust: An Exhibition at the Pierpont Morgan Library, New York* (London: Valmadonna Trust Library, 1989), 10.

context, thus effectively ending its performance as a Jewish object. Its subsequent life in the Munich court library, later state library, spelled its further integration into a Catholic Hebraist and Orientalist context.

I will argue in this essay that Counter-Reformation era collecting of Hebrew (and other languages connected to the "East," e.g., Arabic, Syriac, Ge'ez) manuscripts, like the study of those languages itself, was predicated on a conversionary initiative by the Catholic church directed at or against Judaism, Islam and Eastern Christianities. This Counter-Reformation attitude to non-Catholics was shaped by a sense of Catholic mission, sharpened by the contest with Lutheran and other Protestant Reformations after 1517. The new schism within Christian Europe, and the ensuing wars of religion, made all study, printing and collecting of Eastern/Semitic languages overdetermined. Catholic Orientalism, despite all its admirable learnedness, involved a not inconsiderable measure of epistemic violence against Jews as well as other non-Christians and non-Catholics.

In the modern archive, the aggressive Counter-Reformation spirit of Oriental studies has been naturalized. Through this naturalization, Renaissance Orientalism as merely, and innocently, Oriental Studies (that is the study of "Oriental" languages on the part of Christian westerners) becomes truly haunted by Orientalism in a Saidian sense. My hope is that once we uncover the missionary and universalist-unionist agendas that brought medieval Hebrew (and similarly, Arabic, Syriac, Ge'ez, etc.) manuscripts into Renaissance Christian libraries, we can denaturalize this process. Such a denaturalization might, in the long term, break down the library classification of "Occidental" and "Oriental" manuscripts and towards less binary terms.

While both Christian Kabbalah with its ultimately missionary goals and the Christian suppression of the Talmud have been well studied, the conversionary attention to biblical exegesis has only recently come under scrutiny. Thus, Piet van Boxel has shown that biblical commentaries (like the commentary compilation contained in BSB Cod. Hebr. 5) were in danger of being pulled into the same maelstrom that was destroying Talmudic literature in and after 1553.² This means that BSB Cod. Hebr. 5 escaped confiscation and destruction by a fortuitous series of displacements.

Starting from a single medieval Hebrew manuscript in the Bayerische Staatsbibliothek, this essay is about two aspects of the history of Hebraica collecting and collections: how historic collecting practices' underlying ideologies could change a medieval object materially and affect its radius of agency. And how residual colonialities have continued to affect the access to and understanding of the archive and the object. I am trying to undo the modern-day institutional sanitization of Counter-Reformation Orientalism, while trying to understand the ambiguous position of Hebrew manuscripts in this sanitization process. I aim to show that the Hebrew manuscript collection of Johann Jakob Fugger, which forms one of the core collections of the historic Munich court library, was connected to Counter-Reformation, anti-Jewish-conversionary, and anti-Islam-ist polemic. Ultimately, by questioning traditional library classification categories, I hope to disrupt invocations and political (populist; extreme right wing) mobilizations of "Judeo-Christian civilization."

In my reflections on Cod. Hebr. 5's biography and its part in a continued "ost-westliche" system of archival and library classification, I build on a tremendously rich vein of research on Renaissance Orientalism and Hebraism, especially its Counter-Reformation context in Italy. I am equally indebted to the century and more of research on the history of the Hebrew (printed) book, recently including also considerations of book collecting, which have shown how medieval Hebrew manuscripts were collected, de-accessioned and recollected between the late Middle

---

2   Piet van Boxel, "Robert Bellarmine Reads Rashi: Rabbinic Bible Commentaries and the Burning of the Talmud," in *The Hebrew Book in Early Modern Italy,* eds. Joseph R. Hacker and Adam Shear (Philadelphia: University of Pennsylvania Press, 2011), 121–32, at 122: "What was at stake in the heated discussion was the question of whether rabbinic commentaries on the Bible should undergo the same fate as the Talmud."

Ages and the Counter-Reformation, between South Germany and North Italy.[3]

A Hebrew Manuscript's Afterlife

The object whose biography forms the centre of these reflections is BSB Cod. Hebr. 5/I-II, a thirteenth-century illuminated bible commentary compiled from French and German Jewish authors.[4] Having been copied by a Jewish scribal team in Würzburg (Franconia) in the Hebrew year 4993 corresponding to September 1232 to September 1233 CE, and partially illuminated by a Christian illuminator's workshop active for aristocratic patrons in the same city and region, it belongs to the geographical area called by Jews Ashkenaz (Germany, German-speaking Switzerland, and Austria). We know that it was originally a single, enormous volume of approximately 450 folios. The wander-route Würzburg–Venice–Augsburg–Munich it took after its completion was almost circular. The codex's illumination remained unfinished, leaving numerous empty spaces originally reserved for painting. Sometime around 1400 or during the first half of the fifteenth century, an unknown scribe (or the then owner?) completed the large initial word for Ruth in an "inhabited" ornamental square script and added deer hunt friezes above the Leviticus and Ruth incipits; the Leviticus frieze in-

---

3   David W. Amram, *The Makers of Hebrew Books in Italy* (London: The Holland Press, 1963; repr. 1988; orig. 1909); Paul F. Grendler, *The Roman Inquisition and the Venetian Press, 1540–1605* (Princeton: Princeton University Press, 1977); Marvin J. Heller, *Printing the Talmud: A History of the Earliest Printed Editions of the Talmud* (New York: Im Hasefer, 1992); Amnon Raz-Krakotzkin, *The Censor, the Editor, and the Text: The Catholic Church and the Shaping of the Jewish Canon in the Sixteenth Century* (Philadelphia: University of Pennsylvania Press, 2007); Joseph R. Hacker and Adam Shear, eds., *The Hebrew Book in Early Modern Italy* (Philadelphia: University of Pennsylvania Press, 2011).
4   Elisabeth Klemm, *Die illuminierten Handschriften des 13. Jahrhunderts deutscher Herkunft in der Bayerischen Staatsbibliothek* (Wiesbaden: Reichert, 1998), 198–201, full description with further bibliography.

cludes a horn-blowing hunter in a fashionable tailored outfit, a feather in his hunting hat; he is armed with a sword, which he appears to have drawn and raised above his head. These letters and imagery are of Ashkenazi workmanship, suggesting that the manuscript remained in Ashkenaz at this time (or in Ashkenazi hands, if they had migrated elsewhere).

A fifteenth-century ownership inscription in Ashkenazi semi-cursive script intriguingly connects the book to a conversion to Judaism: "It fell unto my lot — the words of the convert Avram Wich/Weich Bach."[5] Because this ownership mark is inscribed in the outer corner at the top of folio 2, and this folio is quite dirty, we can conclude that by the fifteenth century, the original folio 1 was already missing (this folio 1 was rewritten during the book's acquisition and modification for Fugger in 1549).

In the context of a series of large-scale persecutions and localized expulsions from the major cities of Ashkenaz during the late Middle Ages, it was taken to Northern Italy probably in the 15th century. Thereby, it escaped the confiscation and destruction of Hebrew books in South Germany in 1509/10, mandated by Emperor Maximilian I at the instigation of the apostate Johannes Pfefferkorn.[6] It subsequently made its way to Venice. Along the route that so many Jewish refugees took across the

---

5   נפל לחלקי נאם גר אברם ויך בך

6   Johannes Pfefferkorn's 1510 list of confiscated books has been published in Isidor Kracauer, "Verzeichniss der von Pfefferkorn 1510 in Frankfurt a. M. confiscierten jüdischen Bücher," *Monatsschrift für Geschichte und Wissenschaft des Judentums* 44 (1900): 320–32; 423–30; 455–60. The last installment contains an attempt by Kracauer to list the confiscated books alphabetically. There is no space here to write about the linguistic violence that distorts the Hebrew book titles to gibberish. On the context and scope of the confiscations, see Ilona Steimann, "Jewish Scribes and Christian Patrons: The Hebraica Collection of Johann Jakob Fugger," *Renaissance Quarterly* 70 (2017): 1235–81; Ilona Steimann, "The Preservation of Hebrew Books by Christians in the Pre-Reformation German Milieu," in *Jewish Manuscript Cultures: New Perspectives,* ed. Irina Wandrey (Berlin, Boston: De Gruyter, 2006–7), 203–26, and Avner Shamir, *Christian Conceptions of Jewish Books: The Pfefferkorn Affair* (Copenhagen: Tusculum 2011).

Alps and into the Veneto, ending up in Venice in the tumultuous years of the Wars of the League of Cambrai, which indirectly led to the establishment of the Venice Ghetto in 1516. We have to be aware that the Venetian Jewish community was newly established, under conditions of war, and of tremendous heterogeneity — made up of migrants from the Italian south, Ashkenazi migrants and refugees from Germany and France, and *conversos* from the Iberian peninsula. Venice was the Jewish melting pot of the sixteenth century.

Ten years after the establishment of the Venice Ghetto, an Ashkenazi scribe inscribed in semi-cursive script the confirmation of a transaction centrally below the end of the scribal colophon at the end of what was then still a single comprehensive volume (pandect):

"This commentary on the twenty-four books [of the bible] was sold to the honorable Rabbi Yekutiel son of the late David in a court declaration today Thursday, 13th of Tevet 5286 (December 29, 1526) here in Venice, so says the smallest amongst scholars Hiya Meir ben David of blessed memory."[7]

Despite his hyperbolic modesty, Rabbi Hiyya Meir ben David was by no means "the smallest amongst scholars." He served as one of three judges in the Jewish community of Venice. He is also well known to book historians as an eminent corrector: he corrected the Catholic publisher Daniel Bomberg's first edition of the Babylonian Talmud (1519–23).[8] In this task he joined Bomberg's master printer/corrector Cornelio Adelkind, about whom more below. Although Amram states that Rabbi Hiyya Meir ben David left Venice for Nafpaktos (Lepanto) in Greece immediately after the completion of this Talmud project, i.e., 1523, we see from the sale note in BSB Cod. Hebr. 5 that he re-

---

7 BSB Cod. Hebr. 5/II, fol. 256.
8 Rabbi Hiyya Meir ben David's scholarship extended to other publication projects in parallel: R. Israel Isserlein, *Terumat ha-Deshen* (Venice: Daniel Bomberg, 1519); Joseph Kolon, *Responsa* (Venice: Daniel Bomberg, 1519); R. Solomon b. Adret, *Responsa* (Venice: Daniel Bomberg, 1519); Alfasi, *Code* (Venice: Daniel Bomberg, 1522).

mained in Venice a little longer. This sale may have been connected with preparations for his departure from Venice.

In 1549, the manuscript BSB Cod. Hebr. 5, then still a pandect, was acquired for the rapidly growing Hebrew library of Johann Jakob Fugger von der Lilie (1516–75). Something more needs to be said about Fugger, his library project, and its historical context. Johann Jakob belonged to a (by no means indigent) side-line of the fabled Fugger banking house. The remaining part of my essay will circle around the connections between this manuscript, Fugger, and his Venetian circle of Jewish and Christian scholars, scribes, and printers. My argument is that even where the relationship between Jews and Christians appeared to be amicable, the project of Jewish conversion was always on the horizon. During the Counter-Reformation, we can speak of competitive conversionary projects among Protestant and Catholic intellectuals. Thus Fugger's Hebrew library and, after its 1571 acquisition by Albrecht V of Bavaria, the Munich court library, were integral parts of a Counter-Reformation conception of universal Catholic mission — to Lutherans, Muslims, and last but not least Jews.

Ilona Steimann, in her study of Johann Jakob Fugger's Hebrew manuscripts patronage — the first detailed study of this incredibly important humanist collection — has shown that a complex web of ambivalent relationships enveloped Christian collectors and Jewish scholars and scribes: "[T]heir [Hebraica collections such as Fugger's] place at the intersection of book cultures offers important evidence of deep tensions between Jewish and humanist attitudes toward Hebrew books and scholarship […] Fugger's enterprise eventually disassociated the Hebrew book from Jews and integrated it into universal humanist scholarship."[9] Fugger's Hebrew library was a symbolic gesture because Fugger was not a scholar and could not read the Hebrew books he accumulated with liberality and rapidity. A hired scribal team, all Ashkenazi migrants from German lands, under

---

9   Steimann, "Jewish Scribes and Christian Patrons," 1237.

the overall guidance of the Jewish master printer Cornelio Adelkind, carried out a monumental Hebraica copying enterprise of 270 texts bound into 55 volumes copied between 1548 and 1552 for Johann Jakob Fugger.[10] These codices entered Fugger's library of universal knowledge, and subsequently the Munich court library, today the Bayerische Staatsbibliothek. Fugger relied entirely on Jewish mediators, chief among them Cornelio Adelkind in his capacity as head of the Fugger scribal workshop. As Steimann demonstrated, Fugger's acquisition of BSB Cod. Hebr. 5 was closely associated with this industrial-scale Fugger Hebrew manuscript copying enterprise, resulting in the creation a large collection especially of kabbalistic and philosophical manuscripts. BSB Cod. Hebr. 5 is among the minority of original Hebrew manuscripts Fugger was able to acquire (commissioning new copies was much more efficient and resulted in a satisfyingly uniform format). As the agent and coordinator of the whole collecting and copying enterprise, Steimann has identified precisely Adelkind: none of the colophons of the codices newly copied for Fugger actually name the Augsburg merchant; if they name any patron, it is Adelkind. Adelkind was most likely a frontman to calm the consciences of Jewish scribes who might otherwise have been unwilling to compromise their Jewish careers by copying Hebrew texts for a Christian, and especially not kabbalistic texts which were controversial because of their known missionary potency. This universal humanist scholarship was predicated on the supersessionist project of Christian expropriation of Jewish culture.[11] Adelkind was the most likely

10 Ibid, 1242–43.
11 Kathleen Biddick, *The Typological Imaginary: Circumcision, Technology, History* (Philadelphia: University of Pennsylvania Press, 2003). When King Ludwig of Bavaria erected a monument to the "patron of scholarship" (*Wissenschaft*) Johann Jakob Fugger in Augsburg in 1857, the Bavarian king was invoking a concept of universalized, disinterested scientific activity, carefully ignoring its economic foundations and its ideological interests. At the same time (the mid-nineteenth century), Bavarian Jews did not enjoy civic equality, but had to apply for individual residence and marriage permits.

middleman enabling the acquisition of BSB Cod. Hebr. 5, since he had worked together with its previous owner-but-one Rabbi Hiyya Meir ben David during the years (ca. 1519–26) that both worked at Bomberg's press.

When BSB Cod. Hebr. 5 was acquired for the Fugger library, it was divided into two volumes, which necessitated some violent intervention, but also some restoration. Two Ashkenazi Jewish scribes were entrusted with this modification, who have been identified as Yishai ben Yehiel and Meir (only his first name is known).[12] The already-missing folio 1 containing the beginning of Genesis was now replaced by the scribe Yishai ben Yehiel; the initial word "Bereshit," "In the Beginning," was decorated by another scribe, Meir, with typically Ashkenazi giant letters in a pleated ribbon design that had come into fashion among Ashkenazi scribes around 1400, and saw a revival (always among Ashkenazim) in the early modern period (fig. 1). This calligraphic form was thus understood to be typically Ashkenazi. Because of the division of the pandect into two volumes, the last leaf at the end of the first volume (fol. 218) containing the end of II Kings, was cut off and had to be replaced by Yishai ben Yehiel, also in 1549. The original end of II Kings page was now moved over to the newly created second volume. Its recto was covered over with a recycled medieval Latin(!) flyleaf. Its verso, containing the explicit of II Kings, was pasted over with a newly made title page by the Fugger team scribe Meir. In giant block letters, it announces "LATTER PROPHETS," decorated with skilfully drawn recumbent dog and deer. The original covered-over text is faintly visible underneath (fig. 2). The next folio, containing the beginning of Isaiah, now became the new volume 2's first page. Finally, the two volumes were rebound by a Venetian binder known as the "Fugger binder" into uniform bindings in two volumes. At this time, a single folio from a completely different book was bound in at the end of volume 2: the beginning of the bible commentary by Rashi's grandson Rashbam. This rescued folio is

---

12 Steimann, "Jewish Scribes and Christian Patrons," 1242.

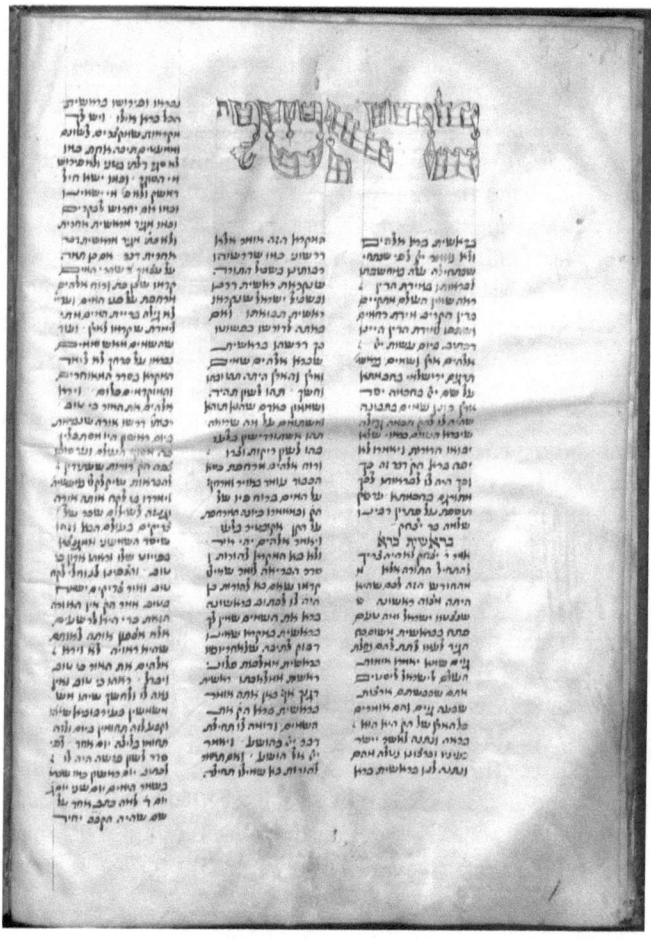

Figure 1. BSB, Cod. Hebr. 5/I, fol. 1v. http://daten.digitale-sammlungen.de/bsb00036330/image_5. Licensed by the Bayerische StaatsBibliothek under a CreativeCommons BY-NC-SA 4.0 license.

Figure 2. BSB, Cod. Hebr. 5/II, fol. 1r. http://daten.digitale-sammlungen.de/bsb00036327/image_6. Licensed by the Bayerische StaatsBibliothek under a CreativeCommons BY-NC-SA 4.0 license.

Figure 3. BSB, Cod. Hebr. 5/I, front cover. http://daten.digitale-sammlungen.de/bsb00036327/image_1. Licensed by the Bayerische StaatsBibliothek under a CreativeCommons BY-NC-SA 4.0 license.

now of the same dimensions (and is likely to have been of similar dimensions originally). It appears to originate in the same scribal environment as the main commentary compilation. It is to date the oldest manuscript witness to the transmission of Rashbam's commentary and plays an important role in modern editions. It appears to have originated in the same scribal team as the bulk of BSB Cod. Hebr. 5. It is impossible to tell why only the first folio of this Rashbam commentary was extant in 1549. Had it become detached from its book?

For the binding, four wooden boards were covered in a medium green (now brown) Morocco which was then gold-tooled (fig. 3). The binder used both ornamental and letter punches, in Greek and in Hebrew. A rhomboid cartouche inspired by Ottoman bindings has been inscribed into a double rectangle whose outer and inner lines intersect to form an overlapping circle based on medieval (though of ultimately late Roman derivation) cosmatesque floor mosaics. The centres front and back, within a circle, enclose the title of the book "Perushim/Commentaries" in Hebrew on the (Hebrew) front and a (blank) heraldic shield in a Northern Renaissance style on the back. Above and below the title, the Fugger library signature has been punched in Hebrew (above the title) and Greek (below the title) respectively.[13]

---

13 This binding is described by Aliza Cohen-Mushlin and Ilona Steimann in the *Ursula and Kurt Schubert Archives,* The Center for Jewish Art, Hebrew University (Jerusalem) thus: "green morocco faded to brown on wooden boards, gold-tooled similarly on front and back with a central roundel in an undulating floral rhomboid within a large rectangle. The latter is decorated with foliate motifs at the corners and with a flower at the center of each side of the frame […]). The central front roundel is inscribed פירושים (Commentaries). Above and below it is Fugger's shelf mark in Hebrew and Latin respectively: ת and Y for volume I […], and ש (*sic*) and Z for volume II. The roundel on the back encloses a shield-like motif. The spine, blind-tooled with hatching, has five hidden cords and head and tail bands. On the front cover are vestiges of four groups of three plaited leather bands: two on the fore-edge and one each at top and bottom, corresponding to holes from four missing nails on the edges of the back cover (see e.g. Cod. Hebr. 301). The edges of leaves are goffered. The binding was done by the Fugger Binder (also called Venetian Apple

The blind-tooled ornaments include at least two Orientalizing elements inspired by Ottoman bindings: the large rhomboid cartouche, and the floral corner motifs. The small rosette medallions formed by the frame's overlapping interlaced bands may allude either to Mamluk or to medieval ornaments, either way introducing exotic elements. It is of course true that Orientalizing bindings were not a defining mark of non-Western books. Western literature was also bound in this style.[14] In this case the additional element of the Hebrew lettering contributed to Orientalizing the books as a whole.

The pastedowns and flyleaves are, surprisingly, from Latin manuscripts. Aliza Cohen-Mushlin and Ilona Steimann not only localized and dated the flyleaves and pastedowns as thirteenth-century Latin leaves written in German lands, but identified their content as a passional (front pastedown and flyleaves in both volumes) and two homiliaries (back pastedowns and flyleaves in both volumes). Some of these are bound upside down. Such use of Latin, indeed liturgical manuscripts as flyleaves in a Hebrew manuscript rebound for a Christian, indeed a Catholic patron, may at first sight seem surprising. But I believe that at work was a renaissance ideology that sought to leave behind as obsolete not only the dark ages of Judaism, but also the aesthetic and scribal culture of the Middle Ages that had lost its value. In

---

Binder) in Venice in 1549" ("Munich Rashi's Commentary on the Bible," *The Center for Jewish Art, Ursula and Kurt Schubert Archives,* http://cja.huji.ac.il/sch/browser.php?mode=set&id=2191). See Bettina Wagner, *Außen-Ansichten: Bucheinbände aus 1000 Jahren aus den Beständen der Bayerischen Staatsbibliothek München* (Vienna: Otto Harrassowitz Verlag, 2006), 84–85. Unlike Steimann ("Jewish Scribes and Christian Patrons," 1264), I believe the letter stamps were applied in Venice, and not in Augsburg. My reassessment is based on their shape, which is distinctly Italian.

14 The same blind-tool ornamental stamps (though not the Hebrew letters) appear in identical form in the British Library's Appian, *Delle guerre civili de Romani* [and] *Historia delle guerre esterne de Romani* (Florence 1526/31), BL Davis 754; and Castiglione, *Libro del Cortegiano* (Venice 1541), BL Davis 794. While Orientalizing bindings were common in Venice, it is important not to normalize them.

addition, passional codices had become obsolete after the introduction of breviaries.¹⁵ So to sum up, the rebinding of BSB Cod. Hebr. 5 into the two volumes we have today involved numerous acts of Orientalist and "medievalist" appropriation.

The Many Names of Adelkind

I have already stated that BSB Cod. Hebr. 5 was acquired for Fugger in Venice. Venice was in Fugger's days Hebrew printing's undisputed center. Venice's laws not only fostered, but in fact enforced close Christian-Jewish collaboration. Although the actual work of printing was carried out by Jews, it was not only not sited in the Jewish Ghetto, but had to be fronted by Christians. No Jewish publisher could obtain a permission to print in Venice. And even for Christians it was not easy to print Hebrew books. No less than the pre-eminent Antwerp Catholic publisher of Hebrew books in Venice, Daniel Bomberg, had to more or less bribe the government into renewing his licence. In 1525/6 and again in 1537 his renewal application met stiff resistance (which had to be bought out at a high price).¹⁶ That Hebrew printing was both lucrative and precarious was demonstrated by the 1553 Talmud burnings, an intellectual conflagration that swept all across Italy, whose fuse was lit in a dispute between two Christian Hebrew printers in Venice, a dispute which escalated to the Roman Inquisition.

The cut-throat world of Venetian publishing, the networks encompassing Fugger's Hebrew manuscript collecting activities

---

15 Nicholas Pickwoad, "The Use of Fragments of Medieval Manuscripts in the Construction and Covering of Bindings on Printed Books," in *Interpreting and Collecting Fragments of Medieval Books,* eds. Linda L. Brownrigg and Margaret M. Smith (Los Altos Hills: Anderson-Lovelace; London: Red Gull Press, 2000), 1–20.

16 Not least on the part of the famous diarist Marin Sanudo, who opposed the renewal of Bomberg's license and who proudly records his fulminations against the printing of books for the benefit of Jews. See Amram, *The Makers of Hebrew Books in Italy,* 173.

in Venice, and the opaque world of Catholic Renaissance Hebraism and Orientalism were connected by the Adelkind family of Hebrew correctors, and in particular the man born as Israel ben Barukh (ha-Levi) Adelkind and who generally signed himself as Cornelio Adelkind (active 1519–54). As a Hebrew corrector and master printer, Adelkind contributed significantly to the quality of Venetian Hebrew printing. In one sense, he was one of the Jewish professionals who made possible the project of Daniel Bomberg, the Catholic Netherlandish entrepreneur who dominated Hebrew printing in Venice from the establishment of a permanent Jewish Ghetto (1516) until the middle of the sixteenth century, when in 1553 the Talmud, for whose publication Bomberg had done so much, went up in flames in the piazzas of Italy, including Piazza San Marco. Although Bomberg knew some Hebrew, Adelkind had responsibility for the sourcing and accuracy of the published texts. He was familiar with the world of Jewish scribes, who then still copied the bulk of Hebrew literature for Jews as well as for some learned Christians. Adelkind was at home in these Christian-run and financed Hebrew printing presses of the high Renaissance from ca. 1519 onwards and until 1553, when he moved to Sabbioneta to work for the Jewish printer Tobias Foa.

Who was Adelkind? And how was his identity affected by the work he did, the people he worked with, and the pressures he was subjected to? Above all, was he a Jew or a Christian? Like a raw nerve or a live wire, the question of Adelkind's conversion to Christianity (Did he? When did he? Why did he? Did he mean it?) runs through the literature on Hebrew printing. Unlike the clear-cut cases of other apostates such as Samuel b. Nissim Bulfarag/Guglielmo Raimondo de Moncada/Flavius Mithridates (ca. 1450–89) or Jacob ben Chaim ben Isaac ibn Adonijah (ca. 1470–before 1538), Adelkind's religious identity has generated more debate than any other. The debate began with Steinschneider in the mid-19th century, who raised the suspicion of Adelkind's apostasy, admittedly then just in the form of a speculation.[17] Since then, the arguments for and against have grown. The issues were laid out in Marvin Heller's classic study of the history of Talmud printing.[18] Heller reviews both the existing evidence and the contentious history of its interpretation, with Steinschneider and Yaari arguing that Adelkind was an apostate, while Rabbinovicz, Berliner and Sonne argue against apostasy. Amram and Bloch remain undecided, and other historians of Hebrew printing conclude that Adelkind converted very late in his career, i.e., that most of his classics were printed while he was still Jewish. Adelkind's language in his prologues, epigraphs and colophons never betrays anything — he uses the Jewish calendar, and overall traditional formulas. But two Christian Frenchmen who were contemporaries of Adelkind's later years assert unambiguously that he converted to Christianity, one of them calling him a "baptised Christian" and the other a "neophyte […] corrected from Judaism," as discussed further below.

An Ashkenazi from Padua, his father Barukh Adelkind is believed to have migrated or fled to Padua from the increasingly hostile German environment that saw the wholesale expulsion of Jews from all major South German cities during the late fifteenth and early sixteenth centuries. His Hebrew names were Israel ben Barukh, sometimes also Israel the Levite, indicating that his father Baruch was a Levi. Most of his book colophons, and also his (Italian) letters, he signed as Cornelio, a humanist-inspired name harking back to Roman antiquity. The secular name Cornelio may also have been a subtle homage to his chief employer Daniel Bomberg, whose father was the Antwerp merchant Cornelius van Bomberghen. In turn, Adelkind named his own son Daniel. And yet, a Cornelius the Centurion appears in the Acts of the Apostles as an early convert by Simon Peter (Acts 10:1–48). On one occasion, he calls himself by a retro-transliter-

---

17   David Cassel and Moritz Steinschneider, *Jüdische Typographie und jüdischer Buchhandel* (Jerusalem: Bamberger & Wahrmann, 1938), 21–94.
18   Marvin J. Heller, *Printing the Talmud: A History of the Earliest Printed Editions of the Talmud* (New York: Im Hasefer, 1992), 159–61 and 416 (footnotes).

ated name Karniel קרניאל. This name, which seems to be the Hebrew aural equivalent of Cornelio, occurs in the fourth printing, third edition of the complete Hebrew Bible with list of Haftarot, published by Bomberg in 1533.[19] The colophon on the last page, after the end of the list of Haftarot (Prophetic portions arranged for liturgical use), states:

> Printed for the third time with much investigation/study by Karniel bar Barukh Adel Ḳind, in the month of Adar [i.e., Feb./March 1528], in the year 1528 in the house of the prince/eminent Daniel Bombergi, may The Rock raise him up.[20]

The main interest is in the name, which skilfully weaves together Hebrew and Latin/Italian onomastics. Karniel translates as ray or rays of God. *Keren* = ray, horn—those are the rays of light that emanated from Moses' face when he descended from Mount Sinai. The name is not biblical; rather, in midrashic literature Karniel appears among the princes of the west wind. It is thus a rather rarefied naming indicative of its owner's and his circle's learning.[21]

---

19 Anthony Grafton is thus quite wrong to assert that "Karniel Adel Kind, the Jewish printer who designed the layout of Bomberg's Talmud editions, converted to Christianity and changed his name to Cornelio, though he continued to turn out editions of the Talmud" ("The Jewish Book in Christian Europe; Material Texts and Religious Encounters," in *Faithful Narratives: Historians, Religion, and the Challenge of Objectivity,* eds. Andrea Sterk and Nina Caputo [Ithaca: Cornell University Press, 2014], 96–114, at 109). Adelkind used both Cornelio and Karniel concurrently and as equivalent *noms de plume*. In fact, no post-conversion Adelkind imprint is known to me.

20 This colophon was actually a 1533 reprint of that third edition of 1528, so we are looking at the fourth printing.

21 *Maaseh Beraishit & Maaseh Merkavah,* in *Otzar Midrashim, a Library of Two Hundred Minor Midrashim,* ed., intro. & notes Judah D. Eisenstein (New York: Eisenstein, 1915), vol. 2, 311–19. My thanks to Isaac Lifshitz for bringing this Midrash to my attention.

The circumstantial evidence that made Steinschneider suspect apostasy was the rhymed epigraph of *Petah Debarai* or *Devari* (1546), set on its own page in large square letters:

ובחן נשלם ספר פתח דברי
בשם האל גואלי חי וצורי
הוא הפרט לשנות ליצירה צורי
יום תשעה ועשרים בתשרי
הוגה על ידי מדקדק בלשון עברי
שמו אליהו לוי איש ערירי
נדפס בבית האדון הנצרי
בווניציאה הבירה שדגלה ארי
המדפיס עתה ספרא וספרי
ועוד ידי לא תמוש מעשות פרי
ישראל היה שמי וקורנילייו זכרי
תם

And thus was finished the book Petah Debarai
In the name of the living god my redeemer and rock
In the year of creation 306
On the 29th day of Tishri
Edited by the Hebrew language grammarian
Elijah the Levite, the lonely man
Printed in the house of the master, the Christian
In Venice the Capital whose standard is a lion
Who is now printing Sifra and Sifre
And may my hand not cease from bringing forth fruit
Israel was my name and Cornelio [will be] my memorial.[22]

The rhyme is on "-ri," hence the final word "zekhri," memorial. Why does Adelkind speak of his name Israel in the past tense?

---

22 Elijah Levita, ed., *Petach Devarai* (Venice: Daniel Bomberg, 1546). A facsimile of the epigraph can be found on the website of the Hathi Trust: https://babel.hathitrust.org/cgi/pt?id=ucm.5320284098&view=1up&seq=161.

We would probably do well not to attempt to resolve all ambiguities in what is after all an artful text that codes its message in rhymed form for the *cognoscenti*. In the colophon of 1546, different temporalities are pitted against each other. And yet even here Adelkind has not abandoned the name his father and community gave him at the age of eight days, when he was brought into the circumcision covenant of his people. This multiplicity of names must lead us to a reflection on the ambiguous and volatile position of Jewish intellectuals in the Renaissance. Adelkind with his many names encapsulates the dangerous terrain of Renaissance Humanist Hebraism and Hebrew book production and collecting during the Counter-Reformation.

The two positive assertions that Adelkind converted to Christianity come from two French sources: the Orientalist–theologian–kabbalist Guillaume Postel (1510–81) and the punchcutter and printer Guillaume Le Bé (1525–98), both of whom knew Adelkind personally. The first source is a 1555 letter by the Oriental linguist, controversial visionary, Christian kabbalist, theologian, and mathematician Guillaume Postel to his fellow Orientalist and Christian kabbalist Andreas Masius. Both were intimately connected to both Widmannstetter and Fugger and both were part of the same northern European Catholic Orientalist circles.

> But hear what happened when I was passing through the area of Cremona [...], I undertook to pass through a small town, previously lowly, Sabbioneta by name, both in order to see the Hebrew press founded there and to visit, for the sake of Bomberg's memory, the *neophyte** Cornelius Adelkind, who has been corrected* from Judaism.[23]

23 The italicized words marked with asterisks are written in Greek in the original Latin letter. "Sed audi quid contigit (ut soli Deo gloria, nobis autem pro summis nostris conatibus confusio videatur meritissima adesse faciei) iter agenti per Cremonense Municipium, alioqui ignobile antea, nomine Sabioneta, quod inditione est D. Vepasiani Gonzaghae Columnae, qua iter institueram, tam ut Typographiam Hebraicam ibi instauratam

The wit of this passage revolves around the wordplay involved in the use of the participle "διορθωτήν," corrected. After all, Adelkind was *the* corrector par excellence with decades of experience in the pre-eminent Bomberg Hebrew press, which had dominated Italy and the Jewish world during the formative first half of the sixteenth century. Through his conversion, the corrector was, so to speak, corrected from his Judaic error.[24] Postel's witty satisfaction needs to be seen in the context of Christian Kabbalah, of which Postel was an avid advocate, and whose theological appropriation of Jewish theologies has come to be clearly recognized:

> Christian kabbalists interpreted these texts as containing hidden evidence for the truth of Christianity, transmitted by Jewish tradition unbeknownst to itself. [...] [M]any Christian kabbalists understood their work in missionary terms. If Jews could be shown that their most sacred and secret traditions confirmed Christian truth, their conversion might finally be achieved. As confessional conflict fractured European Christendom, some even turned to Kabbalah as a means

---

viderem, quam ut Cornelium Adelkindum νεόφυτον ex Judaismo διαρθωτήν [sic in the edition, should be διορθωτήν] inviserem, memoriae Bombergianae gratia. Incidi divinitus in homunculum ferrarium aut ensarium (ut a fabricandis ensibus vocant) quo utebantur ibidem Judaei ad suas operas, tant industria hominem, ut animi magnitude in eo compearit [sic] corporis parvitatem, ita ut hominis ingenio delectatus probari posset, ne exarandis Arabicis characteribus par esset." The letter is dated June 7, 1555 according to the Julian calendar (Jaques George de Chaufepié, *Nouveau dictionnaire historique et critique: pour servir de supplement ou de continuation au Dictionnaire historique et critique, de Mr. Pierre Bayle* [Amsterdam: Chez C. Chatelain, H. Uytwerf, F. Changuion, J. Wetstein, P. Mortier, Arkste et Merkus, M. Uytwerf, et M.M. Rey; The Hague: Chez Pierre de Hondt, 1750–56], vol. 3 [1753], 228). Expanded and minimally corrected after Arthur Spanier, "Note," *Kirjath Sepher* 5 (1928): 278, who quotes the core passage concerning Adelkind. The reference to "previously lowly" Sabbioneta is likely to refer to Duke Vincenzo Gonzaga's foundation of Sabbioneta as an ideal city and ducal residence in 1554/5.

24 I am grateful to Brad Sabin Hill for drawing my attention to this wordplay.

to universal salvation that could heal the fissures within the Church. Perhaps above all, Christian Kabbalah was the appropriation from Jewish esoteric literature of a set of hermeneutic techniques [...] attempted to demonstrate the truth of Christianity from within Jewish esoteric tradition by means of that tradition's own methods.[25]

Although BSB Cod. Hebr. 5 does not contain any kabbalistic texts, it is nevertheless connected to Christian kabbalism. Its acquisition by Fugger stood at the beginning of a large scale collecting endeavor, a very significant portion of which consisted of kabbalistic texts.

Guillaume Le Bé (1525–98) was a (French Catholic) punchcutter who transformed the art of Hebrew printing in France and the Netherlands, inter alia as supplier of Hebrew type to the eminent Antwerp printer Christopher Plantin, publisher of the *Biblia Regia* a.k.a. *Antwerp Polyglot Bible* (1568–72). He is presumed to have met Adelkind during his formative training years spent in Venice (1540s to ca 1550). Sometime between Le Bé's ca. 1550 (?) return from his Italian apprenticeship and his death in 1598, he compiled an album/scrapbook of 48 pages of cut-out and pasted printed specimens cut out from miscellaneous Hebrew books, which he annotated by hand. It is worth pausing to acknowledge the mutilation of Hebrew books committed in the process of assembling the scrapbook. Hebrew books are ascribed a sacrality that prohibits their dismembering and discarding — even disused or defunct Hebrew books should be placed in a Genizah and ultimately buried.[26] A handwritten au-

---

25 Theodor Dunkelgrün, "The Christian Study of Judaism in Early Modern Europe," in *The Cambridge History of Judaism*, vol. 7, *The Early Modern World, 1500–1815*, eds. Jonathan Karp and Adam Sutcliffe (Cambridge: Cambridge University Press, 2017), 316–48, at 323–24.

26 Falk Wiesemann, *Genizah — Hidden Legacies of the German Village Jews = Genisa — verborgenes Erbe der deutschen Landjuden* (Munich: Bertelsmann, 1992); Stefan C. Reif, *A Jewish Archive from old Cairo: The History of Cambridge University's Genizah Collection* (Richmond: Curzon,

tograph rubric in his scrapbook, accompanying a few cut-out lines of Adelkind's typefont, identifies it thus:

> [Taken] from a Hebrew gloss by Messer Cornelio, baptized Christian, corrector at the printing establishment of the Bombergs, quite old and cut by a good master.[27]

By calling Mister Cornelio (without including his surname Adelkind) a "baptized Christian," Guillaume Le Bé is revealing that he was originally Jewish. In effect, Guillaume meant "juif baptise." And what did he mean by "bien antique," given that Adelkind preceded him by barely a generation and actually overlapped with him? Surely what is invoked is a sense that Adelkind's type designs capture a mythical authenticity relating to biblical antiquity. Le Bé's scrapbook may have been compiled some considerable time after his return from Italy, during the latter part of his life. It is thus unlikely that Adelkind converted while le Bé was still in Italy; rather, he may have received the information from Postel, who returned to Paris in 1562. Adelkind's conversion should thus be dated after 1554 (the date of Adelkind's last Hebrew imprint) and before 7 June 1555 (the date of Postel's letter according to the Julian calendar, corresponding to 16 June in the Gregorian calendar). After that, we hear no more of Adelkind, who may have died shortly thereafter. Le

---

2000); Adina Hoffman and Peter Cole, *Sacred Trash: The Lost and Found World of the Cairo Geniza* (New York: Nextbook, Schocken, 2011).

27 "D'une glose hébraïque de messer Cornelio, chrestien baptisé, correcteur en l'imprimerie des Bombergues, bien antique et taillée d'un bon maistre." Guillaume Le Bé (1525–1598). [Spécimens de caractères hébreux gravés à Venise et à Paris par Guillaume Le Bé (1546–1574).] Bibliothèque nationale de France, département Réserve des livres rares, RES-X-1665, fol. 19v, https://gallica.bnf.fr/ark:/12148/bpt6k841173q/f56.image?fbclid=IwAR1J8a-ZVNwseglnıknCg2L39R2Wxjq9TTWVO7tynVzxWuOObZvAoEEDw9M. A reprint was published by Henri Omont, *Spécimens de caractères hébreux gravés a Venise et a Paris par Guillaume le Bé (1546–1574)* (Société de l'Histoire de Paris et de l'Ile-de-France, 1887). My thanks to Noam Sienna, who tracked down the digitized BNF copy of Guillaume's *Specimens*.

Bé's label and Postel's glee at Adelkind's conversion to Christianity should be seen in the context of the conversionary pressure exerted by much of Catholic Orientalism.[28] A significant factor contributing to this pressure was the destruction of Talmud and other Hebrew books in 1553, and the ensuing escalation of the censorship of Hebrew books.

For better or worse, Hebrew books in this era of printing were in the hands of Catholics, who could not help but become implicated in the larger politics of the Counter-Reformation. And the Jews of Italy and their heritage of books and manuscripts were pawns in this larger politics. Controlling, constricting, and eventually converting the Jews — that was the prize that secretly symbolized the superiority of one's Christian confession on all sides of the Reformation — Counter-Reformation divide. Similarly, engaging in late-crusading against the Ottomans was a political act of competitive colonialism that was played out equally in the arena of Orientalist scholarship, printing and publishing.

The Counter-Reformation Persecution of Jewish Books

Hebrew book production was caught between the Scylla of appropriative Christological Kabbalism and the Charybdis of Talmud persecution and censorship. Simultaneously with and at the opposite pole of the avid Christian appropriation of Kabbalah appears the persecution, confiscation and burning of the Talmud, which reached crisis point in Italy in 1553. In a generally volatile atmosphere, a commercial rivalry spun out of control. The two rival Christian printers of Hebrew books in Venice, Marco Antonio Giustiniani (1516–71, active 1545–53) and Alvise Bragadini (ca. 1500–1575) attempted to undercut each other's editions of Maimonides' *Mishneh Torah* (a rewriting of Talmud, of course); they accused each other of publishing Jewish books containing anti-Christian blasphemies (Talmudic literature, in

---

28 Brannon Wheeler, "Guillaume Postel and the Primordial Origins of the Middle East," *Method and Theory in the Study of Religion* 25 (2013): 1–20.

other words). A chain reaction ensued in Rome, fomented by internal rivalries between the Curia and the Holy Office (under the chief inquisitor, the future Pope Paul IV Carafa, the same pope who enclosed the Roman Ghetto in 1555). The outcome of this unwanted inquisitorial attention resulted in a cataclysm of destruction which devoured not only copies of the Talmud printed and manuscript, but also of associated texts such as halakhic compendia and epitomes.

What does any of this have to do with the acquisition and removal from Italy of BSB Cod. Hebr. 5? After all, BSB Cod. Hebr. 5 contains biblical exegesis, not Talmud. Well, one of the debates carried out behind the scenes implicated also the Hebrew biblical commentary tradition. There were voices that alleged that Rashi and his followers were contaminated by Talmudic thinking. Such hardcore thinkers wanted Jews to be able to keep only the Hebrew Bible text itself, without any exegetical aids — in order to all the sooner achieve Jewish conversion to Christianity.[29] Although wholesale destruction of Rashi did not come to pass, nevertheless one may claim that if BSB Cod. Hebr. 5 had not been removed from Italy, and if the proponents of the destruction of all talmudically tainted books had won the upper hand, this massive volume would have escaped this threat with difficulty.

That even the defenders of Talmudic literature were not exempt from supersessionist and conversionary agendas is demonstrated by the case of Andreas Masius (1514–73). This Catholic humanist Hebraist and Syriacist is sometimes considered a hero in Jewish eyes because he spoke up against the destruction of Talmud copies. We mentioned him earlier as a friend and correspondent of Postel and recipient of the gleeful 1555 letter about Adelkind's "correction." But look closely at his defence of the Talmud:

---

29 Boxel, "Robert Bellarmine Reads Rashi," 121–32.

> I have found in this Talmud countless testimonies not against the Christians, but against the Jews […]. No book is more suitable to confound the Jews than the Talmud. To claim the opposite is risible. I had begun to compile materials towards a book which would have won the Jews for Christianity. Out of utter indignation about this thing [(*summa rei indignatione*) the ecclesiastical Talmud destruction], I have thrown the whole thing into the fire.[30]

In other words, while Masius rejects the Talmud persecutions, he is by no means a defender of Judaism; on the contrary, he suggests that the Talmud is an indictment of rabbinic Judaism! So even Andreas Masius, the Netherlandish humanist and friend of many Jewish intellectuals of his day, and staunchest and most outspoken defender of Hebrew printing in the terrible "battle of the printers" of 1553 leading to the confiscation and burning of all Talmudic literature in Italy, was writing at the same time a tract intended to effect the conversion of the Jews, a tract possibly composed of Talmudic excerpts.

Disorienting the Archive

BSB Cod. Hebr. 5, authored in Northern France, copied and collected in Southern Germany, and rebound in Venice, is a thoroughly European product. Yet its language and script (Hebrew) pushes it into the "Oriental" section of the library. Physically, the Bayerische Staatsbibliothek (successor of the Munich court

---

30 Andreas Masius, letter to Cardinal Sebastiano Pighino, December 24, 1553, Bayerische Staatsbibliothek, Ms Clm 23736, nr. 182 (bound folder of numbered original letters). Max Lossen, *Briefe von Andreas Masius und seinen Freunden 1538 bis 1573* (Leipzig: A. Dürr, 1886), nr. 128, 144–45, which is usually called authoritative, leaves out these more controversial portions of Masius's correspondence. Perles's German partial translation in Joseph Perles, "Ungedruckte Briefe aus den Jahren 1517 — 1555", in *Idem: Beiträge zur Geschichte der hebräischen und aramäischen Studien* (Munich: Theodor Ackermann, 1884), 223–25 is actually more complete than Lossen.

library) operates a single manuscript reading room, regardless of language or script. That means that unlike other major libraries who operate separate "Oriental" reading rooms, in Munich all manuscripts are consulted in the same physical space. It is thus possible, again unlike in in other major libraries, to study BSB Cod. Hebr. 5 together with Latin manuscripts illuminated in Wurzburg around the same time, maybe even by the same painting workshop. But when it comes to library classification, and that is all about the production of knowledge, the distinction between Occidental and Oriental manuscripts is upheld, even reinforced by means of the online presentation of the library, which is its twenty-first-century public face. And in terms of classification, BSB Cod. Hebr. 5 is placed firmly in the Orient.

The first encounter with the library's manuscript collections takes place through the collection overview "About the collection."[31] Its titular slideshow of ten images is exclusively Western and predominantly German (9/10), privileging Latin-script manuscripts from present-day Bavarian territories. Notwithstanding its inclusion of two secular texts (Nibelungenlied and Bellifortis), this choice of images establishes a privileged position for Christian objects. The overview of the Munich manuscripts collection thus marginalizes, *inter alia*, Hebraica (as well as Arabica, Persiana, etc). This is all the more ironic as the ducal library's original core was an "Oriental" one: it was founded on the ducal acquisition of two "Oriental"/biblical collections, those of Widmannstetter (acquired 1558) and of Fugger (acquired 1571).[32] The collection overview's binary distinction is

---

31 "About the Collection," *Bayerische Staatsbibliothek,* https://www.bsb-muenchen.de/en/collections/manuscripts/about-the-collection/.

32 "Über die Sammlung," *Bayerische Staatsbibliothek,* https://www.bsb-muenchen.de/sammlungen/handschriften/ueber-die-sammlung/. Widmannstetter's considerable library included ca. 200 manuscripts in Hebrew, Arabic, and Syriac. On the conversionary intention of Widmannstetter, see Robert J. Wilkinson, *Orientalism, Aramaic and Kabbalah in the Catholic Reformation: The First Printing of the Syriac New Testament* (Leiden: Brill, 2007), a book which has profoundly informed my thinking in the present essay.

upheld between the "Over 41,000 Occidental and 18,000 Oriental or Asian manuscripts…" — as if the Bayerische Staatsbibliothek's important other collections did not matter. The twelve highlights of the foundation collection, "Important works from the collection at the time of its foundation," do not include a single Hebrew manuscript (although they do include one Arabic, Armenian, and Ethiopian each).[33] Importance and diversity are clearly at odds in this selection.

The post-foundation historical outline includes among its over eighty highlights two Hebrew items. The two chosen Hebrew highlights are the Babylonian Talmud Cod. Hebr. 95 and the Tegernsee Haggadah BSB Cod. Hebr. 200. Yet the presentation of both of these Hebraica is problematic. Both are cited as part of an alphabetical list of manuscripts that entered the then royal Bavarian court library from monasteries dissolved in 1803 — the Talmud from Polling Abbey, the Haggadah from Tegernsee Abbey. Thereby, the indubitably important Talmud's Jewish, pre-monastic provenance is made invisible;[34] the polem-

---

33 The foundation collection's highlights list (I retain their orthography but have added translations in brackets): *Das Buch der Abenteuer* (The Book of Adventures) (Ms Cgm 1), late 15th century; Andalusian Koran (i.e., Quran) from Seville (Cod.arab. 1), 1226; Armenian four gospels (Cod.armen. 1), 1278; Ethiopian psalter (Cod.aethiop. 1); *Der Ehrenspiegel des Hauses Habsburg* (Mirror of honours of the house of Habsburg) (Ms Cgm 895 and 896); *Das Kleinodienbuch der Herzogin Anna von Bayern* (Book of gems of Duchess Anna of Bavaria) (Cod.icon. 429); Hungarian gospel book (Cod. hung. 1); Omnibus manuscript with astronomical-computational and scientific texts from the library of Schedel (Ms Clm 210); Superb codices of the penitential psalms of Orlando di Lasso (Mus.ms. A I and Mus.ms. A II); Motets of Cipriano de Rore (Mus.ms. B); Terrestrial globe of Philipp Apian (Cod.icon. 129); Celestial globe of Heinrich Arboreus (Cod.icon. 186).

34 This codex, copied in an Ashkenazi script and dated 1342, is of outstanding significance because it is the only surviving complete copy of the entire Babylonian Talmud still extant from before the era of printing. Like a brand plucked out of the fire, it has survived medieval and early modern Talmud burnings. Its provenance however is problematic, and the collection overview's phrasing ensures that such problematic issues are hidden. Judging from its various owners' inscriptions, it was clearly

ical context of the Tegernsee or "Monk's" Haggadah — its provenance from a late medieval missionary Christian milieu connected to blood libel accusations — is equally invisible in this presentation.[35] Its choice seems determined more by its unique position among the Tegernsee Abbey library holdings.

> in Italy during the 15th century, but appears to have left the peninsula before the Talmud persecution of 1553. In 1588, Solomon Ulma/Ulmo from Gunzburg acquired the Talmud, perhaps in Prague. According to Steimann's research, it was still in his possession in 1610. I owe a debt of gratitude to Ilona Steimann for sharing her unpublished cataloguing notes on this codex with me (p.c., May 7, 2019). Until the 18th century, this Talmud belonged to the Ulma/Ulmo/Ullmann family, who after their 1499 expulsion from the eponymous Ulm eventually settled in Pfersee, just outside Augsburg, and became one of the leading Jewish families there. The last ownership entry by the Ulmo family within the codex is from 1772. Ber ben Yona Ulmo/Ber Bernhard Ullmann (1751–1837), the head of the Pfersee/Augsburg Jewish community, was arrested in 1803 on trumped-up charges of monetary forgery. It is unclear how or why the codex moved from Pfersee to the Augustinian priory of Polling (Upper Bavaria, quite distant from Pfersee/Augsburg). Ber Bernhard Ullmann, *Chronicle of the Year 1803*, trans. & ed. Carl J. Ullmann (New York: n.p., 1928). *Tage des Gerichts: Der Bericht des Ber Ulmo aus Pfersee*, ed. & trans. Yehuda Shenef (Friedberg: Kokavim-Verlag, 2012), suggests that the provenance of this codex is doubtful and that it may have been expropriated from Ber Ullmann against his will. See *Lebendiges Büchererbe: Säkularisation, Mediatisierung und die Bayerische Staatsbibliothek* (Munich: Bayerische Staatsbibliothek, 2003).

35 As a recent monograph shows, it may have been written and illuminated for a Christian Hebraist whose aim was to know Jewish rituals for the sake of converting Jews. For this reason, the codex has acquired a new name: "The Monk's Haggadah." See *The Monk's Haggadah: A Fifteenth-Century Illuminated Codex from the Monastery of Tegernsee, with a prologue by Friar Erhard von Pappenheim,* eds. David Stern, Christoph Markschies, and Sarit Shalev-Eyni (University Park: Pennsylvania State University Press, 2015). For the connection with the Trent blood libel of 1475, see Steimann, "The Preservation of Hebrew Books by Christians in the Pre-Reformation German Milieu," 220–21.

To find out more about manuscripts in Hebrew and Jewish languages, one is referred to the languages/regions section.[36] Occidental Manuscripts range at the top of this list, followed by

- African (Ethiopian, i.e., Geʿez and Amharic, Coptic, Punic, and the singular Codex Vai)
- Oriental — (Arabic, Armenian, Hebrew and Yiddish(!), Pashto, Persian, Syriac, Turkish, Zend, as well as one each in Balochi, Kurdish, and Mandaic).
- East Asian — (Korean, Japanese, Chinese — why not alphabetical?)
- South Asian — (no separation into languages, but includes Bengali, Chakma, Gujarati, Hindi, Kannada, Lepcha, Malayalam, Marathi, Nepali, Oriya, Pali, Punjabi, Rajasthani, Sanskrit, Sindhi, Singhalese, Tamil, Telugu, and Urdu)
- South East Asian (Batak, Burmese, Javanese and Balinese, Cambodian, Lampung, Laotian, Malayan, Thai, Vietnamese, and the languages of the Philippines).
- Central Asian (Manchurian, Mongolian, and Tibetan).

It becomes clear that the position of the African manuscripts directly after the occidental ones is due to the predominantly Christian character of the Geʿez, Amharic, and Coptic holdings. This Africa is the Catholic, Christian Africa.

The overview over the Oriental section elides the distinction between alphabet, language and geography. Without pausing to worry about the Quran copied in Seville, the Mishnah with Talmud copied in South East France, or the Yiddish books copied in Southern Germany, the overview of the Oriental section calls them "Manuscripts from the Middle East."[37] In fact, the subsection introducing the Hebrew and Yiddish manuscripts con-

---

36 "Oriental Manuscripts," *Bayerische Staatsbibliothek,* https://www.bsb-muenchen.de/en/collections/manuscripts/languages-regions/oriental-manuscripts/.

37 Ibid.

cedes that, "Although the Hebrew manuscripts are allocated to the group of Oriental works in accordance with their language, the majority of these works was created in Europe (predominantly Germany, France and Spain)."[38] In this way, the classification system denies that Hebrew and Yiddish (as well as Arabic, of course) have historically been among European languages: a form of collective linguistic expatriation (in German, "Ausbürgerung," a historic term connoting the Jewish deprivation of citizenship and residence status by the Nazis). Thus an ambivalent attitude to non-Latin-script languages leads to the Orientalization of Jewish books made in Europe.

The flipside of this Orientalization is the sanitation of the term Orientalism in the online history of the Munich Hebrew and Yiddish manuscript department.[39] In the introductory paragraph concerning the foundation of the "Oriental" collections, the terms "Oriental" and "Orientalist" are used six times in the "innocent" way in which they used to be employed before Edward Said's *Orientalism*.[40] The Orientalist humanist and diplomat Johann Albrecht Widmannstetter (1506–57), rector of Vien-

---

38 Ibid.
39 "The outstanding value of this collection is owed to the acquisition of the libraries of the diplomat and *Orientalist* Johann Albrecht Widmanstetter (1506–57) and of Johann Jakob Fugger (1516–75) at the outset. Widmanstetter is regarded as one of the pioneers of *Oriental studies*. The purchase of the private library of the highly educated and polyglot diplomat and *Orientalist* in the year 1558 by Duke Albrecht V constituted the founding act of the Munich court library at the same time. More than 450 years ago, around 200 — a fairly substantial number at the time — manuscripts in the Hebrew, Arabic and Syrian languages were acquired by the library, among them a number of very important Hebrew works and very rare *Oriental early printed works*. The *Oriental collection* was expanded already in 1571 by the incorporation of the library of Johann Jakob Fugger (1516–75), one of the most prolific book collectors of the 16th century. Fugger's library contained numerous *Oriental works*, in particular Hebrew works of great importance" ("Hebrew and Yiddish," Bayerische Staatsbibliothek, https://www.bsb-muenchen.de/en/collections/orient/languages/hebrew-and-yiddish, emphases mine).
40 Edward Said, *Orientalism* (London: Routledge & Kegan Paul), 1978.

Figure 4. [Syriac New Testament], *Ketaba de'wangeliwan qadisha' demaran wa'lahan yeshu'* ... = Liber sacrosancti evangelii de Jesu Christo Domino & Deo nostro : reliqua hoc codice comprehensa pagina proxima indicabit. Div. Ferdinandi Rom. imperatoris designati iussu & liberalitate, characteribus & lingua Syra, Jesu Christo vernacula divino ipsius ore co[n]secrata, et a Joh. Eva[n]gelista Hebraica dicta, scriptorio prelo dilige[n]ter expressa. Viennae Austriae : Excudebat Michaël Zymmerman, 1562. Leeds, Brotherton Library, University of Leeds, Ripon Cathedral Library XII.E.11: Frontispiece to the Gospel of St. John, appropriating the kabbalistic iconography of the Sefirot Tree into John's vision of the cross. Reproduced with the permission of Special Collections, Leeds University Library.

na University, used his considerable language skills in Hebrew, Arabic and Syriac for ultimately conversionary aims aimed both at European Jews and at Eastern Christians. In the library's presentation, Widmannstetter's linguistic and collecting credentials are endorsed; but he was not only a pioneer of Oriental Studies as in his capacity as Chancellor of Austria and rector of the imperial University of Vienna, he stood at the forefront of the struggle against the Lutheran reformation, and in parallel (and as part of this greater quest for Catholic supremacy) he engaged in anti-Muslim polemics. Widmannstetter's Islamic studies scholarship was not disinterested: he was the author of the 1543 polemical work *Notae contra Mohammedis dogmata,* which accompanied his edition of medieval Quranic excerpts *Mahometis Abdallae filii theologia dialogo explicata* and the *Vita Mohammedis.* All drew heavily on or revived Crusade-era anti-Muslim polemics.[41] When it comes to Widmannstetter's pioneering study of Syriac and Aramaic, its aim was to recuperate ancient Christianity in a quest for Catholic authentication, and to subject the eastern churches to Roman papal authority. He was explicit that his publication of the Syriac New Testament (Peshitta) in 1555

---

41 Hermann of Carinthia, Robert of Chester (fl. 1143), Johann Albrecht Widmanstetter (1506?–57), *Mahometis Abdallae filii theologia dialogo explicate* (Nuremberg: n.p., 1543). Reference: BM STC German, 1455–1600, 634; Christian Friedrich von Schnurrer, *Bibliotheca Arabica* (Halle: C. Hendelii, 1811), 422. A copy in the Bayerische Staatsbibliothek in Munich was owned by Wiguleus Hundt von Lauterbach zu Sulzenmoos, a Bavarian statesman in the service of Duke Albrecht V. That copy has a handwritten note by Widmanstetter on the title page: "Codex iste librariorum culpa, & senatus Norimbergen[sis] iussu deprauatus fuit, maxime ubi Lutheranor[um] haeresis attingi videbatur" ("This codex was ruined by the fault of the publishers, and the command of the Nuremberg city council, especially where it seemed to concern the Lutheran heresy"). "Mahometis Abdallae filii theologia dialogo explicata," *Brill: Early Western Korans Online,* https://primarysources.brillonline.com/browse/early-western-korans/mahometis-abdallae-filii-theologia-dialogo-explicata;epk59.

served conversionary purposes aimed both at Jews and at Muslims as well as non-Catholic Eastern Christians.[42]

The Peshitta's St. John frontispiece, with its almost typological correlation between the crucifixion and the "tree" of ten kabbalistic Sefirot, brings to the fore the appropriation of Kabbalah by Catholic Orientalists (fig. 4).[43] It features the intrusion of Latin and Hebrew into the Syriac context: above the author portrait's head, we read the incipit of St. John, and above the crucifix "Qui expansis in cruce manibus, / traxisti omnia ad te SECULA — You who have stretched out your hands on the cross have pulled towards yourself all the world." These words are taken from the Roman Church's *Tenebrae* for Maundy Thursday.[44] A Hebrew rotulus above Jesus's head is inscribed "ינמה," translating the traditional Latin INRI = Iesus Nazarenus Rex Iudeorum, i.e., Jesus of Nazareth, King of the Jews). Among the pictorially expressed Sefirot, Abraham, Isaac and Jacob feature prominently among the upper spheres. This use of the patriarchs is a form of supercessionist typology. The supersessionist theme is continued with Temple/Sanctuary symbolism: the foot of the cross is flanked by an altar with a fire burning on it and a sacrificial bull. The Menorah (the seven-branched golden Temple candelabrum) features prominently in the left foreground, in front of an image of the heavens. Although not all the details of this ambitious image are decodable, it is evident that Christian Kabbalah is deployed here

---

42 [Syriac New Testament], *Ketaba de'wangeliwan qadisha' demaran wa'lahan yeshu'* … = Liber sacrosancti evangelii de Jesu Christo Domino & Deo nostro: reliqua hoc codice comprehensa pagina proxima indicabit. Div. Ferdinandi Rom. imperatoris designati iussu & liberalitate, characteribus & lingua Syra, Jesu Christo vernacula divino ipsius ore co[n]secrata, et a Joh. Eva[n]gelista Hebraica dicta, scriptorio prelo dilige[n]ter expressa. Viennae Austriae: Excudebat Michaël Zymmerman, 1562. University of Leeds, Brotherton Library, Ripon Cathedral Library XII.E.11.

43 Wilkinson, *Orientalism, Aramaic and Kabbalah in the Catholic Reformation*, 182–85.

44 Fer. 5 in Cena Domini, Holy Thursday (Maundy Thursday). The reference of this antiphon may be to John 12:32: "Et ego, si exaltatus fuero a terra, omnia treham ad meipsum."

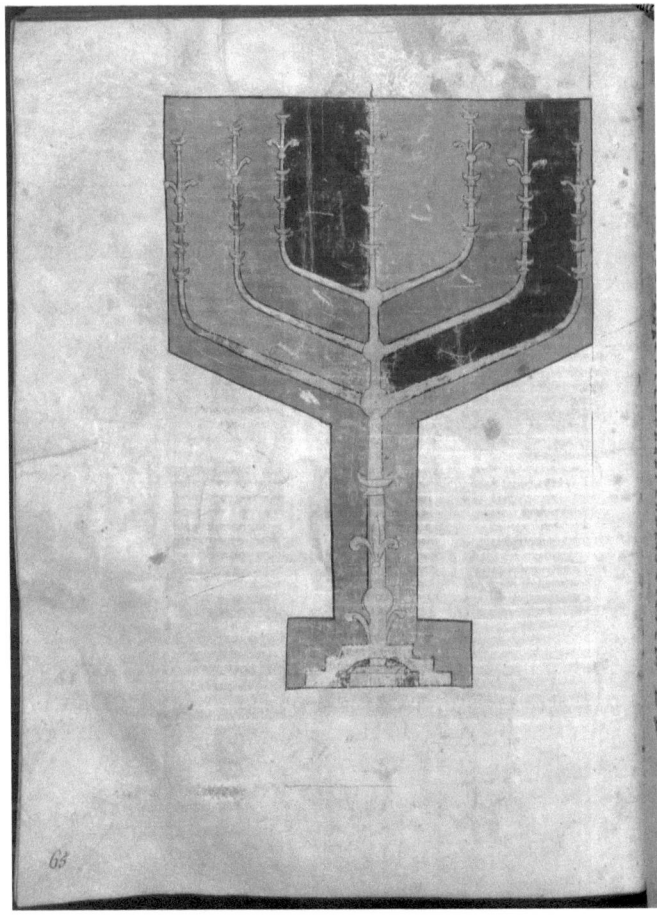

Figure 5. BSB, Cod. Hebr. 5/I, fol. 65. http://daten.digitale-sammlungen.de/bsb00036327/image_137. Licensed by the Bayerische StaatsBibliothek under a CreativeCommons BY-NC-SA 4.0 license.

to expropriate the "Old Testament" (not printed in this book!), all the while depicting its harmony with the New. Thus, Widmannstetter's scholarly work cannot be divorced from his participation in Renaissance anti-Islamism and anti-Judaism. One only needs to peruse Wilkinson's comprehensive study of Syriac studies to discern the entanglement between Renaissance-era Oriental Studies, Christian (ultimately anti-Jewish) Kabbalah and anti-Islamism.[45] As a keen Christian Hebraist with a special interest in Kabbalah (always read christologically), his conversionary agendas are well known — but in the online celebration of this figure, the dark face of Renaissance Orientalism is hidden.

BSB Cod. Hebr. 5, the manuscript with which we started, occupies a prominent place in the Hebrew and Yiddish section of the Oriental Manuscripts collection (among the selection of images here, the illuminated incipit from the book of Daniel is illustrated). It, too makes a visual statement about the continuity of the Temple/Sanctuary imagery, in its monumental full-page image of the Menorah on fol. 65 of the first volume (fig. 5).[46] But at the same time, its angular formation resists the normative roundedness of the Christian seven-branched "Menorah" candelabra of the Middle Ages, such as those in the churches or cathedrals in Essen, Braunschweig, Reims, Klosterneuburg, Prague, Milan, which appropriated this object for claims that their churches replaced/displaced the ancient Temple.[47] The Menorah depicted in the Peshitta's St. John, by contrast, is in-

---

45 Ibid., 29–62; Robert J. Wilkinson, *The Kabbalistic Scholars of the Antwerp Polyglot Bible* (Leiden and Boston: Brill, 2007).

46 Steven Fine, *The Menorah: From the Bible to Modern Israel* (Cambridge: Harvard University Press, 2016). Re the three-stepped stone at the feet of this Menorah, see Babylonian Talmud, Menachot 28b; Maimonides, *Mishneh Torah, Beit Habechira* 3:10: "A stone with three steps was placed before the Menorah. The priest stood on it and kindled the lamps. Also, he placed the containers of oil, the tongs, and the ash-scoops upon it while kindling it."

47 Peter Bloch, "Siebenarmige Leuchter in christlichen Kirchen," *Wallraf-Richartz Jahrbuch* 23 (1961): 55–190; Silvio Leydi, "The Trivulzio

debted to both that sculpted on Titus's triumphal arch erected in celebration of the destruction of the Jerusalem Temple, and to rabbinic Jewish exegesis insisting on its tripod base — a combination then of humanist antiquarianism and of appropriated Hebraic learning.

Conclusion

The conversion of the Jews and that of Muslims, in parallel to the unification of the Eastern churches under the papal banner, was an integral core of Catholic Orientalism. I hope to have demonstrated that BSB Cod. Hebr. 5 carries the scars of such intellectual and political encounters on its leather-bound body. It narrowly escaped being swept up in more than one campaign intended to starve Jews of their traditional textual sources. This conversionary project was an integral part of the Catholic Orientalist project, a grandiose proto-Orientalist scholarly undertaking motivated by a truly Catholic, sometimes also apocalyptic vision of a universal religious unification under the shelter of papal spiritual power. My argument has been that by not critically interrogating these connections in present-day archival organization and classification, we risk sanitizing these extreme pressures on "Renaissance" Jews under the seemingly benign banner of Renaissance Humanism, and that we risk overlooking the chain of actions that at the same time preserved this Hebrew manuscript and removed it from Jewish agency.[48]

How would it be to instead place at the center of our epistemic vision the Ashkenazi synagogue of Venice known as the

---

Candelabrum in the Sixteenth Century: Documents and Hypotheses," *The Burlington Magazine* 153, no. 1294 (2011): 4–12.

48 For the rejection of Hebrew non-biblical learning in an earlier period, see Daniel Stein Kokin, "Giannozzo Manetti in Leonardo Bruni's Shadow: The Formation and Defense of a Humanist Hebraist," *I Tatti Studies in the Italian Renaissance* 19, no. 2 (2016): 309–33.

Figure 6. Scuola Grande Tedesca synagogue, Venice: Facade inscription beneath the roof cornice. Photo: author.

Scuola Grande Tedesca (the Great German School)?[49] This oldest house of Jewish prayer in Venice was founded in 1528/29 by Ashkenazi migrants from hostile environments north of the alps to Venetian-controlled Northern Italy; during the War of the League of Cambrai (1508–16), these Ashkenazi people sought refuge in Venice itself, which then temporarily lifted its embargo on Jewish residence in the lagoon city—only to be contained in the "Getto Novo" in 1516, at the end of the war. Like a book, the synagogue is a body inscribed. The building's west entrance faces the main piazza of the Ghetto Nuovo (that is the oldest part of the Ghetto). An otherwise unremarkable unadorned façade, only the five window arches, solemnly grouped on the third floor above low-ceilinged living quarters, suggest something more than an ordinary dwelling. Above the outer of the five windows, two small inscribed plaques are placed, probably too high up to be read. Using artful allusions so as to code the dates contained in them, the right-hand plaque records the original foundation of the synagogue, and its restoration in the early eighteenth century:

> And when the House was founded, the year was [1528/9]; and when it was rebuilt for the second time, the time had come to rebuild the House of the Lord [1732/3].[50]

---

49 David Cassuto, "The Scuola Grande Tedesca in the Venice Ghetto," *Journal of Jewish Art* 3/4 (1977), 40–57.
50 Cf. Haggai 1:2: "Thus said the LORD of Hosts: These people say, 'The time has not yet come for rebuilding the House of the LORD.'"

Figure 7. Scuola Grande Tedesca synagogue, Venice: Interior north wall of the prayer hall, inscribed frieze, marmorino (faux marble), woodpaneled seat backs. Photo: author, 2019.

The second plaque makes reference to fire damage necessitating this rebuilding (which involved major internal modifications, including the erection of the oval women's gallery). Even higher — very, very high up, just below the roof cornice, almost hiding from passers-by, runs a monumental Hebrew inscription (fig. 6):

> Great House of Assembly, m[ay] G[od] p[rotect it], of the Holy Congregation of the Ashkenazim, may their Rock preserve them, Amen.

Divine protection is invoked twice in this short text, once on the building and once on the community. The particularist identity as "Ashkenazim" suggests a consciousness of the multi-ethnic nature of the population of the Ghetto.[51] This space served as the place of encounter between the various Jewish people who owned or came into contact with BSB Cod. Hebr. 5, among them the rabbi, religious judge and editor Rabbi Hiyya Meir ben David (if he was still in Venice) and the "honorable Rabbi Yekutiel son of the late David," who had bought the book from the former in 1526. This was likely the place where the various editors, typesetters and correctors who worked in the flourishing Hebrew printing industry worshipped, together with the

---

51 Even though the present placement of the inscription above the 18th-century ladies' gallery suggests a later date, the inscription is likely a replica of a 16th-century inscription.

Ashkenazi scribes working for Fugger. Including the master printer Israel ben Barukh alias Karniel Adel Kind alias Cornelio Adelkind, and the scribes who rearranged BSB Cod. Hebr. 5 into two volumes. The interior of the synagogue is also a kind of book: the Ten Commandments are inscribed in gold paint on a crimson band which runs all the way around the hall not much above head height, and originally marked the upper limit of the first, low-ceilinged hall (fig. 7). The leaders of the congregation had plenty of reasons to implore divine protection: not only was the 1516 residence "privilege" for Jewish people in Venice, which enabled the establishment of the Getto Novo, always temporary and threatened by termination upon expiry, but there were plenty of cultural and religious pressures and vulnerabilities in the pressure cooker that was Counter-Reformation Orientalism.

Bibliography

"About the Collection." *Bayerische Staatsbibliothek.* https://www.bsb-muenchen.de/en/collections/manuscripts/about-the-collection/.

Amram, David W. *The Makers of Hebrew Books in Italy.* London: The Holland Press, 1963; rpt. 1988; orig. 1909.

[Bible, New Testament. Syriac]. *Ketaba de'wangeliwan qadisha' demaran wa'lahan yeshu'.* Liber sacrosancti evangelii de Jesu Christo Domino & Deo nostro. Vienna: Michaël Zymmerman, 1562.

Biddick, Kathleen. *The Typological Imaginary: Circumcision, Technology, History.* Philadelphia: University of Pennsylvania Press, 2003.

Bloch, Peter. "Siebenarmige Leuchter in christlichen Kirchen." *Wallraf-Richartz Jahrbuch* 23 (1961): 55–190.

Boxel, Piet van. "Robert Bellarmine Reads Rashi: Rabbinic Bible Commentaries and the Burning of the Talmud." In *The Hebrew Book in Early Modern Italy,* edited by Joseph R. Hacker and Adam Shear, 121–32. Philadelphia: University of Pennsylvania Press, 2011.

Cassel, David, and Moritz Steinschneider. *Jüdische Typographie und jüdischer Buchhandel.* Jerusalem: Bamberger & Wahrmann, 1938; rpt. from Johann S. Ersch and Johann G. Gruber, eds., *Allgemeine Encyclopädie der Wissenschaften und Künste, Ersch und Gruber's Encyclopedia,* vol. 28. Leipzig: F. A. Brockhaus, 1851, 21–94.

Cassuto, David. "The Scuola Grande Tedesca in the Venice Ghetto." *Journal of Jewish Art* 3/4 (1977): 40–57.

Chaufepié, Jaques George de. *Nouveau dictionnaire historique et critique: pour servir de supplement ou de continuation au Dictionnaire historique et critique, de Mr. Pierre Bayle.* Amsterdam: Chez C. Chatelain, H. Uytwerf, F. Changuion, J. Wetstein, P. Mortier, Arkste et Merkus, M. Uytwerf, et M.M. Rey; The Hague: Chez Pierre de Hondt, 1750–56.

Dunkelgrün, Theodor. "The Christian Study of Judaism in Early Modern Europe." In *The Cambridge History of*

Judaism: Volume 7, The Early Modern World, 1500–1815, edited by Jonathan Karp and Adam Sutcliff, 316–48. Cambridge: Cambridge University Press, 2017.

Fine, Steven. *The Menorah: From the Bible to Modern Israel*. Cambridge: Harvard University Press, 2016.

Grendler, Paul F. *The Roman Inquisition and the Venetian Press, 1540–1605*. Princeton: Princeton University Press, 1977.

Hacker, Joseph R., and Adam Shear, eds. *The Hebrew Book in Early Modern Italy*. Philadelphia: University of Pennsylvania Press, 2011.

"Hebrew and Yiddish." *Bayerische Staatsbibliothek*. https://www.bsb-muenchen.de/en/collections/orient/languages/hebrew-and-yiddish.

Heller, Marvin J. *Printing the Talmud: A History of the Earliest Printed Editions of the Talmud*. New York: Im Hasefer, 1992.

Hill, Brad S. *Hebraica from the Valmadonna Trust/ Hebraica (saec. X ad saec. XVI): Manuscripts and Early Printed Books from the Library of the Valmadonna Trust: An Exhibition at the Pierpont Morgan Library, New York*. London: Valmadonna Trust Library, 1989.

Klemm, Elizabeth. *Die illuminierten Handschriften des 13. Jahrhunderts deutscher Herkunft in der Bayerischen Staatsbibliothek*. Wiesbaden: Reichert, 1998.

Kracauer, Isidor. "Verzeichniss der von Pfefferkorn 1510 in Frankfurt a. M. confiscierten jüdischen Bücher." *Monatsschrift für Geschichte und Wissenschaft des Judentums* 44 (1900): 320–32; 423–30; 455–60.

Levita, Elijah, ed. *Petach Devarai*. Venice: Daniel Bomberg, 1546.

Leydi, Silvio. "The Trivulzio Candelabrum in the Sixteenth Century: Documents and Hypotheses." *The Burlington Magazine* 153, no. 1294 (2011): 4–12.

"Mahometis Abdallae filii theologia dialogo explicata." *Brill: Early Western Korans Online*. https://primarysources.brillonline.com/browse/early-western-korans/mahometis-abdallae-filii-theologia-dialogo-explicata;epk59.

"Munich Rashi's Commentary on the Bible." *The Center for Jewish Art, Ursula and Kurt Schubert Archives.* http://cja.huji.ac.il/sch/browser.php?mode=set&id=219.

Lossen, Max. *Briefe von Andreas Masius und seinen Freunden 1538 bis 1573.* Leipzig: A. Dürr, 1886.

Omont, Henri. *Spécimens de caractères hébreux gravés a Venise et a Paris par Guillaume le Bé (1546–1574).* Paris: Société de l'Histoire de Paris et de l'Ile-de-France, 1887.

"Oriental Manuscripts." *Bayerische Staatsbibliothek.* https://www.bsb-muenchen.de/en/collections/manuscripts/languages-regions/oriental-manuscripts/.

Perles, Joseph. *Beiträge zur Geschichte der hebräischen und aramäischen Studien.* Munich: Theodor Ackermann, 1884.

Pickwood, Nicholas. "The Use of Fragments of Medieval Manuscripts in the Construction and Covering of Bindings on Printed Books." In *Interpreting and Collecting Fragments of Medieval Books,* edited by Linda L. Brownrigg and Margaret M. Smith, 1–20. Los Altos Hills: Anderson-Lovelace; London: Red Gull Press, 2000.

Raz-Krakotzkin, Amnon. *The Censor, the Editor, and the Text: The Catholic Church and the Shaping of the Jewish Canon in the Sixteenth Century.* Philadelphia: University of Pennsylvania Press, 2007.

Said, Edward. *Orientalism.* London: Routledge & Kegan Paul, 1978.

Secret, François. *Les Kabbalistes chrétiens de la Renaissance.* Paris: Dunod, 1964.

Shamir, Avner. *Christian Conceptions of Jewish Books: The Pfefferkorn Affair.* Copenhagen, Tusculum 2011.

Spanier, Arthur. "Note." *Kirjath Sepher* 5 (1928): 278.

Steimann, Ilona. "Jewish Scribes and Christian Patrons: The Hebraica Collection of Johann Jakob Fugger." *Renaissance Quarterly* 70 (2017): 1235–81.

———. "The Preservation of Hebrew Books by Christians in the Pre-Reformation German Milieu." In *Jewish Manuscript Cultures: New Perspectives,* edited by Irina Wandrey, 203–26. Berlin & Boston: De Gruyter, 2006–7.

Stein Kokin, Daniel. "Giannozzo Manetti in Leonardo Bruni's Shadow: The Formation and Defense of a Humanist Hebraist." *I Tatti Studies in the Italian Renaissance* 19, no. 2 (2016): 309–33.

Stern, David, Christoph Markschies, and Sarit Shalev-Eyni, eds. *The Monk's Haggadah: A Fifteenth-Century Illuminated Codex from the Monastery of Tegernsee, with a Prologue by Friar Erhard von Pappenheim.* University Park: Pennsylvania State University Press, 2015.

"Über die Sammlung." *Bayerische Staatsbibliothek.* https://www.bsb-muenchen.de/sammlungen/handschriften/ueber-die-sammlung/.

Wagner, Bettina. *Außen-Ansichten: Bucheinbände aus 1000 Jahren aus den Beständen der Bayerischen Staatsbibliothek München.* Vienna: Otto Harrassowitz Verlag, 2006.

Wandrey, Irina, ed. *Jewish Manuscript Cultures: New Perspectives.* Berlin, Boston: De Gruyter, 2017.

Wheeler, Brannon. "Guillaume Postel and the Primordial Origins of the Middle East." *Method and Theory in the Study of Religion* 25 (2013): 1–20. DOI: 10.1163/15700682-12341262.

Wilkinson, Robert J. *The Kabbalistic Scholars of the Antwerp Polyglot Bible.* Leiden: Brill, 2007.

———. *Orientalism, Aramaic and Kabbalah in the Catholic Reformation: The First Printing of the Syriac New Testament.* Leiden: Brill, 2007.

4

The Etymology of *Slave*

Anna Kłosowska

Slavery in the Middle Ages: A Short Summary

Medieval history of the word *esclave* in French and Occitan, informed by Italian *schiavo*, Byzantine *sklavenos*, Arabic *sqaliba*, and Latin *sclavus*, and its derivation from the designation of origin, Slav, is the topic of this chapter. While literary historians Geraldine Heng and Cord Whitaker reshape the scholarship on medieval racism, historians of slavery and servitude in medieval Europe continue to undermine the narrative of the emergence of servitude and decline of slavery that has erased awareness that the medieval world is also a world of slavery. According to a familiar narrative — a narrative that is correct in essentials, except that it obscures the reality of medieval slavery — slavery ended ca. 1100 and a new legal context, servitude, emerged; a transition that the French historian and founder of the Annales school, Marc Bloch, called "one of the most profound transformations known to humans."[1] Scholars including the thirteenth

---

1 Marc Bloch, "Comment et pourquoi finit l'esclavage antique," in *Mélanges historiques*, vol. 1 (Paris: SEVPEN, 1963): 261–85, at 261; Geraldine Heng, *The Invention of Race in the European Middle Ages* (Cambridge: Cambridge University Press, 2018); Cord Whitaker, *Black Metaphors: How Modern*

and fourteenth century-historian of the slave trade in Italy and Egypt, Hannah Barker, the Merovingian and Carolingian historian Alice Rio, and others provide specific studies anchored in time and place, that complicate the narrative that ca. 1100 serfdom replaced slavery as the legal context of unfreedom in many areas of Europe, although not in Scandinavia.[2] They show

> *Racism Emerged from Medieval Race-Thinking* (Philadelphia: University of Pennsylvania Press, 2019).
>
> 2   Alice Rio, *Slavery after Rome, 500–1100* (Oxford: Oxford University Press, 2017); Alice Rio, "Slavery in the Carolingian Empire," in *The Cambridge World History of Slavery*, vol. 2, eds. David Richardson, Stanley Engerman, David Eltis, and Craig Perry (Cambridge: Cambridge University Press, 2019); Alice Rio, "'Half-free' Categories in the Early Middle Ages: Fine Status Distinctions before Professional Lawyers," in *Legalism: Rules and Categories*, eds. P. Dresch and J. Scheele (Oxford: Oxford University Press, 2015), 129–52; Alice Rio, "Penal Enslavement in the Early Middle Ages," in *Global Convict Labour*, eds. Christian Giuseppe De Vito and Alex Lichtenstein (Leiden: Brill, 2015), 79–107; Alice Rio, "Self-sale and Voluntary Entry into Unfreedom, 300–1100," *Journal of Social History* 45, no. 3 (2012): 661–85; Alice Rio, "Byzantine Slavery and the Mediterranean World," *American Historical Review* 115, no. 5 (2010): 1513–14; Alice Rio, "Freedom and Unfreedom in Early Medieval Francia: The Evidence of the Legal Formulae," *Past and Present* 193 (2010): 7–40; Hannah Barker, *That Most Precious Merchandise: Mediterranean and Black Sea Slaves, 1260–1500* (Philadelphia: University of Pennsylvania Press, 2019). Other important new studies of slavery are listed in the excellent general readers' introduction on slavery by Sandrine Victor, *Les fils de Canaan: l'esclavage au Moyen Age* (Paris: Vendémiaire, 2019). They include: Fabienne P. Guillen and Salah Trabelsi, eds., *Les esclavages en Méditerranée. Espaces et dynamiques économiques* (Madrid: Casa de Velazquez, 2012), the work of Mohamed Ouerfelli on diplomacy in the Mediterranean, including Ivan Armenteros Martínez and M. Ouerfelli, "Réévaluer l'économie, l'économie de l'esclavage en Méditerranée au Moyen Âge et au début de l'époque Moderne," *Rives méditerranéennes* 53 (2017): 7–17, at 10; Mohamed Meouak, *Saqâliba, eunuques et esclaves à la conquête du pouvoir. Géographie et histoire des élites politiques marginales dans l'Espagne umayyade* (Helsinki: Soumalainen Tiedakatemia, 2004); Reuven Amitai and Christopher Cluse, eds., *Slavery and the Slave Trade in the Eastern Mediterranean (c. 1000–1500)* (Turnhout: Brepols, 2017); Antoni Josep Furió i Diego. "Una introducció. Treball esclau i treball assalariat a la baixa edat mitjana," *Recerques: Història, economia i cultura* 52/53 (2008): 7–18; Mohamed Meouak, "Esclaves noires et esclaves blancs en

al-Andalus umayyade et en Ifrîqiya fatimide. Couleurs, origines et statuts des élites sûdân et sqâliba," in *Couleur de l'esclavage sur les deux rives de la Méditerranée (Moyen Âge-XXᵉ siècle)*, eds. Roger Botte and Alessandro Stella (Paris, Karthala, 2012), 25–54. For the Mamluks, who ruled the Islamicate califates from 1150–1517 and earlier, see David Ayalon, *Le phénomène mamlouk dans l'Orient islamique* (Paris: Presses Universitaires de France, 1996), and David Ayalon, *Eunuchs, Caliphs and Sultans: A Study in Power Relationships* (Jerusalem: Magnes Press, 1999). For works before 2000, Sally McKee's article contains a handy bibliography. Claude Cahen and Jacques Heers covered the Mediterranean, and the earlier studies included Verlinden and Bloch. Claude Cahen, *Introduction à l'histoire de l'Orient musulman* (Paris: Adrien-Maisonneuve, 1961), Jacques Heers, *Esclaves et domestiques au Moyen Âge dans le monde méditerranéen* (Paris: Fayard, 1981). The general public introduction, Malek Chebel, *L'esclavage en terre d'Islam* (Paris: Fayard, 2007) is not well regarded. Sally McKee, "Inherited Status and Slavery in Late Medieval Italy and Venetian Crete," *Past and Present* 182 (2004): 31–53. These include: Charles Verlinden, "L'esclavage dans le centre et le nord de l'Italie continentale au bas Moyen Âge," *Bulletin de l'Institute historique Belge de Rome* 40 (1969): 93–156; Charles Verlinden, *L'esclavage dans l'Europe médiévale*, 2 vols. (Bruges: De Tempel, 1955; Ghent: Rijksuniversiteit, 1977); Charles Verlinden, "Le recrutement des esclaves à Venise aux 14ᵉ et 15ᵉ siècles," *Bulletin de l'Institut Historique Belge de Rome* 39 (1968): 83–202; Charles Verlinden, "L'origine de sclavus=esclave," *Bulletin Du Cange (Archivum latinitatis medii aevi)* 17 (1942): 97–128; Charles Verlinden, "La Crète, débouché et plaque tournante de la traite des esclaves au 14ᵉ et 15ᵉ siècles," *Studi in onore di Amintore Fanfani*, vol. 3 (Milan: Giuffrè, 1962), 591–609; Charles Verlinden, "Orthodoxie et esclavage au bas Moyen Age," in *Mélanges Eugène Tisserant* (Vatican City: Biblioteca apostolica vaticana, 1964), 5: 427–56; Charles Verlinden, "From the Mediterranean to the Atlantic: Aspects of an Economic Shift (12th–18th Century)," *The Journal of European Economic History* 1 (1972): 625–46; Charles Verlinden, "Encore sur les origines de Sclavus = esclave et à propos de la chronologie des débuts de la traite Italienne en mer Noire," *Cultus et cognitio: Studia z dziejów sredniowiecznej kultury* (Warsaw, Panstwowe Wydawnictwo Nauk, 1976): 599–609; Charles Verlinden, *Précédents médiévaux de la colonie en Amérique* (Mexico City: Instituto panamericano de geografia e historia, 1954); Charles Verlinden, "Le problème de la continuité en histoire coloniale: de la colonisation médiévale à la colonisation moderne," *Revista de Indias* 11 (1951): 219–36; Charles Verlinden, "Les origines coloniales de la civilisation atlantique: antécédents et types de structure," *Cahiers d'histoire mondiale* 1 (1953): 378–98; Benjamin Arbel, "Slave Trade and Slave Labor in Frankish Cyprus (1191–1571)," *Studies in Medieval and Renaissance*

that in reality, slavery continued, while narratives about it were culturally repressed and revised throughout the medieval period and later, especially during and after the Enlightenment. Slavery existed "all around the basin of the Mediterranean, in Latin Europe, in the Northernmost areas, in the Byzantine and Islamicate world, in Jewish, Christian, and Muslim communities," and historians and archaeologists record many deported and enslaved populations: "Slavs in transit towards the South, populations of Black Africa sold by slavers from Iberia, Christians in Islamicate lands, Muslims in Christian lands, [enslaved people] are everywhere, from the countryside to the city, as do-

---

History New Series 14 (1993); Michel Balard, "Giacomo Badoer et le commerce des esclaves," in *Milieux naturels, espaces sociaux. Etudes offertes à Robert Delort* (Paris: Publications de la Sorbonne, 1997), 555–64; Michel Balard, "Esclavage en Crimée et sources fiscales génoises au XVe siècle," *Byzantinische Forschungen* 22 (1996); 77–87; Laura Balletto, "Stranieri e forestieri a Genova: schiavi e manomessi (secolo XV)," in *Forestieri e stranieri nelle città basso-medievali (Atti di Seminario Internazionale di Studio, Bagno a Ripoli (Firenze), 4–8 June 1984)* (Florence: Libreria editrice Salimbeni, 1984), 263–83; Olivia Remie Constable, "Muslim Spain and Mediterranean Slavery: The Medieval Slave Trade as an Aspect of Muslim-Christian Relations," in *Christendom and Its Discontents: Exclusion, Persecution, and Rebellion, 1000–1500*, eds. Scott L. Waugh and Pieter D. Diehl (Cambridge: Cambridge University Press, 1996), 264–84; Domenico Gioffre, *Il mercato degli schiavi a Genova nel secolo XV* (Genoa: Fratelli Bozzi, 1971). Jacques Heers, *Les négriers en terre d'islam: la première traite des Noirs, VIIe–XVIe siècle* (Paris: Perrin, 2003); Jacques Heers, *Esclaves et domestiques au moyen âge dans le monde méditerranéen* (Paris: Fayard, 1981); Iris Origo, *Merchant of Prato: Francesco Di Marco Datini, 1335–1410* (New York: Alfred A. Knopf, 1957); Iris Origo, "The Domestic Enemy: The Eastern Slaves in Tuscany in the Fourteenth and Fifteenth Centuries," *Speculum* 30 (1995): 321–66; Jonathan Phillips, *The Second Crusade: Extending the Frontiers of Christendom* (New Haven: Yale University Press, 2007), 260; William D. Phillips, *Slavery in Medieval and Early Modern Iberia* (Philadelphia: University of Pennsylvania Press, 2014); William D. Phillips, *Slavery from Roman Times to Early Transatlantic Trade* (Manchester: Manchester University Press, 1985); Alfonso Franco Silva, "La esclavitud en la Peninsula Ibérica a fines des Medioevo: estado de la cuestión y orientaciones bibliográficas," *Medievalismo* 5 (1995): 201–10; Alberto Teneti, "Gli schiavi di Venezia alla fine de cinquecento," *Rivista storica italiana* 67 (1955): 52–69.

mestic workers, craftsmen, manufacturers, in various contexts and with various status, which has long prevented historians from considering them in the same category," as Sandrine Victor writes in her recent overview of medieval slavery destined for a general audience.[3]

Given these complexities, in order to examine the Latin word *sclavus* and similar words in French, Occitan, and Italian, it's useful to simultaneously keep in mind several aspects that shape and organize that archive. Firstly, the Latin record is largely archival, including mostly documents that enable people and institutions to retain or transfer legal rights to possess enslaved people, as well as the laws regulating their possession, their families, their descendants, and hagiographical and literary texts (which I have not examined) that relate to the enslaved people. By contrast, the archive for French and other languages used in this essay is largely literary. Therefore, the words that sound like the word *slave* in Latin vs. French, Occitan, and Italian are less a family of words than a similar word in dramatically different contexts. Secondly, this essay summarizes the history of related practices, commercial networks, and legal and other institutions over vast territories and time periods. There is no underlying continuity to the phenomenon of slavery in that context, other than the words used to describe it, and this chapter concentrates on only one of these words. Thus, no overview can emerge, although some generalizations will be suggested.

It is necessary to start with a specific geography and time, a "pointillist approach," as Victor suggests.[4] As she notes, the fact that it is impossible to summarize the issue of medieval slavery has as its corollary the fact that entries on slavery, other than the notion of the decline of slavery and rise of serfdom, are often absent from histories and dictionaries of the Middle Ages and

---

3   Sandrine Victor, *Les fils de Canaan: L'esclavage au Moyen Age* (Paris: Vendémiaire, 2019), 12 and cover text.
4   Ibid. Victor's book, very well written and up to date, contains errors natural in that type of publication; it can serve as an excellent introduction at any level, or a starting point for in-depth research.

similar synthetic works. A further corollary is that in general works on slavery the overviews of its history either skip the medieval period or begin much later.[5] This essay reviews the most recent work on slavery in a similar manner to Victor, however, I double-check her original sources and compare information across in-depth studies by historians of specific locations and periods.

The importance of medieval slavery is undeniable, and it emphatically does not end in 1100. In the 1990s, Michel Balard estimated that enslaved people constituted up to four to six percent of the urban population of the slaver ports of Venice, Genoa, Marseilles, Barcelona, and Valencia; current, lower estimates by Barker (2019) are discussed below.[6] As Ivan Armenteros Martínez and Mohamed Ouerfelli summarize it, slavery was an important axis of Mediterranean and Northern European commerce, as well as Islamicate-Latin diplomacy. It forced the migration of large groups of people of both genders, and served as a model of assimilation of foreigners, transmitted ideas, arts, and technologies.[7] To Armenteros Martínez's and Ouerfelli's picture, the historians of the locations from where the enslaved people were deported add that slave raids left unimaginable suffering, famine and orphans in their wake.

Estimates that put the numbers of enslaved people at about 10% of the population of France until the tenth century, and of England until the eleventh are similar to the estimates for the Roman Empire at large in the first five centuries CE, though not in Italy, where the estimates are at 30–40%, with the top 1–1.5% of the wealthiest population responsible for the ownership of almost half of the enslaved people.[8] In late antiquity and later, on the Southern coast of the Mediterranean, a region that Medieval

---

5   Ibid., 11–12.
6   Michael Balard, "Slavery in the Latin Mediterranean (Thirteenth to Fifteenth Centuries): The Case of Genoa," in *Slavery and the Slave Trade*, eds. Amitai and Cluse, 235–54, at 235.
7   Martínez and Ouerfelli, "Réévaluer l'économie."
8   Victor, *Les fils de Canaan*.

Arabic and subsequently Latin and other languages designate as Ifrīqia, the origins of the enslaved people can be traced to African (in our sense, i.e., the entire continent, not the Ifrīqia, i.e., the coast alone) kingdoms near Lake Tchad, Sudan, and Southern Nile. Concerning the origins of enslaved people, André Maricq notes that in Rome captives were either brought in via commercial networks or enslaved in military campaigns. Depending on the period, they would be of Middle Eastern or, under Caesar, of North- and West-European origin. Scholars assume that in ancient Greece and Rome, most enslaved people were European, North African, and Middle Eastern, although there were also enslaved Africans, for example in Crete, and memorably Homer describes Ulysses' squire and most trusted companion, the herald of the Greeks, Eurybates, as dark-skinned and curly-haired. Nearly half of the Visigothic laws and some 13% of the Salic laws concern slavery, and there are also biblical passages.[9] Since the seventh century, Western synods explicitly prohibit the sale of coreligionaries, which means that Western Christian commercial networks of slave trade reached into pagan and Islamicate territory, enslaving "Muslims, Slavs, Bulgars, and sometimes orthodox Greeks."[10] South and Eastern Europeans and Tatars were sold in Verdun (its location is not established; Meuse, but more likely Burgundy, at the crossroads of several trade routes near Châlon-sur-Sâone) from the eighth to the eleventh centuries. Slavers used their cities' trade networks, for example, Genoans, Pisans, and Venitians, who occupied trading posts on the Black Sea, enslaved and sold Slavs, Finns and Karelians, Cossaks, Tatars, and Black Sea coastal women.[11] Throughout the medieval period, slave trade is present in Constantinople, Venice, Genoa, Marseille, Barcelona, Sevilla, Ceuta, Lisbon, Tunis, Tripoli, Al-

---

9 Juliette Sibon, "Sandrine Victor, Les Fils de Canaan. L'esclavage au Moyen Âge," *Cahiers de recherches médiévales et humanistes*, 2019, http://journals.openedition.org/crm/15603, 2019.

10 Rio, *Slavery after Rome*, 1.

11 Jukka Korpela, *Slaves from the North: Finns and Karelians in the East European Slave Trade, 900–1600* (Leiden: Brill, 2019).

exandria, and Malta where the slave market is active until the mid-eighteenth century.

Terminology Used in this Essay

In this essay I use Islamicate as a designation that does not depend on language and religion, and Latin as a parallel designation of peoples whose literate elites communicated in Latin. Most late antique sources do not know that Africa extends far south of the Equator and the Tropic of Capricorn. Until the late 1400s, Islamicate and Latin sources are chiefly engaged in trade and diplomacy in North Africa or Ifrīqia, a term that designates the area around Carthage, Tunisia, and is later extended to the entire coast, while the lands to the South of the Sahara and the kingdoms around the great lakes are designated as *sûdân,* a distinction also reflected in Pliny the Elder (23–79) who says the river Niger forms the division between Africa and Ethiopia. I use Ifrīqia for the North African coast of the Mediterranean and I reserve Africa for the whole continent. Since my specialty is France, I weakly distinguish different languages and political groups on the territory of Iberia or Africa, but I try to distinguish Al-Andalus from other political entities in the Iberian Peninsula. Unfree people were numerous in Christian, Jewish, and Islamicate households and political entities of the Iberian Peninsula, as elsewhere in Europe, although the reported numbers in Al-Andalus, tens of thousands of *sqâliba* (the word is synonymous with enslaved person, a Slav, and a eunuch, and may have signified any one or any combination of them), are not recorded or mentioned other than in slaving markets of Northern Europe and Scandinavia, in the Mediterranean under Roman, Byzantine, and Islamicate rule, and centuries later, in the Mediterranean isalnds Majorca and Minorca (on the Baleares, see below, David Abulafia and Henri Bresc). They indicate an economy on a different scale and of a different type from the transfer of dominion from a landowner to a convent of two men and their families and descendants skilled in beekeeping and wax production in Upper Austria ca. 768, cited below.

I use the modern terms France and metropolitan, i.e., on the territory of France from the Channel to the Mediterranean. They are handy though problematic, because they use a modern geopolitical situation that imports an already instilled hierarchy and generates imprecisions, that are often the opposite of medieval realities. In the mid- to late Middle Ages, the Southern city of Montpellier is the second most populous city after Paris, while Paris (estimated at 200–270,000 inhabitants in 1328–48, before the plague reduced the numbers, only returning to 250,000 in the early 1500s) possesses only a fraction of the population of Cordoba (200,000 by 800, 400,000 ca. 1000). Cairo (Fatimid capital since 1168), by 1340 was one of the largest cities west of China with 250,000 inhabitants, and Baghdad (from 775–1258 and the destruction by Mongols) had more than a million inhabitants. In the medieval period, France is part of a network reaching into the Mediterranean, with one of its main centers in Northern France. French is only one of the many cultural traditions, languages and dialects spoken in France. Other medieval languages and literatures on the territory of modern France are known from later French, Occitan, and Italian manuscripts.

After 1100, the conglomerate of political entities that today belong to France can be described as part of a cultural and political network including Paris, Montpellier, Acre (the port city of the Latin kingdom of Jerusalem), Cyprus, and Sicily. Last but not least, while the first literary monuments of the French language date to the 800s, the first sizeable corpus of medieval French literature dates to the 1100s. After 1100, the number of manuscripts in French and Occitan allows us to better analyze the written contexts of most words. The rise of serfdom and the proliferation of French literary manuscript witnesses are not directly related, but there are consequences to that parallel. Many French and Occitan texts use the semantic field of *esclave* metaphorically, divorced from the reality of enslavement. And yet, some unexpected cases such as the *esclavine,* the mantle associated with slaves or Slavs, may be vestiges of the reality of medieval slavery.

Slave: Historical Reality, Word Meanings, Terminologies, and Indistinctions

This section focuses on various words used to describe enslaved people, presents some summary facts on slavery, discussed in detail in a later section concerning who was enslaved where and in what proportion to the general population, and comments on the indistinctions between the medieval words slave and serf, and slave and Slav. Indeed, one of the challenges of the topic is that in Latin *servus* means a free person, an unfree person, or both. Similarly, Latin *sclavus* and related words in other languages (French, Italian, Greek, Arabic, etc.) means an enslaved person, a person of Slavic origin, or both. And, *servus* often designates an enslaved person of Slavic origin as well.

Who are the enslaved people in medieval Europe and the Mediterranean, and where do they come from? Since late antiquity, the origins of the enslaved people are often in Eastern Europe, and that is true all through the Middle Ages. Sally McKee provides numbers for every major Italian and Mediterranean city with breakdowns by origin and ethnicity, for example, of the 921 enslaved people sold in Genoa between the 1390s and 1490s, 215 were Russian, 179 Circassian, 138 Tartar, and 118 Moro; while in Venice (1350–1460), out of 948, 206 are Russian, 137 Circassian, and 547 Tartar; Black Africans appear as enslaved people in Italy in the mid-fourteenth century.[12] It is between the eleventh and the thirteenth centuries, that is, during the period that follows 1100 and the transition from slavery to servitude described by Bloch and others, that Latinists indicate a linguistic transition: the term *sclavus* displaced the previous Latin terminology for enslaved people such as *ancilla, serva/servus,* and *familius*. It is important to note that *sclavus* is not the only medieval Latin

---

12 McKee, "Domestic Slavery in Renaissance Italy," 310–11; for a quick overview see Maxime Fulkonis and Catherine Kikuchi, "Vendre des hommes," *Actuel Moyen Âge,* November 23, 2017, https://actuelmoyenage.wordpress.com/2017/11/23/vendre-des-hommes/.

word describing an unfree person, or the most frequently used: *servus* and *ancilla* are frequent. Likewise, medieval French and Occitan *esclave* is not very common in the literal sense of an unfree person. Other descriptors, *villain, meschine, serf, serva* seem more common, a topic I do not explore here.

As Victor notes, diverse terms for *slave* coexist in Ancient Greek: *doulos,* whose derivates, Mycenean Greek, Cannanite, late Babylonian *daggalu,* and Jewish Aramaic *dayyala* designate servants or bondsmen; *andrapodon* (which is supposed to mean a human walking on all fours, indicating the bestial nature and the below-human legal status of the enslaved person); *oeikus* in Crete, related to the household; various categories of debtors and freed men, as opposed to free men (*eleutheros*). In Latin, *servus* is most common, probably originating in Etruscan, followed by *mancipium,* still used in the seventh and eighth century, *famulus, ancilla, verna,* and increasingly *servus* and *sclavus* around 1100. Susan Mosher Stuard emphasizes that the change of meaning in the word *servus* from "chattel slave" to "serf" in the later periods is not reflected in *ancilla,* which continued to describe the enslaved status throughout the medieval period. Except for *ancilla,* the terminology is fluid: *serva* and its synonyms, such as *famula,* may either be used interchangeably with *ancilla* or indicate partly free status, as shown in the designation of a woman as *serva et libera,* "serf and free."[13] According to some explanations, because of the prohibition of enslaving coreligionaries, *sclavus* marked religious others, for instance, Greek orthodox, pagan, or Muslim.[14]

In Arabic as well as other languages, the name of the enslaved man is not followed by that of his son or father, i.e., *abu…*, father of…; *ibn…*, son of… However, an enslaved woman who became *umm walad,* mother of a child, could not be sold or giv-

---

13 Susan Mosher Stuard, "Ancilliary Evidence for the Disappearance of Medieval Slavery," *Past and Present* 149 (1995): 3–28, at 8 and n. 20; Susan Mosher Stuard, "Urban Domestic Slavery in Medieval Ragusa," *Journal of Medieval History* 9 (1983): 155–71.

14 Victor, *Les fils de Canaan*, 22–31.

en away until the death of the man who owned her, and would be freed on his death, although she could be married off and her legitimized child could be raised by the man's family far away; if not legitimized by the father, their child could be enslaved, but could not be sold away until seven or eight years of age.[15] Often, the name of the enslaved person is a designation of that person's collective origin, erasing their individuality, as well as erasing the expression of their belonging to a family.[16] In medieval Latin vocabulary, various words now translated as *slave,* including *sclavus, sarracenus, maurus,* denote the origin or appearance of the enslaved person. Mohamed Meouak shows that words designating unfree persons in a wide variety of texts may refer to their origin or appearance: *zawila* (Libya), *sûdân* (Africa), *sqlâbi/sqâliba* (singular/plural, Slav), *'abd/'abid* (Black), *milk/mamluk* (property). Enslaved people could be described as yellow, *asfar,* a color that designated Byzantines, or red, *ahmar* or *humran* (a color contrasted with black *sûdân*), or combine red hair with blue eyes, *wusafâ/wasîf,* a word that also designated free royal servants in medieval Egypt, as well as specifically designating Black enslaved people based on their appearance.[17]

At the same time, Meouak notes that most Arabic sources — geographies, chronicles, legal, notarial, and literary texts — do not mention "origins or identity" of the enslaved person, making it imperative to always locate the context, and he concludes the designations were often metaphors or should be interpreted in complex geographic and specific ways. Nonetheless, he also lists over 100 names of distinguished individuals

---

15 Hannah Barker, *Egyptian and Italian Merchants in the Black Sea Slave Trade, 1260–1500*. PhD Thesis, Columbia University, 2014, 107–9, https://academiccommons.colombia.edu/doi/10.7916/D8610XH4.

16 Victor, *Les fils de Canaan,* 25.

17 Armenteros Martínez and Ouerfelli, "Réévaluer l'économie." Mohamed Meouak, "Esclaves noirs et esclaves blancs en al-Andalus umayyade et en Ifriqiya fatimide: couleurs, origines, et statuts des élites sudan et saqaliba," in *Couleur de l'esclavage sur les deux rives de la Méditerranée,* eds. Botte and Stella, 25–54, at 26 and 36–40, and Barker, *Egyptian and Italian Merchants in the Black Sea Slave Trade,* 76.

that contain the adjective *al-Saqlabî* (Slav) or *al-aswad* (Black). He also adds that while these and similar designations may have originated in different appearance, they are sometimes used hierarchically, for instance, "red" was preferred both to "Black" and "yellow".[18] Meouak notes the discussion of the binary designations "white" (*al-Bîdân, abyad*) and "Black" (*al-Sûdân, aswad*) already at the origin of Arabic literary and scientific tradition, in the earliest eighth-century Arabic texts authored by the *savant* al Jâhiz (776–868), whose grandfather, incidentally, was a Black cameleer. Al-Jâhiz reflects at length on the origins of skin color and appearance of different peoples. His list of al-Bîdân (white) people includes inhabitants of Fâris (Farsi), Jîbal (mountains, or *jebel*, in western Iran), Khûrasan, Rûm (Byzantium or Christians), Saqâliba, Firania (Francs), and Abar (Avars).[19]

As Barker notes, in Italy a single notary, Bartholomeus Gattus, is responsible for 63% of descriptions of skin color in the slavery archive, and describing a person's color is a practice that drops from 45% (1201–1300) to 3% (1301–1500) of descriptions in Italian notarial documents, perhaps because after 1301 the majority of enslaved people in Italy were Slav and/or Tartar, what Petrarch calls "Scythian" in a passage cited below.[20] Medieval Greek uses *sklavos* and *slavikos*. Old English terms include *theow* (slave) and *thrael*. Along the same lines as *sclavus*, OE *wealh* can mean foreigner, Welsh/Celt, or an enslaved person.

There is an interesting correlation between the three terms, *'abd, mamluk,* and *sqâliba*. As Meouak and Barker note, *'abd*, Black, in most examples, especially earlier ones, denotes "an unfree person" and only later designates high melanin. *Mamluk*, the person who is a property, unfree, underwent the opposite evolution, resulting in the same indistinction as *'abd*: at first denoting an enslaved person with low melanin, but later an enslaved person of any appearance. *Sqâliba*, Slav/slave may

---

18 Meouak, "Esclaves noirs et exclaves blancs," 34.
19 Ibid., 33.
20 Barker, *Egyptian and Italian Merchants in the Black Sea Slave Trade*, 73.

have started as an ethnic origin (a Slav) or an enslaved person of that origin or appearance, and later designates any unfree person with no indication of origin. *Sqâliba* is also a synonym for eunuch.[21]

Wallace and Barker cite the frequently evoked passage from Petrarch's last self-curated collection of letters, *Seniles*, in a letter written from Venice in 1367 to Guido Sette, a childhood friend, then bishop of Genoa, where the poet describes enslaved people that have Slavic or Tartar faces, *scithicis vultibus*. In a passage where foreigners are jostled, narrow passages are plugged up, and filth spills into pure waters, Petrarch combines every stereotypical commonplace of racism and the slave trade. His insistence on the purchaser's eye and delight, his own feelings of repulsion, the language of purity and contamination, and the oppositions he conjures between shapely/unshapely, clean/dirty echo other racist invectives against foreigners. Venice is degraded by slavery, or more precisely by its corollary, the presence of foreigners with their "Scythian faces" and filthy, alluring bodies, but slavery elevates the enslaved people — sold by their parents — who are no longer hungry, bestially rooting in stony, bleached, arid ground with their teeth and claws, as one does in Scythia:

> Nam Grecie calamitas vetus est, sed Scithiarum recens. Ut, unde nuper ingens annua vis frumenti navibus in hanc urbem invehi solebat, inde nunc servis honuste naves veniant, quos urgente fame miseri venditant parentes. Iamque insolita et enextimabilis turba servorum utriusque sexus hanc pulcerrimam urbem scithicis vultibus et informi colluvie, velut amnem nitidissimum torrens turbidus inficit; que, si suis emptoribus non esset acceptior quam michi et non amplius eorum oculos delectaret quam delectat meos, neque

---

21 Meouak, "Esclaves noirs et esclave blancs," 25–54; Meouak, *Sqâliba: eunuques et esclaves*, 73; Barker, *Egyptian and Italian Merchants in the Black Sea Slave Trade*, 71–98.

feda hec pubes hos angustos coartaret vicos, necque melioribus assuetos formis ininameno advenas contristaret occursu; sed intra suam Scithiam cum fame arida ac pallenti lapidoso in agro, ubi Naso illam statuit, raras herbas dentibus velleret atque unguibus.

The fall of Greece is ancient, that of the Scythians recent. While until recently huge quantities of grain were brought each year into the city by ship, today ships arrive laden with slaves [*servis*], sold by their parents pressed by hunger. Already, a strange, enormous crowd of slaves [*servorum*] of both sexes infects this most beautiful city with Scythian faces and misshapen dirt, like a muddy spill that taints a limpid stream. If these repulsive youths were not more acceptable to their buyers than to me, and if they did not delight their [buyers'] eye more than they delight mine, they would not clog our narrow passages; nor would they clumsily jostle and annoy the foreigners used to shapelier beauties. Instead they would be still in their Scythia, hungrily tearing at rare plants with their teeth and nails, as Ovid describes, among stone-strewn fields, arid and yellowed.[22]

Wallace remarks on humanist erudition at work in this passage. Scythians and their wild steppes are the epitome of Barbarians for the Greeks, with whom the image opens.[23] Further, the presence of the repulsive enslaved people elevates Petrarch to the position of power, and they are necessary as the formative elements of prestige. Wallace and Barker add that Genoese notaries owned enslaved people at higher rates than other professions.

I take "the Scythians" to mean people of any origin, Slav, Cossak, Tatar, Finn, Karelian, and others from the Ural to Byzan-

---

22 Petrarch, *Seniles* 10.2, 1116–18; cited by David Wallace, *Premodern Places: Calais to Surinam, Chaucer to Aphra Behn* (Malden: Blackwell, 2004), 191; Barker, *Egyptian and Italian Merchants in the Black Sea Slave Trade*, 79. My translation is adapted from Wallace.

23 Wallace, *Premodern Places*, 191.

tium, who fell into Italian hands in Crimea and were transported to Genoa, and "the fall of Scythians" to mean not only major political upheavals, but also the seasonal, large winter slave raids that characterized the region, and the constant small raids.[24] Slave trade that since the early Middle Ages fed into the vast Islamicate demand for enslaved people, and the much smaller Italian one, seems to have depended on a balance of tribute, pillage, and slave raids that characterized the region, whether in periods of relative political stability under the Crimean Khanate (1441–1783), whose main economic engine was slave trade, or during political changes and upheavals. In the later medieval period, Slave raiders were mostly Tatar, and slave merchants included Italians. At times, that continuous trade had unimaginable consequences. For example, the fall of the Kipçaks to the Mongols resulted in the enslaving of a Kipçak youth named Baybars, or Leopard Bey (1223–1277). He was resold in Aleppo in 1247. Three years later, in 1250, he defeated Louis IX of France in Egypt. In 1260 he repelled the Mongols who sacked Baghdad in 1258 at Ain Jalut. The same year he was crowned sultan at Salihiyah madrasa in Cairo. He eventually reconquered greater Syria from the crusaders.[25] Such dramatic historical consequences aside, slave raids and slave trade seem to be a continuous characteristic of the region and, especially in the early modern period, were on a larger scale. During the Crimean Khanate (1441–1783), beginning with the first documented slave raid of 1468, slave markets at the ports in Cembalo, Soldaia,

---

24 Michael Kizilov, "The Black Sea and the Slave Trade: The Role of Crimean Maritime Towns in the Trade in Slaves and Captives in the Fifteenth to Eighteenth Centuries," *International Journal of Maritime History* 17, no. 1 (2005): 211–35, at 222.

25 See Florin Curta, ed., *East Central and Eastern Europe in the Middle Ages*, 2 vols. (Leiden: Brill, 2008), vol. 2; Florin Curta and Roman Kovalev, eds., *The Other Europe in the Middle Ages: Avars, Bulghars, Khazars and Cumans* (Leiden: Brill, 2008), esp. Dmitri Korobeinikov, "A Broken Mirror: The Kipçak World in the Thirteenth Century," in *The Other Europe in the Middle Ages: Avars, Bulghars, Khazars and Cumans*, eds. Florin Curta and Roman Kovalev (Leiden: Brill, 2008), 379–412.

and the largest, Caffa are estimated to have sold ten thousand people annually, reaching two million from 1500–1700. According to Mikhail Kizilov and Daniel Kolodziejczyk, the Black Sea slave trade at that time (1450–1600) was equivalent in volume to the Atlantic slave trade: two million enslaved people being the estimate for both.[26] The Black Sea slave trade declined in the eighteenth century, unlike the Atlantic and Indian Ocean slave trade, which grew exponentially throughout the eighteenth century, reaching unimaginable levels. Cembalo, Soldaia, and Caffa included Genoese colonies and were inhabited by diverse populations. As Kizilov describes, Caffa, with its satellite ports, founded in the 1260s, was inhabited by a mosaic of populations including the "Genoese, Tatars, Armenians, Greeks, Slavs (Russians and Bulgarians), Syrians, Goths, Alans, Cumans, Caucasians (Georgians, Mingrelians, Circassians, Abkhazians and Lezghins), Hungarians, Persians, Jews."[27] During the 1348 Tatar siege, a plague devastated the city, the beginning of the epidemic that swept the Mediterranean and Africa. In the aftermath of the global epidemic, the prices of enslaved Black Sea people rose. "In 1385–1386, about 530 slaves lived in Caffa," all with Tatar and Circassian names, and 1500 people were sold annually, mostly Abkhaz, Tatar, Circassian, and Mingrelian men sold to Genoa, Cairo, Alexandria and the East, as Kizilov notes.[28] Caffa grew to some hundred thousand people in the early 1400s, but shrunk to one tenth by 1475, the date of the Ottoman takeover of the

---

26 Mikhail Kizilov, "Slaves, Money Lenders, and Prisoner Guards: The Jews and the Trade in Slaves and Captives in the Crimeal Khanate," *Journal of Jewish Studies* 58, no. 2 (2007): 189–207, at 190; Dariusz Kołodziejczyk, "Slave Hunting and Slave Redemption as a Business Enterprise: the Northern Black Sea Region in the Sixteenth to Seventeenth Centuries," *Oriente Moderno* 25, no. 1 (2006): 149–59.

27 Kizilov, "The Black Sea and the Slave Trade," 214–15.

28 Ibid. See also Michel Balard, *La Romanie génoise, 12ᵉ–début du 15ᵉ siècle* (Rome: Ecole française de Rome, 1978), and Charles Verlinden, "L'esclavage et ethnographie sur les bords de la mer Noire," in *Miscellanea Historica in Honorem Leonis van der Essen*, 2 vols., ed. Léon Ernest Halkin (Brussels: Editions Universitaires, 1947), 1:287–98.

Crimean ports. The Ottomans left the rest of the Crimea to the Crimean Khanate.

Barker analyzes at length the relationships between origin, appearance, and terminology used to describe and categorize enslaved people. She notes that Arabic medical texts on inspection of enslaved people show little preoccupation with melanin but are focused on detecting or disguising signs of leprosy, the discolored spots covered by makeup, paint, or tattoos. Barker also cites texts that give examples of enslaved people designated as *mamluk* (in the sense of low melanin), *'abd* (Black), *asmar* (brown), or *raqiq* (an unfree person of any appearance), and she cites, as well, examples where *'abd* designates an enslaved person without indicating appearance. She cites references to *rumi* (Greek), *sindi* (Indian), *nubi* (Nubian), *takruri* (West Africans), and *habashi* (Ethiopian, i.e., Abyssinian) enslaved people, and she especially emphasizes that in both Latin and Arabic sources, the *jins* (origin) of the enslaved people did not always correlate with individual appearance.[29] Rather, origin and appearance "were two distinct elements of a full description [that] were not interchangeable": a *mamluk* (Slav Turkman, Tartar, Circassian, Cuman, Kipchak, Kitai/Chinese, etc.) could be *sawad* (black), *asmar* (dark/brown), *sufrah* (leather), or olive as well as *ashkar* (pale, blond), and conversely a low melanin enslaved person could be a Circassian, a Greek, or a Turk, although a *sudan* would be Black in Arabic sources, while in Latin, *saracenus* could be any complexion from white to indigo. Conversely, a low melanin person could be of "Abkhaz, Bulgar, Circassian, Russian, Saracen, Slavic, Tatar or Turkish" origin.[30] The Latin term *puer* denotes "junior and relatively powerless" status in the household.[31] Other terms denote the location and type of work: *rustici, villani, agricultores*.[32] Terms such as *massarii, manentes,*

---

29 Barker, *Egyptian and Italian Merchants in the Black Sea Slave Trade*, 88–98.
30 Ibid., 71–76; 98.
31 Rio, *Slavery after Rome*, 159–60.
32 Victor, *Les fils de Canaan*, 26.

coloni denote renters without specifying free or unfree status.[33] All these examples come from contexts that are not necessarily comparable. As Rio notes: "Early medieval people took a very creative, pragmatic approach to unfree status, and many of their experiments had very little to do with either the Roman era" and its definitions and contexts of unfreedom, or post-1100 rise of serfdom.[34]

In addition to these complexities and evolutions, just as the word *sclavus* means Slav/slave, the word *servus* that Petrarch uses in the passage cited above meant either a free serf, or an unfree (enslaved) person. Just as in Latin, *servus* is used in the sense of "yours sincerely" in Polish, orally as well as in writing. This and similar issues complicate the attempt to define the terminology of medieval slavery and serfdom.

A good example of the complexity of the issue is the Latin text of a donation to the Benedictine monastery of Saint Michael in Mondsee (Lunaelacensis monastery) in Upper Austria, cited by Victor, dated to "the twenty-first year of the rule of our duke Tassillo," i.e., 768. Since the monastery was founded in 748 by Odilo/Oatilo/Uatilo of Bavaria, the Tassilo mentioned in the document is Tassilo III, who ruled from 748 to 788. The donation is preserved in a twelfth- to thirteenth-century codex that includes a list of early donations. As Victor explains, dependency and enslavement are described in the same language. But, as a closer reading reveals, the document presents complex issues. This case emphasizes that no translation can be attempted without a precise context, including time and geography.[35] Below is the Latin text:

---

33 Rio, *Slavery after Rome*, 201.
34 Ibid., 246.
35 Victor, *Les fils de Canaan*, 35, citing *Urkunden-buch des Landes ob der Enns. Herausgegeben von Verwaltungs-Ausschuss des Museum Francisco-Carolinum zu Linz*, vol. 1 (Vienna: K.K. Hof- und Staatsdruckerei, 1852): 23–24. The text is in *Codex Traditionum Monasterii Lunaelacensis* [Mondsee Abbey in Upper Austria founded in 748], *Ordinis S. Benedicti* manuscript that lists donations to the monastery.

> In nomine domini nostri […] ego hildiroch […] dono de iure mea in potestate et dominacione sancti micahelis monasterii […] cidlarios meos II. Servos, unus est liber et alter est servus, uxores verus eius ambo ancillias et omnes, qui ex ea nati vel procreati fuerint in servicio sancti michaelis persistant cum ipsa marca, qui ad ipsum locum pertinet, hoc est de gaginpah usque in chastorapah ea tamen racione. […] Et ego in dei nomine hrodsuind coniunx hiltirohi cum consensu eius vel filiis meis dedi et ipsi dederunt mihi I. servum itt. Nomine cum uxore sua, filiis et filiabus et cum hopa sua vel omni substancia sua simili modo post excessum meum, quod superius scriptum est de viro meo hiltirochi […] regnante domino nostro tassilone duce anno 21.

> In the name of our Lord […] I Hildiroch […] give from my law into the power and dominion of the monastery of Saint Michael […] my two wax makers, servos (servants/enslaved people/serfs), one is free and the other is servus (servant/enslaved person/serf), verily both their wives, ancilias (enslaved women/servants), all who will be born or procreated from them, will remain in service to the monastery of Saint Michael […][36]

As Victor notes, obviously the word *servus* means both free and unfree in the same sentence. As we see, the rights over both men — the free one and the unfree one, if we are reading correctly — their wives, future sons and daughters, and their possessions, were transferred to the monastery. The consent of the former owner, Hildiroch, and Hildiroch's wife and children was noted, no doubt, in order to prevent the wife and children of Hildiroch or someone else from reclaiming the wax makers. The consent of the wax makers and their wives and children did not pose a threat to the monastery's ownership claim, and it is not recorded. Beekeepers are a special case, since hives and their

---

36 Ibid.

products belonged to the aristocratic landowner, and severe penalties were exacted on poachers, that is those who would divert one part of a splitting hive to create a secret hive and sell its products. Playing loud music was recommended to keep a hive from splitting.[37]

Servus can and does mean simultaneously unfree, enslaved, free, and serf. Interpreting what *sclavus* means, that is determining whether the term was used as a designation of the unfree status, origins, or both, presents a similar danger of circular logic. Victor provides a good example. In an article on the origins of sclavus, Charles Verlinden mentions an 1127 court case, where a person is designated as not enslaved, because only a child of a *sclavus* can be enslaved — unless they are enslaved for a legitimate reason, *legitima culpa,* as in the cases studied by Rio: "ut nullus nullaque qui queve ex christiana religione sunt pro servo et ancilla detineatur, sine legitima culpa, exceptis his qui ex Sclavorum gente geniti sunt" ("for no man or woman of Christian religion can be detained as an unfree man and woman, without a legal reason, except those born of enslaved people/Slavic people").[38] Unless *gente* always means a people in the ethnic sense, and not people who are unfree, we can translate *Sclavorum* as enslaved people/Slavs/enslaved people of Slav origins. Note that in modern French, the noun *gent* means a kind or a group of people without reference to an ethnic commonality, as in the expression *gent feminine* where *gent* is used to elevate "women," to mark the speaker's deference to their special collective with a quaintly archaic word that connotes gentility. Victor uses the citation to demonstrate that only Slavs can be unfree. That is clearly an error. In reality, the question of translating that passage is more complex.[39] And, having one free parent could

---

37 See Emily O'Brock's work on bees, "The Political Animal: The Symbolic Ecology of the Bee in Medieval France," PhD Thesis, NYU, in progress.
38 Charles Verlinden, "L'origine de *sclavus*=esclave," *Bulletin Du Cange. Archivium latinitatis medii aevi* 17 (1943): 97–128.
39 Victor, *Les fils de Canaan,* 28–29. Victor translates *legitima culpa* as "for their sins" and suggests it modifies Slavs. That is clearly an error, corrected

mean a person was born free in some places at some periods. Many documents on unfree people concern people in the possession of the Church. That is partly an accident of preservation: one of the reasons for the staggering wealth of the Church was its well-kept records and if need arose, *post facto* production of forged titles of property. Donations to and purchases by the Church from secular slavers mean that the Church records also shed light on the situation outside of the Church.

Different and not necessarily connected or synchronic aspects of the parallel but unconnected transition from slavery to servitude ca. 1100, and from *servus* to *sclavus* as a frequent designator of an enslaved person in the 1000s–1200s, include textual traditions, geographic and ethnic origins of the enslaved people, and commercial networks. Because the appearance and trajectory of medieval words related to *sclavus* and of the vocabulary of slavery are a complex palimpsest composed of disparate cultural and historical strata, rather than the fruit of an evolution, as with the question of slavery itself, the question of terminology benefits from a "pointillist approach."[40] One important piece of the puzzle is that serfdom often concerns men in agricultural contexts. At the same time women continue to work as domestic and artisanal/industrial enslaved labor, for example in slaver coastal cities of Italy, or in textile production, as in Chrétien de Troyes's (1135–1190) well-known lines of *Yvain ou le chevalier au lion* (ca. 1180): *toz jors le drap de soie tisserons / jamais n'en serons mieux vestues. / toz jors serons povres et nues / tos jors la faim et la soif soffrirons* (*Yvain*, 5298–5324: "we will always weave silk cloth, we will never be dressed better by it, we will always be poor and naked, we will always suffer hunger and thirst"). There, 100 emaciated and unhappy women (*maigres, pales et dolantes,* "skinny pale and suffering," *Yvain*, 5235) are

---

in the translation above. Victor's book's usefulness as an undergraduate level introduction to the topic is not diminished by what I consider the expected errors, since her notes and bibliography allow readers to research and correct them.

40 Ibid., 12.

enslaved as a tribute of thirty maidens annually from the Island of Maidens to the Castle of the Worst Adventure, and they are paid *que quatre deniers de la livre* (*Yvain,* 5310: "only four deniers on each livre"), which does not allow them to eat to satiety or clothe themselves, since even twenty sols a week is insufficient, and none of them earns that much (*Yvain,* 5308–5318). Some unfree people are allowed to retain a part of their earnings, and own possessions whose ownership can be transferred to another owner of enslaved or free people, along with the transfer of the rights over their persons, their wives, and their children, as in the case of the two Austrian wax makers and their families, cited above.

An important aspect that helps distinguish between geographical contexts and legal frameworks of unfreedom is whether, once a person is enslaved, the status of being enslaved is inherited by subsequent generations. The status of the children of an enslaved person could be altered if that person was married to someone of a free or half-free status: "in ninth-century villages on the estates of Saint-Germain-des-Prés a male slave's marriage to a *lida* or *colona* gave his offspring half-free or *colonus* status," however, the same did not apply to the enslaved women: *ancillae* were not sought after in marriage, says Stuard.[41] In medieval French, *villain* designates location, occupation, moral character, or manners and class: an inhabitant of a non-urban locality, a villager, a peasant, a rustic, a serf, a poor person, a vile person, or a lower status person. The permanent trans-generational enslaved status of ancillae was entrenched by the twelfth century canon law that referred to them as res ecclesiae (church property/things). They "continued to live generation after generation [as] chattel slaves," the lowest status persons.[42] When a cleric fathered children with an *ancilla,* the

---

41 Stuard, "Ancilliary Evidence for the Disappearence of Medieval Slavery," 5; Auguste Longnon, ed., *Polyptique de l'Abbaye de Saint-Germain-des-Prés* (Paris: Champion, 1886), 58–61.

42 Ibid., 5, 10.

children were treated as *res ecclesiae*. That was different from secular men who may infrequently free or leave bequests to their children fathered with *ancillae*.[43] In the twelfth century, the Church's unsuccessful policies to suppress clerical marriages multiply, always with the intent of accumulating and preserving ecclesiastical property for the institution, and the law concerning clerical offspring seems a part of that policy. Perhaps the permanent trans-generational enslaved status of *ancillae* in that particular document was less connected to the rise of serfdom and consequent greater distinctions between enslaved and other unfree status, than to the Church's attempts at eradicating clerical marriage.

Esclave, Esclavine in French, Occitan, and Italian, 1100–1500

Attested in manuscripts after 1100, that is, after servitude became the new legal dimension of unfree male labor according to Bloch, the semantic family of *esclave* in Old French and Occitan, from the twelfth century onwards, refers among other things to the form of labor: the meaning "enslaved person" as well as "pirate" is attested. In late medieval Italian, from the late 1200s to the 1500s, the word *schiava* is used in reference to enslaved women, young and old, possibly from Southern Slavic regions of the Adriatic. Sometimes, *esclave* and its variants in French, Occitan, and late medieval Italian refers specifically to the Eastern Slavs of the east coast of the Adriatic, a locality that was more precise in Italian, where it may be used to lend an air of authentic detail to a fictional narrative. By contrast, in French examples, the word appears in lists that mark the provenance of exotic objects, as one far-away, foreign reference among others. Judging from dictionaries, in addition to the use of *esclave* and its family to (1) designate the type of labor (enslaved person, pirate), to (2) connote the fear inspired by that person (pirate), and (3) an exotic origin of a person or object, the word fam-

---

43 Ibid., 12–13.

ily of *esclave* is most strongly embedded in two other places in medieval French and Occitan, starting in the twelfth and continuing in the thirteenth centuries and later: (4) metaphorical *esclave*, in lyric poetry the imaginary relation of dependence between the lover, enslaved by love, and the beloved; and (5) *esclavine*, also common in Latin, a humble, warm, fuzzy cloth or cloak often worn by pilgrims, travelers, and workmen, perhaps of Slav origin. Already when the word *esclave* is first attested in twelfth-century French and thirteenth-century Occitan, the literary semantic field of *esclave* is often disconnected from the contemporary medieval reality of slavery.

In late medieval Italian, especially in prose, we observe in the use of *schiava* and *schiavetta* a possible conflation between the origins of a Slav woman and her enslaved status. That is similar to what we witness centuries earlier in twelfth-century Byzantine *sclavenos* or Ottonian Latin *sclavoni,* and in Al-Andalus Arabic *sqâliba* during the caliphate period. Similar language expresses a similar presence of enslaved people of Slav origin in late medieval, thirteenth- to fifteenth-century Italy, usually women, and eighth- to twelfth-century Byzantium, Germany, and Al-Andalus and the remainder of Iberia, both men and women. For a more detailed discussion of French, Occitan, and Italian literary examples, see below.

Who Are the Sclavoni/Slavs, Scythians, and Kipçaks for Medieval Latins and Byzantines?

Who were the Scythians, Tartars, Kipçaks, and Slavs for Petrarch? In this and the next section, I will evoke two mid-twentieth-century scholars who are, for the historians of slavery, their earliest starting point: Verlinden and the brilliant linguist André Maricq.[44] Verlinden is well known, but Maricq is less commonly

---

44 Verlinden, *L'esclavage dans l'Europe médiévale*; André Maricq and Henri Grégoire, "Notes sur les Slaves dans le Péloponnèse et en Bithynie et sur l'emploi de 'Slave' comme apellatif," *Byzantion* 22 (1952): 337–56.

cited. Verlinden was a historian of colonization and medieval slave trade, and his work from the 1950s to 1970s on the economic shift from the Mediterranean to the Atlantic from the twelfth to the eighteenth centuries is timely again in the context of Geraldine Heng's *Invention of Race* (2018) and Critical Race Studies in general. Maricq was a Persian epigrapher whose life was cut tragically short by illness. He left monumental contributions nonetheless, including authoritative translations of inscriptions that long defeated the concerted efforts of the field: the Kanişka inscription, the Greek version of the Šāpur inscription, and the minaret of Jām. I focus here on his work on the first appearances of the Slavs in Byzantine historiography.

Byzantine, Latin, French, and Italian sources are often vague or wrong on who Slavs are and where they come from, and who they designate as Slav varies through the centuries. Thorir Jonsson Hraundal sheds new light on Islamicate references to the Rus, drawing a distinction between Slav Kievan Rus and the Viking/Scandinavian Volga/Scandinavian Volga/Caspian Rus who, as he notes, assimilated with the Slavs in the early eleventh century.[45] In turn, as Vasilina Sidorova notes in a useful review of French chronicles of Adhemar of Chabannes (near Limoges, 988–1034) and Raoul Glaber (Burgundy and Auxerre, 985–1050), the general Latin ignorance of the Slav world was only slightly altered by direct connections with Polish, Kievan Rus, or Ukranian people, such as the mid-eleventh century presence in Cluny of the Polish king Kazimierz (Casimir I the Restorer), who took the name of Charles as a deacon in Cluny before 1041, or the marriage of Henri I of France to Anna of Kiev (1051), facilitated by Kazimierz who married her aunt Maria and was the father-in-law of Anna's brother, the future prince of Kiev Izyaslav. Note that these Slavic marriages and diplomatic con-

---

[45] Thorir Jonsson Hraundal, "The Rus in Arabic Sources: Cultural Contacts and Identity," PhD Thesis, University of Bergen, 2013, https://pdfs.semantischolar.org/2eb8/7d499a8b645fd5917983e4f497d1b1ce9e92.pdf; Hraundel, "New Perspectives on Eastern Vikings/Rus in Arabic Sources," *Viking and Medieval Scandinavia* 10 (2014), 65–98.

tacts coincide with or closely precede the ca. 1100 transition, in the West, of slavery into serfdom. As Sidorova also notes, these mid-eleventh-century French chronicles are equally vague on Spain, Scandinavia, and England:

> Early medieval French authors knew not very much about the Slavs and the Slavic lands. They were mostly interested in the region in connection with the expansion of the borders of the "Roman world" to the East. Some of them mention Sklavania either as a part of Germany or as an independent territory inhabited by kindred nations or tribes. Despite limited knowledge about the region the authors distinguished well the Slavic peoples first of all by the language but sometimes also by appearance and culture. They indicated the exact tribal names and areas of their settlement as well as reported some very particular episodes of their history. The French chroniclers regarded Central and Eastern Europe as a region where the Western and Eastern Churches struggled for authority. The christianization of the Slavs was considered as a sacred mission of the German emperors while separate cases of conversion to Christianity were perceived as parts of basically one event.[46]

It seems that the knowledge of Slavs that circulated in these Franco-Latin chronicles is, like all narrative geography at the time, a textual tradition that was sometimes accurate but largely divorced from reality, slow to change, and rarely informed by living people or current events.

Overall, just like the question of medieval slavery, the question of medieval understanding of Slavs is best approached in a pointillistic fashion: from a specific time and place. Some

---

46 Vasilina Sidorova, "The Slavic World in French Historical Writings of the Eleventh Century," in *Slovakia and Croatia: Historical Parallels and Connections (until 1780)*, eds. Martin Homza, Jan Lukacka, and Neven Budak (Bratislava: Department of Slovak History, University of Bratislava, 2013), 97–101, at 97.

secondary sources date the use of Slav to designate Venetians, Slavs, and Slovenes to the seventh century. According to Maricq, Slav is used in Byzantium as an ethnic designator as early as the mid-eighth century, while the first attestation of the use of *sclavoni* as "enslaved persons" in Byzantine sources is in the typicon of Pantocrator in 1136. The story that Maricq uncovered of how the Slavs entered onto the Latin and Byzantine historiographic scene is exciting enough to describe in detail.

Maricq discusses *sclavus* in a seventh-century Armenian Ptolemy-based *Geography* that inserts a record of historical events into the basic structure of Ptolemy. That interpolation was previously ascribed to late classical, fifth century Armenian historian bishop Moses of Khoren (410–490s), but is now firmly attributed to the seventh century mathematician and cosmographer Ananias of Shirak (600–650). The events, Maricq says, are not datable based on the text, but appear to be contemporary with the Armenian *Geography*'s composition in the seventh century. Previously, the Byzantinist Henri Grégoire took them to be the earliest extant description of the events of 376, the crossing of the Danube towards the South and the occupation of today's Balkans by twenty-five Slav tribes pushed by the Goths, who were pushed by the Huns. Maricq rejects that hypothesis. In a postscript to Maricq's article, Grégoire agrees with Maricq. The seventh-century Armenian *Geography* describes early Byzantium/Thracia with its capital, the "admirable Constantinople," and places twenty-three (in the text's short recension, twenty-five) Slav tribes in Northern Thracia/Dacia. Pushed out by the "Goths from the isle of Scania [Scandinavia] called Emios by the Germans," the Slavs "passed the Danube and occupied another country in Thrace and Macedonia, and passed into Achaia and Dalmatia."[47] The long recension of the text continues, presenting a section about the Piwki island in the six-branched Danube delta, on which Aspar-hruk fled the Khazar "from the Mount of the

---

47 Maricq and Grégoire, "Notes sur les Slaves dans le Péloponnèse et en Bithynie et sur l'emploi de 'Slave' comme apellatif," 343.

Bulgarians" and repelled the Avars. The Mount of the Bulgarians is part of the Caucasus that descends to the Kuban river. This location of the Bulgarians is confirmed by Byzantine chronicles. "This brief Armenian testimony on the migration of Kuban Bulgarians to Bulgaria" is contemporary with the seventh-century migration it describes, and therefore somewhat more likely to represent actual events.[48] The establishment of Slavs in Bithynia, initially dated 650–710, was narrowed to 694, early in the first reign of Justinian II, who massacred the Slavs for their defection in the lost battle of Sebastopolis in 693, an event recorded by Michael the Syrian, Jacobite patriarch of Antioch (1166–1199) in his Chronicle, 4, 446 [2.470].[49] These citations show that the first Byzantine references to peoples of Slav origin are from the seventh century, as early as these peoples' arrival within the borders of, or proximate to the Byzantine Empire.

Slav and Slave in Slavic Languages

In Slavic languages, by contrast with medieval Latin, Arabic, French, Occitan, and Italian, *slav* means "famous for," *slava* means "fame," and the root *slav* recalls the word *slovo*, "word," "oath," "discourse," and symbolically resonates with the word *swoboda/svoboda*, "freedom," and the semantic field of *slodki*, *slodycz* "sweet, sweetness." The appellation the Slav use for themselves (Slav) designates the category of "people speaking our language," or "understandable language," that is, people using recognizable discourse. On the same principle, in Northern Slavic languages, the Germanic peoples, are designated as *Niemcy*, "people who do not speak": *nie*, the negative prefix and *mowa*, "discourse, speech." Along the same lines, as Mohamed Meouak notes, "in Andalus there was a military corps of non-

---

48 Ibid, 345.
49 Ibid, 349–50.

Muslims including *Sqaliba,* designated as *khurs* (mute) because they spoke no Arabic."[50]

An enslaved or unfree person is, among others, *rab/reb* in Russia and among the Southern Slavs in the Balkans, as well as in Old Polish and Ukrainian, related to modern Russian *ребёнок,* "child." While Russian and Southern Slav retained these words, the northern Slavs now refer to enslaved people as *niewolnicy,* from the negative prefix *nie* and *wola,* "will, free will, command, freedom, franchise, disposition, will/testament." *Wolność* means freedom, *wola* means will, endowment, command, order, preference, disposition, *wolny* means free, deliberate, slow, loose, *pozwolić* is to allow. The discrepancy between the meanings of Slav as an internal or external designation is dramatic. It was the original impetus for this essay, and I set out to identify the earliest attestation of the use of *slave* and *Slav,* starting with Verlinden and Maricq.

In this section, I focus on (a) the origins of the word *esclave,* (b) turn to some uses of the words in the family of *esclave* in the period after 1100, when serfdom, a new legal concept, emerged to cover a variety of practices and institutions that the legal codes of late antiquity defined as slavery, and (c) discuss some details regarding medieval slave trade networks and the history of slavery: (1) thirteenth to sixteenth century trade in women; (2) Central European trade in men through Verdun to Al-Andalus, eighth to tenth century; (3) mass enslavement in the Baleares in the late thirteenth to the early fourteenth century.

The first question is: why was serfdom and not slavery the prevailing medieval condition of unfreedom in agriculture? After all, Roman *latifundia* (large landed estates) depended on labor by enslaved people, and in Roman Gaul in the late antique and medieval periods, that system survives in the gynacea of the rural *villae,* where groups of enslaved women produced and maintained textiles and other products. Why not also men? In the Islamicate world, the development of slave-based planta-

---

50 Meouak, "Esclaves noirs et esclaves blancs," 28.

tion economy was cut short by the Zanj Insurrection in southern Iraq (869–883). The word *zanj,* just as *sqâliba,* denotes both the unfree status and a specific origin: *zanj* is usually identified with East Africa or Bantu-speaking people, for example, Zanzibar is the coast of the Zanji. In the Central Islamicate area, large groups of enslaved men were mamluks forming the amirs' armies and their households.[51] Neither the Latin nor the Islamicate world were a plantation system based on enslaved labor and slave trade, according to Armenteros Martínez and Ouerfelli, although there are important exceptions to that, as shown by David Abulafia and Henri Bresc (on Majorca and Minorca, Sicily, Ibiza), and Sally McKee (on Crete, Cyprus, and Rhodes). Most scholars cite Majorca, Sicily, and Crete as the examples of rural economy based on labor by enslaved people.[52]

The mid-fourteenth century begins a return to large scale economy based on enslaved labor both in terms of the Atlantic and in the Islamicate areas including the Ottoman empire, where some two million Slavs were absorbed into industries including the *kul* system (the service to the amir or sultan, as in the case of Mamluks and Janissaries, recruited through the *devsirme*/tribute system in the Balkans and Anatolia), *kadirga*/galley oarsmen, agricultural, silk and other industries, and domestic labor.[53] The numbers of Lithuanian-Polish losses can be tracked in *iuramenta,* declarations by landowners of loss in their peasant population, intended to lower taxes, amounting to some 7000 annually, with estimated collateral losses to famine and epidemics bringing the total to 10,000 annually. Russian losses were estimated on the basis of declarations of local *voevodas*/governors who declared three to four thousand annually; they had an interest in minimizing losses to prove their own effec-

---

51 Barker, *Egyptian and Italian Merchants in the Black Sea Slave Trade,* 128.
52 Martínez and Ouerfelli, "Réévaluer l'économie de l'esclavage en Méditerranée au Moyen Âge et au début de l'époque Moderne," 9.
53 Kołodziejczyk, "Slave Hunting and Slave Redemption as a Business Enterprise," 157–58.

tiveness. The numbers are confirmed by known major conflicts and the permanent occurrence of small raids.[54]

Again, the pointillist approach is needed. In terms of demography, Barker estimates the enslaved population in Genoa and Northern Italy at 1–2% in the thirteenth century and 4–5% in the fifteenth.[55] As she notes, a 1458 tax record reveals that 95% of Italian slaver households owned one or two enslaved people, with only 1% owning four to six enslaved persons, what she calls a "bourgeois" household pattern of ownership of one or a few enslaved persons and a slightly larger number of servants.[56] These enslaved people were mostly women. The records for Mamluk households imply higher numbers, and the Mamluk army and household of an amir was composed of hundreds to thousands of enslaved people. The total numbers in the sultan household based on anecdotal estimates are 10,000–30,000 throughout the entire Mamluk period (1250–1517), with anecdotal evidence at one point (1384) suggesting 60,000–800,000.[57]

In a 1995 review article Susan Mosher Stuard summarizes work on medieval slavery in Dalmatia, Italy, and Iberia, including Al-Andalus. Among the many studies including Verlinden and later that oppose the notion of an epistemic break that correlates the end of slavery with the divide between antiquity and the Middle Ages, Stuard discusses evidence that contradicts the supposed end of slave trade and documents slave-based rural and urban economies. Stuard shows continuing and, in the case of her main subject, medieval Dubrovnik/Ragusa, largely unchanged "evidence of an East-to-West traffic in Mediterranean slaves."[58] While slave trade persisted, agricultural economy was reshaped, and rural slavery for men became servitude: "changing his status, the *servus,* whose very name lost precise meaning, altered the terms of agricultural production and with that the

---

54 Ibid, 150–52.
55 Barker, *Egyptian and Italian Merchants in the Black Sea Slave Trade*, 123.
56 Ibid, 125.
57 Ibid, 128.
58 Stuard, "Ancilliary Evidence for the Disappearance of Medieval Slavery," 3.

economy and society."[59] By contrast, Stuard shows that the status of the enslaved woman or *ancilla* did not change as dramatically: "medieval traffic in slaves was overwhelmingly a traffic in women"; ninety percent of slaves sold in Ragusa/Dubrovnik were women.[60] The eleventh century is the tipping point in the diminishing role of male slavery in France, according to Bloch and Pierre Bonassie, but in Scandinavia it is the fourteenth century, as Ruth Mazo Karras has shown.[61] The slave trade from the Black Sea and Eastern Mediterranean increased in the thirteenth century.[62] Enslaved people were deported from Africa to Europe in the fifteenth century, followed by massive deportations of enslaved people from Africa to the Americas and the Indian Ocean.[63] After the abolitions of slavery in the 1800s, the same economic networks deported South-East Asian workers along the same routes and under almost unchanged conditions, in spite of the change in the law. The continuity of the practice of unfreedom behind the changes in legal instruments and economic institutions is also noted by historians of the medieval period. As Rio shows, the question of the transition in legal status from slavery to serfdom at the end of antiquity benefits from being reconsidered in terms not of changed legal status, especially after 1100, but of practices, leading her to show diverse modalities of unfree status in specific times and places. Rather than a shift, the overall picture is that of a diversity of conditions, agency, rights, and duties of the unfree: "a proliferation in forms of meanings within what was putatively still a single legal status,"[64] for example, allowing unfree people to keep earnings and create a family. If the twelfth century saw the emergence of

---

59 Ibid.
60 Ibid; Stuard, "Urban Domestic Slavery in Medieval Ragusa."
61 Stuard, "Ancilliary Evidence for the Disappearance of Medieval Slavery," 4.
62 Ibid.; Stuard, "Urban Domestic Slavery"; Ruth Mazo Karras, *Slavery and Society in Medieval Scandinavia* (New Haven: Yale University Press, 1988).
63 Stuard, "Ancilliary Evidence for the Disappearance of Medieval Slavery," 4.
64 Rio, *Slavery after Rome*, 247.

serfdom as a "new legal concept,"[65] the status of the unfree did not dramatically change.

Stuard focused on slave trade in Scandinavia and in the contact zones with Muslims, including the Adriatic. In Dalmatia, she studied the records of the slaving cities of Narenta, Dubrovnik/Ragusa, and Catar. She also cited Greece, Malta, and Castile, where Christian women were sold to Muslims and vice versa. She examined the Italian city states of Venice, Florence, Genoa, and Sicily. The general consensus is that outside of Iberia and particularly the wealthy Al-Andalus, where some sources number enslaved people in the tens of thousands, enslaved people were not exceptionally numerous, but that they existed throughout the medieval period and beyond. Similarly, Barker documents individual Italian slavers importing enslaved individuals or tens of individuals, with entire ships carrying hundreds, and tax rolls and other documents attesting to medieval Italian city populations of enslaved people in the hundreds or at most a few thousand. An enslaved person was often owned jointly or successively by a number of people, and sometimes their labor would be loaned or rented out.[66]

Medieval French fiction includes passing references to slavery. For instance, *Aucassin and Nicolete,* the anonymous late twelfth- or early thirteenth-century musical or *chantefable*, casually mentions that the protagonist, Nicolete, is an enslaved Muslim princess raised as a Christian in a fictional French locale. Such narratives are often based on Arabic or other literary sources, and do not necessarily represent a local practice or a historical reality, but they can. In England, there are references to enslaved persons in wills as late as the 1400s.[67] In 1363, Flo-

---

65 Ibid, 244.
66 Barker, *Egyptian and Italian Merchants in the Black Sea Slave Trade*; Hannah Barker, *That Most Precious Merchandise: Mediterranean and Black Sea Slaves, 1260–1500* (Philadelphia: University of Pennsylvania Press, 2019).
67 Stuard, "Ancilliary Evidence for the Disappearance of Medieval Slavery," 16 n. 46, citing P.J.P. Goldberg, *Women, Work, and Life Cycle in a Medieval*

rentine records show 357 enslaved people, including 120 women under eighteen. Italian and Adriatic *ancillae* (enslaved women) left few records "aside from a few Tartar, Greek and Slavic names and a few verses in *linguaggio di schiave*." According to Stuard, the word *slave* emerges in Latin, English and Romance languages in the thirteenth century, and denotes "women from the Balkans transported around the Mediterranean," destined for household work in Italy, or plantation work in Crete. That statement must be qualified. (1) As already shown, *schiava* does not always denote origin. (2) *Schiava* and related words are attested in Latin, French, and Occitan both earlier and later than the thirteenth century. While the thirteenth century is accurate for Italian, in French and Occitan, the word emerges when the French literary corpus does, in the twelfth century; and in Latin, it emerges at the latest in the seventh or eighth century. (3) *Schiavo* and similar words are often extended to all enslaved people without regard for their place of origin.[68] As mentioned, the same evolution that generalizes esclave to all enslaved people regardless of origin is attested in Arabic. *Sqâliba* (صقالبة, *saqlabi*) first designates the Slavs of Central or Eastern Europe, and later applies to foreign enslaved people in general. Stuard specifically pushes back against an earlier attestation linking *sclavus* to Otto I (912–973) and his campaigns against the Slavs, the razzias in which he enslaved captives. In Arabic sources, Otto I is the emperor of saqâliba, as Meouak notes.[69]

In Byzantium, "the first attestation of 'Slave' as 'enslaved' [...] is from 1136."[70] Maricq proposes the following timeline:

Economy: Women in York and Yorkshire, c. 1300–1520 (Oxford: Clarendon Press, 1992), 182.

68 Stuard, "Ancilliary Evidence for the Disappearance of Medieval Slavery," 27–28; Mario Ferrara, "Linguaggio di schiave nel quattrocento," *Studi di filologia italiana* 7 (1950): 320–28; Verlinden, "La Crète, débouché et plaque tournante de la traite des esclaves au 14e et 15e siècles."

69 Meouak, "Esclaves noirs et blancs," 28.

70 Maricq and Grégoire, "Notes sur les Slaves dans le Péloponnèse et en Bithynie et sur l'emploi de 'Slave' comme apellatif," 354; Maricq cites Dölger.

"'Slav' = 'slave of Slav ethnicity' in the ninth, tenth and eleventh centuries and 'Slave' = slave [of any ethnicity] in the thirteenth."[71] According to Verlinden, *sclavus/a* = enslaved person only appears in the thirteenth century in Western Europe, and quickly becomes common in Italy, France, Germany, Al-Andalus, and other parts of Iberia, suggesting that Venetian and Genoese Black Sea slave trade, trading Slavs from South-Eastern Europe, is responsible. That is not quite correct: the word appears earlier. Maricq points out that the term was used in the sense "enslaved person" in Germany from the ninth century: "in Germany, at a time when a lot of Slavs were sold as enslaved people, *sclavus* appears in documents, not in the sense of 'enslaved person' as Verlinden says, but in the sense of 'an enslaved person of Slav ethnicity.'"[72] Maricq compares three documents that use Slav as (1) proper noun and the two other options, (2) "enslaved person of any kind" and (3) "enslaved person of Slav ethnicity" in the same context: *homi[nibus] liberis vel Sclavis* (853: b/c), *tam Baioarii quamque Sclavi, liberi et servi* (853: a), *aut homines ipsius monasterii tam ingenuos quam servos Sclavos et accolas super terram ipsius commanentes* (857: a/c: *sclavos can be a synonym of servos and accolas or a qualifier of servos*), and *homines ipsius ecclesiae sive accolas vel sclavos* (889: b/c).[73] In the first citation, Sclavi is paired with Baioarii (Bavarians, from *Boii varii*, where *Boii* is the name of the tribe and *varii* is the Latin version of Proto-Germanic *varj*, as in *verja*, Old Norse "protection"), an

---

71 Ibid, 355.
72 Ibid, 354.
73 Verlinden, "L'origine de sclavus=esclave," 125. Maricq and Grégoire, "Notes sur les Slaves dans le Péloponnèse et en Bithynie et sur l'emploi de 'Slave' comme apellatif," 354–55: *Monumenta Germaniae Historica, Diplomata regum Germanorum ex stirpe Karolinorum*: I, 89–8, 18 January 853, Louis le Germanique deeds to the Saint-Emmeran monastery *super homi[nibus] liberis vel Sclavis*; 88–37: *tam Baioarii quamque Sclavi, liberi et servi*; I, 117–26, 21 April 857, Altaich cloister, Louis le Germanique: *aut homines ipsius monasterii tam ingenuos quam servos Sclavos et accolas super terram ipsius commanentes*; III, 99–10, Arnolf, November 21, 889, episcopal church in Würzburg [...]: *aut homines ipsius ecclesiae sive accolas vel sclavos.*

origin designation, but also "Baoiarii et Sclavi" form a pair with "liberi et servi," which may imply that there were free and unfree people of both origins. The second citation can be rendered as "as well as unfree, enslaved, and serfs," where *sclavi* is one of a series of nouns, or "as well as Slav serfs and servants," where *sclavi* modifies the noun(s). In the third case, *sclavus* describes an enslaved person and may also point to their origins. So, in Germany, in the mid-to-late ninth century, *sclavus* is an enslaved person, ethnically Slav, or both. On his part, Verlinden incorrectly says that the word is never used in the sense that links being enslaved and being a Slav in Germany after the tenth or eleventh century because of "the disappearance of a great trade network that spread its use."[74]

That network operating from the eighth to the tenth centuries was recently described by Thomas Freudenhammer in an article on *rafica,* an "enigmatic customs duty recorded in several charters issued by West Frankish kings during the ninth and tenth centuries."[75] As Freudenhammer points out, Arabic *rafik* means friend, companion, and *ravka* (pl. *ravkatim*) is a group of people travelling together, a caravan. The *rafica* or, according to Freudenhammer, the caravan tax is mentioned along the route that the traders from Verdun would take to Al-Andalus, their destination, almost due South until they reached via *Domitia* built by Antoninus Pius (138–161) along the coast of the Mediterranean, connecting Italy to Hispania *via* Galia Narbonensis. Another, Western leg descended from Northern Europe (Meuse Verdun) via Paris, Angers, Bordeaux, and Toulouse. The caravans travelled to Al-Andalus through Barcelona to Tortosa, where the merchants traded for silk, leather, kermes, saffron, ambergris, and other luxury goods against imports of enslaved people, Cornish tin, and Frankish swords.[76] According to Freud-

---

74 Verlinden, "L'origine de sclavus = esclave," 125.
75 Thomas Freudenhammer, "Rafica: Early Medieval Caravan Trade between the West Frankish Kingdoms and Al-Andalus," *Vierteljahrschrift für Sozial- und Wirtschaftsgeschichte* 105, no. 3 (2018): 391–406, at 391.
76 Ibid.

enhammer, that trade starts in the eighth century, flourishes in the ninth, and ends in the tenth. The eleventh century marks three transitions: (1) the transfer of power in Al-Andalus from the Almoravids who built the caliphate to the Almohads; (2) the transition in the East, where the peoples who were previously captured and enslaved become Christian and illegal to enslave; and (3) the rise of serfdom as the legal context of unfreedom, replacing slavery. As do Muslims, Christians are prohibited by their religion from enslaving coreligionaries. The atmosphere of increased orthodoxy in Al-Andalus due to the rise of the Almohads also resulted in the exile of the Jews, culminating in the fall of Cordoba to Almohads in 1148. With the abolition of the *dhimmi* or protected non-Muslim status, Jewish and Christian communities of Cordoba were displaced to Toledo, Fez, Tunisia, and Fustat/Cairo. As Freudenhammer notes, the trade that fueled Carolingian expansion of the ninth century folded, and with it, the *rafica* tax disappeared from charters.

In conclusion, let us turn to the late thirteenth and early fourteenth centuries, which also mark the intensification of European involvement in Atlantic slavery in the Canaries and the east coast African kingdoms, and to the work of David Abulafia and Henri Bresc, the historians of Sicily, the Baleares, and Mediterranean slave trade.[77] Abulafia notes: "Atlantic slave trade developed out of the much older Mediterranean slave trade," and the activity of the Majorcan and Minorcan traders from the Mediterranean to London eventually led them to the Canary Islands, then West Africa and the New World as "labor shortages in the first Spanish colonies created demand for the slaves sold by the Portuguese to replace the notionally free subjects of the

---

77 David Abulafia, "The First Atlantic Slaves, 1350–1520: Conquest, Slavery and the Opening of the Atlantic," in *Western Fictions, Black Realities: Meanings of Blackness and Modernities*, eds. Isabel Soto and Violet Showers Johnson (East Lansing: Michigan State University Press, 2011), 107–28. D. Abulafia, "Sugar in Spain," *European Review* 16, no. 2 (2008), 191–210. Henri Bresc, "Notes de lecture: D. Abulafia, A Mediterranean Emporium: The Catalan Kingdom of Majorca," *Médiévales* 33 (1997), 175–77.

Crown who were worked to death in the *encomienda* system. [...] Spanish authorities in Hispaniola [Haiti] and elsewhere had no qualms about forcibly moving the indigenous population [of Taíno Indians], about separating parents from children for long periods, about making stringent demands for tribute in gold." The Laws of Burgos outlawed physical violence, but "this legislation was generally honoured in the breach," finding justification in Aristotle's concept of "natural slavery" in *Nicomachean Ethics* and *Politics*, texts known since the thirteenth century.[78] A "natural slave" was to be ruled by reasonable humans, ignoring Saint Paul's levelling of such distinctions in Galatians: "there is neither Jew nor Greek, neither slave nor free."[79] As Abulafia describes, Aristotle constructed a scale of humanity where the highest form, men guided by reason and living in society, were opposed to those living asocially. Practicing cannibalism and animal-like barbarity placed some people next to beasts; so did cruelty.[80] The fathers of the Church including Augustine and Isidore of Seville conclude that servitude is a human condition, a result of original sin.[81] Religions may regulate it, or treat it as a stage in conversion. In addition to his own work on Minorca, Bresc reviewed Abulafia's work on the Catalan kingdom of Majorca (1276–1343), a kingdom that Bresc calls a collection of big cities: Montpellier for which the Catalans were the vassals of France, and which was, at the time, the second largest French city after Paris, the Baleares, Perpignan, and northern

---

78 Abulafia, "The First Atlantic Slaves," 107.
79 Ibid, 121; Peter Garnsey, *Ideas of Slavery from Aristotle to Augustine* (Cambridge: Cambridge University Press, 1996), 107–27; Aristotle, *Politics*, 1245a20–24; Gal. 3.28; D. Abulafia, "The First Atlantic Slaves," 124.
80 Aristotle, *Nicomachean Ethics*, 1145a31.
81 Abulafia, "The First Atlantic Slaves," 121; Aristotle, *Politics*, 1280a31–35; Anthony Pagden, *The Fall of Natural Man: The American Indian and the Origins of Comparative Ethnography*, 2nd edn. (Cambridge: Cambridge University Prss, 1986), 18; Aristotle, *Nicomachean Ethics*, 1148b17–19; Aristotle, *Politics*, 1252a1, 125315–10; Isidore of Seville, *The Etymologies of Isidore of Seville*, trans. S. Barney, J. Beach, and O. Berghof (Cambridge: Cambridge University Press, 2006).

Catalonia for which the Catalans were vassals of Aragon. The kingdom of Aragon conquered Minorca in 1287. The entire Muslim population of the island, some 30,000–40,000 people, was enslaved and dispersed. Abulafia and Bresc demonstrate how these kingdoms relied on slave trade and the fleet, as well as the commerce in agricultural products using enslaved labor and producing olives, oil, and figs. Among other documents that testify to their commercial reach, Majorcan ships are recorded buying wool in London in 1281 and 1304. Baleares-based trade also relied on the linguistic diversity of their islander populations, for instance, Arabic-speaking Christians (*Arrom/Rum*), and Arabic-speaking Jews. The Jews fled North Africa/Ifrīqia to Majorca in order to avoid forced conversion by the Almohad rulers. The members of the North African Jewish diaspora in the Baleares not only contributed important elements to the cultural and linguistic commercial networks created in the islands, but they also brought with them the crucial Moroccan trading center of Sijilmasa on the edge of the Sahara, which was central to trans-Saharan trade, including trade in gold and the enslaved people. Most Majorcan trade was with North Africa/ Ifrīqia and Muslim Iberia, which imported French and Burgundian cloth, traded for North African and Sicilian grain. Northern Europe, North Africa, Italian cities, and Sicily are connected to the Baleares through a triangulated trade:

> [A] textile industry develops early north of the Pyrenees. Montpellier, a great center of Italian banking, second largest city in France in terms of population before 1348 has wide horizons that include Romania, Cyprus, and Armenia. Majorca soon establishes links with England, where Majorcan ships come to buy wool in 1281 and 1304, establishing a triangular commerce with Italian cities. Private expeditions of Guillem Pere to the Canaries (1342) and Jaume Ferrer to Rio de Oro (1346) document the Atlantic drive, crowned with the establishment of the Majorcan Lullists in the bishoprics

of the Canary Islands, entrenched in their solid, anti-slavery stance.[82]

The beginning of the fourteenth century, the period that the nineteenth century historian Jacob Burkhardt defined as the birth of the individual and the beginning of the Renaissance in Italy, was also the opening of the transatlantic slave trade, prepared by the medieval slave trade. Anti-slavery stance had little impact.

Semantic Family of Esclave in Medieval French and Occitan

Three functions in the medieval semantic field of *esclave* seem more prominent: (1) geographical location, frequent in Italian and French, usually referring to the Adriatic in Italian, and an unspecified Eastern or Eastern Mediterranean provenance in French; (2) *schiavina* and its family, a fuzzy, warm cape, perhaps the most frequent use; (3) and "slave," used as a metaphor in poetry to represent the relationship between the lover and the beloved. The Italian etymological dictionary lists *schiava* and *Schiava Meranese* as a type of red grape produced in Trentino and Alto Adige. The word is traced to late medieval *schiava* [*vitis*] "[grapes] from Slavonia" on the Adriatic.[83] The use of *schiavo* to designate the Adriatic coast, Slavonia or Sclavonia, including *Mare Schiavo*, the sea that connects Italy to these regions is first attested in the mid-fourteenth-century travelogue of Niccolò da Pogibonsi to the Eastern Mediterranean, the *Libro d'oltramare* (1345–50), where he describes his six companions: Buonacorso da Massa, a man from Toulouse, an Englishman, a Burgundian, a Constantinopolitan, and a Slav. A well-attested late thirteenth century word in Italian and Occitan, *schiavina/sclavina/stiavina* is a humble cape used for protection from the cold, identified

---

82 Bresc, "Notes de lecture," 176.
83 Salvatore Battaglia, *Grande Dizzionario della lengua Italiana*, vol. 17: *Robb–Schi* (Turin: Unione Tipografico-Editrice Torinese, 1994), s.v. *schiava*.

with "travelers and pilgrims" (*Novellino,* ca. 1280–1300).[84] A garment, I imagine, similar to the hooded one in Gallo-Roman iconography that constitutes the identifying garb of the Celts, Lat. *cuculla,* Breton *cougol,* Old Irish *cochall,* Galois *kwcwll,* Cornish *cugol.*

As a descriptor of persons, in Italian, *schiavo* is attested from the late thirteenth century, often in the diminutive form, *schiavetto/a*. It is attested in Giovanni Chellini (1372–1461) in 1455, where Chellini, the Florentine physician, sends "Maria, his *schiavetta*" with two silver bowls to Alberto Tebani.[85] Examples of *schiavóne* used in the sense of an enslaved person from the Adriatic coast include Anonimo Romano (Bartolomeo di Iacovo da Valmonte, ca. 1357). There is also an old cunning woman character in *Il Novelino* by Masuccio Salernitano (published in 1476), and in the first modern historiographer of Italy, Francesco Guicciardini (1483–1540). In the late thirteenth century, *schiavo,* from *sclavo,* Tuscan *stiavo,* is attested in Guido Cavalcanti (ca. 1250–1300):

> Avegna che la doglia i' porti grave
> Per lo sospiro, che di me fa lume
> Lo core ardendo en la disfatta nave
>
> Mand' io a la Pinella un grande fiume
> pieno di lammie, servito da schiave
> belle ed adorne di gentil costume[86]

In A.S. Kline's translation:

> So that the grief I own is more grave;

---

84 Battaglia, *Grande Dizzionario,* s.v. *schiavina,* also meaning "bed cover, horse blanket, rough cloth," whence the metaphorical meaning of "roughing someone up" *fare una schiavina a qualcuno.*

85 Battaglia, *Grande Dizzionario,* s.v. *schiavetto, -a.*

86 Guido Cavalcanti, *Rime* (Turin: Einaudi, 1986), 38, xlivb, *Ciascuna fresca e dolce fontanella,* ll. 9–14.

> With that sigh I gave, that from me lit
> That burning heart in a troubled ship,
>
> I send to Pinella now a tide that's full
> Of hosts of mermaids, served by slaves
> Nobly dressed, adorned, and beautiful.[87]

Cavalcanti's poem is a reply to a sonnet by Bernardo da Bologna to his lady, Pinella, complimenting her for noticing that Guido sighed when he saw her. Here, the word *schiave* is as divorced from reality as the appearance of the mermaids, *lammie*. Together with the mermaids, the beautiful enslaved serving persons in rich clothing designate a fantastical, fictional opulence in this late thirteenth-century poem. An earlier or contemporary attestation belongs to Chiaro Davanzati (d. 1304), a Florentine poet who introduced the Sicilian style to Tuscany and is second only to Guittone of Arezzo (1235–1294) in terms of the size of his corpus, 122 sonnets and sixty-one canzone:

> Pensandomi là dove adimorava [la mia donna]
> E nel pensar di me facea marchese
> E Schiavo […]
>
> I was musing at the place where she caused me to fall in love
> And she made a prince of me
> And slave […]

These late thirteenth century witnesses are followed by Dante (*veggio vender sua figlia e pattegiarne / come fanno i corsar de l'altre schiave,* Purg. 20–81), Boccaccio (Dec. 8–10, I-IV-766), and others.

---

87 Guido Cavalcanti, *Thirty-Six Poems Including "Donna me Prega,"* trans. A.S. Kline, 2007, https://www.poetryintranslation.com/klineascavalcanti.php.

Italian dictionaries trace the provenance of *schiavo* to "prisoner" in Greek (*sclabós,* seventh century) and medieval Latin, and link it to Provençal *esclau,* "pirate" or "Southern Slav." For Occitan and Old French, the examples provided by the early nineteenth-century dictionaries of Raynouard and Levy include the mid-twelfth century Bertran de Born, *Ges de disnar* (1140–1215), which anticipates by a century and more the metaphorical uses of *schiavo* in the late medieval Italian poetry cited above.[88] That is no accident, since later Italian manuscripts preserve and circulate the earlier, Occitan poetic corpus, and Italian poets at the time of Dante often compose in Occitan, not in Tuscan. Bertran de Born's poem uses the word *esclau* as a flattering metaphor that reflects the unlimited power the beloved has over the lover:

> Al dolz esgar que m fes, et ab clair vis,
> En fes amors son esclau.

> With the sweet look that she gave me, and bright face,
> Love made me her slave.

The verb *esclavar* is also attested in Born:

> Pus ilh o a enquest,
> Mi non es greu si m'esclava

> Since she asked,
> I don't care if she enslaves me.

Raynouard lists Catalan *esclau,* Spanish *esclavo,* Italian *schiavo,* and Portuguese *escravo,* as well as the feminine *esclava,* and Por-

---

88 François-Just-Marie Raynouard, *Lexique Roman ou Dictionnaire de la langue des troubadours, comparée avec les autres langues de l'Europe Latine,* vol. 3 (Paris: Silvestre, 1840); Emil Levy, *Provenzalisches Supplement-Wörterbuch, Berichtigungen und ergänzungen zu Raynouards Lexique Roman,* vol. 3 (Leipzig: O.R. Reisland, 1902).

tuguese *escrava*, including the meaning "pirate." There are also words that sounds like *esclau* and may have a meaning that is associated with it, having to do with being locked, enclosed, under key or nail (*clau*).

Let us consider the use of the most popular word in the *esclave* family: *esclavina*, "rough cape," in Marcabru (1100–1150), in a poem tentatively dated to the second quarter of the twelfth century, *Al departir del brau tempier* (1130–1150):

> Neys l'ortolas ab lo clavier,
> Jos ab un vent, s'en fuy huelhs cucx,
> Per esclavina e per trabucx
> An laissat mantelh e caussier.
> Ni ren non ai del estagier.
> Tal hira·m fan sautz' e saucx!
> Si no·ls ten reys o coms o ducx
> Totz temps seran mais caminier.

> There is no gardener and no porter
> I blow away on the wind, I run away with my eyes closed
> In thick cloak and boots
> Leaving behind mantle and shoes
> And I get nothing at all from the tenant.
> The willow and elder tree make me so angry!
> If a king, count, or duke doesn't stop them,
> I will do nothing but walk the roads for all eternity.

The poem participates in a well-established topos, the poet's request for a reward from a miserly and unwilling patron. In the lovely, evocative first verse, Marcabru writes about seasons changing in an orchard, a typical opening that can be a metaphor for love gone wrong or serve as an opening to a political or a moral reflection. The transition at the end of the first, deceptively simple, descriptive strophe: *Suy d'un vers far en cossirier*, "I'm contemplating composing a poem," is a typical turn of phrase that announces the intention to use the description of the weather and nature as a metaphor or an allegory. "They" in the verse above are the people the lyric subject is concerned with, and "they" are not defined until the last lines of the poem, the *envoi* or the short final section where the poet breaks the persona of the lyric subject to directly address his dedicatee. From a lyric subject fully immersed in the poem, he turns into the poet in front of an audience, and directly addresses them. "They" are the *rics malvatz*, the evil rich. Like a well tended orchard, in the time of their glorious predecessors, they were once fruitful, but now, in the current generation, they only make inedible fruit. The orchard's generous fruit trees turned into miserly willow and elder trees. The word *esclavina* appears in the poem in a comparison between two outfits that the poet wears, a change that depicts in concrete terms, through clothing, his degradation and precarity brought on by the unfruitfulness of the *rics malvatz*, that make the poet so angry. The poet used to wear festive, aristocratic, summer, horse riding gear but now wears workmen's, winter, foot-traveler gear — the rough, fuzzy hooded cloak and boots. He may be condemned to forever roam the roads: he will never be paid by the *rics malvatz*.

Tobler-Lommatzsch traces the origins of *esclavina* and its iterations, emphasizing its use by pilgrims and its furry texture.[89] The attestations include Thomas's *Tristan*, one of the most important Anglo-Norman texts of the twelfth century (ca. 1155–1170):

Tristran i ad dormant trové;
Trove s'esclavine [var. eschavine] velue,
crie, a poi n'est del sen esue,
quide que ço deable seit (1903)

---

89 Adolf Tobler and Erhard Lommatzsch, *Altfranzösisches Wörterbuch* (Berlin: Weidmannsche Verlagsbuchhandlung, 1938), s.v. *esclavine*.

She found Tristran sleeping there,
She finds the furry cape,
Cries out, almost out of her mind,
She thought it was a devil.

Esclavine can designate not only the garment, but also the fleecy material, as in *Le roman d'Eustache le moine,* a poem that describes the life of Eustache Busket or the Moine Noir (1170 — 1217), an early thirteenth-century mercenary and pirate of the area between Boulogne, Pas-de-Calais, and Dover: *Une gunele aveit vestue / De un'esclavine bien velue* (777: "wore a tunic / made of thick, fleecy *esclavine*").[90] Another attestation is in *Reynard the Fox,* showing the currency of the term.

Conclusion

French Arabist André Miquel quipped that "as soon as you write the name [Saqâliba], the difficulties start." Mohamed Meouak's book on the *saqâliba* certainly confirms that, as does the present chapter on *slave/Slav.*[91] The question when and in what sense the word slave (*sclavus, esclave, schiavo, sqaliba,* etc), meaning Slav, slave, or both enters the vocabulary has not been reexamined recently, and new observations emerge when we triangulate the previous research of linguists and historians with more recent scholarship and dictionaries, as I have done here. *Slave* is a medieval word *par excellence,* but it does not play the same role in medieval French as it does in modern languages. When *esclave*

---

90 *Le roman d'Eustache le moine, poème anonyme du XIIIᵉ siècle,* ed. Francisque Michel (Paris: Firmin Didot, 1834); *Le roman d'Eustache le moine, Nouvelle édition, traduction, présentation et notes,* eds. A.J. Holden and J. Monfrin (Louvain: Éditions Peeters, 2005).
91 Eduardo Manzano evoked André Miquel's quip in his review of Meouak's book "Mohamed Meouak, Saqaliba: eunuques et esclaves à la conqête du pouvoir," *Mélanges de la Casa de Velázquez* 35, no. 1 (2005): 289–91, at 289; Meouak's full title is *Eunuchs and Slaves Who Conquered Power: Geography and History of "Marginal" Political Elites in Umayyad Spain.* See also Meouak, "Esclaves noirs et esclaves blancs," 41.

first appears in French and Occitan, which is as soon as the first sizeable corpus of French and Occitan texts emerges in manuscript after 1100, the word *esclave* is already a metaphor, for example, expressing the relationship of the lover to the beloved in lyric poetry. It appears too in the more literal meaning "slave," "pirate," and "an object or person of faraway, Slavic origin," but these uses may be less frequent. Other words than *esclave* are more often used in Old French and Occitan to describe unfree people, a matter for another essay.

It is important to note that analysis of language is impossible to separate from the history of slavery and commercial networks. Major in-depth and popular works on medieval slavery, including by Barker, Rio, and Victor appeared in the last few years, making the present chapter more timely. To conclude: (1) as Maricq shows, *sclavus* in the sense of Slav first emerges in Greek and Latin in Byzantine sources in the late seventh century, when Slavs enter Byzantine historiography by crossing into the territory of Byzantium, and when they also settle in Syria with the Arabs with whom they allied themselves against Justinianus II in 694; (2) Because of slave trade, the word *esclavus* is used to signify enslaved people, people of Slav origin, or both, and it is impossible to distinguish which meaning was intended in many cases. As long as there is slave trade, ethnic origin, appearance, and unfree status are conflated in Byzantium, Ottonian Germany, and Al-Andalus (*sûdân, sqâliba*), from the seventh to the thirteenth century, as shown in Byzantine, Ottonian, Frankish, and Islamicate sources; (3) This is no different for *slave* than for other words, including in other languages, that may connote the origins or appearance, including melanin levels, of unfree people, such as *'abd* or *mamluk*; (4) The historical narrative according to which the legal context of unfreedom changed drastically around 1100, transitioning from slavery to serfdom, is complicated by current work on slavery and commercial networks of slavery by Barker, Rio, Freudenhammer, Abulafia, Bresc, Martínez, Ouerfelli, and others, including historians of Russia, Ukraine, and the African kingdoms; (5) The word *schiavo* and its family emerge later in Italian, in the thirteenth century. Some notable Italian characteristics are the frequent use of the diminutive *schiavetta* and the increased likelihood that the word designates not only unfree status but also origin, due to the higher level of Italian involvement in slave trade and the higher proportion of enslaved people in the urban population than in neighboring Occitania or France, as well as to the proximity of Italy to the neighboring Slav city states across the Adriatic; (6) Another feature of Italian is the fact that *schiavo* seems to combine unfree status and origin throughout the Middle Ages; (7) In addition, in Italian, we note a frequent use of the adjective of origin *schiavo*/Slav without any reference to slavery (Slav grapes, Slav sea, etc.). It seems that some aspects of that meaning of Slav as a common adjective of origins, not directly related to slavery are especially well documented in the late medieval period, correlating with the wealth and importance of Ragusa. It appears that, paradoxically, the slave trade that enriched the city of Ragusa caused the word *Schiavo*/Slav in Italian in the late medieval period to become dissociated from the overwhelming association with slavery visible in other medieval contexts, periods, and languages; (8) *Esclave, schiavo* and related words are attested into the 1500s, but are not the most frequent designation of an unfree person; (9) Already in the twelfth century, the French and Occitan *esclave* is disconnected from reality. Even though the meanings "slave" and "pirate" are attested, as well as "Slav," designating the origin of a person or object, the word *esclave* is commonly encountered as a metaphor for the relationship of the lover to the beloved in poetry; (10) One of the most common occurrences is the word *esclavine,* a humble, thick warm cape made of fleecy material. Was the esclavine completely dissociated from the reality of slavery? Pero Tafur, who visited Caffa from Spain in 1435 and purchased three enslaved people, describes the Genoese practice of slave sale: "the sellers make the slaves strip to the skin, males as well as females, and they put on them a cloak of felt, and the price is named."⁹² Perhaps the practice was widespread; perhaps the *esclavine* was not only the shaggy cape that served as traveler's and workmen's apparel throughout Europe, but also a particular garment associated with the sale of an enslaved person.

---

92 Pero Tafur, *Travels and Adventures (1435–1439)*, trans. Malcolm Letts (London: Routledge, 1926), 1323, cited by Kizilov, "The Black Sea and the Slave Trade," 214.

Bibliography

Abu-Lughod, Janet L. *Before European Hegemony: The World System A.D. 1250–1350.* Oxford University Press, 1991.

Abulafia, David. "Sugar in Spain." *European Review* 16, no. 2 (2008): 191–210. DOI: 10.1017/S1062798708000148.

———. "The First Atlantic Slaves, 1350–1520: Conquest, Slavery and the Opening of the Atlantic." In *Western Fictions, Black Realities: Meanings of Blackness and Modernities,* edited by Isabel Soto and Violet Showers Johnson, 107–28. East Lansing: Michigan State University Press, 2011.

Amitai, Reuven, and Christopher Cluse, eds. *Slavery and the Slave Trade in the Eastern Mediterranean (c. 1000–1500).* Turnhout: Brepols, 2017.

Annequin, Jacques, and Olivier Grenouilleau. *Esclavages, de Babylone aux Amériques.* Paris: La documentation photographique, 2014.

Arbel, Benjamin. "Slave Trade and Slave Labor in Frankish Cyprus (1191–1571)." *Studies in Medieval and Renaissance History New Series* 14 (1993): 151–90.

Ashtor, Eliyahu. "Quelques observations d'un orientaliste sur la thèse de Pirenne." *Journal of the Economic and Social History of the Orient* 13 (1970): 166–94. DOI: 10.1163/156852070X00114.

Balard, Michel. "Esclavage en Crimée et sources fiscales génoises au XVe siècle." *Byzantinische Forschungen* 22 (1996): 9–17.

———. "Giacomo Badoer et le commerce des esclaves." In *Milieux naturels, espaces sociaux. Etudes offertes à Robert Delort,* edited by Franco Morenzoni and Elisabeth Mornet 555–64. Paris: Publications de la Sorbonne, 1997, .

———. *La Romanie génoise, 12e–début du 15e siècle.* Rome: Ecole française de Rome, 1978.

———. "Slavery in the Latin Mediterranean (Thirteenth to Fifteenth Centuries): The Case of Genoa." In *Slavery and the Slave Trade Trade in the Eastern Mediterranean (c. 1000–*

1500), edited by Reuven Amitai and Christopher Cluse, 235–54. Turnhout: Brepols, 2017.

Balletto, Laura. "Stranieri e forestieri a Genova: schiavi e manomessi (secolo xv)." In *Forestieri e stranieri nelle città basso-medievali (Atti di Seminario Internazionale di Studio, Bagno a Ripoli (Firenze), 4–8 June 1984),* 263–83. Florence: Libreria editrice Salimbeni, 1984.

Barker, Hannah. *Egyptian and Italian Merchants in the Black Sea Slave Trade, 1260–1500.* Columbia University, PhD Thesis, 2014. https://academiccommons.columbia.edu/doi/10.7916/D8610XH4.

———. *That Most Precious Merchandise: Mediterranean and Black Sea Slaves, 1260–1500.* Philadelphia: University of Pennsylvania Press, 2019.

Barthélemy, Dominique. "Qu'est-ce que le servage en France au XIe siècle?" *Revue historique* 187 (1992): 233–84. https://www.jstor.org/stable/40955432.

———. *The Serf, the Knight, and the Historian.* Ithaca: Cornell University Press, 2009.

Battaglia, Salvatore. *Grande Dizzionario della lengua Italiana,* vol. 17: *Robb–Schi.* Turin: Unione Tipografico-Editrice Torinese, 1994.

Blake, John William, ed. *Europeans in West Africa, 1450–1560: Documents to Illustrate the Nature and Scope of Portuguese Enterprise in West Africa,* 2 vols. London: Hakluyt Society, 1942.

Bloch, Marc. "Comment et pourquoi finit l'esclavage antique." In *Mélanges historiques,* vol. 1, 261–85. Paris: SEVPEN, 1963.

Blumenkrantz, Bernhard. *Juifs et chrétiens dans le monde occidental, 430–1096.* Paris: Mouton, 1960.

———. "Mediaeval 'Inventions.'" In *Land and Work in Medieval Europe: Selected Papers,* trans. J.E. Anderson, 169–85. London: Routledge, 1967.

———. *Slavery and Serfdom in the Middle Ages.* Translated by William R. Beer. Berkeley: University of California Press, 1975.

Blumenthal, Debra. *Enemies and Familiars: Muslim, Eastern and Black African Slaves in Late Medieval Valencia*. Ithaca: Cornell University Press, 2009.

———. *Implements of Labor, Instruments of Honor: Muslim, Eastern and Black African Slaves in Fifteenth-Century Valencia (Spain)*. PhD Thesis, University of Toronto, 2000.

Bonnassie, Pierre. *From Slavery to Feudalism in Medieval Europe*. Cambridge: Cambridge University Press, 1991.

———. "Survie et extinction du régime esclavagiste dans l'Occident du haut moyen âge (IVe–IXe s.)." *Cahiers de civilisation médiévale* 28, no. 112 (1985): 307–43. https://www.persee.fr/doc/ccmed_0007-9731_1985_num_28_112_2302.

Boni, Monica, and Robert Delort. "Des esclaves toscans, du milieu du XIVe au milieu du XVe siècle." *Mélanges de l'école française de Rome* 112 (2000): 1057–77.

Bono, Salvatore. *Corsari nel Mediterraneo: cristiani e musulmani fra guerra, schiavitù e commercio*. Milan: A. Mondadori, 1993.

———. "Schiavi in Europa nell'età moderna. Varietà di forme e di aspetti." In *Serfdom and Slavery in the European Economy, 11th–18th Centuries*, edited by Simonetta Cavaciocchi, 309–36. Florence: Firenze University Press, 2014.

Bresc, Henri. "Notes de lecture: D. Abulafia, A Mediterranean Emporium: The Catalan Kingdom of Majorca." *Médiévales* 33 (1997): 175–77.

Buringh, Eltjo, and Jan Luiten Van Zanden. "Charting the 'Rise of the West': Manuscripts and Printed Books in Europe, a Long-Term Perspective from the Sixth through Eighteenth Centuries." *The Journal of Economic History* 69, no. 2 (2009): 409–45. DOI: 10.1017/S0022050709000837.

Campbell, Gwyn, Suzanne Miers, and Joseph C. Miller, eds. *Women and Slavery*, vol. 1: *Africa, the Indian Ocean World, and the Medieval North Atlantic*. Athens: Ohio University Press, 2007.

Cavaciocchi, Simonetta. *Serfdom and Slavery in the European Economy, 11th–18th Centuries*. Florence: Firenze University Press, 2014.

Cavalcanti, Guido. *Rime*. Turin: Einaudi, 1986.

———. *Thirty-Six Selected Poems Including "Donna me Prega."* Translated by A.S. Kline. 2007. https//www.poetryintranslation.com/klineascavalcanti.php.

Constable, Olivia Remie. "Muslim Spain and Mediterranean Slavery: The Medieval Slave Trade as an Aspect of Muslim-Christian Relations." In *Christendom and Its Discontents: Exclusion, Persecution, and Rebellion, 1000–1500*, edited by Scott L. Waugh and Pieter D. Diehl, 264–84. Cambridge: Cambridge University Press, 1996.

Curta, Florin, ed. *East Central and Eastern Europe in the Middle Ages*. 2 vols. Leiden: Brill, 2008.

———, and Roman Kovalev, eds. *The Other Europe in the Middle Ages: Avars, Bulghars, Khazars and Cumans*, vol. 2. Leiden: Brill, 2008.

Davis, Robert. *Christian Slaves, Muslim Masters: White Slavery in the Mediterranean, the Barbary Coast and Italy, 1500–1800*. London: Palgrave Macmillan, 2004.

DeCorse, Christopher R. *An Archaeology of Elmina: Africans and Europeans on the Gold Coast, 1400–1900*. Washington, D.C.: Smithsonian Institution Press, 2001.

Devroey, Jean-Pierre. "Men and Women in Early Medieval Serfdom: The Ninth-Century North Frankish Evidence." *Past and Present* 166 (2000): 3–30. DOI: 10.1093/past/166.1.3.

Dockès, Pierre. *Medieval Slavery and Liberation*. Translated by Arthur Goldhammer. Chicago: Methuen, 1982.

Duran Duelt, Daniel. "La companyia catalana i el comerç d'esclaus abans de l'assentament als ducats d'Atenes i Neopàtria." In *De l'esclavitud a la lliberta: esclaus i lliberts a l'Edat Mitjana (Actes de colloqui internacional celebrat a Barcelona, 27–29 May 1999)*, edited by Maria Teresa Ferrer i Mallol and Josefina Nutgé i Vivés, 557–71. Barcelona: CSIC, Institucio Milà y Fontanals, 2000.

Epstein, Steven A. *Speaking of Slavery: Color, Ethnicity and Human Bondage in Italy.* Ithaca: Cornell University Press, 2001.

Ferrara, Mario. "Linguaggio di schiave nel quattrocento." *Studi di filologia italiana* 7 (1950): 320–28.

Finkelman, Paul, and Joseph Calder Miller, eds. *Macmillan Encyclopedia of World Slavery*, 2 vols. New York: Macmillan, 1998–99.

Frantzen, Allen J., and Douglas Moffat, eds. *The Work of Work: Servitude, Slavery and Labor in Medieval England.* Glasgow: Cruithne Press, 1994.

Frenkel, Miriam. "The Slave Trade in the Geniza Society." In *Slavery and the Slave Trade in the Eastern Mediterranean (c. 1000–1500 CE)*, edited by Reuven Amitai and Christoph Cluze, 143–62. Turnhout: Brepols, 2018.

Freudenhammer, Thomas. "Rafica: Early Medieval Caravan Trade between the West Frankish Kingdoms and Al-Andalus." *Vierteljahrschrift für Sozial- und Wirtschaftsgeschichte* 105, no. 3 (2018): 391–406.

Fulkonis, Maxime, and Catherine Kikuchi. "Vendre des hommes." *Actual Moyen Âge*, November 23, 2017. https://actuelmoyenage.wordpress.com/2017/11/23/vendre-des-hommes/.

Furió i Diego, Antoni Josep. "Una introducció. Treball esclau i treball assalariat a la baixa edat mitjana." *Recerques: Història, economia i cultura* 52/53 (2008): 7–18.

Gaiser, Adam. "Slaves and Silver across the Strait of Gibraltar: Politics and Trade between Umayyad Iberia and Khārijite North Africa." *Medieval Encounters* 19, nos. 1–2 (2013): 41–70. DOI: 10.1163/15700674-12342124.

Garfield, Robert. "A Forgotten Fragment of the Diaspora: The Jews of Sào Tomé Island, 1492–1654." In *The Expulsion of the Jews: 1492 and After,* edited by Raymond B. Waddington and Arthur H. Williamson, 73–87. New York: Garland, 1994.

Garnsey, Peter. *Ideas of Slavery from Aristotle to Augustine.* Cambridge: Cambridge University Press, 1996.

Gaudioso, Matteo. *La schiavitú domestica in Sicilia dopo i Normanni: legislazione, dottrina, formule.* Catania: Crescentio Galàtola, 1926.

Guillen, Fabienne Plazolles, and Salah Trabelsi, eds. *Les esclavages en Méditerrannée. Espaces et dynamique économiques.* Madrid: Casa de Velazquez, 2012.

Gioffre, Domenico. *Il mercato degli schiavi a Genova nel secolo XV.* Genova: Fratelli Bozzi, 1971.

Goetz, Werner. "Serfdom and the Beginnings of a Seigneurial System in the Carolingian Empire." *Early Medieval Europe* 2 (1993): 29–51.

Goldberg, P.J.P. *Women, Work, and Life Cycle in a Medieval Economy: Women in York and Yorkshire, c. 1300–1520.* Oxford: Clarendon Press, 1992.

Goldenberg, David M. *The Curse of Ham: Race and Slavery in Early Judaism, Christianity, and Islam.* Princeton: Princeton University Press, 2005.

Grégoire, Henri. "Notes sur les Slaves dans le Péloponnèse et en Bithynie et sur l'emploi de 'Slave' comme apellatif." *Byzantion* 22 (1952): 337–56.

Gutierrez, Avelino, and Magdalena Valor. "Trade, Transport and Travel." In *The Archaeology of Medieval Spain 1100–1500*, edited by Gutierrez, Avelino and Magdalena Valor, 117–48. Sheffield: Equinox, 2014.

Harper, Kyle. *Slavery in the Late Roman World, AD 275–425.* Cambridge: Cambridge University Press, 2011.

Heers, Jacques. *Esclaves et domestiques au moyen âge dans le monde méditerranéen.* Paris: Fayard, 1981.

———. *Les négriers en terre d'islam: La première traite des Noirs, VIIe–XVIe siècle.* Paris: Perrin, 2003.

Heng, Geraldine. *The Invention of Race in the European Middle Ages.* Cambridge: Cambridge University Press, 2018.

Heyd, Wilhelm. *Histoire du commerce du Levant au Moyen Age,* 2 vols. Leipzig: Otto Harrassowitz, 1923.

Hoffman, Richard C. "Outsiders by Birth and Blood: Racist Ideologies and Realities around the Periphery of Medieval

Culture." *Studies in Medieval and Renaissance History* 6 (1983): 14–20.

Hraundal, Thorir Jonsson. "New Perspectives on Eastern Vikings/Rus in Arabic Sources." *Viking and Medieval Scandinavia* 10 (2014): 65–98. DOI: 10.1484/J.VMS.5.105213.

———. *The Rus in Arabic Sources: Cultural Contacts and Identity.* PhD Thesis, University of Bergen, 2013. https://pdfs.seanticscholar.org/2eb8/7d499a8b645fd5917983e4f497d1b1ce9e92.pdf.

Isidore of Seville. *The Etymologies of Isidore of Seville.* Translated by S. Barney, J. Beach, and O. Berghof. Cambridge: Cambridge University Press, 2006.

Kaplan, Paul H.D. "Isabella d'Este and Black African Women." In *Black Africans in Renaissance Europe,* edited by T.F. Earle and K.J.P. Lowe, 125–54. Cambridge: Cambridge University Press, 2005.

———. "Titian's Laura Dianti and the Origins of the Motif of the Black Page in Portraiture." *Antichità viva* 21, no. 1 (1982): 11–18 and 21, no. 4 (1982).

Karras, Ruth Mazo. *Slavery and Society in Medieval Scandinavia.* New Haven: Yale University Press, 1988.

Kizilov, Mikhail. "Slaves, Money Lenders, and Prisoner Guards: The Jews and the Trade in Slaves and Captives in the Crimean Khanate." *Journal of Jewish Studies* 58, no. 2 (2007): 189–207.

———. "The Black Sea and the Slave Trade: The Role of Crimean Maritime Towns in the Trade in Slaves and Captives in the Fifteenth to Eighteenth Centuries." *International Journal of Maritime History* 17, no. 1 (2005): 211–35. DOI: 10.1177/084387140501700110.

Klein, Denise, ed. *The Crimean Khanate Between East and West (15th–18th Century).* Forschungen zur osteuropäischen Geschichte 78. Wiesbaden: Harrassowitz, 2012.

Kołodziejczyk, Dariusz. "Slave Hunting and Slave Redemption as a Business Enterprise: The Northern Black Sea Region in the Sixteenth to Seventeenth Centuries." *Oriente*

Moderno 25, no. 1 (2006): 149–59. https://www.jstor.org/stable/25818051.

Korobeinikov, Dmitri, "A Broken Mirror: The Kipçak World in the Thirteenth Century." In *The Other Europe in the Middle Ages: Avars, Bulghars, Khazars and Cumans,* edited by Florin Curta and Roman Kovalev, 379–412. Leiden: Brill, 2008.

Korpela, Jukka. *Slaves from the North: Finns and Karelians in the East European Slave Trade, 900–1600.* Leiden: Brill, 2019.

———. "The Baltic Finnic People in the Medieval and Pre-Modern Eastern European Slave Trade." *Russian History* 41, no. 1 (2014): 85–117. DOI: 10.1163/18763316-04101006.

Lawrance, Jeremy. "Black Africans in Renaissance Spanish Literature." In *Black Africans in Renaissance Europe,* edited by T.F. Earle and K.J.P. Lowe, 70–93. Cambridge: Cambridge University Press, 2005.

Levy, Emil. *Provenzalisches Supplement-Wörterbuch, Berichtigungen und ergänzungen zu Raynouards Lexique Roman,* vol. 3. Leipzig: O.R. Reisland, 1902.

Longnon, Auguste, ed. *Polyptique de l'Abbaye de Saint-Germain-des-Prés rédigé au temps de l'abbé Irminon.* Paris: Champion, 1886–1895.

Lowe, Kate, and Thomas Forster Earle, eds. *Black Africans in Renaissance Europe.* Cambridge: Cambridge University Press, 2005.

Manzano, Eduardo. "Mohamed Meouak, Saqaliba: eunuques et esclaves à la conquête do pouvoir." *Mélanges de la Casa de Velázquez* 35, no. 1 (2005), 289–91.

Maricq, André, and Henri Grégoire. "Notes sur les Slaves dans le Péloponnèse et en Bithynie et sur l'emploi de 'Slave' comme apellatif." *Byzantion* 22 (1952): 337–56.

Martín Casares, Aurelia. "Evolution of the Origin of Slaves Sold in Spain from the Late Middle Ages till the 18th Century." In *Serfdom and Slavery in the European Economy, 11th–18th Centuries,* edited by Simonetta Cavaciocchi, 409–30. Florence: Firenze University Press, 2014.

Martínez, Ivan Armenteros, and Mohamed Ouerfelli. "Réévaluer l'économie de l'esclavage en Méditerranée au Moyen Âge et au début de l'époque Moderne." *Rives méditerranéennes* 53 (2017): 7–17.

Martínez, Ivan Armenteros, and Mohamed Ouerfelli, eds. *L'économie de l'esclavage en Méditerranée médiévale et moderne.* Aix-en-Provence: Presses universitaires de Provence, 2016.

McCoskey, Denise Eileen. *Race: Antiquity and Its Legacy.* London: I.B. Tauris, 2012.

McKee, Sally. "Domestic Slavery in Renaissance Italy." *Past and Present* 182 (2004): 31–53.

———. "Inherited Status and Slavery in Late Medieval Italy and Venetian Crete." *Slavery and Abolition* 29, no. 3 (2008): 305–26.

Meouak, Mohamed. "Esclaves noires et esclaves blancs en al-Andalus umayyade et en Ifrîqiya fatimide. Couleurs, origines et statuts des élites sûdân et sqâliba." In *Couleur de l'esclavage sur les deux rives de la Méditerranée (Moyen Âge-XXe siècle),* edited by Roger Botte and Alessandro Stella, 25–54. Paris, Karthala, 2012.

Meouak, Mohamed. *Saqâliba, eunuques et esclaves à la conquête du pouvoir: Géographie et histoire des élites politiques "marginals" dans l'Espagne Umayyade.* Helsinki: Academia Scientarum Fennica, 2004.

Meyer, Paul. "Explication de la pièce de Peire Vidal, Dragoman Seiner s'agues bon destrier." *Romania* 2, no. 8 (1873): 423–36.

Miller, Kathryn. "Reflections on Reciprocity: A Late Medieval Islamic Perspective on Christian-Muslim Commitment to Captive Exchange." In *Religion and Trade: Cross Cultural Exchanges in World History, 1000–1900,* edited by Francesca Trivellato, Leor Halevi, and Catia Antunes, 131–59. Oxford: Oxford University Press, 2014.

Mueller, Reinhild C. "Venezia e i primi schiavi neri." *Archivio Veneto* 113 (1979): 139–42.

O'Brock, Emily. "The Political Animal: The Symbolic Ecology of the Bee in Medieval France." PhD Thesis in progress, NYU.

O'Callaghan, Joseph F. *Reconquest and Crusade in Medieval Spain*. Philadelphia: University of Pennsylvania Press, 2003.

Oelsner, Toni. "The Place of the Jews in Economic History as Viewed by German Scholars." *Leo Baeck Institute Yearbook* 7 (1962): 183–212.

Origo, Iris. "The Domestic Enemy: The Eastern Slaves in Tuscany in the Fourteenth and Fifteenth Centuries." *Speculum* 30, no. 3 (1955): 321–66. DOI: 10.2307/2848074.

———. *The Merchant of Prato: Francesco Di Marco Datini, 1335–1410*. New York: Alfred A. Knopf, 1957.

Pagden, Anthony. *The Fall of Natural Man: The American Indian and the Origins of Comparative Ethnography*. 2nd edition. Cambridge: Cambridge University Press, 1986.

Phillips, Jonathan. *The Second Crusade: Extending the Frontiers of Christendom*. New Haven: Yale University Press, 2007.

Phillips, William D. *Slavery in Medieval and Early Modern Iberia*. Philadelphia: University of Pennsylvania Press, 2014.

Philips, William D. *Slavery from Roman Times to Early Transatlantic Trade*. Manchester: Manchester University Press, 1985.

Ramey, Lynn. *Black Legacies: Race and the European Middle Ages*. Gainesville: University Press of Florida, 2014.

Raynouard, M. (François-Just-Marie). *Lexique Roman ou Dictionnaire de la langue des troubadours, comparée avec les autres langues de l'Europe Latine*, vol. 3. Paris: Silvestre, 1840.

Rio, Alice. *Slavery after Rome, 500–1100*. Oxford: Oxford University Press, 2017.

Le roman d'Eustache le moine, Nouvelle édition, traduction, présentation et notes. Edited by A.J. Holden and J. Monfrin. Louvain: Éditions Peeters, 2005.

Le roman d'Eustache le moine, poème anonyme du xiiie siècle. Edited by Francisque Michel. Paris: Firmin Didot, 1834.

Rotman, Youval. *Byzantine Slavery and the Mediterranean World*. Translated by Jane Marie Todd. Cambridge: Harvard University Press, 2009.

Ryder, Alan Frederick Charles. *Benin and the Europeans, 1485–1897.* London: Longmans, Green and Co. Ltd., 1969.

Sabaté, Flocel. "Gli schiavi davanti alla giustizia nella Catalogna bassomedievale." In *Serfdom and Slavery in the European Economy, 11th–18th Centuries,* edited by Simonetta Cavaciocchi, 389–407. Florence: Firenze University Press, 2014.

Saunders, A.C. de C.M. *A Social History of Black Slaves and Freedmen in Portugal, 1441–1555*. Cambridge: Cambridge University Press, 1982.

Segal, Ronald. *Islam's Black Slaves: The Other Black Diaspora.* New York: Farrar, Straus and Giroux, 2001.

Sibon, Juliette. "Sandrine Victor, Les Fils de Canaan. L'esclavage au Moyen Âge." *Cahiers de recherches médiévales et humanistes* (2019), http://journals.openedition.org/crm/15603.

Sidorova, Vasilina. "The Slavic World in French Historical Writings of the Eleventh Century." In *Slovakia and Croatia: Historical Parallels and Connections (until 1780),* edited by Martin Homza, Jan Lukacka, and Neven Budak, 97–101. Bratislava: Department of Slovak History, University of Bratislava, 2013.

Silva, Alfonso Franco. "La esclavitud en la Peninsula Ibérica a fines des Medioevo: estado de la cuestión y orientaciones bibliográficas." *Medievalismo* 5 (1995): 201–10.

Snowden Jr., Frank M. *Blacks in Antiquity: Ethiopians in the Greco-Roman Experience.* Cambridge: Belknap Press, 1970.

———. *Before Color Prejudice: The Ancient View of Blacks.* Cambridge: Harvard University Press, 1983.

Stuard, Susan Mosher. "Ancilliary Evidence for the Disappearance of Medieval Slavery." *Past and Present* 149 (1995): 3–28.

———. "Urban Domestic Slavery in Medieval Ragusa." *Journal of Medieval History* 9 (1983): 155–71. DOI: 10.1016/0304-4181(83)90029-5.

Taubira, Christiane. *Baroque Sarabande.* Paris: Philippe Rey, 2018.

Teneti, Alberto. "Gli schiavi di Venezia alla fine de cinquecento." *Rivista storica italiana* 67 (1955): 52–69.

Thompson, Lloyd. *Romans and Blacks.* Norman: University of Oklahoma Press, 1989.

Tobler, Adolf, and Erhard Lommatzsch. *Altfranzösisches Wörterbuch.* Berlin: Weidmannsche Verlagsbuchhandlung, 1938.

Tougher, Shaun. "The Aesthetics of Castration: The Beauty of Roman Eunuchs." In *Castration and Culture in the Middle Ages,* edited by Larissa Tracy, 48–72. Cambridge: D.S. Brewer, 2013.

Valante, Mary A. "Castrating Monks: Vikings, the Slave Trade, and the Value of Eunuchs." In *Castration and Culture in the Middle Ages,* edited by Larissa Tracy, 174–87. Cambridge: D.S. Brewer, 2013.

Vanneste, Tijl. "Slavery in Medieval and Early Modern Iberia." *European Review of History — Revue Européenne d'Histoire* 24, no. 2 (2017): 325–36.

Verhulst, Adrian. "The Decline of Slavery and Economic Expansion of the Early Middle Ages." *Past and Present* 133 (1991): 195–203.

Verlinden, Charles. "Encore sur les origines de Sclavus = esclave et à propos de la chronologie des débuts de la traite Italienne en mer Noire." *Cultus et cognitio: Studia z dziejów sredniowiecznej kultury,* 599–609. Warsaw: Panstwowe Wydawnictwo Nauk, 1976.

———. "From the Mediterranean to the Atlantic: Aspects of an Economic Shift (12th–18th Century)." *The Journal of European Economic History* 1 (1972): 425–646.

———. "La Crète, débouché et plaque tournante de la traite des esclaves au 14e et 15e siècles." In *Studi in onore di*

Amintore Fanfani, 6 vols., edited by Amintore Fanfani, vol. 3: 591–669. Milan: Giuffrè, 1962.

———. "Le problème de la continuité en histoire coloniale: de la colonisation médiévale à la colonisation modern." *Revista de Indias* 11 (1951): 219–36.

———. "Le recrutement des esclaves à Venise aux 14e et 15e siècles." *Bulletin de l'Institut Historique Belge de Rome* 39 (1968): 83–202.

———."L'esclavage dans le centre et le nord de l'Italie continentale au bas Moyen Âge." *Bulletin de l'Institute historique Belge de Rome* 40 (1969): 93–156.

———. *L'esclavage dans l'Europe médiévale.* 2 vols. Bruges: De Tempel; Ghent: Rijksuniversiteit, 1955–77.

———. "L'esclavage et ethnographie sur les bords de la mer Noire." In *Miscellanea Historica in Honorem Leonis van der Essen,* 2 vols., edited by Léon Ernest Halkin, vol. 1: 287–98. Brussels: Editions Universitaires, 1947.

———. "Les origines coloniales de la civilisation atlantique: antécédents et types de structure." *Cahiers d'histoire mondiale* 1 (1953): 378–98.

———. "L'origine de sclavus = esclave." *Bulletin Du Cange (Archivum latinitatis medii aevi)* 17 (1942): 97–128.

———. "Orthodoxie et esclavage au bas Moyen Age." In *Mélanges Eugène Tisserant,* 7 vols., edited by Eugène Tisserant, vol. 5: 427–56. Vatican City: Biblioteca apostolica vaticana, 1964.

Victor, Sandrine. *Les fils de Canaan: l'esclavage au Moyen Age.* Paris: Vendémiaire, 2019.

Wallace, David. *Premodern Places: Calais to Surinam, Chaucer to Aphra Behn.* Malden: Blackwell Publishing, 2004.

Weiss, Gillian Lee. *Captives and Corsairs: France and Slavery in the Early Modern Mediterranean.* Stanford: Stanford University Press, 2011.

Whitaker, Cord. *Black Metaphors: How Modern Racism Emerged from Medieval Race-Thinking.* Philadelphia: University of Pennsylvania Press, 2019.

Whitaker, Cord, ed. *Making Race Matter in the Middle Ages.* Special issue of *postmedieval* 6, no. 1 (2015).

Whitaker, Cord, and Matthew Gabriele, eds. *The Ghosts of the Nineteenth Century and the Future of Medieval Studies.* Special issue of *postmedieval* 10, no. 2 (2019).

Wolf, Kenneth Baxter. "The 'Moors' of West Africa and the Beginnings of the Portuguese Slave Trade." *Journal of Medieval and Renaissance Studies* 24, no. 3 (1994): 449–69. https://scholarship.claremont.edu/pomona_fac_pub/38/.

Wood, Ian. "Social Relations in the Visigothic Kingdom from the Fifth to the Seventh Century." In *The Visigoths from the Migration Period to the Seventh Century: An Ethnographic Perspective,* edited by Peter Heather, 191–208. Woodbridge: Boydell Press, 1999.

Wyatt, David R. *Slaves and Warriors in Medieval Britain and Ireland, 800–1200.* Leiden: Brill, 2009.

5

The Exiles of Byzantium:
Form, Historiography, and Recuperation

Roland Betancourt

In the opening leaves of *The Ornament of the World,* the late María Rosa Menocal dedicates the book to her father, "For *un hombre sincero de donde crece la palma,* / my father, the intrepid Enrique Menocal, / who has lived in lifelong exile / from his own land of the palm trees."[1] Her dedication, derives from the opening lines of the late-nineteenth-century *Versos Sencillos* by the Cuban poet José Martí, composed in the Catskills during Martí's own exile throughout the struggles that led up to the Cuban War of Independence.[2] From that telling dedication, Menocal begins her narrative by staging the first protagonist, the Umayyad prince Abd al-Rahman as an "embittered exile." As the narrative opens up, "Once upon a time in the mid-

1 María Rosa Menocal, *The Ornament of the World: How Muslims, Jews, and Christians Created a Culture of Tolerance in Medieval Spain* (Boston: Back Bay Books, 2002), vi.
2 On exile in the writings of José Martí, see Susana Rotker, "The (Political) Exile Gaze in Martí's Writing on the United States," in *José Martí's "Our America:" From National to Hemispheric Cultural Studies,* eds. Jeffrey Belnap and Raúl A. Fernández (Durham: Duke University Press, 1998), 58–76.

215

eighth century, an *intrepid* young man abandoned his home in Damascus."³ From there, she goes on to recount how the prince, having been forced into exile by the Abbasid Revolution, would come to terms with his new life in Al-Andalus, far away from his own land of palm trees. Menocal characterizes his new home begrudgingly as a "permanent exile in that backwater to which he was condemned," where he was as good as dead.⁴ While she was writing the history of Medieval Spain, attempting to share a vision with us of a convivial medieval world where Muslims, Christians, and Jews existed in tolerance, Menocal was also writing the history of her own family and of all those embittered Cuban exiles. Menocal's choice of words to describe her father through Jose Martí's words have a moving precision since Martí's verses carry a great political force for the Cuban-exile community as they were long-ago adapted into the patriotic Cuban song "Guantanamera," and nostalgically speak to Martí's homeland and his own struggles with nationhood, liberation, and exiles.

Menocal's story is one of people — past *and* present — traversing the sea and finding ways of living-together in exile; it is one of constructing a sense of emplacement across time, through history. How people moved across space, how they interacted with one another, and how art developed in synchronicity with the practices and realities of these traversals. But the proposition of globalism recently in art history is not just a spatial process, but also a temporal one as peoples and things collect in themselves memories, social lives, and affects that come to delineate and demarcate senses of place and belonging, boundaries that can be then traversed and transgressed once again. The sense that "the past is a foreign country" does not so much speak to the alterity of the past as a resolutely *different* and *inaccessible* place, but rather suggests that as a foreign country,

---

3   Menocal, *The Ornament of the World*, 5.
4   Ibid., 8.

it can be inherently visited and experienced.⁵ This inclination is intimately tied to the operations of detrimental movements in the history of art, such as Orientalism and Primitivism, where travel and Grand Tours not only enabled for the encounter with the past in its material ruins, but also with people and places *in the present*. People that because of alleged barbarisms or beliefs might represent a so-called "medieval" state, or that because a non-industrial society could show us an unaltered, simpler moment in a linear human progress.

These reflections lead me to contemplate then the temporal in the global, its ethical implications, and also how the *exile* as a trope could allow us to construct more equitable, global, and less ethnocentric histories. Primarily, I am interested in reframing how we conceive of spatiotemporal markers, such as say Medieval or Byzantine, by radically opening up the types of objects that comprise them. My focus in this essay is Byzantium, an identity that is arguably borne out of a continual state of exile. The Byzantines, as is often remarked, referred to themselves as "Romans" (Ῥωμαῖοι).⁶ Hence, the title of "Byzantine" was one of othering: to distinguish, distance, and define them in opposition to the identity to which they self-identified. For all extents and purposes, as so-called Byzantinists today we study the medieval Roman Empire. Our very notion of Byzantium was birthed from a certain condition of exile when Constantine moved the capital of the Roman Empire from Rome to that backwater port-town of Byzantion. Then, in the thirteenth century Byzantium existed in exile for fifty-seven years during the Latin Conquest of Constantinople. And, finally after the con-

5   For this phrase in debates around cultural heritage, see David Lowenthal, *The Past Is a Foreign Country* (Cambridge: Cambridge University Press, 1985).
6   For a recent assessment on the self-identity and terminologies of the Byzantine Empire, see Anthony Kaldellis, *Romanland: Ethnicity and Empire in Byzantium* (Cambridge: Harvard University Press, 2019). Also, see Averil Cameron, *Byzantine Matters* (Princeton: Princeton University Press, 2014), esp. 26–67.

quest of Constantinople by the Ottomans in 1453, the Byzantine diaspora would fracture and splinter across the region, preserving the knowledge and identity of the empire from Athens to Venice, from North Africa to Russia. In a sense, the notion of Byzantium itself is an embodiment of this exile condition oriented around the losses of centers, once Rome, eventually Constantinople. Ostensibly, there is no Byzantine Empire until the Ottoman conquest of Constantinople, it is an identity birthed by the mourning of exile.

Yet, furthermore, this litany of Byzantium's exiles can also be expanded with the exportation and transmission of Byzantium's culture to other lands far from the capital of Constantinople from the fourth century onward. While still bearing a distinct Byzantine style in their art, religion, and culture, we can see the articulations of the Byzantine in the Ethiopian, Armenian, German, and Coptic worlds, as well as places such as Spain, Italy, and the Slavic world. Once, the envy of the medieval world, today, Byzantium exists in the middle, between various histories and historiographies, often found in the interstices of survey books.[7] In modern popular culture, Byzantium rarely occurs as a clearly defined historical phenomenon or even as "medieval" at all, instead at most one finds it as an adjective, "the Byzantine," which operates to queerly modify and mediate a space between antiquity and the present, Christianity (vaguely conceived), and fanciful articulations of the East.[8] Byzantium then is not so much a region or a temporal bracket, as it is a condition of perpetual exile.

---

7   For a survey of Byzantium's place in art history textbooks, see Robert S. Nelson, "Living on the Byzantine Borders of Western Art," *Gesta* 35, no. 1 (1996): 3–11.

8   For the entanglement of Byzantium with queer subjects, see Roland Betancourt, "The Medium is the Byzantine: Popular Culture and the Byzantine," *The Middle Ages in the Modern World: Twenty-First Century Perspectives,* eds. Bettina Bildhauer and Chris Jones (Oxford: Oxford University Press, 2017), 305–36, pl. 5–16.

Figure 1. Selections from Kehinde Wiley, Iconic series (2014). Courtesy of Kehinde Wiley Studio.

Form

In order to explore this problem, I wish to focus here on an unlikely source: the contemporary African-American artist Kehinde Wiley, whose popular works can be found everywhere from most major museum collections to the hit TV-show *Empire*.[9]

In recent years, Wiley has been catapulted into a household name with the commission and execution of President Barack Obama's portrait for the Smithsonian's National Portrait Gal-

---

9 On the work of Kehinde Wiley, see Eugene Tsai, ed., *Kehinde Wiley: A New Republic* (New York: Brooklyn Museum, 2015) and Thelma Golden et al., *Kehinde Wiley* (New York: Rizzoli, 2012).

Figure 2. Kehinde Wiley, *St. Gregory Palamas,* Iconic series (2014). Courtesy of Kehinde Wiley Studio.

Figure 3. St. Gregory Palamas, Chapel of the Hagioi Anargyroi, Vatopedi Monastery, Mt. Athos, Greece (14th century).

lery. Through a process which he calls "street casting," Wiley selects people off the streets of New York to sit for him in paintings that evoke key works and trends in the canons of art history. His non-white sitters propose a history of art from which people of color have not been excised, reflecting on the tensions between identity and iconography. In his 2014, *Iconic* series, Wiley and his workshop created eight portraits of men depicted upon gold-ground with the gestures and attributes of Byzantine holy figures (fig. 1). As the Kehinde Wiley Studio describes it,

> These intimately scaled portraits use the visual language and gestures of 15th century icons to depict contemporary subjects selected by Wiley from the streets of New York City. The portraits are presented in specially designed frames that are architectural and gilded in the style of their Byzantine forebears.[10]

Wiley's works in this series list the name of their sitters in a medievalizing script at the base of the frame, while the identity of the holy figure that they represent is constructed mainly through gesture.

In Wiley's *St. Gregory Palamas,* a black shirtless man covered in tattoos touches his ring finger to his thumb over his chest with the right hand (fig. 2). This cites a common Byzantine symbol of blessing, as seen for example in the fourteenth-century wall-painting of St. Gregory Palamas in the Chapel of the Hagioi Anargyroi from Vatopedi (fig. 3). In his left hand, Wiley's sitter carries a tome, just as Gregory Palamas does in the Vatopedi image's heavily ornate Gospel book. However, the Wiley sitter instead carries Alfredo Tradigo's *Icons and Saints of the Eastern Orthodox Church* published in translation by the Getty in

---

10 "Iconic: Selected Works," *Kehinde Wiley Studio,* http://kehindewiley.com/works/iconic/.

2006.¹¹ This figure is not costumed, he does not carry a gold, gem-encrusted book, but instead he is depicted as he was on the street, and the book in the artist's studio now finds its way as a stand in for Gregory's accoutrement. Note, the green post-it tabs poking from the top of the well-used text. Here, Wiley spares us the superficial weight of visual or formal citation beyond the posing and gestures of the body, which come to construct the identity of Gregory. The book that he bares figures forth to us the logic of this system of painting, whereby this guide to Byzantine and Post-Byzantine iconography, which presumably serves as the working "Bible" for Wiley's project comes to substitute the Gospels depicted in the medieval portrait. The series works with this eloquent scarcity, whereby it seems that Wiley investigates what the limits of iconography and identity are through this paring down — the sitter's inscribed name below insisting upon our sight.

In his portrait of the *Archangel Gabriel,* Wiley's sitter holds a simple bamboo rod in his right hand, alluding to Gabriel's standard, while his left hand appears at the bottom of the frame (fig. 4). He gestures like the icon of Gabriel from the late fourteenth-century, now in Moscow, which is found in the publication depicted in Wiley's *St. Gregory Palamas.* Yet, Wiley's sources themselves are eclectic. For example, note the slight curvature of the sitter's left hand, which seems to be cupping an invisible object. Compare this to the common depiction of the Archangel carrying a translucent orb, as in an example from the Chora Monastery in Istanbul (fig. 5). Note, how the index finger in Wiley's work balances the hand against that missing orb's shape and weight. Wiley's visual language flitters across various sources, from iconographies that flourished in Constantinople to those that would become prominent in later iterations of Byzantium in the Slavic world.

---

11 Alfredo Tradigo, *Icons and Saints of the Eastern Orthodox Church,* trans. Stephen Sartarelli (Los Angeles: J. Paul Getty Museum, 2006).

Figure 4. Kehinde Wiley, *Archangel Gabriel,* Iconic series (2014). Courtesy of Kehinde Wiley Studio.

Figure 5. Archangel Gabriel, Chora Monastery, Istanbul, Turkey (early 14th century).

Figure 6. Kehinde Wiley, *The Fiery Ascent of the Prophet Elijah,* Iconic series (2014). Courtesy of Kehinde Wiley Studio.

THE EXILES OF BYZANTIUM

Figure 7. Page from A. Tradigo's *Icons and Saints* (Los Angeles, 2006), used by Wiley, featuring the *Icon of The Fiery Ascent of the Prophet Elijah* from Slovychegodsk, Russia (c. 1570)

This is perhaps most evident in his icon of the *Fiery Ascent of the Prophet Elijah* (fig. 6). This scene, while evidenced in the Byzantine tradition, finds its popularity in later Russian icons, as in the well-known fifteenth-century example from Novgorod and another late-sixteenth-century example from Solvychegodsk, again reproduced in Tradigo's *Icons and Saints* used by Wiley (fig. 7).[12] Here the logic of Wiley's citations almost seems to break down: the sitter seems to bear little connection to the icons of Elijah's ascent, beyond perhaps the raised left hand that gestures up to the heavens from the corner where the sitter is being lit, as that manifestation of God's divine light. However, this particular iconography has had an interesting history in modernism, precisely with artists seeking to find a Spartan, yet universal visual language. Consider here Vasily Kandinsky's 1911 *All Saints II,* which depicts a series of holy figures in a taciturn manner. Perhaps, we are seeing an image of Symeon the Stylite upon his column with his hands raised toward the heavens in the lower right-hand corner. Perhaps, we are seeing a figure of St. George upon horseback beside him. And, likewise, on the left it would seem that we are seeing the figure of Elijah ascending upon his chariot, surrounded by that fiery triangular form, which we observe in the Novgorod ascent. Such works question the bounds where we can make secure identifications, an exploration which for Kandinsky culminates in his 1921 *Red Spot II,* which Maria Taroutina has recently suggested, harkens back to the image of Elijah's fiery orb, its uniquely triangular form in the Novgorod example coming to signify this work through synecdoche.[13] All traces of the holy have even been lost in the

---

12 See ibid., 84.

13 For argument and images, see Maria Taroutina, "Iconic Encounters: Vasily Kandinsky's and Pavel Florensky's 'Mystic Productivism,'" *postmedieval: A Journal of Medieval Cultural Studies* 7, no. 1 (2016): 55–65. For an extended discussion of this phenomenon in Kandinsky's work around the Byzantine past, see Maria Taroutina, *The Icon and the Square: Russian Modernism and the Russo-Byzantine Revival* (University Park: Pennsylvania State University Press, 2018).

title, whereby the content of saintly identity is supplanted by the formal identifier, *Red Spot II*.

Returning to Wiley's image of the ascent, we are drawn to ask where and how the limits of this iconography lie, and how do we as viewers — because of its titular identification — become observers, attempting to grasp and comprehend the possibilities of history and citation offered by the image. Looking closely, then, we begin to see — or, perhaps, imagine — how the hands and clock face of his watch allude to the spinning wheels of Elijah's chariot, his robust arm signaling the chariot's body, horses, and their incline; as well as echoing Elijah's own posture with his opened and outstretched hands. And, what about that red orb that subsumes the chariot and critically identifies the scene as that *fiery* ascent? In this questioning, our eye is led right, toward the sitter's prominent bicep, outlined by a glowing red circular contour, which now leaps out at one's sight. Here it seems we have that fiery orb. The hands and minute markers of his watch begin to churn before the eye like the spokes of Elijah's chariot wheel.[14]

The poignant eloquence of Wiley's work, however, is that the identity which the iconography communicates never overshadows, negates, or erases the identity and history of his sitter as a subject. I am particularly drawn to the right hand of this man, which lithely grasps his hip. The most likely source for this gesture is not to be found in any Byzantine artwork, but rather in a painting that our Brooklyn-based artist would be intimately familiar with, Bronzino's *Portrait of a Young Man* from sixteenth-century Florence, now at the Metropolitan Museum of Art in New York (fig. 8). The bravado of his gaze, posture, and demeanor, neatly echoes that of Wiley's Elijah. The two hands upon the waist almost seem to fit upon the same torso. Yet, unlike the *Young Man*'s pinky ring, Wiley's sitter bears a bandage upon his index finger, his knuckles glisten with textured callouses. This roughened skin leads us not to our icon of Elijah,

---

14 I thank Marianna Davison for this observation.

Figure 8. Bronzino, *Portrait of a Young Man,* Florence (1530s) at the Metropolitan Museum of Art, New York.

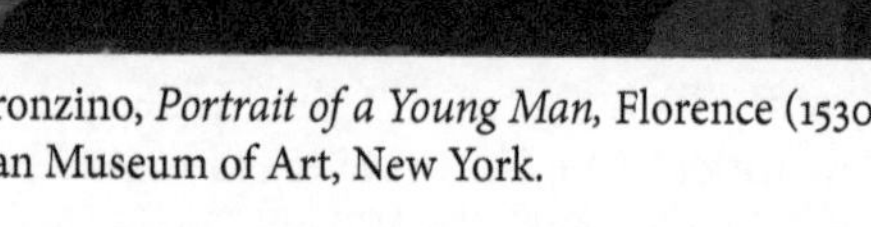

Figure 9. Detail of Kehinde Wiley, *The Fiery Ascent of the Prophet Elijah,* Iconic series (2014). Courtesy of Kehinde Wiley Studio.

but to the name that lies below the image: Chris Norvell, Wiley's sitter for this piece. His wounds here take on a Christomimetic function. They viscerally embody the sufferings of the tortured Christ that so much late-medieval western piety and spectacle were oriented around, drawing viewers toward a "mimetic identification" with the broken body.[15] Here, the C of Chris is inscribed with the Greek abbreviation of Jesus Christ's name (IC XC), as is commonly found framing Byzantine depictions of Christ (fig. 9). A squat cross punctuates the R, while a slanted crucifix, evoking the carrying or raising of the cross, penetrates the S. These flourishes resist the sitter's titular association with Elijah. Instead, they produce a generative friction so as to confront us with the layered histories and excised identities that his works contemplate.

What perhaps draws me the most to Kehinde Wiley's *Iconic* series is its citing of the Byzantine, and all the ways in which it *fails* to do just that. The series' focus on figures like Gregory Palamas, Elijah, or Prince Alexander Nevskii, speaks precisely not to a Byzantine or even fourteenth-century orientation, as his artist's statement would suggest, but rather to the iterations of the Byzantine icon in the Slavic world and modernism. Rather than criticizing Wiley's work as erroneous or misled, what we find in Wiley is an artist contemplating Byzantium through its global history and diaspora, one that may even take us from modern Russia to Baroque Italy.[16]

---

15 On spectacle, see Mitchell Merback, *The Thief, the Cross, and the Wheel: Pain and the Spectacle of Punishment in Medieval and Renaissance Europe* (London: Reaktion Books, 1999), 101–25. On piety and mimetic identification, see Michael Camille, "Mimetic Identification and Passion Devotion in the Later Middle Ages: A Double-Sided Panel by Meister Francke," in *The Broken Body: Passion Devotion in Late Medieval Culture*, eds. A.A. MacDonald, H.N.B. Ridderbros, and R.M. Schlusemann (Groningen: Egbert Forsten, 1998), 183–210.

16 From the perspective of Byzantine architecture, Robert Ousterhout's landmark survey has produced an intricate history of Byzantium's diaspora and dissemination over the centuries, see Robert G. Ousterhout,

Figure 10. Bernardo Daddi, *The Virgin Mary with Saints Thomas Aquinas and Paul,* The J. Paul Getty Museum (c. 1330).

Notably, the intimate devotional frames constructed for Wiley's series eloquently speak to a non-Constantinopolitan vision of Byzantium. These frames are markedly not Byzantine, at least not in a conventional sense. Instead, they evoke the architecture of fourteenth-century Italian altarpieces, such as the triptych by Bernardo Daddi at the Getty (fig. 10). While Wiley has worked

Eastern Medieval Architecture: The Building Traditions of Byzantium and Neighboring Lands (Oxford: Oxford University Press, 2019), esp. 649–713.

Figure 11. Duccio di Buoninsegna, *Maestà* Altarpiece, Siena, Italy (1308–11).

with triptychs before, such as in his *After Memling* series,[17] the individual panels of the *Iconic* series, speak to the compositions of large monumental altarpieces, such as Duccio's well-known *Maestà* in Siena (fig. 11). This is a curious example in its own right since many of the *Maestà*'s individual panels now find themselves scattered across European and American collections. The angels from the pinnacles of the altarpiece particularly bear striking resemblances to Wiley's portraits and their frames, as the example from the Philadelphia Museum of Art demonstrates (fig. 12). Wiley's images then poignantly read as

---

17 On this series, see Sara Cochran, *Kehinde Wiley: Memling* (Phoenix: Phoenix Art Museum, 2013).

Figure 12. Duccio di Buoninsegna, Archangel from the *Maestà* Altarpiece, Philadelphia Museum of Art (1308–11).

fragments of history, connected to lost components and centerpieces. It is *as if* every panel of the *Iconic* series is itself part of a now lost whole, which the museum longingly displays in a quest to reconstitute a body — of an artist or of an artwork — lost or forgotten by the fickleness of history. This mythical fragmentation pins the viewer against that history of racialized erasure that Wiley confronts.

In these gestures, we can appreciate the exiles that artworks suffer as a metaphor for Byzantium's own exiles. After all, these gold-ground panels in Duccio's *Maestà* are derived from the impact of Italian artists borrowing and emulating Byzantine art.[18] It is the Byzantine-inspired gold-grounds and iconographies of these Italian altarpieces and their predecessors that led contemporaries, like Giorgio Vasari, to praise Cimabue and Giotto for eschewing the old "Greek style," or *maniera greca*.[19] These borrowings were themselves sparked by the influx of Byzantine art to sites, such as Venice and Genoa, during the Latin Conquest of Constantinople; and, by the later influx of Greek expatriates to Italy, such as Manuel Chrysoloras and Cardinal Basilios Bessarion, that would make accessible the classics of ancient learning to Europe through the teaching of Greek to the Latin-speaking world.[20] These exiles are historical, but they are also formal and historiographic.

---

18 See J.H. Stubblebine, "Byzantine Sources for the Iconography of Duccio's Maestà," *Art Bulletin* 57 (1975): 176–85.
19 Giorgio Vasari, *Le vite de' più eccellenti pittori, scultori, e architettori : nelle redazioni del 1550 e 1568*, eds. Paola Barocchi and Rosana Bettarini, vol. 2 (Pisa: Scuola Normale Superiore, 1994), 97.
20 See Nigel Wilson, *From Byzantium to Italy: Greek Studies in the Italian Renaissance* (London: Duckworth, 1992); John Monfasani, *Byzantine Scholars in Renaissance Italy: Cardinal Bessarion and Other Émigrés* (Surrey: Ashgate, 1995); Ian Thomson, "Manuel Chrysoloras and the Early Italian Renaissance," *Greek, Roman, and Byzantine Studies* 7 (1966): 63–82.

Figure 13a. Malnazar and Aghap'ir, Solomon Writing, Armenian Gospel Book from Isfahan, The J. Paul Getty Museum (1637–38).

Figure 13b. Malnazar and Aghap'ir, David Praying, Armenian Gospel Book from Isfahan, The J. Paul Getty Museum (1637–38).

Historiography

In an Armenian Gospel Book from New Julfa in Isfahan by the artists Malnazar and Aghap'ir (1630s), now at the Getty, we find the figures of David and Solomon wearing jeweled purple mantles and ecclesiastical garbs reminiscent of late-Byzantine religious dress (fig. 13).[21] Made for Armenian Christians exiled from their homeland, the manuscript not only depicts its images in a Byzantine style, but as an object it works to enfold time so as to imagine a moment back when Armenians were tied to Byzantium and its protections; when an object such as this might have been made for the members of an Armenian court under the aegis of the empire. Much like Wiley's contemporary works, this manuscript works through the trauma of displacement, exile, and erasure by reinserting its contemporaneous viewers, marginalized in their present-day society, into an inclusive and welcoming Byzantine past, as ideated as that past may be.

Byzantium as an empire encompassed various and disparate lands across its history for more than a millennium. Constantly, Byzantine art history has challenged itself to consider the art of spaces, such as the Balkans, Cappadocia, or Armenia, that have been marginalized in relation to the Constantinopolitan center and its dominant narratives. The endurance of Byzantium's artistic culture in modern-day Greece, Serbia, Cyprus, Crete, Armenia, Georgia, and the Slavic world in various forms well after the fall of Constantinople, suggests that Byzantium has always already been far more global and far less temporally bounded than our survey books would like to suggest. Because of its immensely varied history, affiliated lands, and ever-shifting borders, we find that modern historians and critics have often articulated Byzantine art through rubrics that often seem to fit

---

21 Los Angeles, The J. Paul Getty Museum, Ms. Ludwig I 14 (83.MA.63), fols. 320v and 358v. See the recent discussion in Bryan C. Keene, *Toward a Global Middle Ages: Encountering the World through Illuminated Manuscripts* (Los Angeles: The J. Paul Getty Museum, 2019), 109–11.

other areas of artistic production even better than Byzantium. For example, in 1908 Roger Fry would argue that Cézanne and Gauguin were

> not really Impressionists at all, they are proto-Byzantines rather than Neo-Impressionists. They have already attained to contour, and assert its value with keen emphasis. They fill the contour with willfully simplified and unmodulated masses, and rely for their whole effect upon a well-considered coordination of the simplest elements.[22]

Here, Fry's words suggest "the Byzantine" as dominated by a simplicity of form and contour, which pushed against earlier movements rooted on pictorial realism. These are the same qualities that Clement Greenberg would praise of Byzantine art exactly fifty years later, claiming that the Byzantines had achieved what only modern art would later reach, reaffirming the flatness of pictorial space, where, "light and shade were stylized into flat patterns and used for decorative or quasi-abstract ends instead of illusionist ones."[23]

As Robert Nelson has noted, it is the twentieth-century's belief that Byzantine art is flat, linear, and schematic that drew the attention of artists like Vasily Kandinsky, Gustav Klimt, and Fernand Léger.[24] While we regard Byzantine art as non-naturalistic today, as Cyril Mango once noted, the Byzantines themselves "regarded it as being highly naturalistic and as being directly in the tradition of Phidias, Apelles, and Zeuxis."[25] To my mind, this

---

22 Roger Fry, "Letter to the Burlington Magazine (March 1908)," in *A Roger Fry Reader*, ed. Christopher Reed (Chicago: University of Chicago Press, 1996), 73.
23 Clement Greenberg, "Byzantine Parallels," *Art and Culture: Critical Essays* (Boston: Beacon Press, 1961), 168.
24 See Robert S. Nelson, *Hagia Sophia, 1850–1950: Holy Wisdom Modern Monument* (Chicago: University of Chicago Press, 2004), 154.
25 Cyril Mango, "Antique Statuary and the Byzantine Beholder," *Dumbarton Oaks Papers* 17 (1963): 53–75, at 65.

is not so much a "paradox" as an opportunity to seek out this, "Byzantine" art: that is, one that is flat, linear, and schematic.

Recuperation

Rather than finding "the Byzantine" in Byzantium, I find "the Byzantine" more elsewhere: In medieval Spanish works, such as the Beatus Apocalypse at the Morgan Library, which Meyer Schapiro would enthusiastically show to Léger. Or, in the Christ from the Apse of Sant Clement de Taüll in Catalonia, whose image fascinated the likes of Pablo Picasso and Francis Picabia. I find the Byzantine in the post-medieval icons and manuscript illuminations of Ethiopia, such as the sixteenth-century Gospel Book at the Getty (Ms. 102 [2008.15], fol. 19v) with its frontal depiction of the Virgin and Child surrounded by angels, clearly delineated through line-work and brilliant color fields. I even find the Byzantine in the eighth-century Maya murals at Bonampak with their use of color and schematizations of court processions and religious ritual, akin to the interests of Constantinople in the ninth century. Or, I see Hagia Sophia in the squat domes and pendentives of Vittorio Garatti's mid-century School of Ballet in Havana, Cuba.

Why can't all these global works of art be Byzantine? And, how then would we have to re-write the history of art as an act of recuperation through inarticulate absence and unspeakable loss? What the modern historiography of Byzantine art has done is expand (specifically, by virtue of its marginalization and conflations) the Byzantine as a category, releasing it from the strictures of the Byzantine Empire as a spatially and temporally demarcated zone. Rather than attempting to correct this historiography to which Byzantine art history owes so much, my proposition here then is that we deploy this operation of "the Byzantine" *subversively* as a way of re-writing a history that is simultaneously occurring in various spaces at once. This is a proposition of art historical writing that manifests itself as a condition of exile rooted in the crimes of the history of art, a reparative act of resistance. Like Menocal's intrepid Syrian refugee, standing in for her own Cuban exile (and, for me as a reader, my own family's Cuban exile as well), this would be a vision of the Byzantine that has an understanding of a lost and distant homeland, perhaps one that you've never even been to, yet one that may be re-created, re-forged, and re-envisioned in ever new and ever different terrains.

In Kehinde Wiley's art, we find a more articulate vision of these recuperative gestures, which takes on negated figures across different historical pasts to create a room for representation (pasts that are prolific and multifaceted in Wiley's sources). Through gestures of appropriation, Wiley is able to subvert the violences of the history of art by in a sense mimicking its tactics to produce ethical spaces of representation. But, in doing so, his work also demands that we as scholars also begin to perceive figures who have not been so simply absent from Western representation, but rather who historians have willfully ignored, overlooked, or downplayed. In other words, what Wiley's work teaches me as an art historian is a way of looking at the past through the figuration offered by present marginalized subjects. In claiming the Byzantine as an expansive and capacious category, my goal is not to subsume all into simply another empire and its crimes, but rather to embrace a manner of looking.

Inherent in Wiley's *Iconic* series is also a very potent misnomer: that the Byzantines were western and white, and that they fit into a history of western art. As I have alluded to throughout this essay, this is not the case. Unlike Wiley's works that draw on canonical works of art historical surveys by white western male artists, such as Jacques-Louis David or Manet, this is not the case when representing Byzantine art. Byzantine art is often relegated to a single chapter in an art history textbook, akin to the chapters on Islamic, Asian, or African art that cover over a millennium of art, quarantined to itself to suggest its own insularity and irrelevance. What is so potent in Wiley's *Iconic* series is that it finds a place of power and subversion through a field that has enjoyed more privilege than its fellow marginalized fields, but has also been lost in the interstices of the surveys. His ostensible citation of Byzantium through the West's cultural appropriation of its art in the early modern period in Italy is no less pressing and problematic to unpack. There are scars of Byzantine exiles, but also that of the Latin Conquest's plunder and looting of Constantinople. In Wiley's use of light and surface in these images, as Krista Thompson captures it, there is a dynamic of seeing and being seen derived from trends in contemporary popular culture, but these are also dynamics inherent to Byzantine image theory and their conceptualization of the icon itself.[26] Critically, for Thompson this work captures the importance of "being seen being seen," a critical gesture that we undertake as Wiley's sitters are seen by us, being seen by a history of art.[27] It is a moment of recognition and empowerment as Wiley's art reaches poetically across time to embrace both his sitters and the Byzantine together, capturing their united power through the ever-apt title: *Iconic*.

---

26 See Krista Thompson, "The Sound of Light: Reflections on Art History in the Visual Culture of Hip-Hop," *Art Bulletin* 91, no. 4 (2009): 481–505, esp. 489–97.
27 Ibid., 489.

Bibliography

Betancourt, Roland. "The Medium is the Byzantine: Popular Culture and the Byzantine." In *The Middle Ages in the Modern World: Twenty-First Century Perspectives,* edited by Bettina Bildhauer and Chris Jones, 305–36, plates 5–16. Oxford: Oxford University Press, 2017.

Cameron, Averil. *Byzantine Matters.* Princeton: Princeton University Press, 2014.

Camille, Michael. "Mimetic Identification and Passion Devotion in the Later Middle Ages: A Double-Sided Panel by Meister Francke." In *The Broken Body: Passion Devotion in Late Medieval Culture,* edited by A.A. MacDonald, H.N.B. Ridderbros, and R.M. Schlusemann, 183–210. Groningen: Egbert Forsten, 1998.

Cochran, Sara. *Kehinde Wiley: Memling.* Phoenix: Phoenix Art Museum, 2013.

Fry, Roger. "Letter to the Burlington Magazine (March 1908)." In *A Roger Fry Reader,* edited by Christopher Reed, 73. Chicago: University of Chicago Press, 1996).

Golden, Thelma, et al. *Kehinde Wiley.* New York: Rizzoli, 2012.

Greenberg, Clement. *Art and Culture: Critical Essays.* Boston: Beacon Press, 1961.

Kaldellis, Anthony. *Romanland: Ethnicity and Empire in Byzantium.* Cambridge: Harvard University Press, 2019.

Keene, Bryan C. *Toward a Global Middle Ages: Encountering the World through Illuminated Manuscripts.* Los Angeles: The J. Paul Getty Museum, 2019.

Lowenthal, David. *The Past Is a Foreign Country.* Cambridge: Cambridge University Press, 1985.

Mango, Cyril. "Antique Statuary and the Byzantine Beholder." *Dumbarton Oaks Papers* 17 (1963): 53–75. DOI: 10.2307/1291190.

Menocal, María Rosa. *The Ornament of the World: How Muslims, Jews, and Christians Created a Culture of Tolerance in Medieval Spain.* Boston: Back Bay Books, 2002.

Merback, Mitchell. *The Thief, the Cross, and the Wheel: Pain and the Spectacle of Punishment in Medieval and Renaissance Europe.* London: Reaktion Books, 1999.

Monfasani, John. *Byzantine Scholars in Renaissance Italy: Cardinal Bessarion and Other Émigrés.* Surrey: Ashgate, 1995.

Nelson, Robert S. "Living on the Byzantine Borders of Western Art." *Gesta* 35, no. 1 (1996): 3–11.

———. *Hagia Sophia, 1850–1950: Holy Wisdom Modern Monument.* Chicago: University of Chicago Press, 2004.

Ousterhout, Robert G. *Eastern Medieval Architecture: The Building Traditions of Byzantium and Neighboring Lands.* Oxford: Oxford University Press, 2019.

Rotker, Susana. "The (Political) Exile Gaze in Martí's Writing on the United States." In *José Martí's "Our America:" From National to Hemispheric Cultural Studies,* edited by Jeffrey Belnap and Raúl A. Fernández, 58–76. Durham: Duke University Press, 1998.

Stubblebine, J.H. "Byzantine Sources for the Iconography of Duccio's Maestà." *Art Bulletin* 57 (1975): 176–85. DOI: 10.1080/00043079.1975.10787149.

Taroutina, Maria. "Iconic Encounters: Vasily Kandinsky's and Pavel Florensky's 'Mystic Productivism.'" *postmedieval: A Journal of Medieval Cultural Studies* 7, no. 1 (2016): 55–65. DOI: 10.1057/pmed.2015.48.

———. *The Icon and the Square: Russian Modernism and the Russo-Byzantine Revival.* University Park: Pennsylvania State University Press, 2018.

Thompson, Krista. "The Sound of Light: Reflections on Art History in the Visual Culture of Hip-Hop." *Art Bulletin* 91, no. 4 (2009): 481–505. DOI: 10.1080/00043079.2009.10786149.

Thomson, Ian. "Manuel Chrysoloras and the Early Italian Renaissance." *Greek, Roman, and Byzantine Studies* 7 (1966): 63–82.

Tradigo, Alfredo. *Icons and Saints of the Eastern Orthodox Church*. Translated by Stephen Sartarelli. Los Angeles: J. Paul Getty Museum, 2006.

Tsai, Eugene, ed. *Kehinde Wiley: A New Republic*. New York: Brooklyn Museum, 2015.

Vasari, Giorgio. *Le vite de' più eccellenti pittori, scultori, e architettori: nelle redazioni del 1550 e 1568*, eds. Paola Barocchi and Rosana Bettarini, vol. 2. Pisa: Scuola Normale Superiore, 1994.

Wilson, Nigel. *From Byzantium to Italy: Greek Studies in the Italian Renaissance*. London: Duckworth, 1992.

6

Confederate Gothic

Joshua Davies[1]

> *"Style is nonsense unless it develops from historical and racial associations."*
> — Ralph Adams Cram, *The Gothic Quest*[2]

On January 19, 1872, Jubal Early, former Lieutenant General in the Army of the Confederate States, and, since the end of the American Civil War, prolific author and guardian of the memory of the Confederacy, spoke in honor of Robert E. Lee at Washington and Lee University. Lee had died just over a year earlier, in October 1870, in post as president of what was then Washing-

---

1 This chapter began as a paper at the Leeds International Medieval Congress in July 2018. I thank Bettina Bildhauer for organizing and chairing the session. I thank the editors for their invitation to contribute to this volume and their advice and patience during the writing process. This chapter draws on research completed during an AHRC IPS Fellowship at the Smithsonian Institution in early 2018. I thank the AHRC for the opportunity, Clare Lees for support with the application, and Omar Eaton-Martinez, Pamela Henson and Helena Wright for their support at the Smithsonian. I thank Alexis Valentine of the Library of Congress for help with the images.
2 Ralph Adams Cram, *The Gothic Quest* (Garden City: Doubleday, Page and Co., 1915), 157.

ton College. The institution chose to rename itself in Lee's honor soon after his death.

One of the most substantial contributions by Lee as president of the university had been the commissioning of a new chapel, which was completed in 1868 and also renamed in honor of Lee after his death. Early delivered his speech in the chapel — a squat, unpretentious structure, distinguished from the Greek buildings that dominate the campus by its arched windows and the curved taper of its modest spire (fig. 1).

Early framed his celebration of Lee with a melancholy question: "Where shall we turn to find the peer of our great and pure soldier and hero?" He then posited and refused numerous possibilities. "Certainly, we shall not find one among the mythic heroes of Homer," he wrote. "Nor shall we find one among the Grecian commanders of a later period." Alexander, too, fell short because he became "a victim to his own excesses." Hannibal and Julius Caesar were also put forward only to be found wanting, so too were the "Generals of the Empire, either before or after its partition [...and] the barbaric hordes which overran the territories of the degenerate Romans"; the soldiers of "the dark ages"; and "the chieftains of the middle ages." Napoleon, Wellington, and Washington were all named and disregarded.[3]

Early argued that history had no equivalent of Lee. As a way of complimenting Lee's memory the argument is fairly straightforward, but it has a clear ideological agenda, too. One of the effects of Early's argument is to raise Lee above the plane of historical time. He is, Early suggests, beyond all known precedent, which also means that Lee is transported to a pre-political, uncontestable beyond. If he is beyond compare, he is beyond judgment. This rhetorical strategy fits neatly within what Gary Gallagher has called the "interpretive framework" of the Lost

---

3 Jubal Early, *The Campaigns of Gen. Robert E. Lee: An address by Lt. Gen. Jubal A. Early, before Washington and Lee University, January 19th, 1872* (Baltimore: J. Murphy, 1872), 47–50.

Figure 1. Lee Chapel, Washington and Lee University, Lexington, VA. Library of Congress, Prints & Photographs Division HABS VA,82-LEX,2C--1. http://www.loc.gov/pictures/item/va0910.photos.165405p/resource/.

Cause, an ideology fueled by nostalgic fantasy and contradictory claims, so Early's approach is unsurprising.[4]

What is surprising, however, or at least counter intuitive, is that Early made that argument in the Gothic environment of the Lee Chapel. There is something strange and uncomfortable

---

4   Gary W. Gallagher, "Shaping Public Memory of the Civil War: Robert E. Lee, Jubal Early, and Douglas Southall Freeman," *The Memory of the Civil War in American Culture,* eds. Alice Fahs and Joan Waugh (Chapel Hill: The University of North Carolina Press, 2004), 39–63, at 45. On the "Lost Cause" see, among others, Gaines M. Foster, *Ghosts of the Confederacy: Defeat, the Lost Cause, and the Emergence of the New South 1865 to 1913* (Oxford: Oxford University Press, 1987); Charles Reagan Wilson, *Baptized in Blood: The Religion of the Lost Cause, 1865–1920* (Athens: University of Georgia Press, 1980); and David W. Blight, *Race and Reunion: The Civil War in American Memory* (Cambridge: Harvard University Press, 2001).

about the fact that Early's anti-historical fantasies should have been delivered in such a place. Modern Gothic architecture, like other forms of medievalism, is defined by the claims it makes against the past. It derives authority from precedent and presumes that precedent is meaningful and legible. This generates an essentializing power. Unlike Early, modern Gothic generates a sense of commonality with the past.

That Lee commissioned a Gothic chapel should not be surprising. Medievalist aesthetics and practices held a deep significance in the southern states of America in the nineteenth century. This influence runs directly through the antebellum South, the Civil War, to the Lee Chapel and beyond. It moves between the scholarly habits of Thomas Jefferson to the Tournaments, which would feature jousting knights and were popular before and after the Civil War.[5] A biography of Lee, published in 1911, wrote that he was as "unsoiled as the mystic White Knight of the Round Table."[6] Later, Christiana Bond recalled meeting Lee as a medievalist experience: "The man who stood before us," she wrote, "was the embodiment of a Lost Cause, was the realized King Arthur."[7]

---

5   On Jefferson's Anglo-Saxonism see, for instance, Stanley R. Hauer, "Thomas Jefferson and the Anglo-Saxon Language," PMLA 98 (October 1983): 879–98; Allen J. Frantzen, *Desire for Origins: Old English, New Language, and Teaching the Tradition* (New Brunswick: Rutgers University Press, 1990), 15–19; and my own "Hengist and Horsa at Monticello: Human and Nonhuman Migration, Parahistory and American Anglo-Saxonism," in *American/Medieval Goes North: Earth and Water in Transit,* eds. Gillian R. Overing and Ulrike Wiethaus (Göttingen: V&R Unipress, 2019), 167–88. See also Annie Abrams, "'The Miserable Slaves, the Degraded Serfs': Frederick Douglass, Anglo-Saxonism, and the Mexican War," *postmedieval: A Journal of Medieval Cultural Studies* 10 (2019): 151–61. On ring tournaments see Esther J. Crooks and Ruth W. Crooks, *The Ring Tournament in the United States* (Richmond: Garrett and Massie, 1936).
6   Thomas Nelson Page, *Robert E. Lee, Man and Soldier* (New York: Charles Scribner's Sons, 1911), 686.
7   Christiana Bond, "Recollections of General Robert E. Lee," *South Atlantic Quarterly* 24 (1925): 333–48, at 336. Reprinted as Christiana Bond, *Memories of General Robert E. Lee* (Baltimore: Remington, 1926).

The manner in which southern culture was steeped in medievalist habits has been widely studied. As early as 1883 Mark Twain diagnosed the South with what he called "the Sir Walter disease." Without Scott's influence, Twain suggested, the South "would be wholly modern, in place of modern and medieval mixed, and the South would be fully a generation further advanced than it is."[8] More recently, Elizabeth Emery, Robin Fleming, Gregory VanHoosier-Carey, Amy Kaufman, and Tison Pugh, among others, have excavated American medievalisms of the North and South.[9] There has, however, been little work to date on the Gothic architecture of the American South. This stands to reason as Greek Revival was the signature style of the antebellum South and there is no southern equivalent of the Hudson Valley, the stretch of New York State where numerous castle-like Gothic structures were built in the nineteenth century. Patrick Snadon notes that "Gothic plantation houses were a comparative rarity," with slavers preferring what he calls "symbolic ambiguity" of the Greek.[10] But there are many buildings

---

8   Mark Twain, *Life on the Mississippi* (Boston: J.R. Osgood & Co, 1883), 468–69.
9   Elizabeth Emery, "Postcolonial Gothic: The Medievalism of America's 'National' Cathedrals," in *Medievalisms in the Postcolonial Word: The Idea of "the Middle Ages" outside Europe,* eds. Kathleen Davis and Nadia Altschul (Baltimore: Johns Hopkins University Press, 2009), 237–64; Robin Fleming, "Picturesque History and the Medieval in Nineteenth-century America," *The American Historical Review* 100 (1995): 1061–94; Gregory A. VanHoosier-Carey, "Byrhtnoth in Dixie: The Emergence of Anglo-Saxon Studies in the Postbellum South," in *Anglo-Saxonism and the Construction of Social Identity,* eds. Allen J. Frantzen and John Niles (Gainesville: University of Florida Press, 1997), 157–72; Amy Kaufman, "Purity," in *Medievalism: Key Critical Terms,* eds. Elizabeth Emery and Richard Utz (Cambridge: D.S. Brewer, 2014), 199–206; Tison Pugh, *Queer Chivalry: Medievalism and the Myth of White Masculinity in Southern Literature* (Baton Rouge: Louisiana University Press, 2013). See also the two *American/Medieval* volumes edited by Gillian R. Overing and Ulrike Wiethaus.
10 Patrick Snadon, "Gothic Revival architecture," in *The New Encyclopaedia of Southern Culture Volume 21: Art and Architecture* (Chapel Hill: University of North Carolina Press, 2013), 95–102, at 96.

that express the ideological power of Gothic in the slave-holding states, from the fussy Louisiana State Capitol in Baton Rouge to the fortress-like Sugar House in Charleston where enslaved people were tortured and brutalized.

The Lee Chapel is the starting point and destination of this chapter. While it might be tempting to view Confederate Gothic as somehow external to the history of American Gothic, or at least beyond the mainstream of American medievalist practice, this chapter demonstrates its close connections to those broader histories. It plots a path to the Lee Chapel via three very different buildings: Glen Ellen (1832), one of the first examples of domestic Gothic architecture in America; the Smithsonian Institution building (1855), the first large-scale public building built in the Gothic style; and the Confederate Powder Works (1862), a gunpowder factory built in Augusta, Georgia, styled, in part, after the Palace of Westminster in London, UK, and the only permanent structure constructed by the Confederate States.[11]

The history of American Gothic is complex. Different buildings have different histories, different commitments and different contexts. The sheer diversity of American Gothic architecture demonstrates above all the flexibility of medievalist thinking and the breadth of Gothic traditions, but they speak a common language that is premised on an idea of the supremacy of European heritage. One of the ideological functions of Gothic architecture, in both the Middle Ages and modernity, was to make situated and temporary political realities appear transcendent and timeless.[12] From this perspective, the histori-

11 My use of the term "Gothic" is deliberately broad. Among the buildings I discuss in this chapter, for instance, the Smithsonian was described as "Norman" but might be more accurately termed "Romanesque." The questions of classification and terminology are very complex. I have used "Gothic" as a means of emphasizing the shared medieval origins of the architectural forms, in keeping with much of the scholarly and popular literature on these buildings.

12 On the ideologies of medieval Gothic art see, for instance, Michael Camille, *The Gothic Idol: Ideology and Image-making in Medieval Art* (Cambridge: Cambridge University Press, 1989).

cized form of the Lee Chapel has quite a lot in common with Early's anti-historical paean to Lee. As the essays in this volume demonstrate, the intersections among medieval studies, medievalism, nationalism, colonialism and white supremacy are deep and complex. Confederate Gothic forms part of that history.

American Gothic

On July 9, 1864, with the Civil War edging slowly towards its end, Major Harry W. Gilmor of the Confederate Army led a number of small-scale raids around Baltimore. Gilmor had received his orders from Lt. Gen. Jubal Early and the operation, known variously as the Baltimore County Raid, the Magnolia Station Raid and Gilmor's Raid, was considered a success. The aim was to destroy railroad track and disrupt delivery lines between Washington, D.C., and the north. Gilmor achieved his goal with the loss of only one man. His confidence high, in a bravura act, Gilmor took the time to visit his family home while his cavalry was on movements. In his autobiography he relished the irony of meeting with his family while raiding enemy territory, writing that, "I captured the whole party on the front steps — and if I except some perhaps just complaints of my rather severe hugging — I treated them with kindness, and upon detainment of a few hours, paroled and released them and moved on with my command."

The Gilmor family home was named Glen Ellen — "Glen Ellen, the dear old home where I was born," as Harry Gilmor writes — and stood in the Dulaney Valley to the north of Baltimore (fig. 2).[13] It was one of the earliest works of domestic Gothic architecture in the United States — a large, white, crenelated mansion, with tracery, turrets with finials and a tall tower. Its

---

13 Harry Gilmor, *Four Years in the Saddle* (New York: Harper, 1866), 192. After the Civil War, Gilmor was Baltimore City Police Commissioner between 1874 and 1879.

Figure 2. Alexander Jackson Davis, Glen Ellen for Robert Gilmor, Towson, Maryland (perspective, elevation, and plan), 1832. https://www.metmuseum.org/art/collection/search/388434.

architect, Alexander Jackson Davis, called it the "first English Perpendicular Gothic Villa" in America.[14]

Harry Gilmor's father, Robert Gilmor III, was inspired to commission Glen Ellen following a trip to Europe in the early 1830s. Robert Gilmor stayed at a number of Gothic and Gothic Revival houses on the trip, including Horace Walpole's Strawberry Hill House, widely recognized as the first modern Gothic building, and Sir Walter Scott's Abbotsford. He described his visit to Strawberry Hill as "one of the happiest days of my life"[15] and it exerted a strong hold on his imagination. It is the defining influence on Glen Ellen.

Walpole began work on Strawberry Hill in the late 1740s. It was the first building constructed in a medieval style without a medieval origin. Unlike A.W.N. Pugin, the other figure who might stake a claim as an originator of the Gothic Revival, Walpole did not hold well-developed political ambitions for his Gothic studies and designs. He described the architecture of Strawberry Hill as "more the works of fancy than of imitation,"[16] and critical response to his project was and is mixed. When Pugin visited Strawberry Hill he recorded a one-word judgement in his diary: "disgusted."[17] Unlike Pugin, Walpole was not interested in remaking the past. Gothic was an object of study but

---

14 Quoted in Kerry Dean Carso, *American Gothic Art and Architecture in the Age of Romantic Literature* (Cardiff: University of Wales Press, 2014), 65.
15 Quoted in Patrick Snadon, *A.J. Davis and the Gothic Revival Castle in America, 1832–1865,* unpublished PhD Thesis, Cornell University, 1988, 88.
16 Horace Walpole, "To Mary Berry, Friday 17 October 1794," in *Horace Walpole's Correspondence with Mary and Agnes Berry, II,* eds. W.S. Lewis and A. Dayle Wallace, with the assistance of Charles H. Bennet and Edwine M. Martz, *The Yale Edition of the Correspondence of Horace Walpole,* ed. W.S. Lewis, vol. 12 (London: Oxford University Press, 1944), 13. On Pugin, see Rosemary Hill, *God's Architect: Pugin and the Building of Romantic Britain* (London: Allen Lane, 2007).
17 Alexandra Wedgwood, *AWN Pugin and the Pugin Family* (London: Victoria and Albert Museum, 1985), 51.

also a way of generating ideas and feelings that were not necessarily deep or long lasting.[18]

Like Walpole's work, American Gothic architecture was not always about a return to the past and was not always explicitly connected with a well-defined ideological agenda. In 1837, soon after Glen Ellen was completed, Gilmor's architect, Alexander Jackson Davis, published *Rural Residences,* which was both a compendium of Gothic architectural elements and an advertisement of his practice. He celebrated Gothic, what he called the "English collegiate style," not for its historical precedents but for its modest costs and practicality:

> The Greek Temple form, perfect in itself, and well adapted as it is to public edifices, and even to town mansions, is inappropriate for country residences, and yet it is the only style ever attempted in our more costly habitations. The English collegiate style, is for many reasons to be preferred. It admits a greater variety both of plan and outline; — is susceptible of additions from time to time, while its bay windows, oriels, turrets, and chimney shafts, give a pictorial effect to the elevation.[19]

Davis is not concerned with the historical contexts of Gothic, nor even its historical development. He is concerned with effect rather than essence. His Gothic is contemporary.

The Gothic Revival in the United States is bifurcated by the Civil War. What was possibly implicit previously, became explicit afterwards. Glen Ellen captures the latent violence of Ameri-

---

18 For a detailed overview of the development of Gothic in a range of decorative arts see Peter N. Lindfield, *Georgian Gothic: Medievalist Architecture, Furniture and Interiors, 1730–1840* (Woodbridge: The Boydell Press, 2016).

19 Alexander Jackson Davis, *Rural Residences: Consisting of Deigns, Original and Selected, for Cottages, Farm-houses, Villas, and Village Churches with Brief Explanations, Estimates and a Specification of Materials, Construction, etc.* (New York: Dacapo Press, 1980), n.p.

can Gothic eloquently. It is possible to read the history of Glen Ellen's commission and construction as an eccentric and expensive celebration of family heritage, but by the time of the Gilmor family reunion in the summer of 1864, as Harry fought for white supremacy and the preservation and expansion of chattel slavery, innocence or ignorance is not possible. As Harry hugged his family on the steps of their Gothic mansion, the connection between their white European heritage and the enslavement of black people was obvious. Under the logic of American slavery, family was not a right but a privilege held, and withdrawn, by whites. Robert E. Lee, the leader of Gilmor's army, for instance, was an "unsympathetic and demanding master" and broke up enslaved families on his own estate.[20] Glen Ellen's Gothic lines surely generated a sense that the Gilmors' heritage had a deep and lasting meaning. Part of their effect was to move the very production of the Gilmors' identity to the distant past. Glen Ellen's Gothic lines offered an ontological stability to the Gilmors.

In the two decades following the building of Glen Ellen in 1832, the majority of American Gothic architecture was ecclesiastical, with some important exceptions such as the Wadsworth Atheneum. The Smithsonian Institution in Washington, D.C., completed in 1855 by James R. Renwick, Jr., was the first major public building commissioned in the Gothic style and the first substantial Gothic building in the capital (fig. 3). It was only a qualified success and enjoyed a mixed reception upon its completion. In his *North America,* first published in 1862, Anthony Trollope called its style "bastard Gothic"[21] and it remains an anomaly. Today, it stands out as the only Gothic structure on the National Mall.

The beginnings of the Smithsonian Institution are complex. When James Smithson died in 1829 he had never been to the

---

20 Elizabeth Brown Pryor, *Reading the Man: A Portrait of Robert E. Lee through his Private Letters* (New York: Viking, 2007), 145 and 264.
21 Anthony Trollope, *North America* (Harmondsworth: Penguin, 1968), 166. Trollope added that the building was "not ugly in itself" (168).

Figure 3. The Smithsonian Institution, Library of Congress Prints and Photographs Division LC-USZ62-26463 (b&w film copy neg.). https://www.loc.gov/item/cph12156/.

United States and when his nephew died in 1835 to ensure that the bequest was passed on to the US, Congress was unsure how to proceed. The bill that formerly accepted the bequest and established the Institution was only passed in August 1846. Robert Dale Owen, a congressman from Indiana, was instrumental in generating support for the Institution and it was his bill that finally garnered enough votes to pass. Owen then took a place on the Institution's Board of Regents and chaired the Building Committee.

The first proposed design of the building was completed by Robert Mills in 1841 and was in the Gothic style. As he prepared for his Bill to enter Congress, Robert Dale Owen asked his brother David Dale Owen to come up with a new design and enclosed Mills' work which, he wrote, "contains some good hints, though it be incomplete."[22]

In their letters, the brothers record a number of justifications for the necessity of Gothic. None are especially persuasive. Robert Dale Owen suggested to his brother that "[t]he whole should be handsome, but plain, and without unnecessary ornament. I believe that by going back to the pure Norman, with its Saxon arches and simple forms, you may produce something well suited to the purposes in view, and neither commonplace nor over expensive."[23] David Dale Owen offered another rationalisation in his reply, writing that "[c]onsidering, at the same time, the country which gave birth to and cherished, the donor of the bequest, and that our country affords, as yet, few or no marked examples of this oldest English manner, it strikes me that the selection of this style for the Smithsonian Institution is particularly judicious."[24]

Robert Dale Owen provided a more detailed justification of the Smithsonian Institution's form in a book published in 1849, *Hints on Public Architecture*. He wrote about Gothic in aesthetic terms, celebrating "its truth, its candour, its boldness [...] its lofty character, its aspiring lines," but politics is never far away. As he continues: "I like the independence with which it has shaken off the shackles of formal rule, and refused obedience to

---

[22] Robert Dale Owen, "To David Dale Owen, MD, from Robert Dale Owen, New Harmony, (I.A.) August 15 1845," in *Animadversions of the Proceedings of the Regents of the Smithsonian Institution in their choice of an Architect, for their edifice at Washington, founded on observations made during the proceedings, by David Henry Arnot, Architect, prefixed to which is the Act of Congress of the United States of America, incorporating the Institution,* ed. David Arnot (New York: Published for circulation, 1847), 7. This publication, which edited the Owens' correspondence, was published as a result of Arnot's dissatisfaction with the competition to design the Smithsonian building.

[23] Ibid., 8.

[24] David Dale Owen, "To the Hon Robert Dale Owen from David Dale Owen, New Harmony, (I.A.) October 20 1845," in *Animadversions*, 9.

the despotic laws of monotonous repetition."[25] He also repeats Alexander Jackson Davis's language of "flexibility"[26] and presented a comparative analysis of the cost of Greek and Gothic architecture, which proved Gothic to be cheaper.

As with the letters exchanged between Robert and David Dale Owen, the justifications offered in *Hints on Public Architecture* are ultimately unconvincing. Kathleen Curran has offered another explanation that, like the history of Glen Ellen, incorporates family as well as colonial history.

Robert Owen, father of Robert and David, was an entrepreneur, mill owner, utopian socialist and one of the founders of the cooperative movement. In 1825 he used his own funds to purchase a town recently abandoned by George Rapp's Harmony Society in Indiana and renamed it New Harmony. The Harmony Society had settled in 1814, soon after the conclusion of Tecumseh's War that confirmed American possession of the land. The land where Rapp and Owen sited their colonies had been the traditional territory of the Delaware and Shawnee. The Indiana Territory had been established in 1800 and resistance to the white colonizers was sustained.[27] It seems none of this violent history influenced Owen's ambitions, or challenged his conception of justice.[28]

As part of Owen's plans for New Harmony, Thomas Stedman Whitwell produced an architectural vision of the town as it would be. The imagined site is a kind of industrialized monastery, defined by what Kathleen Curran describes as a "medieval-

---

25 Robert Dale Owen, *Hints on Public Architecture, Containing, Among Other Illustrations, Designs and Plans of the Smithsonian Institution* (New York: Putnam, 1849), 63.

26 Ibid., 65.

27 On the settlement of Indiana see Robert M. Owens, *Mr. Jefferson's Hammer: William Henry Harrison and the Origins of American Indian Policy* (Norman: University of Oklahoma Press, 2007). On the history of Indiana see Andrew R.L. Cayton, *Frontier Indiana* (Bloomington: Indiana University Press, 1996).

28 See further Barbara Arneil, *Domestic Colonies: The Turn Inward to Colony* (Oxford: Oxford University Press, 2017), 194–99.

figure 4. "Owen's proposed village." Library of Congress Prints and Photographs Division. LC-USZ62-55096 (b&w film copy neg.). https://www.loc.gov/item/2004673210/.

collegiate character."[29] The complex is set out as a quadrangle, incorporating everything a community might need including dwellings, public buildings, kitchens, baths, gymnasiums, and so on. Gothic detailing abounds: arched doorways, complex patterned tracery, keep-like towers, and, around the site's internal edge, a cloister (fig. 4).[30]

29 Kathleen Curran, *The Romanesque Revival: Religion, Politics, and Transnational Exchange* (University Park: Pennsylvania State University Press, 2003), 242.
30 See further Thomas Stedman Whitwell, *Description of an Architectural Model from a Design by Stedman Whitwell, for a Community Based upon a Principal of United Interests, as Advocated by Robert Owen* (London: Hurst, Chance and Co, 1830). On Robert Owen see Ian Donnachie, *Robert Owen: Owen of New Lanark and New Harmony* (East Linton: Tuckwell Press, 2000), 202–26. On New Harmony see Arthur Bestor, *Backwoods Utopias: The Sectarian and Owenite Phases of Communitarian Socialism in America: 1663–1829* (Philadelphia: University of Pennsylvania Press, 1950), 160–201; Duncan Bowie, *The Radical and Socialist Tradition in British Planning: From Puritan Colonies to Garden Cities* (London: Routledge, 2016); and Anne Taylor, *Visions of Harmony: A Study in Nineteenth-Century Millenarianism* (Oxford: Clarendon Press, 1987).

Curran has made a persuasive case that Whitwell's vision of New Harmony served as an "architectural paradigm in the design development of the Smithsonian Building."[31] The two projects share, as Curran points out, the same approach to education and the same democratic impulse, but all of this is conditioned by their shared use of Gothic forms. While Dale Owen couched his determined used of Gothic in terms of practicality and cost, family history may well have borne a significant influence as well.[32]

The shared formal language between Whitwell's vision of New Harmony and the Smithsonian building reveals the shared interests between utopian thinking and settler colonialism. This is one of the threads that draws together the architecture of the American Gothic Revival, regardless of its precise context. The Gothic architecture of nineteenth-century America tells part of the story of a settler-colonial society importing people, practices and histories while erasing indigenous communities and their histories and cultures.

Confederate Gothic

Until the secession of the southern states in 1861, Jefferson Davis sat on the Smithsonian's Board of Regents. During the war, the first Secretary of the Smithsonian, Joseph Henry, declined to fly the Union flag from the Castle. Although Robert Dale Owen wrote pamphlets in support of emancipation in the later stages of the war, his reputation was clouded by his vote against the

---

31 Curran, *The Romanesque Revival*, 243.
32 See also John F. Sears, "'How the devil it got there': The Politics of Form and Function in the Smithsonian 'Castle,'" in *Public Space and the Ideology of Place in American Culture*, eds. Miles Orvell and Jeffrey L. Meikle (Amsterdam: Rodopi, 2009), 51–80 and Cynthia R. Field, Richard E. Stamm and Heather P. Ewing, *The Castle: An Illustrated History of the Smithsonian Building* (Washington D.C.: Smithsonian Institution Press, 1993).

Wilmot Proviso in 1846, which would have prohibited slavery in new territory acquired by the United States.[33]

As these brief examples demonstrate, in some respects it is easy to overstate the difference between the two sides of the American Civil War as far as attitudes towards race are concerned. The influence of the Smithsonian building is another example of the overlaps in taste between the Union and the Confederates. The influence of Renwick's building on both the Confederate Powder Works and the Lee Chapel is widely acknowledged.

When the Civil War began, Jefferson Davis instructed Colonel George W. Rains to manage the production of gunpowder for the Confederacy. Rains settled on Augusta, Georgia, as the best site to build his Powder Works.[34] There is little evidence that much thought was given to the architectural form of the works but, regardless, the decision was made to build in a castellated Gothic style (fig. 5). In the only study of the Powder Works, Stephanie Jacobs notes the influence of the Smithsonian building, but also suggests that, "The Norman style was probably chosen for one practical reason," which was cost.[35] Jacobs credits Robert Dale Owen's financial analysis of the Gothic in *Hints on Public Architecture* with establishing the economic sense of the

---

33 Kenneth Hafertepe, *America's Castle: The Evolution of the Smithsonian Building and its Institution 1840–1878* (Washington, D.C.: Smithsonian Institution Press, 1984), 78. On the history of enslaved people working at Seneca Quarry, where the stone used to build the Smithsonian building was quarried, see Mark Auslander, "Enslaved Labor and Building the Smithsonian: Reading the Stones," *Southern Spaces*, 2012, https://southernspaces.org/2012/enslaved-labor-and-building-smithsonian-reading-stones.

34 See C.L. Bragg, "An Urgent and Critical Need: The Confederacy's Gunpowder Crisis," in *Never for Want of Powder: The Confederate Powder Works in Augusta, Georgia*, eds. C.L. Bragg et al. (Columbia: University of South Carolina Press, 2007), 1–10.

35 Stephanie A.T. Jacobs, "An Incredible Task," in *Never for Want of Powder*, 31–70, at 36.

Figure 5. Confederate Powder Works, Augusta, GA. Photographed between 1861 and 1865, printed between 1880 and 1889. https://www.loc.gov/item/2014645944/.

style. But the ideological dimensions to the design are undeniable.

It is striking that the language of practicality is threaded through the critical histories of the Smithsonian and the Confederate Powder Works as well as the work of Alexander Jackson Davis and Robert Dale Owen. Arguments about practicality are a well-worn tool against progressive thinking. Indeed, many arguments against the abolition of slavery focused on its impracticality. To take just one example, Robert E. Lee acknowledged that "slavery as an institution, is a moral & political evil in any Country," but also claimed that "[t]he blacks are immeasurably better off here [in the United States] than in Africa" and believed that "[t]heir emancipation will sooner result from the mild & melting influence of Christianity, than the storms & tempests of fiery Controversy."[36] Lee's self-serving fantasies bring to mind what Lucia Stanton has called the "psychological buffers" slaveholders needed to protect themselves "from the realities of owning human beings."[37] Claims about practicality or providence or suggestions like Lee's that "blacks are immeasurably better off here than in Africa" were a means of denying the brutal choices that allowed slavery to exist and enabled whites to profit from it. They were one way in which, to use Eduardo Bonilla-Silva's language, "the ruling ideology [expressed] as 'common sense' the interests of the dominant race."[38] Similarly, to argue for the practicality of Gothic is to deny or disguise, psychologically and politically, the ideological work the form was put to in the US.

Some of the ideological power of Gothic is confirmed by a lament recorded by George Rains following Lee's surrender at Appomattox:

> Sadly I took down the last beloved flag and folded it away; the fires went out in the furnaces; the noise of the mills ceased; one by one the workmen slowly went away, and once more I stood on the banks of the canal alone — all lost save honor.

---

36 The letter is widely discussed. See, for instance, Charles P. Roland, *Reflections on Lee: A Historian's Perspective* (Baton Rouge: Louisiana State University Press, 2003), 17–19.

37 Lucia Stanton, *"Those who Labor for my Happiness": Slavery at Thomas Jefferson's Monticello* (Charlottesville: University of Virginia Press, 2012), 18.

38 Eduardo Bonilla-Silva, *Racism without Racists: Color-Blind Racism and the Persistence of Racial Inequality in America* (Lanham: Rowman and Littlefield, 2017), 9.

> The beautiful buildings have been torn down to build drains and ditches; their ruins mark the spot where they once existed. The tall grand obelisk alone remains, mutely pointing to Heaven amid the surrounding desolation, an emblem of the pure faith and upright hearts of the heroes who died for the Lost Cause. Take it in charge, Confederate Survivors embellish it; consecrate it to their memory, and let it remain undesecrated forever.[39]

As with Early's speech at the Lee Chapel, this is a fine example of the mythmaking of the Lost Cause. Rains recalls the "workmen" walking away but doesn't note whether they were free or enslaved. Enslaved workers were essential to the construction and running of the Confederate Powder Works. After the war, freed people took shelter in the works and later part of the site was converted to a cotton mill. The obelisk that served as the vehicle of Rains's lament is the only surviving element of Powder Works today.[40]

Despite Rains's hopes, it was the Lee Chapel that became the shrine to the Confederacy. The history of the design of the chapel is as unclear as that of the Powder Works. Credit has often been distributed between Lee, his son George Washington Custis Lee and Thomas H. Williamson, an engineer who taught at the Virginia Military Academy. But it is generally accepted now that Williamson did the majority of the work.[41] As with the Powder Works, numerous critics have suggested that the Smithsonian was the dominant context of the design. Pamela Simpson

---

39 George Washington Rains, "Col. Rains' Appeal for the Powder Works Obelisk (n.d.)," quoted by C.L. Bragg and Theodore P. Savas, "The Tall Grand Obelisk Alone Remains: The Confederate Powder Works after the War," in *Never for Want of Powder*, 235–46, at 235–36.
40 See further "Sibley Mill and Confederate Powder Works Chimney," *National Park Service*, https://www.nps.gov/nr/travel/Augusta/sibleymill.html.
41 See, for example, Calder Loth, ed., *The Virginia Landmarks Register* (Charlottesville: University of Virginia Press, 1999), 263.

writes that the Chapel "was probably influenced" by Renwick's work, notes that "Williamson was well aware of" *Hints on Public Architecture* and suggests it is likely Custis Lee knew Owen's book as well.[42] R. David Cox has demonstrated that Owen's book provided the models for the Lee Chapel's windows and spire.[43]

Upon Lee's death, his body lay in state at the Chapel. His funeral took place there as well, and the Chapel was slowly transformed into a memorial to Lee. A mausoleum was constructed in the chapel's basement and Edward Valentine was commissioned to design a monument to Lee. Valentine's work spoke the same medievalist language as the Chapel. The monument he made, known as the "Recumbent Figure," depicts Lee in his military uniform, as if asleep on the battlefield (fig. 6). Although the monument and the other elements of Lee's memorial were managed by a committee, it was claimed that Mary Custis Lee was inspired to commission the tomb after seeing Christian Daniel Rauch's tomb of Queen Louisa of Prussia.[44] Rauch's work is itself a homage to the tomb effigies of late medieval Europe. Lee's tomb therefore forms part of what Alexander Nagel and Christopher Wood have called "a diachronic chain of replicas" that links the Confederate cause to the royal families of Europe and the knights of the Middle Ages.[45]

---

42 Pauline H. Simpson, "The Great Lee Chapel Controversy," in *Monuments to the Lost Cause: Women, Art, and the Landscapes of Southern Memory*, eds. Cynthia Mills and Pamela H. Simpson (Knoxville: The University of Tennessee Press, 2003), 85–99, at 86–87.

43 R. David Cox, *The Lee Chapel at 150: A History* (Buena Vista: Mariner Publishing, 2018), 22 (window) and 29 (spire).

44 *Ceremonies Connected with the Inauguration of the Mausoleum and the Unveiling of the Recumbent Figure of General Robert Edward Lee at Washington and Lee University* (Lynchburg: J.P. Bell & Co, 1883), 5. On the Lee Memorial Association see Wilson, *Baptized in Blood*, 156.

45 Alexander Nagel and Christopher Wood, *Anachronic Renaissance* (New York: Zone Books, 2010), 29–30. On the medieval traditions see, amongst others, H.A. Tummers, *Early Secular Effigies in England* (Leiden: Brill, 1980) and Paul Binski, *Medieval Death* (London: British Museum, 1996).

Figure 6. Recumbent Robert E. Lee, Washington & Lee University, Lexington, Virginia. Library of Congress, Prints & Photographs Division. Photograph by Carol M. Highsmith. LC-DIG-highsm-11812.

The historicizing impulse of the Recumbent Figure approaches the problem of Lee's memory from the opposite direction that Jubal Early adopted in his memorial speech of 1872. While Early claimed Lee had no historical equivalent, Valentine's tomb celebrated Lee as an echo from the past. But these apparently contradictory tactics share a common political purpose. In his study of the medievalist aesthetics of Lee's memorials, Christopher Lawton notes that, "Former Confederates, especially those of Lee's socio-economic background, knew all too well the constant struggle between the humiliating realities of defeat and the unquenchable desire to vindicate their history."[46] There was an urgency, in the immediate aftermath of the war, to take control

---

46 Christopher Lawton, "Constructing the Cause, Bridging the Divide: Lee's Tomb at Washington's College," *Southern Cultures* 15 (2009): 5–39, at 6.

of the narrative of the defeat. As early as March 1866 Lee had written to Early of his desire that "the world shall know what my poor boys, with their small numbers and scant resources, succeeded in accomplishing."[47] Focusing attention on Lee and his "poor boys" allowed supporters to sideline the political aims of the Confederates. Lee was presented, as David Blight puts it, as a "blameless Christian soldier, a paragon of manly virtue and duty who soared above politics."[48] The effect of all this was that the question of slavery was displaced.[49] The complex temporalities of the medievalist imagination were an essential part of this process. Medievalist aesthetics was a means of generating an imprecise sense of historicity. A diversion tactic. Confederate Gothic was a means of not thinking about history.

Gothic Lines

The medievalist aesthetics of Confederate Gothic flow through some of the most horrific episodes of post-Civil War history such as the rise of the Ku Klux Klan and the Knights of the White Camelia.[50] By the twentieth century, Gothic could be read as signifying a kind of transcendent, ontologically stable, whiteness.

One of the reasons for this was the rapid spread of Collegiate Gothic in the last decades of the nineteenth century. For

---

47 "Robert E. Lee to Jubal Early, March 15, 1866," in *Personal Reminiscences, Anecdotes and Letters of Gen. Robert E. Lee*, ed. J. William Jones (New York: D. Appleton & Co., 1875), 180, quoted by Gallagher, "Shaping Public Memory of the Civil War," 41.
48 Blight, *Race and Reunion*, 267.
49 See Gallagher, "Shaping Public Memory of the Civil War," 45.
50 Paul Christopher Anderson, "Rituals of Horsemanship: A Speculation on the Ring Tournament and the Origins of the Ku Klux Klan," in *Weirding the War: Stories from the Civil War's Ragged Edges*, ed. Stephen Berry (Athens: The University of Georgia Press, 2011), 215–33. On the emergence of the Klan see also Elaine Frantz Parsons, *Ku-Klux: The Birth of the Klan During Reconstruction* (Chapel Hill: The University of North Carolina Press, 2015).

example, in 1903, as President of Princeton University, Woodrow Wilson claimed that, "we have added a thousand years to the history of Princeton by merely putting those [Gothic] lines in our buildings." For Wilson, the value of Gothic was that it pointed "every man's imagination to the historical traditions of learning in the English-speaking race." Moreover, the Gothic of Princeton wasn't just about the past. "We have declared and acknowledged our derivation and lineage," Wilson continued, but the Gothic lines also formed a connection with "classes yet to be graduated."[51] For Wilson, Gothic was about preserving the past as a means of fashioning the racial future.[52]

The architect and critic Ralph Adams Cram was more precise than Wilson, writing that Cope and Stewardson's Gothic work at the University of Pennsylvania succeeded in part because it confirmed that "American heroism harks back to English heroism; the blood shed before Manila and on San Juan Hill was the same blood that flowed at Bosworth Field, Flodden, and the Boyne." He wrote that this bloody history meant that "the British base of the design is indispensable, for such were the racial foundations."[53] Shared racial inheritance trumped national borders for Cram, and architecture was an ideal expression of this. Later, Cram wrote that "style is nonsense unless it develops from historical and racial associations."[54] Again, the association

---

51 Woodrow Wilson, "President Wilson's Address," *Princeton Alumni Weekly* 3 (1903): 199–204, at 199–200.
52 On Princeton's Gothic architecture see Johanna G. Seasonwein, *Princeton and the Gothic Revival 1870–1930* (Princeton: Princeton University Art Museum, 2012). On the history of African Americans at Princeton, see April C. Armstrong, "Erased Pasts and Altered Legacies: Princeton's First African American Students," *Princeton & Slavery,* https://slavery.princeton.edu/stories/erased-pasts-and-altered-legacies-princetons-first-african-american-students. For an overview of the history of slavery and the American university see Craig Steven Wilder, *Ebony and Ivy: Race, Slavery, and the Troubled History of America's Universities* (London: Bloomsbury, 2013).
53 Ralph Adams Cram, "The Work of Messrs. Cope and Stewardson," *The Architectural Review* 16 (1905): 407–38, at 417.
54 Cram, *The Gothic Quest,* 157.

is instructive. For Cram, "historical and racial associations" are both an expression and a foundation of Gothic, both a cause and an effect. Another way to phrase Cram's claim would be to state that it is not possible to think about style without thinking about history and race. As with Jubal Early's celebration of Lee, for Cram, Gothic emerges from history but is not only of the past. It is transcendent, even as its historical origins are enumerated. In these American contexts, this generates a sense that whiteness, too, is somehow double: old as well as new, defined by and defining the past and future.

But it wasn't just whites who engaged medievalist culture in the United States. To take one example, in 1871 a Tournament took place in Wilmington, North Carolina. Tournaments in which "knights" jousted and "queens" were crowned were a common element of antebellum culture and a prime symptom of "Sir Walter disease."[55] What distinguished the Wilmington Tournament Association was that it was a Black organization and Matthew X. Vernon has examined the influence of medieval culture on African American thought more broadly.[56] Similarly, it was not only Confederates who adopted medieval forms. The Soldiers' and Sailors' Memorial Arch in Hartford, Connecticut, built in 1886, is one example of Union Gothic (fig. 7). The lines of Gothic are open and reveal traditions and possibilities that undercut the racist fantasies it sometimes served. Still, often, the lines of American Gothic gave shape and succour to otherwise nebulous and changeable ideas of white identity.

There are many other Gothic lines that might be traced, mapping subject-formation, exchange and appropriation across time and space. For example, one of the most significant early

---

55 The Tournament is recorded in *The Daily Journal* (Wilmington, North Carolina) May 2, 1871, Tuesday, 3. See further Eric Foner, *Reconstruction: America's Unfinished Revolution, 1863–1877* (New York: Perennial Classics, 2002), 130 and James L. Roark, *Masters without Slaves: Southern Planters in the Civil War and Reconstruction* (New York: Norton, 1977), 203–4.

56 See Matthew X. Vernon, *The Black Middle Ages: Race and the Construction of the Middle Ages* (Basingstoke: Palgrave Macmillan, 2018).

Figure 7. Soldiers' and Sailors' Memorial Arch, Hartford, Conn. Library of Congress, Prints & Photographs Division, LC-DIG-det-4a17503. http://www.loc.gov/pictures/item/2016809404/.

works of domestic Gothic in America was Edwin Forrest's Fonthill Castle, built in 1852 in the Hudson Valley. Forrest was one of the pre-eminent American actors of his generation and his home was a powerful statement of cultural worth and belonging. It was named for an earlier Gothic home in Britain: William Beckford's Fonthill Abbey. Kerry Dean Carso has excavated this micro-history of transatlantic influence, but it was conditioned by an altogether larger transatlantic phenomenon: the slave trade.⁵⁷ Beckford's architectural ambitions were funded by his family's Jamaican sugar plantations, which were established soon after England's invasion of the island in 1655.⁵⁸ This line of Gothic is intertwined, as Confederate Gothic is, with colonization and enslavement.

Gothic is a transnational and transtemporal form. Its origins are complex and its methods and effects are diverse. It exceeds definition. That was obviously part of its appeal in nineteenth-century America. The flexibility of Gothic, which was so valued by Alexander Jackson Davis and Robert Dale Owen, is a product of its long and complex history. Paradoxically, however, Gothic was used in the United States to generate fantasies of singular, unchanging and unquestionable truths. It was a cog in the wheel of what bell hooks has named the "white capitalist patriarchy."⁵⁹

Conclusion: Overrepresentations

In her essay, "Unsettling the Coloniality of Being/Power/Truth/Freedom," Sylvia Wynter offered the insight that "[m]an [...] overrepresents itself as if it were the human itself."⁶⁰ It barely needs to be said the European Middle Ages has been and continues to be overrepresented as white and male. To phrase the point slightly differently would be to suggest that the white man has overrepresented itself as if its medieval heritage was unique

---

57 Carso, *American Gothic Art and Architecture*, 115–44. On Fonthill Abbey see Caroline Dakers, ed., *Fonthill Recovered: A Cultural History* (London: UCL Press, 2018).

58 See, for instance, the Beckford family entries in the *Oxford Dictionary of National Biography*, beginning with, Sheridan, Richard B. 2004 "Beckford, Peter (bap. 1643, d. 1710), planter in Jamaica and politician." *Oxford Dictionary of National Biography*, June 1, 2019, https://www.oxforddnb.com/view/10.1093/ref:odnb/9780198614128.001.0001/odnb-9780198614128-e-50424.

59 bell hooks, *Ain't I a Woman: Black Women and Feminism* (New York: Routledge, 2015), 145.

60 Sylvia Wynter, "Unsettling the Coloniality of Being/Power/Truth/Freedom," CR: *The New Centennial Review* 3 (2003): 257–337, at 260.

and uniquely valuable. Viewed from this perspective, there is no way to disentangle the scholarly history of medieval studies from the history of popular representations of the medieval past. Confederate Gothic is an important part of both those histories.

This overrepresentation is part of the reason why white supremacists marching in Charlottesville in August 2017 can adopt the standard of St Maurice, or at least an image that very closely resembles it: because of their lack of historical understanding but also because of the apparently common sense connection between the Middle Ages and whiteness.[61] The history of Confederate Gothic forms part of the history of how that common sense connection was produced. Those white supremacists in Charlottesville were after all marching to a route determined by the site of a statue of Robert E. Lee.

The aesthetic pleasures of the Gothic are not neutral. The affective charge generated by the Gothic is not neutral. That does not mean that it should be ignored. An alternative method is suggested by an event in Charleston in the immediate aftermath of the Civil War.

The Union Army took Charleston on February 18 1865. On March 21, a parade took place in the city to mark the defeat of the Confederacy and the end of slavery, even though it was still three weeks before Lee's surrender at Appomattox. Thousands of the city's black population gathered at the Citadel Green, which is now named Marion Square, and took a route round the city to the waterfront before returning to the green. As Ethan Kytle and Blain Roberts write:

> It was a scene laden with irony. For decades the park had served as a parade ground for the adjacent South Carolina Military Academy, also known as the Citadel. But now the

---

61 See Josephine Livingstone, "Racism, Medievalism, and the White Supremacists of Charlottesville," *The New Republic,* August 15, 2017, https://newrepublic.com/article/144320/racism-medievalism-white-supremacists-charlottesville and @medievalpoc, *Twitter,* August 14, 2017, 8:47 AM, https://twitter.com/medievalpoc/status/897122421353918464.

Figure 8. Charleston, SC. The Citadel seen across Marion Square, April 1865. Library of Congress Prints and Photographs Division. LC-B811-3113 [P&P]. https://www.loc.gov/pictures/item/2018666930/.

square where white cadets charged with protecting the city against slave insurrection had conducted public exercises became the gathering point for a parade of black Union soldiers and countless African Americans.[62]

The Green where the rally gathered stood in the shadow of the Gothic form of the Citadel, a large, squat, fort-like, castellated

---

62 Ethan Kytle and Blain Roberts, *Denmark Vesey's Garden: A 150-year Reckoning with America's Original Sin* (New York: The New Press, 2018), 42.

structure with turrets enclosing a rounded arch entryway (fig. 8). This piece of American Gothic had been built in the 1820s in the aftermath of the rebellion led by Denmark Vesey. It had originally housed the State Arsenal. From 1842 it was occupied by the South Carolina Military Academy.[63]

As part of the parade, a variety of re-enactments were performed, among them a mock slave auction and coffle. The parts of the enslaved were played by those whose freedom had been established with Union victory. Other freed people in the crowd which lined the street were invited to bid. It was too much for some. James Redpath, a reporter for the *New-York Tribune,* recorded that some observers "burst into tears as they saw this tableau."[64] As Mark Auslander writes, however, the performance seems to have occasioned "a kind of metamorphosis, transmuting a tragic all-too-recent memory into a dramatic and comedic vignette."[65] It appears to have been a cathartic, communal event that centred and respected personal experience, that offered a means of moving on without forgetting the past. The performance provides a model for anyone who wants to work with the past without repeating it, a model which privileges community, inclusivity and the transformative potential of the historical imagination while acknowledging individuals' different histories and biographies.

There is a striking discordance between the mock medieval form of the Citadel and the mock horrors performed in the street. The building and parade offer two types of historical performance and two models of historical engagement: one in

---

63 See "National Register Properties in South Carolina: South Carolina State Arsenal, Charleston County (2 Tobacco St., Marion Square, Charleston)," *South Carolina Department of Archives and History,* http://www.nationalregister.sc.gov/charleston/S10817710017/index.htm.
64 James Redpath, "From South Carolina. Grand Procession of Colored Loyalists," *New-York Tribune,* April 4, 1865, quoted by Kytle and Roberts, *Denmark Vesey's Garden,* 43.
65 Mark Auslander, "Touching the Past: Materializing Time in Traumatic 'Living History' Reenactments," *Signs and Society* 1 (2013): 161–83, at 167.

stone, the other in flesh; one repeating historical forms in order to justify contemporary horrors, the other horrifyingly contemporary but designed to initiate a sense of pastness; one desiring replication, the other change; one predicated on similarity, the other difference; one a relic of a racist past, the other a means of beginning a radical future.

Bibliography

Abrams, Annie. "'The Miserable Slaves, the Degraded Serfs': Frederick Douglass, Anglo-Saxonism, and the Mexican War," *postmedieval: A Journal of Medieval Cultural Studies* 10 (2019): 151–61. DOI: 10.1057/s41280-019-00121-3.

Anderson, Paul Christopher. "Rituals of Horsemanship: A Speculation on the Ring Tournament and the Origins of the Ku Klux Klan." In *Weirding the War: Stories from the Civil War's Ragged Edges,* edited by Stephen Berry, 215–33. Athens: The University of Georgia Press, 2011.

Armstrong, April C. "Erased Pasts and Altered Legacies: Princeton's First African American Students." *Princeton & Slavery.* https://slavery.princeton.edu/stories/erased-pasts-and-altered-legacies-princetons-first-african-american-students.

Arneil, Barbara. *Domestic Colonies: The Turn Inward to Colony.* Oxford: Oxford University Press, 2017.

Arnot, David, ed. *Animadversions of the Proceedings of the Regents of the Smithsonian Institution in their choice of an Architect, for their edifice at Washington, founded on observations made during the proceedings, by David Henry Arnot, Architect, prefixed to which is the Act of Congress of the United States of America, incorporating the Institution.* New York: Published for circulation, 1847.

Auslander, Mark. "Touching the Past: Materializing Time in Traumatic 'Living History' Reenactments." *Signs and Society* 1 (2013): 161–83. DOI: 10.1086/670167.

———. "Enslaved Labor and Building the Smithsonian: Reading the Stones." *Southern Spaces*, 2012. https://southernspaces.org/2012/enslaved-labor-and-building-smithsonian-reading-stones.

Bestor, Arthur. *Backwoods Utopias: The Sectarian and Owenite Phases of Communitarian Socialism in America: 1663–1829.* Philadelphia: University of Pennsylvania Press, 1950.

Binski, Paul. *Medieval Death.* London: British Museum, 1996.

Blight, David W. *Race and Reunion: The Civil War in American Memory.* Cambridge: Harvard University Press, 2001.

Bond, Christiana "Recollections of General Robert E. Lee." *South Atlantic Quarterly* 24 (1925): 333–48.

Bowie, Duncan. *The Radical and Socialist Tradition in British Planning: From Puritan Colonies to Garden Cities.* London: Routledge, 2016.

Bragg, C.L., et. al. *Never for Want of Powder: The Confederate Powder Works in Augusta, Georgia.* Columbia: University of South Carolina Press, 2007.

Carso, Kerry Dean. *American Gothic Art and Architecture in the Age of Romantic Literature.* Cardiff: University of Wales Press, 2014.

Cayton, Andrew R.L. *Frontier Indiana.* Bloomington: Indiana University Press, 1996.

Ceremonies Connected with the Inauguration of the Mausoleum and the Unveiling of the Recumbent Figure of General Robert Edward Lee at Washington and Lee University. Lynchburg: J.P. Bell & Co, 1883.

Cox, R. David. *The Lee Chapel at 150: A History.* Buena Vista: Mariner Publishing, 2018.

Cram, Ralph Adams. "The Work of Messrs. Cope and Stewardson." *The Architectural Review* 16 (1905): 407–38.

———. *The Gothic Quest.* Garden City: Doubleday, Page and Co., 1915.

Crooks, Esther J., and Ruth W. Crooks. *The Ring Tournament in the United States.* Richmond: Garrett and Massie, 1936.

Dakers, Caroline, ed. *Fonthill Recovered: A Cultural History.* London: UCL Press, 2018.

Davies, Joshua. "Hengist and Horsa at Monticello: Human and Nonhuman Migration, Parahistory and American Anglo-Saxonism." In *American/Medieval Goes North: Earth and Water in Transit,* edited by Gillian R. Overing and Ulrike Wiethaus, 167–88. Göttingen: V&R Unipress, 2019.

Davis, Alexander Jackson. *Rural Residences: Consisting of Designs, Original and selected, for Cottages, Farm-houses, Villas, and Village Churches with Brief Explanations,*

Estimates and a Specification of Materials, Construction, etc. New York: Dacapo Press, 1980.

Donnachie, Ian. *Robert Owen: Owen of New Lanark and New Harmony.* East Linton: Tuckwell Press, 2000.

Early, Jubal. *The Campaigns of Gen. Robert E. Lee: An Address by Lt. Gen. Jubal A. Early, before Washington and Lee University, January 19th, 1872.* Baltimore: J. Murphy, 1872.

Emery, Elizabeth. "Postcolonial Gothic: The Medievalism of America's 'National' Cathedrals." In *Medievalisms in the Postcolonial Word: The Idea of "the Middle Ages" outside Europe,* edited by Kathleen Davis and Nadia Altschul, 237–64. Baltimore: The Johns Hopkins University Press, 2009.

Field, Cynthia R., Richard E. Stamm, and Heather P. Ewing. *The Castle: An Illustrated History of the Smithsonian Building.* Washington, D.C.: Smithsonian Institution Press, 1993.

Fleming, Robin. "Picturesque History and the Medieval in Nineteenth-century America." *The American Historical Review* 100 (1995): 1061–94. DOI: 10.2307/2168201.

Foner, Eric. *Reconstruction: America's Unfinished Revolution, 1863–1877.* New York: Perennial Classics, 2002.

Foster, Gaines M. *Ghosts of the Confederacy: Defeat, the Lost Cause, and the Emergence of the New South 1865 to 1913.* Oxford: Oxford University Press, 1987.

Frantzen, Allen J. *Desire for Origins: Old English, New Language, and Teaching the Tradition.* New Brunswick: Rutgers University Press, 1990.

Gallagher, Gary W. "Shaping Public Memory of the Civil War: Robert E. Lee, Jubal Early, and Douglas Southall Freeman." In *The Memory of the Civil War in American Culture,* edited by Alice Fahs and Joan Waugh, 39–63. Chapel Hill: The University of North Carolina Press, 2004.

Gilmor, Harry. *Four Years in the Saddle.* New York: Harper, 1866.

Hafertepe, Kenneth. *America's Castle: The Evolution of the Smithsonian Building and its Institution 1840–1878.* Washington, D.C.: Smithsonian Institution Press, 1984.

Hauer, Stanley R. "Thomas Jefferson and the Anglo-Saxon Language." PMLA 98 (October 1983): 879–98.

Hill, Rosemary. *God's Architect: Pugin and the Building of Romantic Britain.* London: Allen Lane, 2007.

hooks, bell. *Ain't I a Woman: Black Women and Feminism.* New York: Routledge, 2015.

Jones, J. William, ed. *Personal Reminiscences, Anecdotes and Letters of Gen. Robert E. Lee.* New York: D. Appleton & Co., 1875.

Kaufman, Amy. "Purity." In *Medievalism: Key Critical Terms,* edited by Elizabeth Emery and Richard Utz, 199–206. Cambridge: D.S. Brewer, 2014.

Kytle, Ethan, and Blain Roberts. *Denmark Vesey's Garden: A 150-year Reckoning with America's Original Sin.* New York: The New Press, 2018.

Lawton, Christopher. "Constructing the Cause, Bridging the Divide: Lee's Tomb at Washington's College." *Southern Cultures* 15 (2009): 5–39. DOI: 10.1353/scu.0.0059.

Lewis, W.S., ed. *Horace Walpole's Correspondence with Mary and Agnes Berry, II,* edited by W.S. Lewis and A. Dayle Wallace, with the assistance of Charles H. Bennet and Edwine M. Martz, *The Yale Edition of the Correspondence of Horace Walpole,* Volume 12. London: Oxford University Press, 1944.

Lindfield, Peter N. *Georgian Gothic: Medievalist Architecture, Furniture and Interiors, 1730–1840.* Woodbridge: The Boydell Press, 2016.

Loth, Calder, ed. *The Virginia Landmarks Register.* Charlottesville: University of Virginia Press, 1999.

Livingstone, Josephine. "Racism, Medievalism, and the White Supremacists of Charlottesville." *The New Republic,* August 15, 2017.

@medievalpoc. *Twitter,* August 14, 2017, 8:47AM. https://twitter.com/medievalpoc/status/897122421353918464.

Nagel, Alexander, and Christopher Wood. *Anachronic Renaissance.* New York: Zone Books, 2010.

"National Register Properties in South Carolina: South Carolina State Arsenal, Charleston County (2 Tobacco St., Marion Square, Charleston)." *South Carolina Department of Archives and History.* http://www.nationalregister.sc.gov/charleston/S10817710017/index.htm.

Overing, Gillian R., and Ulrike Wiethaus, eds. *American/Medieval: Nature and Mind in Cultural Transfer.* Göttingen: V&R Unipress, 2016.

Owen, Robert Dale. *Hints on Public Architecture, Containing, Among Other Illustrations, Designs and Plans of the Smithsonian Institution.* New York: Putnam, 1849.

Owens, Robert M. *Mr. Jefferson's Hammer: William Henry Harrison and the Origins of American Indian Policy.* Norman: University of Oklahoma Press, 2007.

Page, Thomas Nelson. *Robert E. Lee, Man and Soldier.* New York: Charles Scribner's Sons, 1911.

Parsons, Elaine Frantz. *Ku-Klux: The Birth of the Klan During Reconstruction.* Chapel Hill: The University of North Carolina Press, 2015.

Pryor, Elizabeth Brown. *Reading the Man: A Portrait of Robert E. Lee through his Private Letters.* New York: Viking, 2007.

Pugh, Tison. *Queer Chivalry: Medievalism and the Myth of White Masculinity in Southern Literature.* Baton Rouge: Louisiana University Press, 2013.

Redpath, James. "From South Carolina. Grand Procession of Colored Loyalists." *New York Tribune,* April 4, 1865.

Roark, James L. *Masters without Slaves: Southern Planters in the Civil War and Reconstruction.* New York: Norton, 1977.

Roland, Charles P. *Reflections on Lee: A Historian's Perspective.* Baton Rouge: Louisiana State University Press, 2003.

Sears, John F. "'How the devil it got there': The Politics of Form and Function in the Smithsonian 'Castle.'" In *Public Space and the Ideology of Place in American Culture,* edited by Miles Orvell and Jeffrey L. Meikle, 51–80. Amsterdam: Rodopi, 2009.

Seasonwein, Johanna G. *Princeton and the Gothic Revival 1870–1930.* Princeton: Princeton University Art Museum, 2012.

"Sibley Mill and Confederate Powder Works Chimney." *National Park Service*. https://www.nps.gov/nr/travel/Augusta/sibleymill.html.

Simpson, Pauline H. "The Great Lee Chapel Controversy." In *Monuments to the Lost Cause: Women, Art, and the Landscapes of Southern Memory,* edited by Cynthia Mills and Pamela H. Simpson, 85–99. Knoxville: The University of Tennessee Press, 2003.

Snadon, Patrick. *A.J. Davis and the Gothic Revival Castle in America, 1832–1865,* unpublished PhD Thesis, Cornell University, 1988.

———. "Gothic Revival Architecture." *The New Encyclopaedia of Southern Culture Volume 21: Art and Architecture,* 95–102. Chapel Hill: University of North Carolina Press, 2013.

Stanton, Lucia. *"Those who Labor for my Happiness": Slavery at Thomas Jefferson's Monticello.* Charlottesville: University of Virginia Press, 2012.

Taylor, Anne. *Visions of Harmony: A Study in Nineteenth-Century Millenarianism.* Oxford: Clarendon Press, 1987.

The Daily Journal (Wilmington, North Carolina) May 2, 1871, Tuesday, 3.

Trollope, Anthony. *North America.* Harmondsworth: Penguin, 1968.

Tummers, H.A. *Early Secular Effigies in England.* Leiden: Brill, 1980.

Twain, Mark. *Life on the Mississippi.* Boston: J.R. Osgood & Co, 1883.

VanHoosier-Carey, Gregory A. "Byrhtnoth in Dixie: The Emergence of Anglo-Saxon Studies in the Postbellum South." In *Anglo-Saxonism and the Construction of Social Identity,* edited by Allen J. Frantzen and John Niles, 157–72. Gainesville: University of Florida Press, 1997.

Wedgwood, Alexandra. *AWN Pugin and the Pugin Family.* London: Victoria and Albert Museum, 1985.

Whitwell, Thomas Stedman. *Description of an Architectural Model from a Design by Stedman Whitwell, for a Community*

Based upon a Principal of United Interests, as Advocated by Robert Owen. London: Hurst, Chance and Co, 1830.

Wilder, Craig Steven. *Ebony and Ivy: Race, Slavery, and the Troubled History of America's Universities*. London: Bloomsbury, 2013.

Wilson, Charles Reagan. *Baptized in Blood: The Religion of the Lost Cause, 1865–1920*. Athens: The University of Georgia Press, 1980.

Wilson, Woodrow. "President Wilson's Address." *Princeton Alumni Weekly* 3 (1903): 199–204.

Wynter, Sylvia. "Unsettling the Coloniality of Being/Power/Truth/Freedom." cr: *The New Centennial Review* 3 (2003): 257–337. DOI: 10.1353/ncr.2004.0015.

7

"Die, defenceless, primitive natives!": Colonialism, Gender, and Militarism in *The Legacy of Heorot*

Alison Elizabeth Killilea

Introduction

According to Marijane Osborn's "Annotated List of *Beowulf* Translations," over one hundred full translations of the poem have appeared since the 1800s, and at least the same number of adaptations, ranging from novels to operas, have appeared since the second half of the nineteenth century. The popularization of the poem in the Victorian era, beginning with Turner's interpretation of a number of passages in 1805 and the first full translation into English by Kemble in 1837, is intrinsically linked to the rise of British nationalism during its "imperial century" and the search for an exclusively English national epic. This Romantic nationalism which spurred interest in the poem shows evidence in numerous of its translations and adaptations, some of which obsessively stress the "Anglo-Saxons" as "our ancestors" (as repeated throughout Conybeare's translation) or use the poem as a didactic piece in which Britain's colonial pursuits are justified (as seen in H.E. Marshall's retelling).[1] While the use of *Beowulf* as a means to promote problematic aspects of English heritage has long been challenged, the topic of colonialism and genocide, especially in adaptations of the poem, has proven to be somewhat challenging.

While the issues of colonialism and genocide are challenged in some later translations and adaptations (Gardner's *Grendel,* Gunnarsson's *Beowulf and Grendel,* and Heaney's translation of *Beowulf*) and the question of gender roles has been a growing focus since the 1970s, one adaptation stands out as being particularly problematic in these areas. *The Legacy of Heorot,* a science fiction novel written by Larry Niven, Jerry Pournelle, and Steven Barnes in 1987, appears to promote a system of ideologies echoing those in early retellings of the poem, including the pro-imperialistic justification of colonialism, the celebration of female passivity, and the triumphalism of war.

As with all adaptation, "like the work it adapts, [it] is always framed in a context — a time and a place, a society and a culture; it does not exist in a vacuum."[2] *The Legacy of Heorot* is no different here; it uses *Beowulf* as a blueprint on which to lay out fears and desires of its own cultural and historical context. This chapter aims to show how this retelling of *Beowulf,* and its justification of imperialism, machoism, and militarism, is not only an attempt to rehash the story for a modern audience, but the ideologies it expresses are intrinsically shaped by the zeitgeist of the Reagan era, the cultural context of the time, and the personal political leanings of the authors. Through a comparison of the problematic aspects of the novel to sentiments expressed in Victorian retellings of *Beowulf,* this chapter also aims to highlight the common areas of misappropriation by conservative

---

1   The use of the term "Anglo-Saxon" has in recent months come under critical scrutiny due to its historical use in white supremacist discourse, both in the UK and the US. In this chapter, the use of the term "Anglo-Saxon" is reserved only where it is tied intrinsically to nationalistic identities, and were it is referring to an imagined and imaginary past.
2   Linda Hutcheon, *A Theory of Adaptation* (London: Routledge, 2015), 142.

and right-wing groups so that current and future misuses of the poem (and the medieval) may be more easily identified and tackled.

The Legacy of Heorot

Written during the conservative Reagan era, *The Legacy of Heorot* focuses on the colonization of the seemingly ideal "Avalon" and the colonists' eventual struggles with the indigenous "grendels," reptilian-type creatures who prove to be deadly predators for the humans. While the novel may appear and is often treated as an escapist piece with little substance, it is important to reconsider the traditional dismissal of the science fiction genre, one which Spinrad claims is "an ignorant dismissal that has never developed a comprehensive or remotely intelligible overview of what is actually being written."[3] As Le Guin argues, "science fiction is not predictive; it is descriptive,"[4] its narratives of distant futures closely echoing those of the past and present. Through the use of cognitive estrangement (to use Darko Suvin's terms), we are able to consider societal concerns from a distance, and thus, anew; "Sf is not about the future; it uses the future as a narrative convention to present distortions of the present."[5] An example of such "descriptive" rather than "predictive" science fiction writing, to use Le Guin's terms, is seen in one of the most important works of the genre, *The War of the Worlds* by H.G. Wells; written at a time when the British Empire had colonized dozens of territories throughout the world, Wells's novel "asks his English readers to compare the Martian invasion of Earth with the Europeans' genocidal invasion of the Tasmanians, thus demanding that the colonizers imagine themselves as the colo-

---

3   Norman Spinrad, *Science Fiction in the Real World* (Carbondale: Southern Illinois University Press, 1990), 8.
4   Ursula K. Le Guin, "Introduction to the Left Hand of Darkness," in *The Language of the Night: Essays on Fantasy and Science Fiction* (Berkley: Berkley Books, 1979), 155–59, at 156.
5   Samuel R. Delany, *Starboard Wine* (New York: Dragon Press, 1984), 48.

nized, or the about-to-be-colonized."⁶ As with countless science fiction works that came beforehand, *The Legacy of Heorot* uses a possible and distant future to promote its ideological beliefs, albeit ones that prove unsurprisingly problematic, coming from two (Niven and Pournelle) of science fiction's most influential right-wing authors.⁷

The ideological intent behind the novel is expressed through a retelling of events surrounding the taking of the western frontier, albeit further retold through the lens of science fiction. As Abbott notes, the novel is one which explores the "Western American Past in the Human Future,"⁸ a science fiction trope popularised by Ray Bradbury (*The Martian Chronicles*) and Robert A. Heinlein (*Farmer in the Sky*) in the 1950s, where the American tradition of homesteading is explored in an extraterrestrial setting. In short, *The Legacy of Heorot*, as with much first-contact and colonial based science fiction, is a frontier novel, the plains of the western Americas substituted for those of Camelot island on the fourth planet of Tau Ceti. As Abbott notes:

> Because these stories of the West are so powerful in the American imagination, they echo and re-echo in imaginative writing about the future [...]. Because the imagery and mythology of the western frontier so pervade American culture, science fiction repeatedly internalizes the stories that Americans tell about the development of the West and writes them forward for places and times yet unknown.⁹

---

6   John Rieder, *Colonialism and the Emergence of Science Fiction* (Middletown: Wesleyan University Press, 2008), 5.
7   African-American author Steven Barnes, speaking of his collaborations with Niven and Pournelle has noted that he "had some pretty profound differences with both Larry and Jerry politically [...] [I]t was sort of like going incognito into the enemy camp" (Greg Beatty, "Interview: Steven Barnes," *Strange Horizons*, July 29, 2002, http://strangehorizons.com/nonfiction/articles/interview-steven-barnes/).
8   Carl Abbot, "Homesteading on the Extraterrestrial Front," *Science Fiction Studies* 32, no. 2 (2005): 240–64, at 243.
9   Ibid.

Of course, *The Legacy of Heorot* not only casts forward the story of the western frontier into the far off reaches of the future, it simultaneously moulds it into the early medieval story of *Beowulf,* as well as making numerous other allusions to British literary history, notably Arthurian legend. It is here that we see the first, most basic commonalities between the novel and the medieval revivalist literature of late eighteenth- and early nineteenth-century Britain, which was intrinsically linked to the rise of conservatism and nationalism during Britain's "imperial century."[10] *Beowulf* itself is at the core of this debate, and as Nokes states, "claims upon *Beowulf* have often served as proxies for claims on national identity, whether English or otherwise."[11] As with much medieval and folkloric literature throughout the world, works of the Anglo-Saxon tradition were used to legitimize British identity and, therefore, are vulnerable to being used as propagandist pieces when it comes to the ideas of racial and cultural superiority and colonialism.

Zafirovski argues that the conservatism of British medievalism "has subsequently and enduringly [...] been rediscovered and even become a sort of retrieved and perennial model [...] for American conservatism" and that the "'new nation' has become, by the 21st century [...] more politically and cultur-

---

10 The roots of Victorian medievalism appear varied, but a likely origin appears with the poets of the Age of Transition, who were "disgusted with the excesses of neo-classical traditions prevalent in that age [i.e., The Enlightenment]" and who "sought inspiration in the past." See R.R. Agrawal, *The Medieval Revival and its Influences on the Romantic Movement* (New Delhi: Abhinav Publications, 1990), vii. From a political and sociological point of view, Zafirovski makes a similar contention, arguing that "medieval traditionalism" arose from the social-historical situation of the Enlightenment and the French Revolution and the attempt to "return to what [Mannheim] describes as the 'security of a dead past.'" See Milan Zafirovski, "Contemporary Conservatism and Medievalism: 'Nothing New under the Sun'?" *Social Science Information* 50, no. 2 (2011): 223–50, at 230.
11 Richard Scott Nokes, "*Beowulf: Prince of the Geats,* Nazis, Odinists", *Old English Newsletter* 41, no. 3 (2008), http://www.oenewsletter.org/OEN/print.php/essays/nokes41_3/Array.

ally polarized, more traditionalist, religious, fundamentalist or theocratic than the 'Old World'."[12] Just as the British turned to the Anglo-Saxons in their desire to understand their perceived ancestral origins, so too did White Americans in America.

Through early influential figures like Thomas Jefferson, the Anglo-Saxon past became an integral part of US national identity, and thus, the study of early medieval literature and Old English was used to strengthen belief in national destiny,[13] much in the same way as it was used in Britain. Horsman argues that the idea of Anglo-Saxon superiority was especially well-embraced in an America that had engaged in war with Native American peoples and enslaved people of color,[14] and as with figures like Scott, Byron, and Morris in Britain, early medieval English literature saw a similar romanticization in the States during the mid-1800s with, for example, poets like Henry Longfellow, who recommended Old English as "a moral corrective against the affectation of foreign fashion."[15] These racial ideas of superiority continued, and arguably strengthened, after the American Civil War; as Kaufman states, the emancipation and social and political progression of the Black population, along with the push for women's suffrage, were central in the creation of the Ku Klux Klan in 1865. With the threat to the long-standing hierarchy of race and gender, "the myth of a white, patriarchal Middle Ages became a fantasy and a refuge."[16] The appropriation of (an imagined and mythological) medieval imagery has characterized the KKK from their foundation through to their numerous eras and offshoots and is also a feature of more recent hate groups

---

12 Zafirovski, "Contemporary Conservatism and Medievalism" 229, 235.
13 Maria Jóse Mora and Maria José Gómez-Calderón, "The Study of Old English in America (1776–1850): National Uses of the Saxon Past," *The Journal of English and Germanic Philology* 97, no. 3 (1998): 322–36, at 322.
14 Reginald Horsman, *Race and Manifest Destiny: The Origins of American Racial Anglo-Saxonism* (Cambridge: Harvard University Press, 1981), 100.
15 Mora and Gómez-Calderón, "The Study of Old English in America," 327.
16 Amy Kaufman, "The Birth of a National Disgrace: Medievalism and the KKK," *The Public Medievalist*, November 21, 2008, https://www.publicmedievalist.com/birth-national-disgrace/.

across America and Europe. Examples can be seen in the Finnish anti-immigrant group "Soldiers of Odin," the Virginia-based "Wolves of Vinland," and, of course, in the runic insignia of the Schutzstaffel which were based on mysticist Guido von Lists's Armanen runes, the supposed "primeval system from which all other runic systems were derived," but which are closely based on the Younger Futhark runic system.[17]

In common with the misappropriation of the Middle Ages from the end of the Enlightenment to the present day, *The Legacy of Heorot* appropriates medieval imagery in a way that glorifies a mythological, rather than historical, past as a means to purport a certain ideology of supposed racial superiority. The novel is laced with allusions to British literary history; the maps contained in the first number of pages reveal the colonized planet is named Avalon after the legendary island of the Arthurian mythos, while the occupied island is named Camelot after Arthur's court; the protagonist's name — Cadmann Weyland — evokes both the first English poet Cædmon (as attested in Bede's *Historia ecclesiastica* at least), as well as the legendary smith of Germanic tradition, Wayland,[18] and indeed, many of the chapter epigraphs contain quotations from British authors and poets, many from the Victorian literary tradition, as well as numerous biblical quotations. Interestingly, while the tale of colonial voyage is told through the lens of *Beowulf* (as well as the story of the western frontier), the novel makes numerous self-conscious allusions to the poem, firstly in its decision to name

---

17 Mark McGlashan, "The Branding of European Nationalism: Perpetuation and Novelty in Racist Symbolism," in *Analysing Fascist Discourse: European Fascism in Talk and Text*, eds. Ruth Wodak and John E. Richardson (New York: Routledge, 2013), 297–314, at 303.

18 Cadmann's surname may also refer to the Weyland-Yutani Corporation of the *Alien* franchise, with which the novel shares numerous similarities. There is no evidence to suggest that *Alien* writers Dan O'Bannon and Ronald Shusett were referencing Wayland the Smith, however.

the native creatures "grendels" after "the old legend," and later in Cadmann's inheritance of the moniker "Beowulf."[19]

Because of *The Legacy of Heorot*'s dual status as *Beowulf* adaptation and western frontier novel, it is possible to read the grendels, the creatures native to Avalon, as a physical manifestation of the wild lands the pioneers would have to tame, or perhaps, more specifically, the Native Americans who inhabited those lands. While this is never expressly stated, the bafflingly unironic war-cry of "Die, defenceless, primitive natives!"[20] combined with similarly racist overtones in the authors' earlier works,[21] and the historical tendency of colonizing nations to construe the oppressed in certain terms, lends plausibility to this theory.

While traces of sympathy towards the grendels are discernible in the first few chapters, any compassion towards the creatures is overwhelmed by their overtly monstrous characterization as blood-thirsty reptiles whose victims include a young baby. As critical theorist Homi Bhaba notes, it is typical of the colonizing nation "to construe the colonized as a popula-

---

19 Larry Niven, Jerry Pournelle, and Steven Barnes, *The Legacy of Heorot* (London: Sphere Books, 1988), 224 and 255. This moment in the novel reflects the ignorance (whether or not on the authors' parts) surrounding *Beowulf* and its detachment from later medieval tradition, as one of the characters states that Cadmann is "sometimes *yclept* Beowulf" (emphasis my own).
20 Ibid., 323.
21 Pournelle and Niven's 1977 novel *Lucifer's Hammer* is so aggressively conservative and racist that it almost borders on satire. The novel describes a majority white stronghold which is attacked by a cannibalistic group made up of environmentalists and socialists, led by two Black men, presumably some of the "city niggers, whining about equality," referenced earlier in the novel. Niven himself is also on record as telling a Department of Homeland Security conference in 2008 that "the problem [of hospitals going broke] is hugely exaggerated by illegal aliens who aren't going to pay for anything anyway," and suggested the spread of rumours in the Latino community that hospitals in the US were killing patients to harvest organs (Stew Magnuson, "Science Fiction Mavens Offer Far Out Homeland Security Advice," *National Defense Magazine*, March 1, 2018, http://www.nationaldefensemagazine.org/articles/2008/2/29/2008march-science-fiction-mavens-offer-far-out-homeland-security-advice).

tion of degenerate types on the basis of racial origin, in order to justify conquest and to establish systems of administration and instruction."[22] As a means to justify the conquest of Ireland, for example, English discourse needed to demonstrate that the Irish were a savage and backwards people; Andrew Trollope, the early Tudor propogandist, stated that the Irish were "not [...] human creatures, but heathen or rather savage and brute beasts," sentiments which were later echoed by Charles Kingsley in 1861 describing the Irish as "human chimpanzees."[23] This discourse is not restricted to Irish history of course, and as Canny notes, "we find the colonists in the New World using the same pretexts for the extermination of the Indians as their counterparts had used in the 1560s and 1570s for the slaughter of numbers of the Irish."[24] As in Ireland, the colonizers of the "New World" first claimed that reformation of the Native Americans was their primary mission; however, this notion was abandoned and the colonized were quickly described in brutish terms in order to justify the mass slaughter that ensued.[25] We can see a parallel to this in *The Legacy of Heorot,* where both the protagonist, Cadmann Weyland, and the authors quickly abandon any real moral

---

22 Homi Bhabha, "The Other Question: Difference, Discrimination and the Discourse of Colonialism," in *Out There: Marginalization and Contemporary Culture*, eds. Russell Ferguson et al. (Cambridge: MIT Press, 1990), 71–88, at 75.
23 Trollope, qtd. in Elsie B. Michie, *Outside the Pale: Cultural Exclusion, Gender Difference, and the Victorian Woman Writer* (Ithaca: Cornell University Press, 1993), 93, and Kingsley qtd. in Nicholas Canny, *Making Ireland British: 1580–1650* (Oxford: Oxford University Press, 2001), 133. Seamus Heaney, in his celebrated yet controversial 1999 translation of *Beowulf,* plays with this historic colonizing discourse; writing from within the English canon, Heaney adopts an English perspective and writes Grendel in the same fashion that the English had written the Irish.
24 Nicholas Canny, "The Ideology of English Colonization: From Ireland to America," *The William and Mary Quarterly* 30, no. 4 (1973): 575–98, at 596. See also, David Harding, "Objects of English Colonial Discourse: The Irish and Native Americans," *Nordic Irish Studies* 4 (2005): 36–60.
25 Canny, "The Ideology of English Colonization," 596.

stance regarding the massacre of the creatures in favor of a celebratory "winning of the west" type narrative.

The justification for the killing of the grendels in the novel is analogous to earlier retellings of *Beowulf* for children, particularly those associated with the romantic medievalism of Victorian Britain. As Smol argues, retellings of the poem offered children a means to learn about the professed origins of their nation and acted as pedagogic instruments through which "the hero [was] highlighted and simplified in his solitary fight against 'Others.'"[26] This cultural experience of Imperial Britain and colonial rule is expressed quite clearly in H.E. Marshall's 1908 adaptation of *Beowulf*; Hawes explores the adaptation alongside Marshall's publication of the same year, *Our Empire Story*, a history book for children. She outlines the striking similarities between the language used of Grendel and the colonized peoples in *Our Empire Story*, as well as changes made to Beowulf's character to make him a more acceptable nineteenth-century hero — for instance, Beowulf does not boast in Marshall's retelling, but is rather "proudly humble,"[27] a characteristic we see repeated in Cadmann Weyland's figure. Of particular interest are the similarities drawn between Grendel and the colonized, however. In her *Beowulf*, Marshall describes Grendel as being animal-like, having "thick black hair" and "wild demon laughter," "howling with wicked joy," descriptions which cannot help but be compared to the description of the Afghans in *Our Empire Story* as "cursing howling brutes," and the Indians as people who want to "fill the land with lawlessness and bloodshed."[28] Hawes argues that Marshall's *Beowulf* was "meant in part to support the imperialistic cause of Great Britain by emphasising the chivalric code as rendered through a British imperial lens." This is much in the

---

26 Anna Smol, "Heroic Identity and the *Children's Beowulf*," *Children's Literature* 22 (1994): 90–100, at 98.

27 Janice Hawes, "Beowulf as Hero of Empire," *Teaching Medieval and Early Modern Cross-Cultural Encounters*, eds. Katrina F. Attar and Lynn Shutters (New York: Palgrave, 2004), 179–96, at 188.

28 Ibid., 191–92.

same way that Niven's (and his associates') novels are "obviously the literature of an Imperial power still confident of its right to dominate the rest of the world, still certain of its manifest destiny," which play into the social fear exploited by the likes of Reagan, Bush, and Newt Gingrich.[29]

In a manner similar to Victorian imperialist literature, *The Legacy of Heorot* follows the same first-contact narrative that, as Michelle Raheja argues:

> Transform[s] settler colonial space into what is perceived as domestic and white homelands through the use of non-Native characters as the primary points of entry for the reader/spectator, while Aboriginal people are metaphorized as terrify [sic], primitive, alien and non-individual others that require subjugation or annihilation (thus justifying violence and genocide).[30]

While Raheja uses Ridley Scott's *Alien* (1979) to express this point, *The Legacy of Heorot* may just as easily be held up as an example where exploration (or expansion) becomes a euphemism for invasion. Attebery similarly argues that when American writers like Edgar Rice Burroughs "sent their heroes to other planets, the beings they encountered on these worlds were frequently Native Americans in disguise."[31] In these types of narratives, the indigenous are, as Raheja notes, "rendered violent, villainous, and cannibalistic, in a narrative that mirrors Christopher Columbus's representations of Indigenous people

---

29 John Newsinger, "'The Universe is Full of Warriors': Hard Science and War in Some Novels by Larry Niven and his Accomplices," *Foundation* 67 (1996): 47–55, at 47 and 51–52

30 Michelle Raheja, "Future Tense: Indigenous Film, Pedagogy, Promise," in *Sources and Methods in Indigenous Studies*, eds. Chris Andersen and Jean M. O'Brien (New York: Routledge, 2017), 239–46, at 242.

31 Brian Attebery, "Aboriginality in Science Fiction," *Science Fiction Studies* 32, no. 3 (2005): 385–404, at 390.

as radically 'Other' in what is now known as the Caribbean."[32] Interestingly, Columbus's tentative claims regarding the Island Caribs as cannibalistic appears echoed in *The Legacy of Heorot*; just as claims of cannibalism provided European colonizers of the Americas with a "metaphorical and a reality-based justification for imposing their own forms of cruelty,"[33] the grendels' "nasty habit" of eating their young — which makes the motive of revenge, as with Grendel's mother in *Beowulf*, obsolete — adds extra justification to the Avalon colonizers' slaughter of the creatures. By the end of the novel, the colonists and grendels (their numbers significantly depleted) reach a mostly peaceful existence, albeit importantly, with the residents of Avalon in complete control. Echoing Native American subjugation, the novel stresses a narrative that attempts to legitimize the false idea that peace can only be brought about through a necessary culling, and thus, "taming," of the aboriginal.

As in Ridley Scott's *Alien,* the grendels' status as "Other" is further solidified in their femaleness. This depiction of the native creatures as female is important in terms of postcolonial discourse; as Ashis Nandy points out in the context of Indian colonisation, colonial vilification involved the assimilation of cultural hierarchies and sex hierarchies in which the indigenous peoples are feminized and emasculated,[34] often through the literal loss of land, but also in the surrounding discourse.[35] Spencer-Wood notes how "the social institution of patriarchy,

---

32 Raheja, "Future Tense," 242.
33 Jerry M. Williams and Robert E. Lewis, *Early Images of the Americas: Transfer and Invention* (Tucson: University of Arizona Press), xxiv.
34 Ashis Nandy, *The Intimate Enemy: Loss and Recovery of Self under Colonialism* (Oxford: Oxford University Press, 1988), 4–11.
35 The feminization of indigenous men may be seen in Giraldus's *Topography,* where the Irish men are described as "pass[ing] their water sitting" (75). See Giraldus Cambrensis, *The Topography of Ireland,* trans. Thomas Forester, ed. Thomas Wright (Cambridge: In Parenthesis Publications, 2004), 55. As Cohen notes, Giraldus "deciphers the alphabet of Irish culture — and reads it backwards, against the norm of English masculinity." See Jeffrey Jerome Cohen, "Monster Culture (Seven Theses),"

including sexual relationships, was fundamental to European military conquest, colonization, economic exploitation of indigenous people, and cultural entanglement";[36] the colonized, as with women, are both feminized and infantilized, which meant "that they were to accept without argument the verities and the laws laid down for them by other men."[37] The feminization of the grendels and the passivity of the female colonists appears to be a tactic used by the authors as a means to validate the hypermasculine society embodied by Cadmann Weyland; Newsinger, in an article exploring numerous works by Larry Niven, notes, "Niven's protagonists have struggled against adversity, sustained by the warrior qualities and patriarchal relationships that he identifies as necessary for survival in a hostile universe […] women's liberation is not a viable proposition where the warrior virtues prevail and masculine triumphalism is the order of the day."[38]

While the start of the novel shows men and women as equal in the colonists' society, the struggle for survival means (for the authors at least) that traditional gender roles must be reasserted; as Cadmann himself states:

> Women have never loved being kept from education and treated as second-hand citizens. Men have never enjoyed having their balls shot off in wars. Men and women didn't fall into their roles accidentally […] it happened because for

---

Monster Theory: Reading Culture, ed. Jeffrey Jerome Cohen (Minneapolis: University of Minnesota Press, 1996), 3–25, at 11.

36 Suzanne M. Spencer-Wood, "Feminist Theorizing of Patriarchal Colonialism, Power Dynamics, and Social Agency Materialized in Colonial Institutions," *International Journal of Historical Archaeology* 20, no. 3 (2016): 477–91, at 470.

37 Simone De Beauvoir, *The Second Sex,* ed. and trans. H.M. Parshley (Middlesex: Penguin, 1984), 725.

38 John Newsinger, "'The Universe Is Full of Warriors': Hard Science and War in Some Novels by Larry Niven and his Accomplices," *Foundation* 67 (1996): 47–55, at 47, 53.

a thousand generations, that was the best way we knew to build a civilization.[39]

While he admits that women have historically been treated as "second-hand citizens," his reflection makes it clear that, in order for civilization to survive, a return to traditional gender roles is the only viable solution. Thus, by the end of the novel, the women have become dependents of "brawny self-sufficient warrior[s]" and little more than propagators of the human race.[40] The progression from autonomous female to a vessel through which the race may be continued shows unsettling similarities to a controversial early-twentieth-century novel, *The Clansman: A Historical Romance of the Ku Klux Klan* by Thomas Dixon Jr. (which also notably appropriates medieval imagery in its portrayal of the Klansmen). As Kaufman notes, "the novel's racial hierarchy is exceeded only by its fear of the feminine,"[41] and, as mirrored in the women of *The Legacy of Heorot,* the quasi-feminist Elsie, in order for the white race to triumph, submits to a role of subservience.

Not only is the patriarchal desire of traditional gender roles reasserted, but a male fantasy of multiple wives is also borne out, as many of the men have died in their heroic travails against the grendels. Despite the apparent urgency for repopulation, however, Niven, Pournelle, and Barnes do not miss the opportunity to assert archaic gender expectations by only rewarding the more passive women with men (and thus, children); Carolyn, who is "sallow in both complexion and personality," who shouts "too loudly" and too "shrilly,"[42] and who is arguably one of the most skilled warriors in the colony, is the only woman who does not end up with a man, despite her obvious desire to have one

---

39 Niven, et al., *The Legacy of Heorot,* 244.
40 Ibid., 158.
41 Amy Kaufman, "Anxious Medievalism: An American Romance," in *The Year's Work in Medievalism 2008,* ed. M.J. Toswell (Eugene: Wipf & Stock, 2009), 10
42 Ibid., 20, 52, 302.

("It isn't fair [...]. You've got men").[43] The ideal woman here is one who knows her place and who will "love, honor and obey" her man, and any transgression is punished through denial of what all women apparently want: babies ("You want a baby. We all do").[44] This is not necessarily surprizing when we look at some of the authors' body of published work. Sexism reveals itself also in a number of other works by the authors; Niven and Pournelle's *The Mote in God's Eye* (1974) features only one female human character, who, in a display of conservative sexual politics, tells one of the alien "moties", that "nice girls" do not use birth control, as they save themselves for marriage,[45] a line which anticipates the Reagan administration's fears regarding women's sexual liberation. Niven's *Ringworld* (1970) also reveals an issue with women; only two female characters feature in the novel, Teela, a vapid woman and sexual partner of the protagonist, Louis, and Prill, a prostitute who replaces Teela's place as Louis's mistress.

As with the novel's imperialist undertones, its treatment of the female characters similarly reflects conservative Victorian values regarding women; as nineteenth-century art critic John Ruskin declared, a woman's "power is not for rule, not for battle, and her intellect is not for invention or creation, but for sweet ordering." Man's power, on the other hand is "active, progressive, defensive. He is eminently the doer, the creator, the discoverer, the defender."[46] The celebration of the passive Mary Ann and Sylvia and the punishment of the autonomous Carolyn in *The Legacy of Heorot* brings to mind nineteenth-century novels, such as Thackeray's *Vanity Fair* (1848), wherein the passive Amelia Sedley is contrasted to the autonomous Becky Sharp. Becky's transgression from the ideal feminine role leads to her

---

43 Ibid., 391.
44 Ibid., 150, 395.
45 Larry Niven and Jerry Pournelle, *The Mote in God's Eye* (New York: Simon and Schuster, 1974), 349.
46 John Ruskin, "Lecture II: Lilies of Queen's Gardens," in *Sesame and Lilies* (Rockville: Arc Manor, 2008), 66.

being described as "diabolically hideous and slimy," and as having a "monster's hideous tail."[47] Similar descriptions may be found in the work of Dickens, who portrayed couples in which the "lady reigns paramount and supreme" as unnatural, like "hideous births" or "monstrous deformities."[48] Of course, the same moral conservatism regarding women also manifested in translations and retellings of *Beowulf*; Wealhtheow serves as a contrast to Grendel's mother, and in many cases her appearance in the poem is often summed up in one sentence, the emphasis on her beauty and good influence,[49] and her diplomatic role regarding her sons' futures reduced or cut altogether.[50] In a similar fashion, Grendel's mother is arguably demonized to an excessive extent in such translations and adaptations, her active and autonomous role rendering her physically monstrous to a Victorian age in which the pseudo-science of physiognomy was experiencing a re-popularization.[51] In the 1800s, women who

---

47 William Makepeace Thakeray, *Vanity Fair* (Ware: Wordsworth Classics, 2001), 607.
48 Charles Dickens, *Sketches of Young Couples* (London: Chapman and Hall, 1840), 78.
49 Smol, "Heroic Identity and the *Children's Beowulf*," 96.
50 See, for example, W. Wägner and M.W. MacDowell, *Epics and Romances of the Middle Ages,* 2nd edn. (London: W. Swan Sonnenschein and Co., 1884). The exaggerated passivity of Wealhtheow's character is not relegated to the Victorian era, of course. Josephine Bloomfield addresses the Victorian influence on Klaeber's construction of her character, who has been "diminished by kindness" in his glossary. See Josephine Bloomfield, "Diminished by Kindness: Frederic Klaeber's Rewriting of Wealhtheow," *Journal of English and Germanic Philology* 93 (1994): 183–203. More recently, we see Andy Orchard's description of her as a shallow, meddling, and rather ineffectual figure, more active than Victorian depictions of her character, yet just as chauvinistically stereotyped. See Andy Orchard, *A Critical Companion to Beowulf* (Cambridge: D.S. Brewer, 2003), 220, 226.
51 Physiognomy involved the assessment of an individual's character based on their outward appearance. The popularity of this pseudo-science can be seen in the publications of the time, with over 150 editions of Lavater's works being published by the middle of the nineteenth century. See Jonathan Smith, *Charles Darwin and Victorian Visual Culture* (Cambridge: Cambridge University Press, 2006), 199.

did not fit into the mould of the ideal woman, the "angel in the house," were often ascribed physically unattractive features as an outward expression of their inner characters, as can be seen in many anti-suffragette caricatures of the time and in Thackeray's description of Becky Sharp.[52]

The return to Victorian-like ideals isn't restricted to Niven, Pournelle, and Barnes's novel, but is part of a wider moral conservatism of the 1980s, the architects of which situated themselves against the 1970s rise of feminism and sought a return to more conservative gender roles. As Faludi argues, this backlash shaped much of Hollywood's portrayal of women in this era. Speaking of films like Adrian Lyne's 1987 *Fatal Attraction,* she argues that "women's lives were framed as morality tales in which the 'good mother' wins and the independent woman gets punished […] Hollywood restated and reinforced the backlash thesis: American women were unhappy because they were too free; their liberation had denied them marriage and motherhood."[53] We see a direct example of this in *The Legacy of Heorot* when, towards the end of the novel, after traditional gender roles have been enforced, the women (with the exception of Carolyn) appear content with their newfound focus on motherhood and repopulating the human race on Avalon.

This return to conservative values is intrinsically tied to the Reagan administration and his 1980 presidential campaign which held a strong anti-feminist component; as Balser notes:

> [T]he year 1980 represented a major turning point for the women's movement. The election of Ronald Reagan, the rise of right-wing governments throughout the world (often with anti-women agendas), the defeat of the ERA [Equal Rights Amendment] in the United States, and the emergence of the

---

52 For a discussion of the demonization of Grendel's mother in the Victorian era, see Alison Killilea, "The Monster in the House: Grendel's Mother and the Victorian Ideal," *Sibéal* 1, no. 1 (2015): 10–22.

53 Susan Faludi, *Backlash: The Undeclared War Against American Women* (New York: Three Rivers Press, 2006), 126.

> Gender Gap were all crucial phenomena [...]. No presidential candidate had ever made women's issues (such as *anti*-ERA, *anti*-choice, and return to the "traditional family") so prominent as Ronald Reagan did.[54]

Reaganism appeared as the antithesis to the liberal 1960s and the feminism of the 1970s, which Reagan's spokeswoman Faith Whittlesey described as being a "straitjacket" for women, who should rather "go home and look after their own children."[55] The Reagan administration's backing of a "Human Life Amendment" and the banning of some types of birth control appears to be connected with fears surrounding the declining birth-rate in the United States, which was conveniently blamed on women's liberalization by Ben Wattenberg.[56] Fears surrounding the loss of power by the United States and the decline of America's average IQ levels (due to "brighter women neglecting their reproductive responsibilities in favor of degrees and careers")[57] should the population decline echo earlier fears of "race suicide" and the demise of the nation by Theodore Roosevelt, who blamed the declining birth-rate (of the white population) on the loss of traditional family values.[58] The two anxieties presented here are transposed in *The Legacy of Heorot,* when the women of the novel abandon their focus as scientists in order to dedicate their time to repopulating the now much-declined colonial community.

Just as women were encouraged to return to more traditional, domestic roles, so too was a pro-military, hyper-masculine role encouraged for men. As Jeffords notes, "the depiction of the

---

54 Diane Balser, *Sisterhood & Solidarity: Feminism and Labour in Modern Times* (Boston: South End Press, 1987), 11.
55 Quoted in Faludi, *Backlash,* 4, 270.
56 Ibid., 248, 48.
57 Richard J. Herrnstein, "IQ and Falling Birthrates," *The Atlantic* 263, no. 5 (1989): 72–79, at 73.
58 Elaine Tyler May, *Barren in the Promised Land: Childless Americans and the Pursuit of Happiness* (Cambridge: Harvard University Press, 1995), 61.

indefatigable, muscular, and invincible masculine body became the linchpin of the Reagan imaginary; this hardened male form became the emblem not only for the Reagan presidency but for its ideologies and economies as well."[59]

We can see this "hardened body" in scores of popular Hollywood heroes of the time, such as Sylvester Stallone in the *Rambo* franchise (1982–) and Bruce Willis in *Die Hard* (1988).[60] We likewise see this "muscular, unbending masculine body"[61] in *The Legacy of Heorot* in the figure of Cadmann Weyland; after all, as Newsinger notes, "war, according to Niven, is what men are all about."[62] Cadmann embodies the traditional, strong, silent male, at odds with the other figures in the novel; he is the only person on the colony planet who is not an intellectual or a scientist, and his main duty of protection is one that isolates him from the rest of the formally educated population. However, it is only through Cadmann's masculinity, which is stressed through his military background (as well as his "broad, strong handwriting"),[63] that any of the colonists survive at all. As with a number of Niven's works specifically, such as *Protector* (1973), the protagonist is one whose military background and staunch independence isolates him from the other figures of the text; Cadmann is treated with suspicion, and his ideas regarding the grendels are ridiculed, until of course, the "warrior's way is recognised as the only way, his virtues are acknowledged and his role is celebrated."[64]

The characterization of Cadmann as lone warrior once again reflects the Victorian ideal of Beowulf as the "solitary" hero who

---

59 Susan Jeffords, *Hard Bodies: Hollywood Masculinity in the Reagan Era* (New Brunswick: Rutgers University Press, 1994), 25.
60 Sergio Hernández López, "Reagan's Era: Return to the Macho Future," *Revista Canovia de Estudios Ingeses* 67 (2013): 193–202, at 198–99.
61 Ibid., 199.
62 Newsinger, "'The Universe is Full of Warriors,'" 48.
63 Niven et al., *The Legacy of Heorot*, 320.
64 Newsinger, "'The Universe is Full of Warriors,'" 48.

fights against "Others."⁶⁵ Just as nineteenth-century children's retellings of the poem promoted a chivalric warrior ethos for the "future soldiers of the Empire,"⁶⁶ *The Legacy of Heorot* promoted a similar type of pro-militarism that glorified a certain type of masculine warrior figure in the Reagan years of the Cold War.⁶⁷ As Auerbach notes, Pournelle and Niven, amongst other science fiction writers of the time, "all envisioned the best of a militarized humanity breaking away from the evils of bureaucracy and bleeding-hearts."⁶⁸

The idea that Cadmann is the only competent figure amongst a cast of scientists and intellectuals appears as a reflection of the anti-intellectualism of the conservative Reagan era. As Shogan argues, Reagan's "leadership posturing" places him on the "explicitly anti-intellectual end of the spectrum,"⁶⁹ he was considered by Democratic advisor Clark Clifford to be an "amiable dunce"; by journalist Haynes Johnson as being neither intellectually curious or well-read; and Reagan's biographer noted "a growing suspicion that the president ha[d] only a passing acquaintance with some of the most important decisions of his administration."⁷⁰ His targeting of academics, and his "coun-

---

65 Smol, "Heroic Identity and the *Children's Beowulf*," 98.
66 Ibid., 98.
67 References to a possible future conflict were also present in other Victorian retellings of medieval myth and history. G.A. Henty (who is described by Guy Arnold as a "propagandist — for Empire and British interests") goes as far as to compare King Alfred's campaigns against the invading Danes to measures the English may undertake in a potential Indian uprising. See G.A. Henty, *The Dragon and the Raven* (Auckland: Floating Press, 2012), 79. For Arnold's criticism of Henty, see Guy Arnold, *Held Fast for England: G.A. Henty, Imperialist Boys' Writer* (London: Hamish Hamilton, 1980), 4.
68 David Auerbach, "The Sci-Fi Roots of the Far Right — From 'Lucifer's Hammer' to Newt's Moon Base to Donald's Wall," *Daily Beast*, September 17, 2017, https://www.thedailybeast.com/from-lucifers-hammer-to-newts-moon-base-to-donalds-wallthe-sci-fi-roots-of-the-far-right.
69 Colleen J. Shogan, "Anti-intellectualism in the Modern Presidency: A Republican Populism," *Perspectives in Politics* 5, no. 2 (2007): 295–303, at 295.
70 Qtd. in Shogan, "Anti-intellectualism in the Modern Presidency," 298.

teroffensive on that last Leftist redoubt, the college campus," fostered an anti-intellectual and anti-academic reputation that stayed with him throughout his political career.[71]

Reagan's anti-intellectualism is only one aspect for which he has since been remembered. Perhaps more notable is his initiation of the Strategic Defence Initiative in 1983, which soon after became derisively nicknamed the "Star Wars" project. This plan, which aimed to put in place a system of satellites to shoot potential Soviet ballistic missiles out of the sky, was based on the 1980s report, *Space: The Crucial Frontier,* written by the Citizens' Advisory Council on National Space Policy, the chairman of which was none other than Jerry Pournelle, with Larry Niven as one of the members on the council.[72] Not only were Larry Niven and Jerry Pournelle regarded as dominant figures in the military science fiction genre, but their science fiction crossed the boundaries into potential reality, albeit a reality which fellow author Isaac Asimov regarded as unfeasible and not to be taken seriously.[73] As John Wenz argues, the SDI was "the speculative, ideology-fueled fantasy of two famed science fiction authors with the imaginations to dream of creating real-life laser guns and space missiles," and whose "plan was simply to propel right-wing American agendas off Earth: extract resources and build military might."[74] While not as blatant as novels like

---

71 T. Kenneth Gribb, qtd. in Henry A. Giroux, "The U.S. University under Siege: Confronting Academic Unfreedom," *A Concise Companion to American Studies*, ed. John Carlos Rowe (Chichester: Wiley-Blackwell, 2010), 407–31, at 411. See also Shogan, "Anti-intellectualism in the Modern Presidency," 298, and Elvin T. Lim, *The Anti-Intellectual Presidency: The Decline of Presidential Rhetoric from George Washington to George W. Bush* (Oxford: Oxford University Press, 2008), 29.

72 Robert A. Heinlein (*Starship Troopers, Stranger in a Strange Land, The Moon Is a Harsh Mistress*) appears also on this list. A huge influence on both Niven and Pournelle, Heinlein is known for his far-right libertarian fiction.

73 Thomas Bodenheiner and Robert Gould, *Rollback! Right-Wing Power in U.S. Foreign Policy* (Boston: South End Press, 1989), 45.

74 John Wenz, "How Two Sci-Fi Writers Fueled a U.S. President's Wild Quest to Weaponize Space," *Thrillist*, November 10, 2017, https://www.thrillist.

Footfall, which Booker describes as "very much in tune with the 'Star Wars' fantasies of the Reagan administration in its vision of the development of a super-weapon,"[75] *The Legacy of Heorot* expresses the same pro-military, alarmist, and nationalist ideology expressed by the far-right factions of the Reagan era, while appropriating medieval imagery in an attempt to legitimize claims to superiority. By the end of the novel, Cadmann Weyland (the roots of whose name should not be forgotten), becomes the leader of the colonists, replacing the aptly named Zack Moscowitz. Weyland's militaristic and machoistic qualities — which reflect the manufactured self-image pushed by Reagan — prove him the most suitable for the role.

Conclusion

Like the Victorian reincarnations of *Beowulf* in the nineteenth century, *The Legacy of Heorot* expresses a misogynist, pro-colonial, and pro-militaristic appropriation of the poem in order to serve its own ideological intent. Like the translations and adaptations of Britain's Imperial century, the novel is a "self-conscious celebration of the American Empire," one which is framed by its colonial past and a conservative present.[76] Just as the Grendel-kin are paralleled with colonized natives in H.E. Marshall's *Beowulf* and *Our Empire Story*, *The Legacy of Heorot* uses the same tactic of transforming "troublesome natives […] into aliens" as a means to justify invasion and annihilation of what appear here, to be a stand in for the indigenous Native Americans.[77] The novel similarly reflects sentiments expressed by the Victorians regarding traditional gender roles, sentiments

---

com/entertainment/nation/strategic-defense-initiative-reagan-star-wars-jerry-pournelle-larry-niven.

75 M. Keith Booker, *Historical Dictionary of Science Fiction in Literature* (London: Rowmann & Littlefield, 2015), 179.
76 Newsinger, "'The Universe is Full of Warriors,'" 48.
77 Brian Attebery, "Aboriginality in Science Fiction," *Science Fiction Studies* 32, no. 3 (2005): 385–404, at 390.

which are also in line with the patriarchal backlash against feminism in the Reagan era (and also, troublingly reflect sentiments expressed by the KKK and other white supremacist groups in what Kaufman calls their "fear of the feminine").[78] On the other side of this is the novel's depiction of the "muscular and invincible masculine body" which is intrinsically tied into the Reagan presidency and pro-militaristic ideology.[79] As Newsinger notes of Niven's [and Pournelle's] work, "war […] is what men are all about,"[80] and this obsession with militarism almost literally becomes a reality when we examine the two authors' intimate relationship with the "Star Wars" Strategic Defense Initiative.

Beowulf has, since the very beginnings of its translation in the nineteenth century, been received and reappropriated in ways which reflect (and sometimes either challenge or affirm) the historical context of the time. Often this is accomplished through the figures of Grendel and Grendel's mother, who undergo various changes in order to express different fears or desires of the mind and era that produces them. This is no different in *The Legacy of Heorot* wherein the Grendel-kin are utterly bestialized as a means to justify the imperialist desires of the Avalon colony, and symbolically, the US. While the adaptation is by no means a very popular one, and one which is often ignored in *Beowulf* scholarship, it is important to recognize that this vein of far-right science fiction, as with the misappropriation of medieval imagery, has made a return in the present day. A pertinent example can be seen in the manipulation of the 2013–16 Hugo award nominations by groups the Sad Puppies, and their more extreme counterpart, the Rabid Puppies (led by alt-right activist Vox Day), whose goals were to strike back against what they saw as a predominance of "social-justice fiction" at the Hugo awards.[81]

---

78 Kaufman, "Anxious Medievalism," 10.
79 Jeffords, Hard Bodies, 25.
80 Newsinger, "'The Universe is Full of Warriors,'" 48.
81 Greg Bechtel, "Our Villains, Ourselves: On SF, Villainy, and…Margaret Atwood?" *The Word Hoard* 1, no. 5 (2016): 115–30, at 120.

Just as the science fiction world has "endemic problems with racism,"[82] so too does the sphere of medievalism, as seen in the adoption of heraldic crests, Celtic crosses (such as by white nationalist forum Stormfront) and Thor's hammers by white supremacist groups. We see the alt-right obsession with *Beowulf* in the backlash against diverse casting choices in adaptations (such as in *Beowulf: Prince of the Geats*) and in the likening of Trump to Beowulf's character on sites like *Stormfront*.[83] As Josephine Livingstone laments, "what once felt like a fringe research topic has become a site of violent, ugly conflict in America's public forum, brought out from the cultural subconscious by an administration which has legitimized hate speech."[84] Through appreciating the cyclical nature of this appropriation, and how current misuses of *Beowulf* and other medieval texts reflect the imagery of the Victorian era, the post-Civil war era, and the neo-conservative Reagan era, we can more easily tackle the racist and misogynist discourse that surrounds the misappropriation of the medieval.

---

82 David Forbes, "The Secret Authoritarian History of Science Fiction," *Motherboard,* June 19, 2015, https://motherboard.vice.com/en_us/article/9ak7y5/the-secret-authoritarian-history-of-science-fiction.

83 For the backlash against *Beowulf: Prince of the Geats,* see R.S. Nokes. The bizarre comparison of Trump to the character of Beowulf can be found in Machelson, "Re: Stan Lee, Legendary Marvel Superheroes Creator, Dead at 95," *Stormfront,* November 18, 2018, https://web.archive.org/web/20190120192506/https://www.stormfront.org/forum/t1263139-4/.

84 Josephine Livingstone, "Racism, Medievalism, and the White Supremacists of Charlottesville," *The New Republic,* August 15, 2017, https://newrepublic.com/article/144320/racism-medievalism-white-supremacists-charlottesville.

Bibliography

Abbott, Carl. "Homesteading on the Extraterrestrial Frontier." *Science Fiction Studies* 32, no. 2 (2005): 240–64. http://archives.pdx.edu/ds/psu/8555.

Agrawal, R.R. *The Medieval Revival and Its Influences on the Romantic Movement.* New Delhi: Abhinav Publications, 1990.

Arnold, Guy. *Held Fast for England: G.A. Henty, Imperialist Boys' Writer.* London: Hamish Hamilton, 1980.

Attebery, Brian. "Aboriginality in Science Fiction." *Science Fiction Studies* 32, no. 3 (2005): 385–404. https://www.jstor.org/stable/4241374.

Auerbach, David. "The Sci-Fi Roots of the Far Right — From 'Lucifer's Hammer' to Newt's Moon Base to Donald's Wall." *Daily Beast,* September 17, 2017. https://www.thedailybeast.com/from-lucifers-hammer-to-newts-moon-base-to-donalds-wallthe-sci-fi-roots-of-the-far-right.

Balser, Diane. *Sisterhood & Solidarity: Feminism and Labour in Modern Times.* Boston: South End Press, 1987.

Beatty, Greg. "Interview: Steven Barnes." *Strange Horizons,* July 29, 2002. http://strangehorizons.com/non-fiction/articles/interview-steven-barnes/.

Bechtel, Greg. "Our Villains, Ourselves: On SF, Villainy, and… Margaret Atwood?" *The Word Hoard* 1, no. 5 (2016): 115–30.

Bery, Ashok. *Cultural Translation and Postcolonial Poetry.* New York: Palgrave, 2007.

Bhabha, Homi. "The Other Question: Difference, Discrimination and the Discourse of Colonialism." In *Out There: Marginalization and Contemporary Culture,* edited by Russell Ferguson, Martha Gever, Trihn T. Mihn-ha, and Cornell West, 71–88. Cambridge: MIT Press, 1990,

Bodenheiner, Thomas, and Robert Gould. *Rollback! Right-Wing Power in U.S. Foreign Policy.* Boston: South End Press, 1989.

Booker, M. Keith. *Historical Dictionary of Science Fiction in Literature.* London: Rowmann & Littlefield, 2015.

Bradbury, Ray. *The Martian Chronicles.* New York: Doubleday, 1950.

Canny, Nicholas. "The Ideology of English Colonization: From Ireland to America." *The William and Mary Quarterly* 30, no. 4 (1973): 575–98. DOI: 10.2307/1918596.

———. *Making Ireland British: 1580–1650.* Oxford: Oxford University Press, 2001.

Citizens' Advisory Council on National Space Policy. *Space: The Crucial Frontier.* L-5 Society, 1981.

Cohen, Jeffrey Jerome. "Monster Culture (Seven Theses)." In *Monster Theory: Reading Culture,* edited by Jeffrey Jerome Cohen, 3–25. Minneapolis: University of Minnesota Press, 1996.

De Beauvoir, Simone. *The Second Sex.* Translated and edited by H.M. Parshley. Harmondsworth: Penguin, 1984.

Delany, Samuel R. *Starboard Wine.* New York: Dragon Press, 1984.

Dickens, Charles. *Sketches of Young Couples.* London: Chapman and Hall, 1840.

Dixon, Thomas. *The Clansman: A Historical Romance of the Ku Klux Klan.* New York: Doubleday, 1905.

Conybeare, John Josias, trans. *Illustrations of Anglo-Saxon Poetry,* edited by William Daniel Conybeare. London: Harding and Lepard, 1826.

Faludi, Susan. *Backlash: The Undeclared War Against American Women.* 2nd edition. New York: Three Rivers Press, 2006.

Forbes, David. "The Secret Authoritarian History of Science Fiction." *Motherboard,* June 19, 2015. https://motherboard.vice.com/en_us/article/9ak7y5/the-secret-authoritarian-history-of-science-fiction.

Gardner, John. *Grendel.* New York: Picador, 1973.

Giraldus Cambrensis. *The Topography of Ireland.* Translated by Thomas Forester. Edited by Thomas Wright. Cambridge: In Parenthesis Publications, 2000.

Giroux, Henry A. "The U.S University Under Siege: Confronting Academic Unfreedom." In *A Concise*

Companion to American Studies, edited by John Carlos Rowe, 407–31. Chichester: Wiley-Blackwell, 2010.

Gunnarsson, Sturla, dir. *Beowulf and Grendel.* Truly Indie, 2005.

Harding, David. "Objects of English Colonial Discourse: The Irish and Native Americans." *Nordic Irish Studies* 4 (2005): 36–60. https://www.jstor.org/stable/30001519.

Hawes, Janice. "Beowulf as Hero of Empire." In *Teaching Medieval and Early Modern Cross-Cultural Encounters,* edited by Katrina F. Attar and Lynn Shutters, 179–96. New York: Palgrave 2004.

Heaney, Seamus, trans. *Beowulf: A Verse Translation.* London: W.W. Norton, 2002.

Heinlein, Robert A. *Farmer in the Sky.* New York: Scribner's and Sons, 1950.

Henty, G.A. *The Dragon and the Raven.* London: Blackie and Son, 1886.

Herrnstein, Richard J. "IQ and Falling Birthrates." *The Atlantic* 263, no. 5 (1989): 72–79.

Horsman, Reginald. *Race and Manifest Destiny: The Origins of American Racial Anglo-Saxonism.* Cambridge: Harvard University Press, 1981.

Hutcheon, Linda. *A Theory of Adaptation.* London: Routledge, 2005.

Jeffords, Susan. *Hard Bodies: Hollywood Masculinity in the Reagan Era.* New Brunswick: Rutgers University Press, 1994.

Kaufman, Amy. "Anxious Medievalism: An American Romance." In *The Year's Work in Medievalism 2008,* edited by M.J. Toswell, 5–13. Eugene: Wipf & Stock, 2009.

———. "The Birth of a National Disgrace: Medievalism and the KKK." *The Public Medievalist,* November 21, 2017. https://www.publicmedievalist.com/birth-national-disgrace/.

Kemble, John M., trans. *A Translation of the Anglo-Saxon Poems of Beowulf.* London: William Pickering, 1837.

Killilea, Alison Elizabeth. "The Monster in the House: Grendel's Mother and the Victorian Ideal." *Sibéal* 1, no. 1 (2015): 10–22.

Kristeva, Julia. *Powers of Horror.* Translated by Leon S. Roudiez. New York: Columbia University Press, 1982.

Le Guin, Ursula K. "Introduction to the Left Hand of Darkness." In *The Language of the Night: Essays on Fantasy and Science Fiction,* 155–59. Berkley: Berkley Books, 1979.

———. *The Word for World Is Forest.* London: Gollancz, 1972.

Lim, Elvin T. *The Anti-Intellectual Presidency: The Decline of Presidential Rhetoric from George Washington to George W. Bush.* Oxford: Oxford University Press, 2008.

Livingstone, Josephine. "Racism, Medievalism, and the White Supremacists of Charlottesville." *The New Republic,* August 15, 2017. https://newrepublic.com/article/144320/racism-medievalism-white-supremacists-charlottesville.

López, Sergio Hernández. "Reagan's Era: Return to the Macho Future." *Revista Canovia de Estudios Ingeses* 67 (2013): 193–202.

Machelson, "Re: Stan Lee, legendary Marvel superheroes creator, dead at 95." *Stormfront,* November 18, 2018. https://web.archive.org/web/20190120192506/https://www.stormfront.org/forum/t1263139-4/.

Magnuson, Stew. "Science Fiction Mavens Offer Far Out Homeland Security Advice." *National Defense Magazine,* March 1, 2018. http://www.nationaldefensemagazine.org/articles/2008/2/29/2008march-science-fiction-mavens-offer-far-out-homeland-security-advice.

Marshall, H.E. *Our Empire Story.* London: T.C. & E.C. Jack, Ltd, 1908.

———. *Stories of Beowulf Told to the Children.* Edinburgh: Thomas Nelson and Sons, Ltd., 1908.

May, Elaine Tyler. *Barren in the Promised Land: Childless Americans and the Pursuit of Happiness.* Cambridge: Harvard University Press, 1995.

McGlashan, Mark. "The Branding of European Nationalism: Perpetuation and Novelty in Racist Symbolism." In *Analysing Fascist Discourse: European Fascism in Talk and Text,* edited by Ruth Wodak and John E. Richardson, 297–314. New York: Routledge.

Michie, Elsie B. *Outside the Pale: Cultural Exclusion, Gender Difference, and the Victorian Woman Writer.* Ithaca: Cornell University Press, 1993.

Mora, Maria Jóse, and María José Gómez-Calderón. "The Study of Old English in America (1776-1850): National Uses of the Saxon Past." *The Journal of English and Germanic Philology* 97, no. 3 (1998): 322–36. https://www.jstor.org/stable/27711681.

Nandy, Ashis. *The Intimate Enemy: Loss and Recovery of Self under Colonialism.* Oxford: Oxford University Press, 1988.

Newsinger, John. "'The Universe Is Full of Warriors': Hard Science and War in Some Novels by Larry Niven and his Accomplices." *Foundation* 67 (1996): 47–55.

Niven, Larry. *Protector.* New York: Ballantine Books, 1973.

———. *Ringworld.* New York: Ballantine Books, 1970.

Niven, Larry, and Jerry Pournelle. *Footfall.* New York: Ballantine Books, 1997.

———. *Lucifer's Hammer.* Leander: Futura, 1978.

———. *The Mote in God's Eye.* New York: Simon and Schuster, 1974.

Niven, Larry, Jerry Pournelle, and Steven Barnes. *The Legacy of Heorot.* London: Sphere Books, 1988.

Nokes, Richard Scott. "*Beowulf: Prince of the Geats,* Nazis, and Odinists." *Old English Newsletter* 41, no. 3 (2008). http://www.oenewsletter.org/OEN/print.php/essays/nokes41_3/Array.

Orchard, Andy. *A Critical Companion to Beowulf.* Cambridge: D.S Brewer, 2003.

Osborn, Marijane. "Annotated List of Beowulf Translations: The List." *ACMRS.* https://acmrs.org/academic-programs/online-resources/beowulf-list.

Raheja, Michelle. "Future Tense: Indigenous Film, Pedagogy, Promise." In *Sources and Methods in Indigenous Studies,* edited by Chris Andersen and Jean M. O'Brien, 239–46. London: Routledge, 2017.

Rieder, John. *Colonialism and the Emergence of Science Fiction.* Middletown: Wesleyan University Press, 2008.

Ruskin, John. "Lecture II: Lilies of Queen's Gardens." In *Sesame and Lilies*, 261–68 Rockville: Arc Manor, 2008.

Scott, Ridley, dir. *Alien*. 20th Century Fox, 1979.

Shogan, Colleen, J. "Anti-intellectualism in the Modern Presidency: A Republican Populism." *Perspectives in Politics* 5, no. 2 (2007): 295–303. DOI: 10.1017/S153759270707079X.

Smith, Jonathan. *Charles Darwin and Victorian Visual Culture*. Cambridge: Cambridge University Press, 2006.

Smol, Anna "Heroic Identity and the Children's *Beowulf*." *Children's Literature* 22 (1994): 90–100.

Spencer-Wood, Suzanne M. "Feminist Theorizing of Patriarchal Colonialism, Power Dynamics, and Social Agency Materialized in Colonial Institutions." *International Journal of Historical Archaeology* 20, no. 3 (2016): 477–91. DOI: 10.1007/s10761-016-0356-3.

Spinrad, Norman. *Science Fiction in the Real World*. Carbondale: Southern Illinois University Press, 1990.

Suvin, Darko. *Metamorphoses of Science Fiction: On the Poetics and History of a Literary Genre*. New Haven: Yale University Press, 1979.

Thackeray, William Makepeace. *Vanity Fair*. Ware: Wordsworth Classics, 2001.

Turner, Sharon. *The History of the Manners, Landed Property, Government, Laws, Poetry, Literature, Religion and Language of the Anglo-Saxons*. London: Longman, Hurst, Rees, and Orme, 1805.

Wägner, W., and M.W. MacDowall. *Epics and Romances of the Middle Ages*. 2nd edn. London: W. Swan Sonnenschein and Co., 1884.

Wells, H.G. *War of the Worlds*. London: William Heinemann, 1898.

Wenz, John. "How Two Sci-Fi Writers Fueled a U.S. President's Wild Quest to Weaponize Space." *Thrillist*, November 10, 2017. https://www.thrillist.com/entertainment/nation/strategic-defense-initiative-reagan-star-wars-jerry-pournelle-larry-niven.

Williams, Jerry M., and Robert E. Lewis. *Early Images of the Americas: Transfer and Invention.* Tucson: University of Arizona Press, 1993.

Zafirovski, Milan. "Contemporary Conservatism and Medievalism: 'Nothing New under the Sun'?" *Social Science Information* 50, no. 2 (2011): 223–50. DOI: 10.1177/0539018410396617.

8

Twenty-five Years of "Anglo-Saxon Studies": Looking Back, Looking Forward

Catherine A.M. Clarke with Adam Miyashiro, Megan Cavell, Daniel Thomas, Stewart Brookes, Diane Watt, and Jennifer Neville

Prologue

Catherine Clarke

It's October, 2019, and I'm looking at the edited copy of the essay you're about to read: a multi-authored piece which captures a discussion about one field within Medieval Studies, conducted at a specific moment in time. The date of that discussion — at the Leeds International Medieval Congress, July, 2018 — suddenly feels a long time ago. A great deal has happened in the field of early medieval English studies since then, and most visibly over the summer of 2019. Scholars including Adam Miyashiro, one of this essay's authors, as well as, perhaps most prominently, Mary Rambaran-Olm, have called for radical change in our field. Vigorous discussion has ranged from conference presentations to social media to the mainstream press. In September 2019, the organization formerly known as the International Society of Anglo-Saxonists voted to change its name (at the time of writing still to be decided). In the summer of 2018 at the International Medieval Congress (IMC), our round-table session looked back over the last twenty-five years of "Anglo-Saxon Studies": today, the context of that discussion is receding fast, with a new landscape emerging for our field.

After careful reflection, I feel this essay should stand as written, without excessive interventions, amendments or updates from my vantage-point here in autumn 2019. Why, then, leave this essay as it was written, representing a discussion in 2018, before so many major upheavals and transformations in our field? First, this essay should remain an accurate reflection of a discussion which took place at a specific historical moment. Future scholars, themselves looking back at the history of our field, should be able to see the processes involved in its change — from major interventions to small, incremental steps such as this round table session. More importantly, to elide these small steps with major moments of transformation — such as that of summer 2019 — would erase the labor and efforts of scholars (such as Adam Miyashiro, included here) who have worked tenaciously, over many years, for change. It is also right that this piece should accurately represent — albeit signaled as problematic — the vocabulary used in our field at that moment in 2018. "Anglo-Saxon Studies" was the name of the IMC programming strand in 2018, and that was the terminology we engaged with in our conversation: I have left this language here, but in quotation marks, to signal its problems and to indicate that I am quoting from a now-historical event. Finally, many of the co-authors of this piece raise challenges and difficulties within the field of early medieval English studies which are far from resolved. Their concerns, fears, aspirations, and hopes still stand. We have traveled far, but have a long way yet to go.

In Leeds, West Yorkshire, the evening of Monday July 2, 2018, was warm and muggy: in the midst of a lingering heatwave, temperatures hovered around the upper-twenties Celsius. At seven o'clock, delegates at the Leeds International Medieval Congress cooled down with beers and iced drinks in the campus courtyards, or crowded into bars to watch Belgium play Japan in the FIFA World Cup. At the same time, around fifty participants gathered in the Stage@Leeds Theatre Building for a round table session, which I organized in my role as "Anglo-Saxon Studies" Strand Co-ordinator to connect with celebrations around the conference's twenty-fifth anniversary. "Anglo-Saxon Studies at IMC#25: Looking Back, Looking Forward" aimed to look back at "Anglo-Saxon Studies" over the past twenty-five years, using the subject's changing presence at the Leeds International Medieval Congress (IMC) as a focus and a lens for examining developments and transformations in the field over the past decades. This focus on a major annual conference in Medieval Studies — the largest in Europe, involving 2900 medievalists from over sixty countries in 2018 — also opened discussion around the role of such landmark events in the formation of fields of enquiry within Medieval Studies, in the careers of academics, and in the profession. Members of the panel were invited to respond to a paper or session from the very first International Medieval Congress in 1994, reflecting on questions such as: How has thinking in our disciplines changed or developed since then? What conversations are continuing, and where have agendas shifted? The discussion also foregrounded the future of "Anglo-Saxon Studies," and the challenges it faces. How can we better foster inclusivity and diversity? What new conversations do we need to open up? Where do we hope to see the field in another twenty-five years?

The round table remit, then, was very broad, and members of the panel discussed a wide range of aspects of "Anglo-Saxon Studies," with attention to their own areas of research interests. But much of the discussion focused around interrogating and de-centering historical or existing power structures and lines of authority within the field, identifying lines of exclusion and attending to marginalized voices across our early medieval disciplines and profession. This included explicit discussion of racism and white supremacy in contemporary culture and politics, and the need for "Anglo-Saxon Studies" to engage politically. But these issues surfaced repeatedly in other areas, too. Panellists reflected critically on the historical centering of the field in areas of core canonical focus, and the associated hierarchies (or asymmetries) of research prestige — these changing emphases unpacked most strikingly in Peter Darby's discussion of the first IMC program, with its dominant focus on Gregory of Tours, compared with the lack of presentations on the same figure today.[1] Other panelists highlighted the historical displacement or marginalization of particular groups and concerns from the field of "Anglo-Saxon Studies," evidenced by their invisibility in early conference programs: from questions of gender and sexuality, to the ideology of human exceptionalism underpinning Medieval Studies and the Humanities in their entirety, only lately being challenged by attention to the non-human and animal in the early medieval world. Discussion about increasing interdisciplinarity or newly emerging digital methods also served as an implicit challenge to historical models of authority, regulation, and power across the field. Following the panel presentations, whole-room discussion turned to topics such as the place of early-career scholars and those on precarious contracts in the field: their marginalization and sometimes exclusion from centers of academic power and their existence at the peripheries of academic institutions and traditional career models — though often at the heart of risk-taking, pioneering new work which moves the discipline forward.

This essay brings together contributions from members of the round table panel (short speaker biographies are collected at the end of the essay). Just as with the IMC session, the brief for these written contributions was kept open and the authors have responded in their own, varying ways. I have not attempted to homogenize the style and tone of the pieces: again, as with the variety of voices in a round table discussion, I wanted to retain the diversity and distinctiveness of the pieces here. They remain

---

1   Peter Darby (Department of History, University of Nottingham) participated in the round table session but was unable to contribute to this essay.

largely in the present tense, retaining the immediacy and informality of the roundtable discussion itself. I have not bedded the contributions into an artificial narrative or central line of argument, and I will not attempt to draw conclusions. Instead, after the individual contributions, this essay will close with a reflection on what this conversation might bring to ongoing efforts to critique and re-shape Early Medieval English Studies, and where it has already effected small but significant change.

Reading the Runes:
"Anglo-Saxon Studies," Race and Colonialism

Adam Miyashiro

In the twenty-five years since the first International Medieval Congress in Leeds, it seems as if, on the one hand, Old English Studies haven't changed that much. Panels on "Anglo-Saxon" manuscripts and their relationship to continental writing traditions are represented strongly in the field. The medieval Digital Humanities was in its (quaint) infancy in 1994 — the term "Digital Humanities" had not yet been coined — with a panel on medieval Danish murals on Laserdisc, and it promised a CD-ROM and video. Medieval feminist work was taking place, though not explicitly.

The last year (2017–18), however, also shows how much has, indeed, changed. Looking back at the inaugural IMC program, instead of paper titles, I decided to read a session title: "Appropriating the Middle Ages" (session 205).[2] The titles of the papers for this session were "Whatever Happens to the Armour?" by

---

2   The program for the first International Medieval Congress (1994) is archived online at https://www.imc.leeds.ac.uk/wp-content/uploads/sites/28/2018/05/IMC_Programme_1994.pdf. The 2018 IMC programme is fully searchable online at https://www.imc.leeds.ac.uk/imc/imc-2018/.

Rosamund Allen, "Ivanhoe" by Erik Cooper, and "How Medieval Is Spanish Religious Festive Drama?" by Pamela King. Today, however, when we hear of medieval appropriations, we're now faced with the fast onset of fascist symbols, which include runic letters. In 1994, the study of runic characters was imagined as belonging to the domain of epigraphy, paleography, and perhaps Dungeons and Dragons and other fantasy genres. But today, runic letters constitute one aspect of fascist appropriation in the US, Canada, and in Northern Europe.

The runic character ᛟ (*ethel*) has been associated with German nationalism and other, more contemporary, white supremacist nationalist groups in the United States. The modern German name for the runic letter *ethel, Odal,* was used as the title of a German nationalist magazine called *Odal Monatsschrift für Blut und Boden* ("Odal: Monthly Magazine for Blood and Soil") in the 1930s and 1940s. Next to the swastika, the runic character *ethel,* while somewhat obscure to mainstream audiences, has become a common symbol in the circles of white supremacist Germanic nationalist groups and has become symbolically connected to "Blut und Boden." At the Charlottesville "torch march" in August 2017, the gathering of the white supremacists led by Richard Spencer chanted "White Lives Matter," "Jew Will Not Replace Us," and "Blood and Soil." At the "Unite the Right" rally on August 12, 2017, a day which saw the tragic vehicular homicide of activist Heather Heyer in an attack that also injured dozens of others, the National Socialist Movement, a neo-Nazi group, displayed a banner featuring the *ethel* rune. A CNN reporter even called it "the new swastika," reporting that the NSM chose the rune instead of the swastika because the latter distracts from their message. The NSM's website prominently displays the ethel on a shield incorporating the flag of the US.

White supremacist deployment of the "Anglo-Saxon" Old English language is common in various subcultures, such as Gothic and heavy metal communities. Old English, like Latin before it, has become a kind of "sacred" language that contains mystical or esoteric meanings and significances. Just as the runic alphabet has been viewed as magical in popular fantasy literature, the Old English language has been featured in television shows and popular music. The Swedish heavy metal band Ghost exploits this symbolic association with Old English, mingling Satanism, the Church, and Goth subculture with white supremacy. One of Ghost's most popular songs is called "Cirice" (pronounced by the band and their fans as "si-ri-sa"), which is the Old English word for "church." It won a 2016 Grammy award for Best Heavy Metal Performance. The lead singer, who wears make-up and a mock mitre, is known as Papa Emeritus III, a kind of counter-cultural pontiff. Another song, "Square Hammer," contains themes about Satanic rituals and sacrifices: "Are you on the square? / Are you on the level? / Are you ready to swear right here right now before the Devil?" A "square hammer" may be a reference to the lyrics, but also to Mjölnir, the hammer of Thor, which is widely used among Odinists and other white nationalists, symbolized in pewter pendants worn around the neck. Yet Ghost's mainstream popularity is often attributed to their style being so flamboyant as to be camp. You can't take Ghost seriously, it's claimed, because it is so over-the-top. The large upside-down Christian cross on stage is "ironic": many people in the audience casually accept it as part of the act. But the connection between Satanism and white supremacy goes deeper than that. In 2006, it was revealed that the co-founder of the American Nazi Party (NSM) and wife of their chairman emeritus Cliff Herrington was the "High Priestess" of the "Joy of Satan Ministry," and that her satanic church shared an address with the Tulsa, Oklahoma, NSM chapter. This controversy exposed the split in the NSM between the Christian Identity and the Odinists and Satanists. One offshoot, called "Wotansvolk," is an Asatru form of neo-paganism founded by David Lane, a member of the white terrorist group "The Order," who murdered a Jewish talk show host in Denver and coined the "14 words" ("We must secure the existence of our people and a future for white children"). A variation of Odinism, Wotanism — a neo-pagan religious movement that centered on white nationalism and pan-European racial identity — played on the Old English and Nordic names for the god Odin/Wotan, for

"Will Of The Aryan Nation" or "WOTAN." Other forms of neo-pagan imagery and narrative have also invoked the language of indigenous studies.

Hegemonic Anglophone settler colonialist societies like the United States, Canada, Australia, and New Zealand all share and claim the epithet "Anglo-Saxon" among their peoples and have a deep attachment. The linguistic supremacy of English — in government, culture, business, finance, the military — in these societies is attached to foundational texts like *Beowulf,* which occupy a central place in their education systems. "Anglo-Saxon," in today's Oceania, for example, explicitly signifies a racialized identity: that of white settler colonials — *haole* (Hawai'ian for "foreigner") or *pākehā* (Māori for white New Zealanders) — who deploy cultural, economic, and military means to displace *kanaka maoli* (Hawai'ians), Māori, Micronesians, and other Pacific peoples. In many of these places, the English language was brutally imposed on the native populations, and native languages of the Americas, Oceania, and Australia were almost completely destroyed.

When medievalists discuss "decolonizing" the field, we must always look toward indigenous and non-European scholars who call attention to the ways in which academic decolonization has become a metaphor. As Tuck and Yang point out, "decolonization in a settler context is fraught because empire, settlement, and internal colony have no spatial separation. Each of these features of settler colonialism in the US context — empire, settlement, and internal colony — make it a site of contradictory decolonial desires."[3] So when medievalists discuss "decolonizing" the field, we must be aware of the settler colonial politics that govern the historical parameters of what coloniality exactly is. Nadia Altschul and Kathleen Davis remind us that

---

3 Eve Tuck and K. Wayne Yang. "Decolonization Is Not a Metaphor," *Decolonization: Indigeneity, Education & Society* 1, no. 1 (2012): 1–40, at 7.

if we keep in mind that the idea of the Middle Ages did not in any simple way precede colonization, that it took shape with both colonial conquest and active struggles of resistance, and that colonial subjects contributed to the early formation of academic medieval studies […] then the Eurocentric status of the Middle Ages becomes more complicated.[4]

The more we as medievalists engage with scholars outside of our field — those working in Critical Race Theory and Indigenous Studies — the clearer we can see the challenges that face Medieval Studies as it looks toward the global world.

Non-human Pasts and Futures

Megan Cavell

My contribution aims to reflect on how Early Medieval Studies engages with the non-human world, especially in relation to the fields of Animal Studies and Ecocriticism. Naturally (pun wholeheartedly intended), I was unable to find a paper title from the first International Medieval Congress to respond to. The fields of Animal Studies and Ecocriticism are both relatively new, although the latter in particular was certainly picking up steam in the 1990s (let's not forget that the film *Free Willy* was released only one year before the first IMC in 1993!). And yet, these fields have only started to take hold in Medieval Studies — especially among those working on "Anglo-Saxon" literature and culture — in the past decade or so.

Because I was unable to find a particular title to use as a prompt, I instead searched the original program for sessions

---

4 Kathleen Davis and Nadia Altschul, eds., *Medievalisms in the Postcolonial World: The Idea of "the Middle Ages" outside Europe* (Baltimore: The Johns Hopkins University Press, 2009), 8.

and papers that showed some — any — interest in non-humans and the natural world. My search yielded two sessions that included a paper on landscape (519, 1316), two sessions on animal fables and fabliaux (912, 1212), and one session on animal symbolism (909). All of these were focused on high/late medieval contexts, and encompassed a number of linguistic and cultural perspectives largely centered on Western Europe. The titles of papers in these sessions suggest an interest in issues of translation, genre, metaphor, and place. Even the sessions with "animal" in the title suggest a treatment of the non-human world as ancillary to human literary and cultural perspectives, which is perhaps to be expected before the "animal turn" had reached Medieval Studies.

With the results of my search of the original IMC program in mind, I turned with excitement to the 2018 program; I knew there would be something a little more up my street since I had already signed up to speak in a session on ecocriticism! This was by no means the only session focused on the non-human and natural worlds. In the 2018 program, I found three sessions devoted to animals (208, 708, 1206) and one stray paper on animals hiding in an unrelated session (1002), three sessions on climate and disaster (301, 549, 649), three sessions on water, landscape, and natural resources (504, 602, 1751), as well as two sessions organized by the Medieval Animal Data Network (108 and 408), and two by the Medieval Ecocriticisms group (1649, 1749). Given that I undertook keyword searches rather than reading the IMC online program in full, I may well have missed additional papers on relevant topics. On the whole, the session and paper titles listed above indicate an interest in the following topics: beauty, bodies, animality and dehumanization, transformation, neglect, complicating binaries, and climate, the elements, and weather.

What is immediately apparent when analyzing data from the two Congresses is that — whether governed by theoretical frameworks or not — the 2018 sessions cover the entire medieval period (from early to late), include all manner of disciplines within Medieval Studies, and represent a truly international cohort of speakers and topics. There are also now scholarly groups dedicated to working in the areas of Ecocriticism and Animal Studies, which bring these varied perspectives into conversation with one another. While Medieval Studies as a field tends to pick up new theoretical perspectives after its contemporary colleagues (with the early medieval often lagging far behind later periods), the 2018 IMC program makes it clear that there is a healthy scepticism of human exceptionalism and a response to human impacts on the natural world taking root across the entire field of Medieval Studies.

This change cannot be rejected as simply a trend: it is a direct response to the damage humans have inflicted on the world. Given that we humans have not yet reacted, in any sustained way, to the ecological crises we have set in motion — to the threats of climate change, environmental degradation, species loss, and so on — medievalist scholars will, I believe, continue to organize, respond, historicize, critique, and, I hope, cooperate with other disciplines across the Humanities and Sciences to foster change.

Part of this organizing must acknowledge the disproportional blame that lies with privileged groups and the disproportional effect that ecological crises have on marginalized peoples around the world. A speaker in another IMC session I attended in 2018 referred to ecocritical work in Medieval Studies — not unjustly — as the "safe" option among politicized and activism-oriented approaches. And yet, efforts to re-make the theoretical fields my contribution reflects on have already manifested in hybrid approaches and methodologies like Green Postcolonialism. Embracing this hybridity and bringing Ecocriticism and Animal Studies into conversation with the study of race, racism, postcolonialism, and global medievalisms is the future of the eco movement in our little corner of academia.

Shaping the Field: Then and Now

Daniel Thomas

For my contribution, I chose to reflect upon the developing interests and scholarly preoccupations which have shaped and continue to shape our field of "Anglo-Saxon Studies." Rather than taking a single paper or session from the 1994 International Medieval Congress program as my focus, I looked across the 1994 and 2018 programs in their totality to consider what they might tell us about how particular aspects of our field are valued and how this might (or might not) have changed over the past twenty-five years.

Being primarily a literary scholar, I chose as one example the very important, but persistently under-studied, corpus of anonymous "Anglo-Saxon" vernacular homilies (especially those surviving outside major collections such as the Vercelli and Blickling manuscripts). A survey of the program from 1994 showed that while the conference included two power-packed sessions on vernacular homilies — comprising papers by Jon Wilcox, James Earl, Clare Lees, Joyce Hill, Charles Wright, and Mary Swan — four of these six speakers focused on the work of Ælfric and Wulfstan, the two major stylists of late Old English homiletic prose. Of the remaining two papers, that of Mary Swan ("Memorialised Readings: Investigating Old English Homily Compilation") did not announce a specific textual basis in the title, leaving Charles Wright's paper ("Vercelli Homily XII on the Fear of God: Source and Audience") as the only contribution to the conference that declared an explicit interest in anonymous Old English homilies. Turning to the 2018 program, I am surprised and disappointed to be unable to find a single paper whose title suggests a focus on anonymous vernacular homilies.

It is, of course, quite possible that this fact may simply be an anomaly, and it is to be hoped that the work of the "Electronic Corpus of Homilies in Old English" project (hosted at the University of Göttingen) will act as a significant stimulus for renewed scholarly activity and interest in anonymous homilies.

But the apparent lack of papers at the 2018 conference raises for me questions about how the shape of the corpus of "Anglo-Saxon" literature is reflected in scholarship, and how that scholarship is itself reflected in the programs of conferences such as the IMC.

Writing now, looking back at the 2018 roundtable session, it is striking that much of the most interesting discussion emerged not during the formal presentations themselves, but in the subsequent discussion, including responses to these questions of how the study of different aspects of our field is valued, and how this might change or develop over time. One thing which came out of this discussion very clearly was the fact that many scholars are reluctant to present on the main topic of their research for fear that it be considered too "niche" to be of interest to a wider audience. For early career academics especially, the IMC offers a welcome opportunity for greater exposure for their research, but also, with an eye on the increasingly congested job market, an important chance to speak before and become known to a wider academic audience. As became clear in the course of the discussion, the pressure to attract a substantial audience, and the feeling that papers or sessions on particular topics are unlikely to be well attended, may be a significant factor in the choice of material for a presentation. Furthermore, at least some early career scholars are being actively dissuaded, by those advising them, from submitting papers on particular topics on the grounds that they are unlikely to be given equal consideration alongside more "popular" submissions.[5]

Such concerns are, no doubt, not new, and it must be said here that, during the roundtable session, participants who had been involved with the organization of the IMC were at pains to stress that all submitted abstracts were judged on scholarly

---

5   It should be noted here that this is a misapprehension, and there is no policy of preference or noticeable bias towards particular topics or areas of scholarship in the paper selection and programming process at the IMC — Catherine Clarke.

merit alone. But the very fact that there is obviously a common perception that this is not the case is a cause for concern. At the heart of the discussion is an issue that goes beyond the relatively specific observation of the lack of papers on "Anglo-Saxon" vernacular homiletics in the 2018 program. In the current academic climate, it is particularly important that we are conscious of how biases at all levels — including judgements about the inherent interest or worth of particular methodologies or fields of study — affect the development and shape of our discipline. In the UK, and presumably elsewhere, this question of conscious or unconscious biases on the basis of methodology, theoretical standpoint, or simply topic of study is of wider importance in relation to funding models—the impact of which on the ongoing development of the field is obvious. It is also, of course, at the heart of recent concerns about the role of peer review in academic publishing.

At a time when practices and politics of scholarly canon formation are under more scrutiny than ever before, and when hard and necessary questions of disciplinary equality are being asked more persistently than ever before, it is especially important that the programs of major conferences like the IMC both reflect and encourage breadth, range, and diversity of scholarship. More than this, however, it is surely incumbent on all of us to interrogate the practices and processes by which value is ascribed to particular topics, issues, or scholarly approaches.

Reflecting on the differences between the conference program in 1994 and that in 2018, one is most immediately and most forcefully struck by the difference in the number of sessions and the number of papers. At a "mere" ninety-nine pages, the 1994 program is somewhat less than two-thirds the length of the 2018 version. The increasingly wide scope of the conference as a whole should be a sign of the health of the wider field of Medieval Studies, but it also emphasizes the importance of the IMC and similar conferences as platforms for diverse voices and perspectives. It is difficult not to look at the list of participants at that first conference and be struck by the number of speakers who have gone on to be major figures in the discipline over the last quarter of a century. Many of the paper titles are familiar from now-classic studies. What this suggests, I think, is that, for good or ill, agendas governing the development of such major conferences, including the inclusion or exclusion of particular papers or sessions, can impact upon the developing shape of the discipline in years to come. The influence of such conferences is, in itself, not unproblematic, especially given issues of equality of access and opportunity and issues over the transparency of programming such as those that have recently been raised with regards to the International Congress on Medieval Studies at Kalamazoo. Nevertheless, programming of major conferences offers a concrete opportunity to pay careful attention to the biases inherent in our own approaches to our chosen discipline, and to think about how such biases shape future engagement with the subject.

Database Then, Digital Now

Stewart Brookes

I'd like to invite you to travel back in time with me to the first International Medieval Congress in Leeds. It's July 1994. Wet Wet Wet have topped the UK singles chart for weeks with "Love Is All Around;" the FIFA World Cup is in full flow in the US, but England have failed to qualify; and it's the very day that Jeff Bezos is launching Amazon.com (an Internet book retailer, apparently). Now that you've got all of the time-space co-ordinates and cultural context that you need, I'd like you to visualize a young postgrad in pursuit of papers relating to his obsession with computers and how they might be used to study medieval texts and manuscripts. Thirteen papers in the program look promising in this regard. Three are surveys (917: Thomas Bestul, "Electronic Databases and Chaucer Studies;" 1217: Seamus Ross, "New Tools for Studying Medieval Sculpture;" 1307: Sherry Reames, "Hagiographical Research and Computers in the United States"). One pedagogic (1317: Daniel Farkas and Martha Driver, "Creating Multimedia Applications for the Classroom: The Pace University Medieval Women Project"). Five tantalize with the promise of future digital resources (717: Joy Jenkyns, "Computerized Charter-Bounds: A Project Report;" 717: Carole A. Hough, "Computerising Place-Names: A Project Report;" 917: Sally-Beth MacLean, "REED Patrons Database: Notes Towards a Biography;" 917: Marilyn Deegan, "Hidden Treasures: The Problems and Prospects of Creating Manuscript Databases;" 1217: Virginia Davies, "Computerizing the Medieval English Clergy"). One is dictionary-based (117: Tanneke Schoonheim, "The Role of the Computer in the Making of Vroegmiddelnederlands Woordenboek"). Two showcase nascent commercial database products (1317: Steven Hall, "Why Do Migne? The Creation of the *Patrologia Latina Database;*" 1317: Dominique Poirel, "Placing In Principio on CD-ROM"). And one introduces a new classification system for iconography (1217: Hans Brandhorst, "ICONCLASS and the Study of Medieval English Psalters"). The postgrad leaves that first Leeds inspired by these examples of computer-assisted research but sadly aware also that most of the projects were descriptive databases, lacking images of manuscripts (or other artifacts).

Time to go back to the future (to borrow a phrase) and reflect on how things have changed in the field of Humanities Computing (or Digital Humanities, as we call it now). I'm going to take 1994's session 1317 and its discussion of the *Patrologia Latina* database as my springboard. When Chadwyck-Healey launched their database in 1996, two years after that Leeds presentation, it represented a significant achievement, offering a searchable full-text corpus of all 221 volumes of Jacques-Paul Migne's *Patrologia Latina* (covering the writings of the Church Fathers and their successors from the years 200 CE to 1216 CE). It was a Windows-only offering that required a top-of-the-range machine with at least 8MB of RAM, plus a CD-ROM stack for searching across the multiple CD-ROMs (I think there were five of them). If the computing requirements weren't enough of an expense to deter the average researcher, then the price certainly was: *Patrologia La-*

tina cost £27,000. At Leeds in the latter years of the 1990s, Chadwyck-Healey offered taster sessions in one of the alcove rooms in the university's Weetwood Hall, designed to promote their software product but also to instruct people in how to use it. Training was necessary, for while *Patrologia Latina* both promised and delivered much, the complex search syntax had a learning curve attached, as was common for software of the time.

Patrologia Latina is, of course, still around, and still has a hefty price tag (via an institutional subscription) but is primarily an online experience now. The Leeds IMC experience has shifted direction from those early days, however. Rather than offering spaces where publishers can demonstrate their products, increasingly the programming team have accepted workshops designed to encourage academics to create and share resources using open source software. My favorite example of that from 2018 is the trio of "Manus-On Manuscripts" ("Hands-on," pun noted) workshops in which Abigail G. Robertson, Dorothy Carr Porter, and Anya Adair described their experiences of working with digital editing and data creation platforms (sessions 553, 653, and 753). Participants were then shown how to apply these tools to their own research and teaching, having gained first-hand experience of ViSColl,[6] Digital Mappa,[7] and EVT.[8] A particular strength of the workshop format is that it allows for discussion and the sharing of ideas, rather than just reporting findings (compare this to Session 1317 from 1994 on multimedia applications for the classroom) and the IMC team's decision to schedule the sessions back-to-back in the same room added to the sense of community that the organizers wished to build. It is important to note that workshops of the sort just mentioned can have a levelling effect, allowing PhD students and early career researchers to engage in research that has typically been

---

6   ViSColl Github repository: https://www.github.com/leoba/ViSColl.
7   Digital Mappa, An Open-Source Digital Humanities Platform for Open-Access Workspace, Projects and Publications: https://www.digitalmappa.org/.
8   Edition Visualization Technology: http://evt.labcd.unipi.it/.

the domain of funded projects (of which the "project reports" of Session 717 from 1994 were an early taste) and move from being content consumers to being content curators and creators.

Looking through the programs subsequent to 1994 confirms how significant a part of the IMC computer-related and Digital Humanities sessions have become. In that first IMC of 1994 there is not even a computing-related "strand" in the thematic index and the closest thing to what we want is "Sources and Resources," which lists ten sessions, four of which are computing-related. Reading through the program suggests that six of the 231 sessions (= 2.6%) in 1994 had a computer-related component. The indexing term "Sources and Resources" was dropped for the 1995 IMC, and we find the more promising "Computing in Medieval Studies," which listed 8 sessions (of 234 total sessions = 3.4%). In 1996, the strand was renamed "Computing for Medievalists," weighing in at only six sessions (of 250 at the Congress = 2.4%). I couldn't identify the number of sessions that were indexed as computing-related in the years 1997–2001 because the online archive for that period only offers a single page format and doesn't reproduce the thematic strands that were in the printed originals. From 2002, thematic strands and keywords are back in the online archive and we find that "Computing in Medieval Studies" has thirteen sessions (of 318 sessions = 4.1%). The numbers continued to increase year on year, and in 2018 this has risen to sixty-three sessions (of a total of 796 sessions = 8%). Looking ahead to the IMC 2019, the figure leaps to 111 sessions (from a Congress total of 771 sessions = 14.4%).

The above gives us a good idea of the growth of computer-related sessions at the Congress, but not the technologies in use in 1994. There were no laptops in sessions. Nor WiFi. Nor Twitter. The computer cluster offered banks of Windows 3.1 machines with their WIMP (Windows, Icons, Menus, Pointer) interface, but many medievalists were still more comfortable with DOS and typing in commands manually ("copy nostalgia.txt c:\not\so\good\old\days" anyone?). Those who'd made it into the brave new world of mice and WYSIWYG (What You See Is What You Get) had to deal with slow processors, noisy cooling fans, and cramming their data onto 3.5" diskettes. VDUS occupied a large chunk of the desk space in return for comparatively small screen sizes, and just sixteen colours. Yes, sixteen, including the memorably named olive, navy, teal, and fuchsia. So, What You Saw Wasn't In Reality Very Much (though nobody coined an acronym for that, unsurprisingly). Consequently, there were very few images of manuscripts online and those that were available were grainy, low resolution and often in black-and-white. It is worth reflecting that today's Smartphones can often do more than the highest-end computers you were likely to have encountered then.

Despite the comparatively modest number of sessions with a computing focus in 1994, it was apparent even then that medievalists were innovators in the field of Humanities Computing. One of the visionaries of that period was Patrick W. Conner (who, not so incidentally, was in Session 103 at Leeds in 1994 with fellow pioneers Kevin Kiernan, of *Electronic Beowulf* fame [1999], and Bernard J. Muir who went on to edit the *Exeter Anthology of Old English Poetry* with its digital facsimile on CD-ROM [2006]). In 1991, Conner both anticipated and influenced much of what was to come with his Beowulf Workstation, an Apple Macintosh HyperCard application that offered different views of the Old English poem, plus a glossary, notes, and images. The software made innovative use of the technologies available at the time and made the case for a pedagogic role for computers. And in 1996, Conner set-up Ansaxnet, the first electronic discussion list for the humanities, with the intention of creating a "social network" (as he called it) of students and scholars.[9]

Perhaps the most significant desideratum of those early years was the wish to interact with high quality images of manuscripts. With this in mind, and only a few months before that first Leeds, Murray McGillivray had gazed into a future in which scholars of *The Book of the Duchess* would enter a cubicle and don

---

9 Patrick W. Conner, "Networking in the Humanities: Lessons from ANSAXNET," *Computers and the Humanities* 26 (1992): 195–204, at 196.

sensory-input devices and for an hour or two enjoy the experience of "flipping the virtual pages of Bodleian MS Fairfax 16." McGillivray argued that examining a manuscript is an experience "involving several of the senses: vision above all, of course, but the feel of the parchment or paper, the sound of a turning page, and even the smell of the codex are part of examining a manuscript."[10] This immersive experience was one that McGillivray suggested had much in common with researchers into virtual reality who liked to think about a possible future in which "we will be able to have sex with remote or artificial partners by electronic means, presumably by strapping on visors, gloves and other sensory input devices. This imaginary future technology," McGillivray argued, "is the kind of thing medievalists need."[11] Twenty-five years on, using virtual reality for scholarship is still in an experimental phase. A promising success story, however, is Brent Davis's use of the technology for "object-based learning" with his Egyptology students.[12] In general, though, we have moved away from attempts to model the flipping of virtual pages — as exemplified by the "Turning the Pages" of the early 2000s used by the British Library[13] — toward technologies for comparison of images from multiple manuscripts using IIIF.[14]

The IMC 2018 program reflects the variety of thinking that is going on in Digital Humanities, whether it's about metadata, Big Data, visualization, network analysis, machine learning, or digital preservation. Another theme was shared standards (e.g., TEI,

---

10 Murray McGillivray, "Electronic Representation of Chaucer Manuscripts: Possibilities and Limitations," in *Computer-Based Chaucer Studies,* edited by Ian Lancashire (Toronto: Centre for Computing in the Humanities, University of Toronto, 1993), 1–15, at 2.
11 Ibid., 2.
12 Arts Unimelb, "Learning Hieroglyphics in the Tomb of Nefertari in Virtual Reality," *Vimeo,* November 13, 2018, https://vimeo.com/300627980.
13 "Turning the Pages™," *British Library,* http://www.bl.uk/turning-the-pages/.
14 A strong example of the potential offered by IIIF is provided by Ben Albritton's comparison of Chaucer manuscripts: Benjamin L. Albritton, "Fellow Travelers: The Canterbury Tales and IIIF," July 14, 2015, http://blalbrit.github.io/2015/07/14/fellow-travelers-the-canterbury-tales-and-iiif.

XML, IIIF, Iconclass) and the importance of sustainable practices. A salutary lesson from 1994 is that our whizziest software will before long seem primitive or may not even run on newer systems, and so it is open standards and the separation of data and interface that will preserve our research.

That digitally-informed research has turned out to be an increasingly important topic at the IMC is not, of course, a massive surprise. We've reached the stage where we couldn't do most, perhaps any, of our research as effectively without computer-based resources. That's only the surface story, however. This look backwards to 1994 has served as a reminder of the degree to which computer-assisted tools are changing the way that we do our research and encouraging us to ask more ambitious research questions. Sure, we still use the full-text corpora that were works-in-progress in 1994. But these were often a way of testing (or proving) a hunch or offering us further examples of what we already knew. In recent years, we've moved more and more towards creating tools designed explicitly for exploration and discovery, that disrupt our assumptions by offering wider contexts, that trigger an awareness of further questions. Hand-in-hand with that has been creating resources that are about evidence-based scholarship, open research methods and allowing others access to the data behind our assertions, with transformative impacts on knowledge, research processes, and lines of authority in the academy today.

Intersectional Feminisms and "Anglo-Saxon" Futures

Diane Watt

I am currently (July 2018) lucky enough to be researching full time on my project Women's Literary Culture Before the Conquest, funded by a Leverhulme Major Research Fellowship

(MRF-2016-014).[15] I am exploring works by and for women in the period 650–1150, focusing on women in England and English women who traveled to the continent, either as part of Boniface's missions to Francia, or because of other later connections with Europe. Looking through the first International Medieval Congress program to find a paper to which I could respond, I inevitably gravitated towards the Old English session entitled "Rewriting *Judith*: Anglo-Saxon Responses to the Old Testament Figure" (403), and to the most explicitly feminist presentation, Ruth Evans's theoretically sophisticated paper on "The Dangers of Being *Judith*."[16]

I am particularly pleased to contribute to this discussion because I have, in a sense, grown up with the IMC. In 1994 I was embarking on what was to become my first permanent lectureship, at the University College of Wales, Aberystwyth (now Aberystwyth University). I was invited to the inaugural congress by Rosalynn Voaden, who was organizing two sessions on the "Influence of Continental Holy Women in Medieval England" (416 and 515). These included papers on some of the heavyweights of late medieval women's mysticism, such as Hildegard of Bingen, Mechtild of Hackeborne, and Julian of Norwich. I was asked to step in and replace Felicity Riddy, who was unable to attend, and in my paper I spoke about the influence of Bridget of Sweden and Catherine of Siena on Elizabeth Barton, the Holy Maid of Kent (died 1534), work which subsequently fed into some articles and essays as well as a chapter of my first book, *Secretaries of God: Women Prophets in Late Medieval and Early Modern England*.[17]

My own career has, inevitably, moved on since then. For many years I have been on the programming committee at the

---

15 "Women's Literary Culture before the Conquest," *University of Surrey*, https://www.surrey.ac.uk/womens-literary-culture-before-conquest.
16 I am grateful to Ruth Evans for supplying me with a scanned copy of the full paper, which was delivered in abridged form at the conference.
17 Diane Watt, *Secretaries of God: Women Prophets in Late Medieval and Early Modern England* (Cambridge: D.S. Brewer, 1997)

IMC, organising the "Gender and Sexualities" strand (formerly "Women's and Gender Studies"). This strand has grown immensely and over the last two decades has enjoyed close links with organizations such as the Society of Medieval Feminist Scholarship, the Gender & Medieval Studies group, and the Society for the Study of Homosexuality in the Middle Ages. Unfortunately, its connection with the Medievalists of Color group was brought to an abrupt halt following the 2017 IMC on the theme of "Otherness," which Geraldine Heng rightly condemned as "another spectacular moment of racial-neocolonial privilege."[18]

While my research has hitherto focused on women, gender and sexuality in late medieval England, I am pleased now to be working on the early Middle Ages. With my own current research interests in mind I could have chosen from several other sessions and papers. Some of the major names in the field today participated in that first IMC. Clare A. Lees, for example, spoke about Ælfric's prose writings in session 1003 ("Late Old English Prose Styles: Language, Politics, Belief"), while Elaine Treharne talked about copying Old English in the twelfth-century in session 1203 ("Anglo-Norman Attitudes to Anglo-Saxon Vernacular Writings"). So why Ruth Evans and why *Judith*? Ruth Evans, like me, is primarily a late medievalist but one whose interests range much further and who isn't constrained by traditional period boundaries. This is significant. To some extent the sort of theorized, and in this case postcolonial, feminism that characterizes Ruth Evans's work is still not mainstream in early medieval English literary studies. In her paper Ruth Evans paid particular attention to the body in the Old English poem, pointing out that within it "ethnic and 'racial' identity […] significantly

---

18 Geraldine Heng, "Who Speaks for Us? Race, Medievalists and the Middle Ages," *Medievalists of Color*, April 3, 2018, https://medievalistsofcolor.com/race-in-the-profession/who-speaks-for-us-race-medievalists-and-the-middle-ages/.

intersects with issues of gender." Her approach might now be described as intersectional feminist.

The *Judith* narrative itself appeals to me for a number of reasons. It has proven to be very popular amongst students on my own Old English modules. Judith, part hero, part monster, is often regarded as the female counterpart to Beowulf, and of course both poems, *Judith* and *Beowulf* are found in the famous late ninth- or early tenth-century Nowell Codex (London, British Library, Cotton Vitellius A.xv). The biblical Judith also resonates with contemporary culture. In a 2014 conference presentation, "The Legacy of Artemisia, or Why We Should Care that Someone Was Raped," the graphic artist and novelist Una examined the strikingly innovative paintings of Judith by Artemisia Gentileschi in relation to the Baroque artist's own life.[19] Una revisited Gentileschi's Judith in *Becoming Unbecoming*, an autobiographical account of abuse and rape that she experienced growing up (coincidentally) in West Yorkshire at the time of Peter Sutcliffe's atrocities; a work which reflects movingly on the pervasiveness of violent antifeminism. Una uses the figure of a mace-carrying troll to illustrate the observation that "those everyday acts of misogyny have always been around, but now they are visible to all."[20] (As an aside, I am conscious that the so-called Yorkshire Ripper's reign of terror provided the backdrop of the formative academic careers of Ruth Evans and Clare Lees, who were both students at Leeds University in the 1970s.) For Una, and many others, Judith is a figurehead of resistance to sexual violence and female oppression. She is a feminist superhero. At the time of writing (in 2018) Judith's story clearly also speaks to the #MeToo movement.

But I am also drawn back to Ruth Evans's paper on "The Dangers of Being *Judith*" because I recognize the importance

---

19 Una, "The Legacy of Artemisia, or Why We Should Care That Someone Was Raped," November 19, 2014, https://unacomics.com/2014/11/19/comics-forum-presentation-the-legacy-of-artemisia-or-why-should-we-care-that-someone-was-raped/.

20 Una, *Becoming Unbecoming* (Brighton: Myriad Editions, 2015), 117.

of thinking across defined literary and historical periods, as argued by feminist scholars such as Lees (with Gillian R. Overing) and Treharne, as well as Catherine A.M. Clarke and, most recently, Elizabeth M. Tyler. This is an imperative that has become all the more urgent in the context of conservative, fascist and white supremacist misappropriations of "Anglo-Saxon" history and culture. In my own research career I started off working across the medieval/early modern divide; now my focus is on the early/late medieval split. It is important that we, as researchers, are willing to engage with scholarship in other areas within and beyond our own (sub)disciplines, to work with modern creative and cultural responses, to challenge and to dismantle established and restrictive teleologies, to accept the politically-necessary strategic anachronisms of queer theory, transgender studies, and critical race theory, and to resist gate keeping. Only by so doing can we ensure a future for what we still, perhaps ill-advisedly, refer to as "Anglo-Saxon Studies."

Talking about our generations

Jennifer Neville

I was a PhD student in the Department of Anglo-Saxon, Norse, and Celtic at Cambridge University in 1994, but I had attended the Kalamazoo conference while doing my MA at the University of Toronto, so I thought that I had a sense of what this new International Medieval Congress at Leeds was going to be. It was, of course, both similar and different. For me, half-way through my PhD, it was a thing of wonder: I ran from session to session (there were no mini-buses in the first year, despite the huge playing fields that needed to be traversed), always arriving breathless — not because of the physical exertion, but rather because everyone I had ever read seemed to be there. Looking back at the program now, I experience that feeling again: session after session contains names to be reckoned with, a roll-call of the great and the good, names that have remained important to this day. Even the chairs were star-studded. The IMC 1994 thus served to showcase world-leading scholarship in "Anglo-Saxon Studies."

I was a spectator of, not a participant in, that performance. That is the most important difference between then and now that I would like to highlight. Twenty-five years ago, PhD students watched in awe while the grown-ups showed them what they could do; now, as one of those (supposed) grown-ups, I almost feel surplus to requirements at that same conference. That is not to say that I feel unwelcomed, but now the Leeds IMC is a place where new people demonstrate new things, where the community fosters, accepts, and applauds scholars who may not yet be very good at presenting their ideas and do not yet have jobs, alongside those who are and those who do. Despite the melancholy reality that the competition for jobs is even worse now than it was then, this conference seems to me to demonstrate an important support for newcomers among the scholarly community that attends it. That is, we have removed boundaries between young and old, between a certain kind of "haves" and "have-nots."

That scholarly community of "Anglo-Saxon Studies" was and is, of course, only a part of the wider community of the International Medieval Congress. In 1994, thirteen out of 240 sessions were labeled "Anglo-Saxon Studies"; although I think that some sessions may have been mislabeled, that means that "Anglo-Saxon Studies" constituted about 5% of the whole. In 2018, the proportion was about 12%. That is, not only has the conference grown larger, but the proportion of the conference populated by our field has grown, too. That may or may not be a change to be celebrated. On the one hand, that growth is frankly astonishing given the dwindling presence of Old English in undergraduate English degrees (in the UK, at least). On the other, it seems odd and slightly worrying in the context of the necessary diversification of Medieval Studies as a whole. I wonder whether this shows early medievalists, despite our best efforts, retrenching rather re-making our field.

On the other hand, what we talk about within "Anglo-Saxon Studies" has changed and become more varied. In 1994 we talked about a wide variety of texts, but we did not talk about riddles; in 2018 we still talk about *Beowulf,* of course, but the Exeter Book Riddles now seem to be main-stream, perhaps even canonical. In 1994 Elaine Treharne spoke in a session about Anglo-Norman literature; now we know that Old English continues up into the twelfth century. In 1994 a key focus of attention was Orality and Oral Formulaic Theory; I still remember how stimulating and productive those ideas were, but we seem to have run out of things to say about them (for the moment), and so now we have eco-criticism and thing-theory and many, many other new things. Yet at the same time we still have manuscript studies. We may even see a new explosion of these, sparked by the 2018–19 British Library exhibition, "Anglo-Saxon Kingdoms." Overall, I would say that we have not lost any threads from twenty-five years ago; rather, we have added new colors and textures and materials.

I am not that worried that we still puzzle over *Beowulf* and other old, dated things; we have new trends, fads, innovations, and cutting edges that we can try out on our old things, and, indeed, old ways of doing things that still work very well. In terms of our community, however, there is more that we can do. Even after doing it myself twice, I still cannot see how the parent of a small child can participate fully in this world. The roundtable that spawned this collection of reflections reminded me of the invisible barriers that prevent disabled people from fully joining in. I am painfully aware of how painfully unaware I am about the effects of race and sexuality. And yet, the change that I mentioned first, that transformation of the listening audience into participating members, the de-centering from the "grown-ups" to the new scholars who are not simply our future but also part of our present, makes me hopeful that we can and will transform ourselves in many, many ways — not to play the game to make our scholarship "relevant," but rather so that it will be better.

❦

In the whole-room discussion which followed the IMC round table presentations, several features were very striking. One was the level of genuine affective investment in the conversation, sometimes spilling out in displays of emotion which challenged, bravely, the narrow norms of academic discourse and conference protocol. Also noticeable was the mutual kindness present in the room (and in the corresponding discussion on Twitter, using hashtag #s401). I'm conscious that the notion of kindness, especially in professional contexts, is complex and not unfraught: too often it is attendant on models of hierarchy and patronage or, conversely, it forces additional burdens on (or, indeed, silences) marginalized and less advantaged groups and individuals. In the session discussion, though — both formally, and over drinks — this kindness seemed to rest in mutual respect and a willingness to listen to alternate views. Finally, one point of consensus, amongst those in the room, stood out clearly. Those present agreed, in general, that the established term for our field — "Anglo-Saxon Studies" — was exclusionary, carried connotations of colonialism and racism, and included language with the capacity to cause hurt. The discussion stalled here, however: there was no consensus around an alternative title which could accommodate the diverse strands of the field. "Old English Studies" privileged the vernacular at the expense of the Latin; "Early Medieval North Atlantic Studies" was geographically vague and leaned away from continental Europe; "Early Medieval Insular Studies" carried its own sense of narrowness and inwardness. However, the need to develop a new term for our field was agreed.

What did this discussion, looking back at twenty-five years of "Anglo-Saxon Studies," change? What might it help to nuance or shift in future? Its inclusion in this volume highlights its participation in a far wider, timely, and important conversation about the future of Medieval Studies and concerted attempts to critique and renew the curriculum, academic research, and the academy. More specifically, the round table discussion has led directly to a change in the published "strand definition" for "Anglo-Saxon Studies" at the International Medieval Congress. In early 2019, I submitted a revised definition to the IMC, removing all uses of the troubling term "Anglo-Saxonist" (for a scholar or practitioner in the field), and adding the following statement:

> We recognise and acknowledge the problems of "Anglo-Saxon Studies" as the established name for our field and strand, as well as its sometimes exclusionary histories and contemporary appropriations. We welcome and seek to foster ongoing conversations around alternative terms and approaches, with attention to all facets of our multi-disciplinary, multilingual, diverse field.

I sent this revised text to the IMC in March, 2019, by chance just two days before the terrorist attacks on the Al Noor Mosque and Linwood Islamic Centre, New Zealand, in which the attacker carried weapons inscribed with symbolic medievalist, white supremacist references. More than ever, now is the time for us to engage politically as medievalists, and to pay attention to the ways in which our fields can be misappropriated and twisted. We are learning from each other, and especially from those with more direct personal experiences of exclusion and marginalization within the academy. A reflective addition to the strand description for an academic conference is of course only a small, intermediary step. But this process of reflection and — potentially — change is not over. Plans are in place for further discussion and consultation at the Leeds International Medieval Congress and across the wider community of early medievalists, over the coming months, to examine and review the name of our field and the IMC thematic "strand." We enter the next twenty-five years of our field alive to its shortcomings and the challenges for our scholarly practice and community — and ready to forge opportunities for change and transformation.

Epilogue

Catherine Clarke

Back to this autumn day in 2019. As I send this essay to press, I'm involved in discussions with the Standing Committee at the International Medieval Congress over the name of the "Anglo-Saxon Studies" strand, in the hope of changing it for the summer of 2020. Today's snapshot, in October 2019, is far from the last word on the future of our discipline, but I hope that this essay helps readers navigate some of its past and continuing journey.

Bibliography (curated by all co-authors)

The programme for the first International Medieval Congress (1994) is archived online at https://www.imc.leeds.ac.uk/wp-content/uploads/sites/28/2018/05/IMC_Programme_1994.pdf. The 2018 IMC programme is fully searchable online at https://www.imc.leeds.ac.uk/imc/imc-2018/.

Albritton, Benjamin L. "Fellow Travelers: The Canterbury Tales and IIIF," July 14, 2015. http://blalbrit.github.io/2015/07/14/fellow-travelers-the-canterbury-tales-and-iiif.

Arts Unimelb. "Learning Hieroglyphics in the Tomb of Nefertari in Virtual Reality." *Vimeo,* November 13, 2018. https://vimeo.com/300627980.

Breay, Claire, and Joanna Story. *Anglo-Saxon Kingdoms: Art, Word, War.* London: British Museum, 2018.

Clarke, Catherine A.M. "Literary Production Before and After the Conquest." In *The History of British Women's Writing, 700–1500,* edited by Liz Herbert McAvoy and Diane Watt, 40–50. Basingstoke: Palgrave Macmillan, 2012.

———. *Writing Power in Anglo-Saxon England: Texts, Hierarchies, Economies.* Cambridge: D.S. Brewer, 2012.

Conner, Patrick W. "Networking in the Humanities: Lessons from ANSAXNET." *Computers and the Humanities* 26 (1992): 195–204.

Crane, Susan. *Animal Encounters: Contacts and Concepts in Medieval Britain.* Philadelphia: University of Pennsylvania Press, 2013.

Dale, Corinne. *The Natural World in the Exeter Book Riddles.* Cambridge: D.S. Brewer, 2017.

Davis, Kathleen, and Nadia Altschul, eds. *Medievalisms in the Postcolonial World: The Idea of "the Middle Ages" Outside Europe.* Baltimore: The Johns Hopkins University Press, 2009.

Dockray-Miller, Mary. "Old English Has A Serious Image Problem." *JSTOR Daily,* May 3, 2017, https://daily.jstor.org/old-english-serious-image-problem/.

Ellard, Donna Beth. *Anglo-Saxon(ist) Pasts, postSaxon Futures.* Earth: punctum books, 2019.

Estes, Heide. *Anglo-Saxon Literary Landscapes: Ecotheory and the Environmental Imagination.* Amsterdam: Amsterdam University Press, 2017.

Evans, Ruth. "Historicizing Postcolonial Criticism: Cultural Difference and the Vernacular." In *The Idea of the Vernacular: An Anthology of Middle English Literary Theory, 1280–1530,* edited by Jocelyn Wogan-Browne, Nicholas Watson, Andrew Taylor, and Ruth Evans, 366–70. University Park: Penn State Press; Exeter: Exeter University Press, 1999.

Frank, Roberta. "The Search for the Anglo-Saxon Oral Poet." In *Textual and Material Culture in Anglo-Saxon England: Thomas Northcote Toller and the Toller Memorial Lectures,* edited by Donald Scragg, 137–60. Cambridge: D.S. Brewer, 2003.

Griffith, M.S. "Convention and Originality in the Old English 'Beasts of Battle' Typescene." *Anglo-Saxon England* 22 (1993): 179–99. DOI: 10.1017/S0263675100004373.

Heng, Geraldine. *The Invention of Race in the European Middle Ages.* Cambridge: Cambridge University Press, 2018.

———. "Who Speaks for Us? Race, Medievalists and the Middle Ages." *Medievalists of Color,* April 3, 2018. https://medievalistsofcolor.com/race-in-the-profession/who-speaks-for-us-race-medievalists-and-the-middle-ages/.

Kim, Dorothy. "The Unbearable Whiteness of Medieval Studies." *In the Middle,* November 10, 2016. http://www.inthemedievalmiddle.com/2016/11/the-unbearable-whiteness-of-medieval.html.

Lee, Christina. "Body Talks: Disease and Disability in Anglo-Saxon England." In *Anglo-Saxon Traces,* edited by Jane Roberts and Leslie Webster, 145–64. Essays in Anglo-Saxon Studies 4. Tempe: Arizona Center for Medieval and Renaissance Studies, 2011.

Lees, Clare A., and Gillian R. Overing. *Double Agents: Women and Clerical Culture in Anglo-Saxon England*. Philadelphia:

University of Pennsylvania Press, 2001. Reprinted with a new preface, Cardiff: University of Wales Press, 2009.

———. "Still Theoretical after All These Years, Or, Whose Theory Do You Want, Or Whose Theory Can We Have?" *The Heroic Age* 14 (2010). https://www.heroicage.org/issues/14/lees&overing.php.

———. "Women and the Origins of English Literature." In *The The History of British Women's Writing, 700–1500,* edited by Liz Herbert McAvoy and Diane Watt, 31–40. Basingstoke: Palgrave Macmillan, 2012.

McGillivray, Murray. "Electronic Representation of Chaucer Manuscripts: Possibilities and Limitations." In *Computer-Based Chaucer Studies,* edited by Ian Lancashire, 1–15. Toronto: Centre for Computing in the Humanities, University of Toronto, 1993.

Mukherjee, Pablo Upamanyu. *Postcolonial Environments: Nature, Culture and the Contemporary Indian Novel in English.* Basingstoke: Palgrave Macmillan, 2010.

Niles, John D. "The Myth of the Anglo-Saxon Oral Poet." *Western Folklore* 62 (2003): 7–61.

O'Keeffe, Katherine O'Brien. *Visible Song: Transitional Literacy in Old English Verse.* Cambridge Studies in Anglo-Saxon England 4. Cambridge: Cambridge University Press, 1990.

Paz, James. *Nonhuman Voices in Anglo-Saxon Literature.* Manchester: Manchester University Press, 2017.

Phelpstead, Carl. "Beyond Ecocriticism: A Cosmocritical Reading of Ælfwine's Prayerbook." *The Review of English Studies* 69 (2018): 613–31. DOI: 10.1093/res/hgy037.

Rambaran-Olm, Mary. "Anglo-Saxon Studies, Academia and White Supremacy." *Medium,* June 27, 2018. https://medium.com/@mrambaranolm/anglo-saxon-studies-academia-and-white-supremacy-17c87b36obf3.

Swan, Mary, and Elaine Treharne, eds. *Rewriting Old English in the Twelfth Century.* Cambridge: Cambridge University Press, 2000.

Treharne, Elaine. *Living Through Conquest: The Politics of Early English, 1020–1220.* Oxford: Oxford University Press, 2012.

Tuck, Eve, and K. Wayne Yang. "Decolonization Is Not a Metaphor." *Decolonization: Indigeneity, Education & Society* 1, no. 1 (2012): 1–40. https://jps.library.utoronto.ca/index.php/des/article/view/18630.

Tyler, Elizabeth M. *England in Europe: Royal Women and Literary Patronage c.1000–c.1150*. Toronto: Toronto University Press, 2017.

Una. "The Legacy of Artemisia, or Why We Should Care That Someone Was Raped." November 19, 2014. https://unacomics.com/2014/11/19/comics-forum-presentation-the-legacy-of-artemisia-or-why-should-we-care-that-someone-was-raped/.

———. *Becoming Unbecoming*. Brighton: Myriad Editions, 2015.

Watt, Diane. *Secretaries of God: Women Prophets in Late Medieval and Early Modern England*. Cambridge: D.S. Brewer, 1997.

"Women's Literary Culture before the Conquest." *University of Surrey.* https://www.surrey.ac.uk/womens-literary-culture-before-conquest.

9

The Medieval Literature Survey Reimagined: Intersectional and Inclusive Praxis in a US College Classroom

Carla María Thomas

Introduction

In recent years, medievalists and other premodern scholars, such as classicists, have drawn attention to the striking lack of diversity and inclusivity in our academic fields that enable white supremacists to misappropriate the past for their bigoted ends. Just two examples include the historical whitewashing of Greek and Roman statues that Sarah Bond has made more publicly known and Dorothy Kim's call for an overt rejection of white supremacist ideology by medievalists in the classroom after the violent riot in Charlottesville, VA, in 2017.[1] While vari-

---

1   See Sarah Bond, "Whitewashing Ancient Statues: Whiteness, Racism and Color in the Ancient World," *Forbes,* April 27, 2017, https://www.forbes.com/sites/drsarahbond/2017/04/27/whitewashing-ancient-statues-whiteness-racism-and-color-in-the-ancient-world/#1fec550f75ad, and "Why We Need to Start Seeing the Classical World in Color," *Hyperallergic,* June 7, 2017, https://hyperallergic.com/383776/why-we-need-to-start-seeing-the-classical-world-in-color/; and Dorothy Kim, "Teaching Medieval Studies in a Time of White Supremacy," *In the Middle,* August 28,

ous fields within academia, especially sociology and law, have long understood and researched organizational, structural, and institutional exclusionary practices, leading to the crucial work done by Kimberlé Williams Crenshaw, Patricia Hill Collins, and Sara Ahmed, among others, colleges and universities in the United States still "perform" diversity work without successfully becoming truly inclusive for students, faculty, and staff in those institutions.[2] As the editors of *Intersectionality and Higher Education: Identity and Inequality on College Campuses* argue, this disparity in supposed diversity work comes from a misunderstanding, or a complete lack of understanding, of "intersectionality," which must be engaged in both theory and praxis to achieve both a diverse and inclusive higher education environment.[3] Further, Collins seeks to reveal the "matrix of domination" that is the other side of the intersecting structures of oppression articulated through intersectional work.[4] Without identifying the forms of power within such a matrix, we cannot fully recuperate the damage done within the college classroom to intersectional, particularly racialized, bodies, both those who teach and who are taught, those who inhabit the ivory tower and who seek to enter it — the medievalist scholar-teacher and the medievalist novice-student.

2017, available at http://www.inthemedievalmiddle.com/2017/08/teaching-medieval-studies-in-time-of.html. This is just one example of public academic engagement aimed at both educating the public and encouraging academic colleagues to be more mindful.

2 See, for example, Kimberlé Williams Crenshaw, "Mapping the Margins: Intersectionality, Identity Politics, and Violence Against Women of Color," *Stanford Law Review* 43, no. 6 (1991): 1241–99; Patricia Hill Collins, *Black Feminist Thought: Knowledge, Consciousness, and the Politics of Empowerment*, 2nd edn. (New York: Routledge, 2000); and Sara Ahmed, *On Being Included: Racism and Diversity in Institutional Life* (Durham: Duke University Press, 2012).

3 W. Carson Byrd, Rachelle J. Brunn-Brevel, and Sarah M. Ovink, eds., *Intersectionality and Higher Education: Identity and Inequality on College Campuses* (New Brunswick: Rutgers University Press, 2019).

4 Collins, *Black Feminist Thought*, 18.

In this chapter, I encourage an intersectional approach paired with an understanding of critical race pedagogy to teaching the Medieval Literature survey in an English department, which is ubiquitous in the college curriculum in the United States, and I draw on my own experience and struggle with developing an intersectional pedagogical theory and praxis. Further, while I understand that each institution and program have their own requirements for what such a survey should include, I encourage a form of classroom-based activism and radically compassionate feminism that resists institutionalized white supremacy through a decentering of white male Anglophone literature as well as decentering my own power within the classroom as the professor. Instead, I strive to center the multilingual — or, if we take Jonathan Hsy's term, appropriated from sociolinguistics and applied to polyglot writers of late medieval London, *translingual*[5] — and multicultural Middle Ages in conjunction with making space for and honoring the epistemological and ontological pluralities of my students' lived realities at a Hispanic-serving institution (HIS)[6] in south Florida. In what follows, I rely upon not only current work on intersectionality studies and inclusivity in higher education, such as the examples already cited, but also on my experience teaching medieval literature courses at three different universities in the United States and

---

5 Jonathan Hsy, *Trading Tongues: Merchants, Multilingualism, and Medieval Literature* (Columbus: Ohio State University Press, 2013), 6–7. In distinguishing between "multilingual" and "translingual," Hsy writes, "If 'multilingual' denotes the fact that languages coexist and occupy the same di- or triglossic space, then 'translingual' emphasizes the capacity for languages within such spaces to interact: to influence and transform each other through networks of exchange" (7).

6 According to the United States Code, a "Hispanic-serving institution" is defined as "an eligible institution" (e.g., accredited, degree-awarding) that "has an enrollment of undergraduate full-time equivalent students that is at least 25 percent Hispanic students at the end of the award year immediately preceding the date of application." See Higher Education Opportunity Act of 2008, 20 U.S.C. (2008), §§1101a, http://uscode.house.gov/view.xhtml?req=granuleid:USC-prelim-title20-section1101a&num=0&edition=prelim#effectivedate-amendment-note.

my constantly evolving pedagogical theory and praxis. Finally, for the sake of pragmatism and transparency, I conclude with an appendix containing an abridged syllabus that includes my statement of inclusivity, ungrading policy, reading list, and a formal assignment.

Intersectionality and Inclusivity

More often than not, discussions of intersectionality begin with the origin of the term, which goes back to two of Kimberlé Williams Crenshaw's legal writings: "Demarginalizing the Intersection of Race and Sex: A Black Feminist Critique of Antidiscrimination Doctrine, Feminist Theory and Antiracist Politics" published in the *University of Chicago Legal Forum* in 1989 and, more famously, "Mapping the Margins: Intersectionality, Identity Politics, and Violence against Women of Color" published in the *Stanford Law Review* in 1991. Crenshaw's early work on developing a "Black feminist criticism" that became what is known today as intersectionality studies, especially these two essays, addressed the particular challenges for Black women who report workplace discrimination not simply as women or as Black but as Black women (1989) and violence against Black women (1991). Black feminists like Angela Davis and Black feminist legal theorists especially influenced Crenshaw's conception of intersectionality as centered on the experience of American Black women. In her 1989 piece, Crenshaw specifically credits the feminist legal theoretical work of Judy Scales-Trent, Regina Austin, Angela Harris, and Paulette M. Caldwell.[7]

---

7 Judy Scales-Trent, "Black Women and the Constitution: Finding Our Place, Asserting Our Rights (Voices of Experience: New Responses to Gender Discourse)," *Harvard Civil Rights-Civil Liberties Law Review* 24, no. 9 (1989), https://digitalcommons.law.buffalo.edu/articles/792; Regina Austin, "Sapphire-Bound!" *Wisconsin Law Review* (1989); Angela P. Harris, "Race and Essentialism in Feminist Legal Theory," *Stanford Law Review* 42, no. 3 (1990): 581–616; and Paulette M. Caldwell, "A Hair Piece: Perspectives on the Intersection of Race and Gender," *Duke Law Journal* 40, no. 2

In a more recent essay, Sumi Cho, Crenshaw, and Leslie McCall provide not only a summary of current debates within intersectional studies but also a broader definition of intersectionality as they understand it today: "Intersectionality has, since the beginning, been posed more as a nodal point than as a closed system — a gathering place for open-ended investigations of the overlapping and conflicting dynamics of race, gender, class, sexuality, nation, and other inequalities."[8] Furthermore, Crenshaw has done more than "coin" the term intersectionality in her earlier essays noted above; she "identifies an important marker that shows not only intersectionality's growing acceptance in the academy, but also how this acceptance subsequently reconfigured intersectionality as a form of critical inquiry and praxis."[9] We can understand intersectional theory as an analytic for both the way we conduct research within academia and the way we move through and interact with the world as it acts upon us. In this chapter, I am interested specifically in the ways that instructors can work towards embodying intersectionality within their own pedagogical practice in the Medieval Literature classroom in the United States.

However, Sara Ahmed's sociological work on diversity initiatives within universities in the United Kingdom and Australia has proven that such initiatives are a kind of "phenomenological practice: a way of attending to what gets passed over as rou-

---

(1991): 365–96. These sources are cited in Crenshaw, "Demarginalizing," 139, n2 where Harris's and Caldwell's pieces were not yet published.
8 Sumi Cho, Kimberlé Williams Crenshaw, and Leslie McCall, "Toward a Field of Intersectionality Studies: Theory, Applications, and Praxis," *Signs: Journal of Women in Culture and Society* 38, no. 4 (2013): 785–810, at 788. At the end of this sentence, Cho, Crenshaw, and McCall cite Nina Lykke, "Intersectional Analysis: Black Box or Useful Critical Feminist Thinking Technology," in *Framing Intersectionality: Debates on a Multi-faceted Concept in Gender Studies*, eds. Helma Lutz, Maria Teresa Herrera Vivar, and Linda Supik (Farnham: Ashgate, 2011), 207–21.
9 Patricia Hill Collins and Sirma Bilge, *Intersectionality* (Cambridge: Polity, 2016), 81.

tine or an ordinary feature of institutional life."[10] That which is "passed over as routine," of course, is the very racist, sexist, ableist, homophobic, and other forms of marginalization of those who identify outside of normative culture. Even more disconcerting is the fact that, although "a typical goal of diversity work is 'to institutionalize diversity,'" this may not be the goal of a given institution such that "having an institutional aim to make diversity a goal can […] be a sign that diversity is not an institutional goal."[11] For example, if there is legislation requiring an institution of higher education to have at least one faculty of color on a hiring committee, the presence of that faculty member may "represent the absence of wider support for diversity," and it certainly enacts the very definition of tokenism.[12] This "absence of wider support for diversity" and institutional tokenism lends itself to a lack of inclusivity in which microaggressive comments, exclusive syllabi, and other discriminatory practices find a happy and uncontested resting place in the classroom specifically and the university more broadly. Rather than striving for diversity in our classrooms, such as including only one reading by a person of color — which would be another kind of tokenism — we should strive to be truly inclusive, which requires those in the dominant, non-marginalized groups to give up space to make their environment welcoming for those in minority and marginalized groups. Ahmed concludes that "diversity is exercised as a repair narrative in the context of institutions: a way of re-centering on whiteness, whether as the subject of injury who must be protected or as the subject whose generosity is 'behind' our arrival."[13] Therefore, an emphasis on inclusivity rather than diversity is key, and the conjoining of an intersectional approach with an inclusive mindset is what will ultimately enact meaningful change in our classrooms and institutions.

10 Sara Ahmed, *On Being Included*, 22, her emphasis.
11 Ibid., 22–23.
12 Ibid., 23.
13 Ibid., 168.

While I understand that the racial politics within the United States are particular to the country's origin and subsequent history, I believe it is important for instructors in European institutions of higher education to reflect on their own country's complex past as it relates to historically minoritized peoples, and not just non-white peoples but also those who identify as non-Christian, disabled, socio-economically disadvantaged, women, and/or queer. The significance of an intersectional approach is that it acknowledges that any number of these categories may intersect to oppress a person while a person who does not experience the same reaps the benefits — that is, has *privilege* because — of that person's oppression. My identity and life experiences, for example, inform the way that I interact with the world and the way that others respond to me. I have an enormous amount of privilege because I am white and married to a cisgender heterosexual white man, but as a polyamorous queer woman who grew up as a Spanish heritage speaker in a working-class and middle-class split home, I have experienced, and continue to experience, for example, homophobia, misogyny, classism, and linguistic prejudice routinely, especially within academia. Moreover, because I am white, my Latinidad is often erased because I do not look or sound stereotypically Puerto Rican, a topic to which I will return below, but while I can recognize the denial of my ethnic background as problematic for me, I also acknowledge that Black Latinx peoples are not only erased from their Latinidad but also violently discriminated against because of the persistence of epidermal racism in the United States and much of Latin America, including the Caribbean.

Individual and Institutional Positioning

My home institution of Florida Atlantic University (FAU) currently has 25.88 percent of all enrolled students, undergraduate and graduate alike, self-identifying as "Hispanic or Latino," or

Latinx[14], as of the preliminary Spring 2019 Census.[15] If we breakdown the demographic statistics to distinguish between the undergraduate and graduate student populations, which is important because the Medieval Literature survey that I reimagine in this chapter is for an upper-level *undergraduate* course, the percentages become 27.38 and 20.31 percent, respectively. This difference demonstrates the difficulty Latinx students have in accessing not only postsecondary education but also (and especially) graduate education, and further, when combined with students who identify as "Black or African-American," the percentage breakdowns become more striking.[16] Black undergradu-

---

14 In adherence to my intersectional approach as well as the use in current Latinx Studies, I use the gender-neutral "Latinx" instead of "Latino/a," "Latin@," and "Latine" — which, while trying to be more inclusive, still relies on an artificial gender binary of masculine/feminine endings — as a pan-ethnic term to encompass all those who identify as Latin American (i.e., not just descendant from Spanish-speaking countries). However, "Latinx" itself has met with criticism because it is seen as a colonizer naming the colonized from its origin in the United States, as well as the simple fact that the /x/ in Spanish is not voiced, leaving the final syllable of the word unheard in Spanish. I would like to note here that there still is no consensus regarding what various Latinx peoples prefer to self-identify as and whether or not such pan-ethnic terms as "Latinx" or "Hispanic" are ultimately helpful or simply reductive. For example, my mother is from Puerto Rico, and she prefers to identify as Puerto Rican, Hispanic, or Caribbean but not as a Latina or Latin American. As many, such as G. Cristina Mora, have pointed out the three major Latinx groups in the United States (Cubans, Mexicans, and Puerto Ricans) had different needs when the term "Hispanic" first came into use, and they still have them. See G. Cristina Mora, *Making Hispanics: How Activists, Bureaucrats, and Media Constructed a New American* (Chicago: University of Chicago Press, 2014).
15 CENSUS Spring 2019 (Preliminary), Division of Student Affairs and Enrollment Management, Florida Atlantic University, https://www.fau.edu/student/assessment/data-dashboard.php.
16 Like Kimberlé Williams Crenshaw and others before me, I capitalize "Black" because it is a specific ethnoracial group, like Latinx and Asian. I maintain a lower-case "w" in "white" as an attempt to decenter whiteness not only within this chapter but also within my pedagogy and other scholarship. See Crenshaw, "Mapping the Margins," 1244, n. 6.

ate and graduate students combined total 19.15 percent of the entire FAU student population, but separated into undergraduate and graduate, the numbers change to 20.11 and 16.68 percent, respectively. When we add the Latinx and Black percentages together, we find that Latinx and Black undergraduate students outnumber the non-Latinx white students with 47.49 percent (compared to the 40.13 percent of non-Latinx white undergraduates). However, when the same math is applied to the graduate student population, the numbers are not only reversed but also the degree of difference increases: non-Latinx white graduate students make up 47.48 percent while Latinx and Black students make up 36.99 percent.

This kind of census may be helpful on a superficial basis in tracking diversity (or the lack thereof) at an institution; however, it does not consider the geographic and linguistic multiplicities of, as well as their impacts on, south Floridians, who are the majority of undergraduate students enrolled at FAU (91.14 percent). Nowhere are students able to indicate that they are "Afro-Caribbean" or a "white Latino" on the census, which affects the ways that the university may choose to develop its diversity and inclusivity training and programming to the extent such exist. This lack of specificity or even ability to self-identify as one chooses beyond what is reduced to essentialized categories founded on the outdated and erroneous concept of biological (or "scientific") race skews the numbers in significant ways.[17] For example, I identify as a white Puerto Rican who is a

---

17 In *Nature's Body: Gender in the Making of Modern Science* (Boston: Beacon Press, 1993), Londa Schiebinger writes: "While biologists today recognize that humans are differentiated along geographic lines, most argue that distinct races do not exist, that geographical groups exhibit tremendous individual variation and are constantly undergoing modification as they migrate and mingle with people from other areas" (119). Schiebinger cites Richard Lewontin, *Human Diversity* (New York: Scientific American Books, 1982), 11–134; and Anthony Appiah, "The Uncompleted Argument: DuBois and the Illusion of Race," in *"Race," Writing, and Difference*, eds. Henry Louis Gates, Jr. and Kwame Anthony Appiah (Chicago: University of Chicago Press, 1986), 21–37, at 21.

Spanish-heritage speaker, and my skin color provides me with white privilege while my lack of Spanish-accented American English provides me with Anglophone privilege. These aspects of my identity allowed me to navigate my private school in north Florida, which was filled with non-Latinx white students who were more socio-economically privileged than I was. However, my upbringing emphasized the linguistic, cultural, and even metaphysical or spiritual significance of descending from twice-colonized Caribbean islanders, and this, in turn, provided me with a different set of perspectives (epistemological and ontological) than a non-Latinx white person would have. At that private school, I received my first lesson in code-switching from a best friend who asked "Why do you talk like that?" when I mentioned anything related to Puerto Rico and my Puerto Rican family. Unbeknownst to me, I was automatically speaking Spanish or pronouncing Spanish names and places in my mother's Puerto Rican accent, and this first lesson in the importance of code-switching, of Anglicizing Spanish names and places in addition to censoring my word choice, affected my subsequent engagement with language as well as my confusion over my own ethnoracial identity—I looked like my best friend in a superficial way (light skin, blue eyes, dark blond hair), but I was ethnically and linguistically different from her and our peers in what were clearly significant ways.

This background also serves to connect me to my students more easily as most end up revealing otherwise concealed parts of themselves to me, both ethnoracially and linguistically, such as the Francophone Haitian-American, bilingual Black Puerto Rican, monolingual white Mexican, or biracial and multilingual Caribbean-American students who excitedly share their stories with me.[18] What I take into account in my classroom is

---

18   I would like to add that they also out themselves in terms of gender and sexuality because, on the first day of class, I identify myself as queer (pansexual and genderfluid) and share my personal pronouns with them in an effort to make my queer students, especially those who identify as trans*, comfortable sharing their realities with me and, hopefully, the class.

not simply ethnoracial diversity, but also geographic origin and language(s) spoken in the home, among other considerations.[19] As my friend and colleague Nahir I. Otaño-Gracia has so eloquently related to me, being from the small Caribbean island of Puerto Rico, she felt a certain connection reading the Old English elegies when she was younger, bound by the shared experience as an islander at the mercy of the sea.[20] Therefore, I continually strive to become a more inclusive (thus, more effective) teacher by being mindful of the intersectional realities of my students, which may resemble my Puerto Rican colleague's, or my own mother's, experience. While this is particularly true because I teach at an HSI, those who identify as non-Latinx white instructors who teach at historically black colleges and universities (HBCUs) and especially at historically white colleges

---

    This is another way of making the classroom more inclusive although it is not the primary focus of this chapter.

19 For example, see the above footnote. In addition to adding lives of queer saints and more writings by or centered on women to my syllabus, I also include texts in Arabic, French, Irish, Italian, German, Norse, Spanish, and Welsh to demonstrate how much more connected and dynamic the medieval world was than non-specialists often think. I anticipate these languages and readings to continue changing over time, and I am always open to recommendations.

20 Nahir I. Otaño Gracia, p.c., July 2017. In addition to her brilliant scholarship — such as her first monograph, which is currently under review with Boydell and Brewer, *The Other Faces of Arthur: Medieval Arthurian Texts from the Peripheries of Europe* — Otaño Gracia has also published on prejudice and racism in both the Middle Ages and the field of medieval studies. See "Constructing Prejudice in the Middle Ages and the Repercussions of Racism Today," co-written with Daniel Armenti, *Medieval Feminist Forum* 53, no. 1 (2017): 176–201; "Lost in Our Field: Racism and the International Congress on Medieval Studies," *Medievalists of Color,* July 24, 2018, http://medievalistsofcolor.com/uncategorized/lost-in-our-field-racism-and-the-international-congress-on-medieval-studies/, and "Welcome to a New Reality! Reflections on the Medieval Academy of America's Panel: 'Inclusivity and Diversity: Challenges, Solutions, and Responses,'" *Medievalists of Color,* April 27, 2018, http://medievalistsofcolor.com/race-in-the-profession/welcome-to-a-new-reality-reflections-on-the-medieval-academy-of-americas-panel-inclusivity-and-diversity-challenges-solutions-and-responses/.

and universities (HWCUS) would do well to keep this approach in mind.[21] Further, I am aware that the (violently) racist history and ethnoracial demographics of the United States, as well as the subsequent contemporary racism, differs from that of the United Kingdom and other colonizing countries; however, I ask that my colleagues reflect deeply on their own ethnoracial and linguistic privileges to understand how those privileges affect their students as well as their peers. Those of us descendant from colonizers have a moral obligation to do so.

Praxis: The Medieval Literature Survey Reimagined

On the first day of class, we read aloud certain portions of my syllabus and course policy, which includes my "Statement of Inclusivity" (see Appendix), but we also do introductions and icebreakers to get to know one another on a more dynamic level, not simply as instructor and students. At this point on the first day is when I reveal that I'm a Spanish heritage speaker, half Puerto Rican, and queer, as well as encourage "mental health" days due to my own ongoing healing from childhood trauma.

---

21 I take the phrase "historically white colleges and universities" from Kristen A. Clayton, "Biracial College Students' Racial Identity Work: How Black-White Biracial Students Navigate Racism and Privilege at Historically Black and Historically White Institutions," *Intersectionality and Higher Education*, eds. Byrd, Brunn-Brevel, and Ovink, 73–87, 86n. Additional essays in *Intersectionality and Higher Education* that would be helpful on this particular topic include Marcela G. Cuellar and R. Nicole Johnson-Ahorlu, "The Contingent Climate: Exploring Student Perspectives at a Racially Diverse Institution," 27–43; Deborah M. Warnock, "Race-Based Assumptions of Social Class Identity and Their Consequences at a Predominantly White (and Wealthy) Institution," 58–72; Victor E. Ray, "The Still Furious Passage of the Black Graduate Student," 88–103 — I urge my colleagues to read the essay by Douglas Davidson titled "The Furious Passage of the Black Graduate Student" (*Berkeley Journal of Sociology* 15 [1970]: 192–211) that is the inspiration of Ray's essay — and Orkideh Mohajeri, Fernando Rodriguez, and Finn Schneider, "Pursuing Intersectionality as a Pedagogical Tool in the Higher Education Classroom," 166–78.

Being open about my background, including being a child of divorce, allows my students to find some common thread to grasp, to link themselves to me that first day, whether that's through their own mental health history; coming from a Christian family but no longer Christian themselves; identifying as queer; or, like most of my students, especially the white and Black Caribbean students, through their experience of language. Many excitedly tell me later "I'm Puerto Rican/Cuban/Mexican/Jamaican/Haitian, but you wouldn't guess it. It's so nice to meet someone who understands." Here, read "someone" as a "professor" who understands that our bodies do not tell the whole story about who we are, especially a professor of a body of literature associated, often, with monolingualism and white nationalism. Because we tend to break down most of the stubborn walls of propriety and authority on the first day, my classes are usually willing and eager to see where this unconventional class in an otherwise conventional subject is going to lead them.

One of the unconventional assignments that I ask my students at FAU to complete before the middle of the term is a three-part creative translation project with a partner. I randomly pair them up in the first week and ask them to choose either one long, or two or three short Middle English lyrics that total approximately 25–30 lines from the selection provided in the *Broadview Anthology of British Literature, Volume One: The Medieval Period*. The three steps that they must follow to complete this project, which is assessed simply as complete/incomplete with written feedback rather than a "grade" in accordance with my ungrading policy (see Appendix), include: a literal/conservative modern vernacular translation; a meeting with me about their translation and to discuss their plan for the third step; and a creative adaptation, interpretation, or response to the lyric, which can be, but does not have to be, in poetic form. By explaining to my students what I mean by a "modern vernacular" for their first step, I introduce to them the potential for translating Middle English in any of the three most commonly spoken languages at FAU: English, French, or Spanish. These include any variations of those languages, including Jamaican Patois, Haitian Creole (or *kreyòl ayisyen*), and Spanglish. Most of the time, however, students are too cautious to attempt a non-English translation in the first step because it is early in the semester and I am still a relatively unknown entity, despite the decimated walls. By the time we have made it a quarter of the way through the semester, though, they have emerged from their protective shells and begin to take chances, which is why the last step in the project is the most exciting for us all. In the past, my students have adapted the lyrics in many different ways, ranging from a short story in English influenced by a love lyric to a macaronic modern adaptation of a misogynistic lyric in English and Spanish with the languages performing different rhetorical and tonal purposes. Additionally, I have been happily surprised to receive creative options that were not limited to the three languages previously mentioned. For example, one couple turned a long lyric into a macaronic French and Hebrew translation in which I had to enlist my Jewish student's help and authority in Hebrew to educate me in his poetic creation. Further, they remind me of different non-verbal languages that are just as significant today: one couple reconceived of a Middle English lyric, which seemed to praise women and was only revealed to be misogynistic in a Latin refrain that undermined all of the lyric's praise, by modernizing the forms of praise to fit a college cisgender heterosexual man in the United States and undermined it with a complex series of emojis. While I originally conceived of this multilingual translation project to allow my students with Caribbean backgrounds a way to draw on their own linguistic realities, assert their own knowledge in a way familiar to me, and enable them to see themselves in the temporally, geographically, linguistically, and ethnoracially unfamiliar literature in a Medieval Literature course in English, they wound up teaching me and each other just as much, if not more, than I taught them about what it means to be human, then and now.

As one might expect, then, other than making this project multilingual, the single most important element of the project is its collaborative nature. By giving my students a partner to work with, who became their "buddy" in class so that they could also get notes or inform me that they would be tardy, they also seemed more inclined to take greater risks in class, even if their partner did not know the language they wanted to translate the lyric into. In fact, this seemed to encourage greater collaborative work and dialogue because they taught each other throughout the process, and they brought the confidence built from an assertion of their own knowledge and validation of their expertise into class discussion. My bilingual and multilingual students constantly bring in observations from their own linguistic backgrounds when reading the Middle English. For example, one student in fall 2018 noted in class one day, when pointing out a false cognate between the Middle English and Modern Spanish, "I don't know if this is what the Middle English is trying to convey, but in Spanish…" While the words they were pairing up had no lexical or etymological connection, the interpretation to which it provided my student access was insightful and based singularly on their raciolinguistic[22] background, an interpretation that would not have been possible in a less inclusive classroom. By opening up my translation projects to include languages other than English, my students are more comfortable bringing those variously influenced readings into class discussion and journal entries. Even more encouragingly, this multilingual approach to a collaborative translation project, as well as my openness regarding my background as a Spanish heritage speaker who values and respects linguistic pluralities, instilled in my students a desire to tackle more translations, as the many final projects demonstrated. In spring 2019, one student, who

---

22 In his essay in *Raciolinguistics* (Oxford: Oxford University Press, 2016), H. Samy Alim notes that, in discussions about race and ethnicity, "language is often overlooked as one of the most important cultural means that we have of distinguishing ourselves from others" (4–5). Further, in *Looking like a Language, Sounding like a Race* (Oxford: Oxford University Press, 2019), Jonathan Rosa argues, "the co-naturalization of language and race is a key feature of modern governance, such that languages are perceived as racially embodied and race is perceived as linguistically intelligible, which results in the overdetermination of racial embodiment and communicative practice" (2).

did not know French, taught themselves enough to translate and adapt a Christine de Pizan poem ("Seulete sui") into multiple poetic forms in Modern English. Moreover, a few students who had never taken an Old English language course translated selections from *The Dream of the Rood* and *Beowulf,* another student translated the French feminine pronouns for "la bête" into English feminine pronouns in Marie de France's *Bisclavret* to analyze the possible transgender reading that provided, and many more translated *Sir Orfeo* and selections from *Sir Gawain and the Green Knight*. Another of my students wrote their final research paper on *The Arabian Nights* and expressed a desire to learn Arabic so that they could get closer to that text as well. The common thread, here, is a desire to form a deeper understanding of the medieval past through the language and literature by removing at least one level of mediation, the translator, in addition to their bringing the text closer to them and their own linguistic realities.

Conclusion

One of the most common questions I ask myself whenever I enter a large crowd is "Where are my people?" That is, where are the Latinx folx? Naturally, the answer to this question became consistently "not here" whenever I asked it of medieval English literature classrooms specifically—both the ones in which I was a student *and* an instructor—and medieval studies conferences generally. After completing an undergraduate minor in Spanish and writing an *English* honors thesis on contemporary Latin American women's literature, feminist theory (in which I combined French, Black, and Latin American feminist theories), and magical realism, I transitioned into Early Middle English literature and manuscript studies in my Master's program. I have always had a knack for gravitating towards the in-between spaces, those texts and people that seem to dwell forever in hybridity and, therefore, often in obscurity, so I suppose it only made sense — Early Middle English is both Old English and Middle English and neither simultaneously, and it is often overlooked in the study of the English Middle Ages. In my entering Early Middle English and manuscript studies, I found myself turning away from my Spanish heritage speaker background and embracing the languages of Old and Middle English, French, Latin, and even some reading knowledge of German and Italian. Now that I have returned to Florida, my home state, as an assistant professor at a public university that is an HSI, I have found myself joyfully returning, literally, to my mother's tongue, which has even more poignancy now than ever before because I hope to share his abuelita's tongue with my son, to encourage a complex linguistic and cultural view of both himself and the world around him before he ever steps foot into a college classroom.

Appendix: Abridged Syllabus[23]

Statement of Inclusivity

Since the violent events at Charlottesville, VA, in 2017, the field of Medieval Studies has been hotly discussing the misappropriation of medieval signs, symbols, and history in the narratives of white supremacy and white nationalism. We have seen a surge in public medievalist engagement with blogposts, opinion pieces, Twitter threads, and more to resist these racist deceits. However, pointing out misappropriations only does so much, especially because medieval studies was founded on white nationalist desire to define the American nation and link it to a "superior," "Anglo-Saxon" past. Thus, as Professor Dorothy Kim writes in a blogpost titled "Teaching Medieval Studies in a Time of White Supremacy," "What medieval studies do you[24] imagine is going to be erased if the field is inclusive? What is so difficult to understand that white supremacists have had a stake in medieval studies for a long time? Medieval studies is the go-to subject for white supremacists who want to uphold their belief about the 'pure white' Middle Ages. [...] So, what are you doing to overtly signal that your medieval studies class is not going to implicitly or explicitly uphold the tenets of white supremacist ideology?"[25]

---

23 I have yet to teach the same Medieval Literature survey twice, and my syllabus continues to evolve, sometimes in the middle of the semester, which is why I include a comment at the top of my formal syllabus that reads: "This syllabus is subject to change at any time, but I will do so only in consultation with you." Further, here, I have only included my ungrading policy, reading list for a 15-week course, and a major assignment description. All references to specific university (and personal) policies and course information have been removed.

24 Please note that all instances of the second person that Professor Kim uses are directed at her (white) colleagues in teaching positions in Medieval Studies, such as myself, not you (students) personally.

25 Dorothy Kim, "Teaching Medieval Studies in a Time of White Supremacy," *In the Middle,* August 28, 2017, http://www.inthemedievalmiddle.com/2017/08/teaching-medieval-studies-in-time-of.html.

As a white Latina, I must demonstrate overtly that I am "not a white supremacist and how [my] medieval studies is one that does not uphold white supremacy" because "[n]eutrality is not optional." I am personally and professionally invested in being explicit in my approach to studying the medieval period, which is anti-racist and intersectional feminist while simultaneously drawing on historicist and materialist methods. If your personal worldview conflicts with this approach, then I invite you to talk to me privately or withdraw from the course.

Ungrading Policy

In his blogpost "How to Ungrade," Jesse Stommel writes, "Grades are a morass education has fallen into that frustrates our ability to focus on student learning," and they weren't even a common element of student assessment in the US until the 1940s.[26] The concept of "ungrading" encourages self-assessment, collaborative peer feedback, and a democratization of power in the classroom whereby the professor becomes more like a facilitator rather than a strict authoritative figure who wields the power of grading like a weapon, striking fear and anxiety into the hearts of their students. You'll notice that, unlike other course syllabi with which you may be familiar, I do not include a percentage breakdown for the assignments, only the deadline that each assignment is due. My pedagogy, beyond my "Statement of Inclusivity," includes a student-centered approach in which I become a co-participant with you in our collaborative construction of knowledge. I believe strongly in intersectional feminist principles, which asks that we see each other as experiencing multiple interlocking structures of oppression and privilege that act upon us simultaneously, thus ensuring that we all experience the world differently and similarly in variously intersecting ways (e.g., race, gender, class, religion, ability, and others).

---

26 Jesse Stommel, "How to Ungrade," *Jesse Stommel*, March 11, 2018, https://www.jessestommel.com/how-to-ungrade/.

This approach means that we will build a class "ungrading contract" together to develop a set of community principles and standards on what it means to earn an "A," "B," and so on in the class, which, in addition to your self-assessments, written feedback from me, and conferences with me, will determine the letter grade I submit to the university registrar at the end of the semester. These will be agreed upon as a collective in the first week, and in the second week, we will meet one-on-one to discuss your individual goals in class: What do you hope to get out of this class? What is the minimum grade you hope to achieve and why? How can we ensure that you meet your own expressed learning goals? This pedagogical approach also encourages honesty, transparency, and communication on both our parts, and it requests that you, as student–scholars, take a greater interest and responsibility in your education by asking you to hold yourself accountable. I also ask that you hold me and your classmates accountable so that we all adhere to the collaborative course contract.

Inevitably, someone may be dissatisfied with their progress in the class—I will email you all a midterm "grade" to give you an idea of how I think you're progressing that will be based partially on your own midterm self-assessment; also, we can meet individually to discuss your progress further if necessary — or disagree with their final grade. Before final grades are submitted to registrar, each of you should have a general idea of how you've done throughout the semester, but if your grade comes as a surprise, please email me first to discuss. I am not opposed to reconsidering a grade if you can present me with compelling evidence (note that I said evidence, not feelings — this includes consistently seeking help in my office hours, emailing me for clarification, marked improvement in my written feedback to you, peer feedback on assignments, and your own self-assessments). However, please refrain from breaking the chain of command by going "over my head" to the chair of the department — this potentially creates not only mistrust and hard feelings on both our parts but also forces us down a bureaucratic tangent that isn't necessary. When in doubt, always talk to me.

The (Ever-Evolving) Reading List[27]

- Gildas, *The Ruin of Britain* (excerpt)
- Bede, *The Ecclesiastical History of the English People* (excerpt)
- Geoffrey of Monmouth, *The History of the Kings of Britain* (excerpt)
- Old English elegies (*The Wanderer* and *The Wife's Lament*)
- *The Poetic Edda* (selections)
- *The Legend of Ḥayy ibn Yaqẓān* (excerpts)
- *The Vision of Paul*
- *St. Brendan's Voyage*
- *The Wonders of the East*
- *The Book of Aḥmad Ibn Faḍlān*
- *The Travels of Sir John Mandeville* (excerpts)
- *The Arabian Nights* (selections)
- Boccaccio, *The Decameron* (selections)
- Chaucer, *The Canterbury Tales* (selections, including "The Prioress's Tale")
- Old English saints' lives (St. Euphrosyne and St. Mary of Egypt)
- Middle English *Life of St. Margaret*
- Hildegard von Bingen, *Scivias* (excerpts)
- *Lives and Sayings of the Sufis* (Rābiʿa al-Adawiya)
- Julian of Norwich, *Showings* (excerpts)
- *The Siege of Jerusalem*
- *Y Gododdin* (selections)
- *Havelock the Dane*
- *The Song of Roland*
- *The Song of the Cid*
- Marie de France, *Bisclavret* and *Yonec*
- St. Augustine, *The City of God against the Pagans* (excerpts)

---

[27] I use this list to choose my readings for any given semester, not to use in its entirety in a single semester course. I emphasize depth in my courses, not breadth, which our students receive through their period requirements.

- Ancient and Medieval Misogynistic Writings (short excerpts from Ovid, St. Augustine, Galen, St. Jerome, Jean de Meun taken from Alcuin Blamires, *Woman Defamed, Woman Defended*)
- Christine de Pizan, *The Book of the City of Ladies* (excerpts)

Partnered Translation Project

Overview

This is a three-part collaborative project that will conclude at the Midterm. In week 2, you will sign up for a Middle English lyric (or two or more) with a partner, which you will translate into a modern vernacular language together, meet with me together about your translation, and then adapt into a contemporary form (prose or poetry) based on your translation. This project is meant to help you get to know a classmate that you can rely on for notes or support in class as well as foster a sense of collaboration while teaching you about translation, interpretation, and creative adaptation. More importantly, though, this is your chance to play and teach us something about how you interact with language.

Vernacular Translation

To begin this project, you and your randomly assigned partner must translate 27–36 lines of Middle English lyrical poetry (from our anthology, beginning on p. 250) into a modern vernacular language (English, French, or Spanish). You have two options: you may choose to translate one long lyric (listed below) or you may choose to translate two or more short lyrics to reach the 27–36 total. Please be sure to include the titles of the poems you translated in your submitted assignment (remember, the titles should *also* be translated).

One long lyric:

1. *Betwene Mersh and April* — 36 lines
2. *Lenten is come with love to toune* — 36 lines
3. *Maiden in the mor lay* — 28 lines
4. *Bring us in good ale* — 27 lines
5. *Of all creature women be best* — 28 lines

Or two or more short lyrics:

1. *Sumer is icumen in* — 15 lines
2. *Now goth sonne under wod* — 4 lines
3. *Foweles in the frith* — 5 lines
4. *I lovede a child of this cuntree* — 14 lines
5. *Erthe tok of erthe erthe with woh* — 4 lines
6. *The Lady Dame Fortune is both frende and foe* — 4 lines
7. *Adam lay ibounden* — 16 lines
8. *To dy, to dy. What haue I* — 8 lines
9. *My lefe is faren in a lond* — 7 lines
10. *A god and yet a man* — 12 lines

I will be assessing based on accuracy of translation and flow of the modern vernacular (i.e., did you place it into intelligible word order?).

Creative Poetic Adaptation, Interpretation, or Response

Per our mandatory brainstorming meeting in Weeks 5 and 6, you and your partner will use the work done on your translation, which is an act of interpretation, to turn your chosen lyric(s) into a whole new creature. As I showed you in class from the few excerpts of Miller Oberman's *The Unstill Ones*, a creative adaptation can take many shapes.

Remember how in his non-translation of the Old English *Wulf and Eadwacer*, Miller showed us the various interpretations of the short riddling poem in a breathless display of poetic prowess, ending with what was clearly his own interpretation of the poem that began to turn into something else entirely?

Or what about his poem "The Grave" that was influenced by the Early Middle English poem after the same title, but was not about burying someone's father — instead, the older poem was simply about the inevitability of death, captured in the description of the lonely, worm-ridden grave?

Therefore, in this part of the project, you may take this in whichever direction you'd like: a poetic interpretation of the source, a literal response to the source in poetic form, a poem influenced by the theme of the source, a reworked translation that mimics the rhyme scheme and/or alliteration, a macaronic poem that uses more than one language for specific effect, and so much more.

I will be assessing based on adherence to the directions of the assignment (e.g., Did you incorporate the original Middle English poem into your new creation in some way, whether that be as an influence, the subject of the response, etc? Did you and your partner work on this *together*?).

Bibliography

Ahmed, Sara. *On Being Included: Racism and Diversity in Institutional Life*. Durham: Duke University Press, 2012.

Alim, H. Samy. "Introducing Raciolinguistics: Racing Language and Languaging Race in Hyperracial Times." In *Raciolinguistics: How Language Shapes Our Ideas About Race*, edited by John R. Rickford, and Arnetha F. Ball, 1–30. Oxford: Oxford University Press, 2016.

Appiah, Anthony. "The Uncompleted Argument: DuBois and the Illusion of Race." In *"Race," Writing, and Difference*, edited by Henry Louis Gates, Jr. and Kwame Anthony Appiah, 21–37. Chicago: University of Chicago Press, 1986.

Austin, Regina. "Sapphire-Bound!" *Wisconsin Law Review* (1989). https://scholarship.law.upenn.edu/faculty_scholarship/1347.

Bond, Sarah. "Whitewashing Ancient Statues: Whiteness, Racism and Color in the Ancient World." *Forbes*, April 27, 2017. https://www.forbes.com/sites/drsarabond/2017/04/27/whiteswashing-ancient-statues-whiteness-racism-and-color-in-the-ancient-world/#1fec550f75ad.

———. "Why We Need to Start Seeing the Classical World in Color." *Hyperallergic*, June 7, 2017. https://hyperallergic.com/383776/why-we-need-to-start-seeing-the-classical-world-in-color/.

Byrd, W. Carson, Rachelle J. Brunn-Brevel, and Sarah M. Ovink, eds. *Intersectionality and Higher Education: Identity and Inequality on College Campuses*. New Brunswick: Rutgers University Press, 2019.

Caldwell, Paulette M. "A Hair Piece: Perspectives on the Intersection of Race and Gender." *Duke Law Journal* 40, no. 2 (1991): 365–96. https://scholarship.law.duke.edu/cgi/viewcontent.cgi?article=3147&context=dlj.

CENSUS Spring 2019 (Preliminary). Division of Student Affaris and Enrollment Management. Florida Atlantic University. https://www.fau.edu/student/assessment/data-dashboard.php.

Cho, Sumi, Kimberlé Williams Crenshaw, and Leslie McCall. "Toward a Field of Intersectionality Studies: Theory, Applications, and Praxis." *Signs: Journal of Women in Culture and Society* 38, no. 4 (2013): 785–810. DOI: 10.1086/669608.

Clayton, Kristen A. "Biracial College Students' Racial Identity Work: How Black-White Biracial Students Navigate Racism and Privilege at Historically Black and Historically White Institutions." In *Intersectionality and Higher Education: Identity and Inequality on College Campuses,* edited by W. Carson, Rachelle J. Brunn-Brevel, and Sarah M. Ovink, 73–87. New Brunswick: Rutgers University Press, 2019.

Collins, Patricia Hill. *Black Feminist Thought: Knowledge, Consciousness, and the Politics of Empowerment.* 2nd edition. New York: Routledge, 2000.

Collins, Patricia Hill and Sirma Bilge. *Intersectionality*. Cambridge: Polity, 2016.

Crenshaw, Kimberlé. "Demarginalizing the Intersection of Race and Sex: A Black Feminist Critique of Antidiscrimination Doctrine, Feminist Theory and Antiracist Politics." *University of Chicago Legal Forum* (1989): 152–60.

———. "Mapping the Margins: Intersectionality, Identity Politics, and Violence Against Women of Color." *Stanford Law Review* 43, no. 6 (1991): 1241–99. DOI: 10.2307/1229039.

Davidson, Douglas. "The Furious Passage of the Black Graduate Student." *Berkeley Journal of Sociology* 15 (1970): 192–211. https://www.jstor.org/stable/41035174.

Harris, Angela P. "Race and Essentialism in Feminist Legal Theory." *Stanford Law Review* 42, no. 3 (1990): 581–616. https://www.jstor.org/stable/pdf/1228886.pdf.

Higher Education Opportunity Act of 2008, 20 U.S.C. § 1101a (2008). http://uscode.house.gov/view.xhtml?req=granuleid:USC-prelim-title20-section1101a&num=0&edition=prelim#effectivedate-amendment-note.

Hsy, Jonathan. *Trading Tongues: Merchants, Multilingualism, and Medieval Literature.* Columbus: Ohio State University Press, 2013.

Kim, Dorothy. "Teaching Medieval Studies in a Time of White Supremacy." *In the Middle*, August 28, 2017. http://www.inthemedievalmiddle.com/2017/08/teaching-medieval-studies-in-the-time-of.html.

Lewontin, Richard. *Human Diversity.* New York: Scientific American Books, 1982.

Lutz, Helma, Maria Teresa Herrera Vivar, and Linda Supik, eds. *Framing Intersectionality: Debates on a Multi-faceted Concept in Gender Studies.* Farnham: Ashgate, 2011.

Lykke, Nina. "Intersectional Analysis: Black Box or Useful Critical Feminist Thinking Technology." In *Framing Intersectionality: Debates on a Multi-faceted Concept in Gender Studies,* edited by Helma Lutz, Maria Teresa Herrera Vivar, and Linda Supik, 207–21. Farnham: Ashgate, 2011.

Mora, G. Cristina. *Making Hispanics: How Activists, Bureaucrats, and Media Constructed a New American.* Chicago: University of Chicago Press, 2014.

Otaño Gracia, Nahir. "Lost in Our Field: Racism and the International Congress on Medieval Studies." *Medievalists of Color,* July 24, 2018. http://medievalistsofcolor.com/uncategorized/lost-in-our-field-racism-and-the-international-congress-on-medieval-studies/.

———. "Welcome to a New Reality! Reflections on the Medieval Academy of America's Panel: 'Inclusivity and Diversity: Challenges, Solutions, and Responses." *Medievalists of Color,* April 27, 2018. http://medievalistsofcolor.com/race-in-the-profession/welcome-to-a-new-reality-reflections-on-the-medieval-academy-of-americas-panel-inclusivity-and-diversity-challenges-solutions-and-responses/.

Otaño Gracia, Nahir, and Daniel Armenti. "Constructive Prejudice in the Middle Ages and the Repercussions of Racism Today." *Medieval Feminist Forum: Journal of the*

Society of Medieval Feminist Scholarship 53, no. 1 (2017): 176–201.

Rosa, Jonathan. *Looking like a Language, Sounding like a Race: Raciolinguistic Ideologies and the Learning of Latinidad.* Oxford: Oxford University Press, 2019.

Scales-Trent, Judy. "Black Women and the Constitution: Finding Our Place, Asserting Our Rights (Voices of Experience: New Responses to Gender Discourse)." *Harvard Civil Rights-Civil Liberties Law Review* 24, no. 9 (1989). https://digitalcommons.law.buffalo.edu/articles/792.

Schiebinger, Londa. *Nature's Body: Gender in the Making of Modern Science.* Boston: Beacon Press, 1993.

Stommel, Jesse. "How to Ungrade." *Jesse Stommel,* March 11, 2018. https://www.jessestommel.com/how-to-ungrade/.

Printed in Poland
by Amazon Fulfillment
Poland Sp. z o.o., Wrocław

22082691R10218